# To the Golden Shore

*The Life of Adoniram Judson*

# To the Golden Shore

*The Life of Adoniram Judson*

by
COURTNEY ANDERSON

BOSTON · Little, Brown and Company · TORONTO

*Published simultaneously in Canada*
*by Little, Brown & Company (Canada) Limited*

PRINTED IN THE UNITED STATES OF AMERICA

*For*
*KIT*
*with love*

I long to reach the Golden Shore.

—ADONIRAM  JUDSON


In what torne ship soever I embarke,
That ship shall be my embleme of Thy Arke;
What sea soever swallow mee, that flood
Shall be to me an embleme of Thy blood;
Though Thou with clouds of anger do disguise
Thy face; yet through that maske I know those eyes,
    Which, though they turne away sometimes,
        They never will despise.

—JOHN DONNE, *A Hymne to Christ*

# Author's Note

THIS narrative is fact, not fiction. The only inventions are the author's conjectures and opinions, and these, it is hoped, are clearly evident as such. A few liberties have been taken in paragraphing and spelling. For instance, it has seemed best to make the same word, as heard and written differently by different individuals, or by the same individual at different times, sufficiently consistent in spelling so that the general reader can recognize it *as* the same word. The result is unscholarly in the strict sense but offers less interruption to the story.

It goes without saying that there are errors. For these, as for his opinions, the author offers neither defense nor excuse except that he has presented a great man as faithfully as has lain within his powers.

# Foreword

*So reads the plate affixed to the inconspicuous stone on the neat green lawn in front of the white house facing the traffic of Malden's Main Street. And in truth, that was the trajectory of his life: in navigator's language, from latitude 42° 25.75′ North, longitude 71° 04.4′ West, to latitude 13° North, longitude 93° East.*

*The great circles of his navigation on our globe had certain intersections: at an unidentified inn in western Massachusetts; in a grove behind the Academy at Andover; in the front room of a commodious house in Bradford; in the Death Prison at Ava on the Irrawaddy; beside a long-open grave in the tigerish jungle below Moulmein; in the harbor of the island of St. Helena; in the city of Philadelphia; at the seaport of Amherst by the Gulf of Martaban.*

*And there is a final trajectory on a curve only one Navigator can draw, to an intersection only one Navigator can locate.*

*This One issued a command:*

ALL POWER IS GIVEN UNTO ME IN HEAVEN AND IN EARTH. GO YE THEREFORE, AND TEACH ALL NATIONS, BAPTIZING THEM IN THE NAME OF THE FATHER, AND OF THE SON, AND OF THE HOLY GHOST: TEACHING THEM TO OBSERVE ALL THINGS WHATSOEVER I HAVE COMMANDED YOU: AND LO, I AM WITH YOU ALWAY, EVEN UNTO THE END OF THE WORLD.

*He obeyed it.*
*The question remains: Why?*

# Contents

# PART ONE
# The Embarkation
## [ *1788–1812* ]

# CHAPTER I
# The Frame
## [ *1788* ]

IT must have been love for Abigail Brown that decided the Reverend Adoniram Judson, Senior, to become a candidate for the pastorate of the First Church in Malden. Hardly anything else could explain it.

True, to anyone but a Congregational minister — particularly to one of Mr. Judson's character — Malden would have seemed as pleasant a town to live in as any in Massachusetts. The nearly two hundred families who farmed the fertile slopes below its low, verdant hills almost all lived in solid comfort. The total population of about a thousand was ample to support a church and minister in appropriate if not lavish style. In size and prosperity it compared favorably with such communities as Concord and Lexington and it had a real advantage in location, for it was scarcely five miles north of Boston, that flourishing center of culture and wealth which was now reputed to have achieved the fabulous population of some twenty thousand. Of course, to reach Boston from Malden, one had to ferry across two rivers, the Mystic and the Charles; but plans were already in the making for bridging both.

To a minister minded to matrimony, however, Malden's greatest attraction would have been its parsonage, which was a large, square, two-story house with a pitched roof, and with an ell at the rear — built in the old style of the early 1700's and having two huge chimneys, one on each side of the hall, which divided the house from front to back.

To be sure, the parsonage was more than sixty years old that summer of 1786 when Mr. Judson began to imagine his children playing about its doorstep; but its construction was so solid and honest that it showed hardly any signs of deterioration. During the years huge elms and evergreens had grown up to shade the broad lawns which sloped gently to the rough stone wall by the side of the road. Across the road stood the church, a hundred yards or so away. Not far from the church a spring of pure water bubbled out of the ground at the foot of Bell Rock, where in generations past the town bell had hung suspended from a tripod of huge timbers. Wells might run dry, but the spring had never been known to fail.

This was what Mr. Judson saw every Sunday that summer when he preached as a candidate for the pastorate of the church. Seeing it, he wanted more and more to occupy its study permanently, to live in it with Abigail Brown, to have his children born in it and grow up in it; perhaps, even, like the beloved divine for whom it was erected, to die in it.

His scruples against accepting calls that were less than unanimous faded and finally vanished altogether.

He was thirty-six years old, this Adoniram Judson, Senior, the father of our subject; he was a medium-sized, stocky man. He had preached in many pulpits since graduating from Yale in fateful 1776. But never yet had he accepted a call from a congregation. The First Congregational Church of Scituate, some ten miles south of Boston and nearly three times the size of Malden, had called him in 1784. He had declined. Hardwick, farther west in Worcester County and almost twice the size of Malden, had called him twice, the second time in the spring of 1785. He had declined. Wrentham, some thirty miles southwest of Boston and larger than Malden, had called him, and this call too he had declined.

All these calls he declined because they were not unanimous. For Mr. Judson wanted not merely a church, but one in which every member subscribed to his views. Since the Revolution, such churches had become increasingly hard to find. The ferment that led to a rejection of the divine right of kings and to eventual independence from England had led to a questioning of the old Puritan Calvinist theology. In worldly Boston there were prosperous Unitarian churches, amply supported by the rich and powerful, teaching a creed that seemed to him scarcely better than infidelism; and in nearby Cambridge the Congregationalism taught at Harvard had undergone a sad watering-down. Even in the outlying rural villages, the Hardwicks, Wrenthams, and Maldens, a growing number of church members were moving toward the conclusion that God had created the world for the happiness of men as much as for His own glorification, and that the damnation of sinners was not part of His original plan.

To Mr. Judson, once a pupil of the noted Joseph Bellamy and an exponent of the views of Samuel Hopkins — both doctrinal heirs of Jonathan Edwards — such assertions were rank heresy, defying logic and Scripture alike.

But he declined to engage in controversy. He preferred not to be pastor of a church in which it was necessary.

That is, not until he became a candidate for the pulpit of Malden. Yet Malden was divided by far worse disagreements than the churches whose calls he had declined. Its First Church suffered from not *one* dispute, but *two*.

One, of course, was the old matter of creed. To a substantial minority (consisting mainly of the more prosperous and substantial citizens) Mr. Judson's old-line Congregationalism was an affront and an abomination. They had listened to him nearly all that summer of 1786 with growing disapprobation. But to their dismay, when the congregation met on Friday the seventh of July to decide the candidate's fate, a majority voted to extend him a call. Mr. Judson preached the undefiled faith of their forefathers. Moreover, the church needed a minister badly, and Mr. Judson seemed as good as any under the peculiar circumstances existing. The minority argued vociferously, but to no avail. Even so, the last diehards went down fighting. On the church record for that day still stands the sentence: *Capt John Dexter desired that his Protest Might be entered against Settling a Minister of the Bade Hopkintonian Principels.*

But there was a second, even more serious, matter dividing the First Church; and this one had been making trouble for generations beyond memory. It concerned the location of the church, which had been determined long ago when the first settlers from Charlestown crossed the Mystic River to found Malden on the northern side. Those who had remained closest to the river always felt that the church had been built altogether too far north for convenience or even common sense. The issue had smoldered quietly during the half century from 1721 to 1767, when the pulpit had been filled by the beloved Joseph Emerson — he for whom the capacious parsonage had been erected in 1724. Beloved as he was, he had powers to inspire awe which quelled the merest murmur of disunion. As his son wrote of him, he was "a Boanerges, a son of thunder, to the workers of iniquity; a Barnabas, a son of consolation, to the mourners in Zion." When, white of hair and rich in redeeming grace, he was gathered to his reward, the congregation searched three years before it found a suitable successor in the brilliant Peter Thacher, who had been ordained at a precocious eighteen and called "Young Elijah" by no less than the great evangelist Whitefield. Thacher gave universal satisfaction, but times and tempers had changed. The dissidents who wanted their own church in the South Parish began to raise their voices.

In 1785, his renown having spread to Boston, Thacher received a call from the influential Brattle Street Church. He accepted, probably thinking himself well out of Malden, for presently the South Parishers by the Mystic withdrew and set up their own church. Now Malden had two weak churches where had flourished a single strong one under Emerson. At this point the First Church called the Reverend David Avery. He declined, with motives which are understandable.

This, then, was the situation when the senior Mr. Judson became a candidate for the vacant pulpit of the First Church. He knew, that summer of 1786, that a substantial minority disapproved heartily of his doctrines. He knew they were convinced he was not the man to bring the two enfeebled churches together. He could not have helped knowing — for Captain Dexter spread it on the records that Mr. Judson's installation as minister would prove *an Effectual Barrier in Preventing the mutually wished for Union of the Two Parishes in this town both of which have severely felt their Separation, and this Remaining will probibly terminate in the Ruin of Both.*

What Mr. Judson thought, it is hard to say. To those who knew him his personality was one with his creed. Both were stoical, forbidding, and austere. His judgments were scrupulously fair; but he had great determination — obstinacy, his enemies would have called it. Probably, thinking of that comfortable parsonage — and Abigail

Brown — he closed his eyes to circumstances that ordinarily would have made him hesitate.

For at thirty-six he was not yet married. Abigail was ten years younger. They would surely have children. He could not condemn his dependents to the precarious life of an itinerant preacher. He needed to settle down. And snug inside that attractive parsonage he could find peace and security with his wife and children, whatever storms might rage outside.

He accepted the call. In October the church met, with Mr. Judson as moderator, to plan his ordination. The date was set for November fifteenth. He and Abigail were to be married the twenty-third, a week later.

At the meeting the congregation did what it could — short of withdrawing its call to Mr. Judson — to allay the swelling discontent of the minority, by voting that *Such Persons as disented from the vote might have liberty of Conscience to Do as they Pleased without Giving Offense to the Church*. This conciliatory gesture had no effect whatever. The minority would have none of Mr. Judson. If they could not prevent his call, they could make trouble over his ordination. When the council which was to ordain him met at Captain William Wait's house such a heated dispute arose that Mr. Judson had to ask that it be dissolved, *Altho the Diffecultyes did not Immediately relate to him*. The church had no choice but to meet again five days later and vote to call another ordination council — this one for the seventh of December.

It was in this embarrassing situation that Abigail Brown became Mrs. Adoniram Judson, and the couple moved into uneasy occupancy of the parsonage, hoping that everything would go off better next time. But even nature seemed to conspire against them. For on December 7 Malden, along with all the surrounding towns, was buried under such a tremendous snowstorm that neither on horse nor foot could any of the members of the council move out of their snowbound parishes. The ordination could not be held until January 23, 1787. This time it went off at least approximately as planned.

*The Council were then made Acquainted with the Circumstances of the Church and Parish; and Notwithstanding there were found*

*some Objections against the Ordination, they Deemed it their*
*Duty to Proceed to the Examination of the Pastor Elect. And having*
*heard his Confession of Faith, and a Relation of his Religious Ex-*
*periences, and Carefully Examined thereon, the Council were*
*Unanimously Satisfied with his qualifications for the Gospel Minis-*
*tery. Accordingly, on the 24th Instant, they Ordained him to the*
*Pastoral Office Agr[ee]able to the Request of the Church.*

The defeated minority had one last shot in their locker. Immediately after the ordination, a score of them — the leading members
of the church — withdrew and joined the South Parish.

Thus ominously began Mr. Judson's ministry to the shrunken
First Church of Malden. But though he suffered disappointments
in his pastoral life, he found loving consolation within the walls of
the parsonage. And in due time — on Saturday, August 9, 1788 —
Abigail presented him with a son. The baby was given the name of
his father, Adoniram.

Looking at the little boy asleep in his cradle the father resolved,
like so many fathers before and since, that his son should be what
he was not. He had met disparagement. His son should win the
praise of multitudes. He knew now that his life would be spent
in village pulpits. But his son should have fame.

Somewhere deep in his mind may have stirred a desire to make
this his revenge for the slights and rejections he had suffered. Now,
in his son's person, he had an opportunity to live his own life over
again from the beginning, and in the son's life achieve the ambitions
he had renounced in his own.

## CHAPTER II

# Clouds
## [ *1789–1792* ]

THE infant Adoniram remained serenely unconscious of the trials his father was having with the First Church of Malden. He slept and waked, cried and smiled, or merely lay in his cradle surveying with round eyes his baby world. He fed and grew. He busied himself with the primary distinctions of babyhood: what was himself, and what was not; what was person, and what was thing. Sometimes there stirred in him a fleeting feeling that something was expected of him, but this was no more than a brief, shadowy intimation. He was occupied with other more important matters.

A cold fall gave way to a bitter winter — the twenty winters between 1779 and 1799 were remembered for their unusual severity. On Sundays, while the congregation shivered in spite of their foot-warmers, the baby's father persevered at the task of propounding to his shrunken congregation the Hopkinsian God — a God Whose vindictiveness was part of His justice, to Whom holiness was universal benevolence or friendly affection to all intelligent beings. This God was a God Whose motive in making man was to provide a being who should glorify Him, no other. Yet the world God made, with all its apparent imperfections, was the best of all possible worlds: for God in the beginning was the only Being; He was perfect; He had an infinity of choices as to what kind of world He would create; He created this one; this must be the best world possible. Q.E.D.

When February's blasts tore with strong fingers at the creaking steeple and the driving snow tumbled in white drifts over the frozen churchyard, the members of the congregation must have listened uneasily to the tumult outside and wondered, their breaths

floating in frosty plumes, whether winter itself were not proof
enough of Samuel Hopkins's vindictive justice of God.

But on warm summer Sundays, when the sweet grass-scented air
stole gently through the open windows, and the men sank drowsily
back in their pews, lulled into lethargy, after a week's hard labor on
farm or at bench, by the faint humming of bees and the distant bells
of grazing cattle and the pastor's measured words, they must have
been inclined to reject a theology so dismal, so sourly flavored with
infant damnation, and so thinly sweetened with "universal benevolence."

Certain it was that, as the winter wore on to spring and the snow
melted and the buds appeared and the songbirds returned, the
contending elements within Malden's church felt less and less
universal benevolence toward each other, and still less toward their
pastor, Mr. Judson.

But of what went on in the church a few hundred yards away,
the baby Adoniram knew nothing. Within the parsonage, however,
he was learning all the time. He sat on his striped blanket on the
kitchen floor — not dreaming it would be preserved a century and
a half later — watching the flames roaring bright in the fireplace.
The fire was pleasantly warm from where he sat, but when he
crawled too close he found that it could hurt.

Good came from this fire. Huge joints were roasted in front of
it. Occasionally he was allowed a delicious taste of the roasting
meat. More often, when he was old enough, he was given a mouth-
ful of vegetables pulped after being ladled from the huge iron
kettle that swung from a hook at the corner of the hearth. There
were other things to see and smell: the corn his mother pounded in
the wooden mortar; the apples sputtering in a row before the
glowing coals. Sometimes his mother sprinkled sand on the floor.
He tasted it and found it gritty and unpleasant to the tongue. There
was a difference in texture and tastes, he realized. Some were undesirable. His mother had even more decided ideas about what was
undesirable. He found out early that dirty things were bad, clean
things good. And the word "dirty" meant far more than the simple
soil of earth.

Very early, much earlier than most babies, he became aware of
sounds. There was a pattern in the sounds made by humans. It had

a meaning, but what it was he did not know as yet. He listened carefully for some clue. His first attempt to reproduce the sounds had instant results. He was praised and smiled upon, picked up and petted. The results encouraged him to try harder; but he suspected there was more to sounds than that they brought forth approval.

He crawled into his second summer and toddled out of it. His world was expanding. From the sloping ground in front of the parsonage he saw, that summer, the traffic on the dusty road through Malden — people walking, people in carriages, boys driving cows, slow spans of oxen so massive that even the heavy wooden yokes seemed to rest lightly on their necks. He saw other animals on the road and on the parsonage grounds — dogs, chickens, but no pigs, for in the summer of 1788 the Selectmen had decreed that swine were not to run loose any more, but must be shut up during the months of August, September, and October. Still, he must have been carried in his father's arms to see the pigs in the sty behind the house; for Mr. Judson, like other ministers, kept cows and pigs and cultivated his own crops. Ministers were still partly farmers, and farm work in no way detracted from the dignity of their profession.

At this age, his mother was the center of his life. She fed him, warmed him, soothed him, cared for him. Second to her came the black-clad person called variously "your father," "Sir," "Mr. Judson," and — rarely — "Adoniram." This last was baffling, for he had learned to associate the word "Adoniram" with himself. There was something strange about this person. He was friendly, yet remote. He was to be loved, yet there was something about him that called forth fear.

When his third winter was nearly over and he had become familiar with snow, another person came to live in the house besides his father and mother and the three women who were "the help." This was a smaller person than he, who lay in a cradle most of the day. She received a great deal of attention — sometimes too much, he thought, since to that degree he himself received less. But on the whole he felt a kinship with her because her size was more like his own. Later, when she had learned to walk, she followed him around like an adoring puppy.

She was born March 21, 1791. Her full name was Abigail Brown

Judson, after her mother and grandmother; but Adoniram used for her the names he heard more often: "sister," or "Abby," or "Nabby."

By now Adoniram must have attended a number of church services. There were some interesting things about going to meeting, although the whole business took an awfully long time.

The church was very much in his mind, because he could see it looming in the distance on the other side of the road, not far from craggy Bell Rock. From the outside it looked rather like a big square box. It was boxlike on the inside, too. Inside, the worshipers took their places in other boxes — "pews." In the pew, Adoniram sat on a stool like the other children; the walls of the pew were higher than his head — to see out he had to stand on the stool on tiptoe, but this was usually forbidden. Surely he did have opportunities, though, to see that the men in each pew sat in the back, the women in front. Ahead of the pews were rows of seats for the singers, and in the very front of the church a few seats for old people who could not see or hear well. The seats for the singers were hinged. When the singers stood up for prayers, they raised the seats. At the final "Amen," when they sat down, the seats fell down too with a delicious thundering clatter.

But the most important thing about church was Adoniram's father. He was more important than anybody. He stood all by himself in the pulpit up front and talked to the people, very loudly. Adoniram took a good deal of satisfaction in his father's importance. It seemed to him that his father was master of all the people, because they had to come to his church every week and listen to what he said.

Sometimes, though, Adoniram's father did not talk to people but to Somebody Else Adoniram could not see, Who seemed to be up on the roof, or even higher, out of sight. This Person had a good many names. He was called "Our Heavenly Father," "God," and "Jehovah." Adoniram had never seen Him, but when he asked he was told he would see Him someday, in a delightful place called "heaven."

Meanwhile, Adoniram's father could, evidently, see Our Heavenly Father — because he talked to Him often, at home as well as in church. The Heavenly Father was obviously someone to be feared.

The consequences of disobeying Him were even more frightful than the cold disapproval Adoniram's disobedience brought from his own father. For, although He liked most people, people He did not like or who had offended Him He put in a hot fire, even bigger and hotter than the hottest fires in the parsonage fireplaces.

Much of the importance of Adoniram's father resided in books, particularly one Book which he used in church, and into which he would look for hours in the parsonage. This was the Bible, and Adoniram's mother and father read parts of it aloud to him nearly every evening. Some of the stories were interesting. Others he could not quite understand, but he liked to hear them anyway. At still other times, his father would sit at a table and cover page after page with black marks that flowed from a sharpened goose quill. When his father had finished a page he would sprinkle sand over it, and shake it back and forth and then pour the sand back into its container. This was called "preparing the sermon." It had something to do with his father's power, and was very important. In fact, it was so important that Adoniram's father usually closed the door and Adoniram seldom had a chance to see him use the goose quill. Sometimes Our Heavenly Father would be in there behind the closed door, helping. At least, Adoniram thought so, because once in a while he could hear his father talking to Someone of that name.

Unfortunately, nothing could have been further from the truth than the boy's conception of his father's power. His opponents had never stopped trying to oust him, and at last they were beginning to succeed. By the spring of 1790 William Bentley, pastor of the East Church in sophisticated Salem, was able to note with satisfaction that Mr. Judson, one of the Hopkinsian "schemers," had "become uncomfortable at Malden."

In another year Mr. Judson's position became untenable. In early April of 1791, less than two weeks after the birth of little Abigail, he received his "Dismission." In the tactful words of the official resolution voted by the church: *As it is proposed for Mr. Judson to leave us, we think it to be our Duty, & we feel disposed to be explicit upon the occasion to declare to the world that Mr. Judson has during his ministry among us, conducted agreeably to his profes-*

*sion as a christian, & as a minister of Jesus Christ & as such we do
recommend him to the world of our fellow christians at large.*

He was not to rear his family in that comfortable parsonage after
all. But a minister could not be turned off on a moment's notice like
a farm laborer — particularly not a man like Mr. Judson, who had
a keen sense of what was due him in honor and justice, and who,
with a wife and two small children dependent upon him, was disposed to insist on his rights.

Certainly even his bitterest opponents could not blame him for
standing true to the principles that had brought him a call in the
first place. He had not changed; the congregation had changed. And
in any case, the controversy had been caused fully as much by parish geography as by anything else.

Armed thus, he was able to make an agreement with the church
which provided that although he should cease to be pastor at the
end of September, he should have *the sole & uninterrupted use, &
improvement of the sd. parsonage, without any reserve, one whole
Year from the day of his sd. dismission.*

This agreement was confirmed and ratified in August, when
Adoniram had reached the age of three, by an ecclesiastical council
consisting of the Third Church of Salem, the Brattle Street Church
of Boston and the Stoneham Church. At least the Judsons would
have a roof over their heads for more than a year, while Mr. Judson
looked for another pulpit.

The search was a long one. Often during the next year the father
was away for days at a time supplying pulpits, undergoing inter-
views with church committees, calling on his ministerial brethren.
Again and again he returned home, tired and anxious, having to
admit no success.

It must have been while he was away on one of these expeditions
that Abigail prepared for him the one surprise that she knew would
encourage him most. For on his return, most likely when he had
stabled the horse, refreshed himself and eaten a little and settled
down in a chair by the fire, she opened the Bible and handed it to
three-year-old Adoniram. And while the father's jaw fell slack in
amazement, the little boy read aloud a whole chapter. His mother
had taught him to read in a week — at the age of three!

Tenderly, perhaps almost tearfully, the Reverend Mr. Judson took his son in his lap and with pride and assurance in his voice told him that surely he would be a great man someday. Anyone who could learn to read at three could not fail to accomplish great things and become a man of note.

The event was to live long in family tradition. Once again it reinforced the father's ambition for his son. He himself might remain obscure. But his son would make a brilliant name for himself. Adoniram the younger would someday have the world at his feet.

As for the little boy seated on his father's lap, he listened earnestly and pridefully to his father's praise. Many of the words he did not understand. But he did understand, somehow, that great efforts were expected of him. Great efforts would win him more praise. He understood that he too was to lead the people, and with greater success than his father. He began, perhaps — for sometimes these things are sensed early — to understand that a way might open by which he could surpass his father and win his praise, and his mother's praise, in the doing. The foundations of a powerful determination were building in him.

But none of this found a new church for the Judsons.

## CHAPTER III

# Wenham

[ *1792–1799* ]

MR. Judson was without a charge for more than a year. It was late in 1792 before he was able to return home from one of his trips with the good news that he had received an acceptable call.

The church was the one at Wenham, at the base of Cape Ann, five miles north of Salem in Essex County. Its previous pastor, Mr. Swain, had served it more than forty years until his death. Now the congregation had voted unanimously, the last day of November, to extend a call to Mr. Judson. At the same meeting it had also voted to do away with the "halfway covenant," which had long been a thorn in the flesh of ministers of his persuasion. No longer could a man or woman expect to become a member of the church merely by being of good moral character and a believer in God. From now on the church would go back to the practice of old New England, which required that a candidate must also testify to the satisfaction of the minister and the congregation that he had experienced "Redeeming Grace." And from now on only those in full membership could have their children baptized, although nonmembers would not be barred from attending church. All in all, it was a great triumph for the new minister.

In Wenham the church chose the pastor but the town employed him and paid his salary. Immediately after the church made its decision, a town meeting was held. The town voted to invite Mr. Judson to be its minister, and to offer him the use of the town's parsonage plus a "free contribution" and "Sixty pounds Lawfull money" for settling in Wenham. His salary was to be ninety-five pounds a year, but since money values were fluctuating as the new national currency began to be minted, if he were not paid in pounds he could be paid in some current form of money of an equivalent value. Mr. Judson wasted no time accepting the call. A little more than two weeks later he presided at his first church meeting. On December 26, 1792, he was formally installed. Dr. Bentley, watching events from nearby Salem, noted in his diary that: "This day is to be ordained Judson, lately from Malden. His council are Cleveland, Oliver, & Parish. He will not trust an enlightened clergy after the trouble they gave him in Malden."

A few days later, January 10, 1793, Mr. Judson bundled his family into a sleigh, gathered up the reins, clucked to the horse, and on whispering runners they sped over the snowy roads to Wenham.

Wenham was scarcely half the size of Malden. Its five hundred inhabitants occupied fewer than seventy-five houses strung out along the Old Bay State Road, oldest highway in Massachusetts, which meandered north from Beverly to Ipswich and then up the seacoast to the Merrimack River. But to a small boy of four, Wenham could not have been very different from Malden. The parsonage, similar to the Malden one, stood on a gentle rise just east of the Old Bay State Road. The church was across the road and a few hundred yards to the north. A spired structure with a bell in the belfry, it was about the same size as the Malden church. The pews were the same square, high-backed kind Adoniram had seen before. Probably the only important difference, to a boy's eyes, was that the choir took its place in the gallery instead of forward on the ground floor.

The father would have been aware of other differences. Wenham was slowly declining in population, and the church had been allowed to fall into rather poor repair since its construction in 1748. Against this disadvantage was the immense advantage of a united congregation. For a few years, at least, the Judsons should enjoy peace.

And so they did. And it was here, on May 28, 1794, that another son was born to them, Elnathan, named for his paternal grandfather, Captain Elnathan Judson of Woodbury, Connecticut, of whom Adoniram, Senior, was the seventh child and sixth son.

The boy Adoniram flourished in Wenham. He began to assume individuality. At four he had been imitative, aping his father by collecting the neighboring children and preaching to them. The hymn he gave out to his youthful congregation, his parents remembered, was usually the one beginning "Go preach my Gospel, saith the Lord." But by six or seven, perhaps when he began going to Master Dodge's school, he had begun to display interests and abilities unlike those of the other boys in the neighborhood.

For that matter, his personality was different. It had a peculiar vividness. He was unusually high-spirited, enthusiastic in anything he did, active and energetic. He had complete self-confidence. Yet, on the whole, he preferred books to play. During the years of his boyhood he read everything he could lay hands on, from his father's religious books to Ben Jonson's plays — which he borrowed in the neighborhood — to the novels of Richardson and Fielding, the best sellers of their time.

This avid devouring of everything in print would have marked him in any typically ingrowing, gossipy village like Wenham. But to this was added a curious flair for puzzle-solving, for inquiry, for testing, that today would convince parents they were rearing a born scientist.

Once, very early, he nearly blinded himself peering at the sun through a small hole he cut in the crown of his hat — to solve the problem of the sun's motion, he told Abigail. As she could not have been much more than five, she believed him when he avowed he had succeeded.

At Master Dodge's school he impressed — and undoubtedly irritated — the other boys by his uncanny ability to solve riddles. He simply could not be stumped. Eventually he accumulated a large collection of brain-twisters with which he loved to confound his schoolmates.

At eight or nine his mental cockiness nearly got him in trouble with his father. A newspaper printed what it called an "enigma," which it defied its readers to solve. Adoniram looked at it, decided he had succeeded with others just as hard, and promptly set to work. Presently he had the solution, copied it neatly, addressed it to the editor, and — probably with Abigail tagging along — walked up the shady street beyond the church to the post office in the general store. He gave it to the postmaster, forgetting, in those days before postage stamps, that the newspaper would have to pay the postage, which would have been a goodly sum — fourpence to Boston, about a quarter in today's values. The postmaster quietly put the letter aside without forwarding it, and later gave it to Adoniram's father.

The person Adoniram feared above all others was his father. It was not only that he was a minister. It was not even that he was Adoniram's father in a day when fathers ruled their children with an iron hand. It was the sheer awesomeness of the man himself. He was nearly incapable of humor. He was just, but with the retributive justice of God Himself. He was stern, austere; and as God did not overlook the sparrow's fall, so Mr. Judson did not overlook trifles. In fact, deep in Adoniram's mind God and his father could hardly help taking on identity.[1]

At any rate, when Adoniram came home for tea later that day and saw the letter on the tea table, his face paled. Mr. Judson indicated the letter. "Is that yours, Adoniram?"

"Yes, sir," faltered the boy.

"How came you to write it?"

"Please read it, Father."

"I do not read other people's letters. Break the seal and read it yourself."

With trembling fingers the boy broke the seal, mumbled through the contents, and gave the sheet to his father, who received it in silence and read it to himself. But the expected wrath did not descend. Mr. Judson asked Adoniram for the paper containing the puzzle. Adoniram gave it to him, then hastily retreated to the far side of the room beyond the fireplace. From this distance he watched his father's face, trying unsuccessfully to read his thoughts. All he saw was his father reading the enigma in the paper, comparing it with Adoniram's solution, rereading the enigma, and recomparing

---

[1] If so, the fearsomeness of that identity may have been deepened by the fact that about this time, in February of 1796, Adoniram's mother had borne another child, Mary, who died after less than seven months of life — too young to repent Original Sin and acquire Redeeming Grace by conscious choice. The boy Adoniram, steeped in his father's creed, must have pondered the infant's destination with some unease. What was it? Automatic forgiveness? Or, as the poet Wigglesworth had suggested more than a century before, "the easiest room in hell"?

it with the solution with expressionless countenance. At length Mr. Judson placed both on the table, and crossing his hands on his knees stared thoughtfully into the fire for a long time.

In a few minutes Mrs. Judson tactfully brought up a new topic of conversation. Adoniram — his feelings obscurely tinged with guilt — went to bed without knowing the verdict.

Next morning at breakfast his father said, "Adoniram, I have purchased a book of riddles for you. It is a common book, but when you have solved them all I shall get you a more difficult one." Adoniram beamed; and beamed more when his father patted him on the head with rare warmth and added, "You are a very acute boy, Adoniram, and I expect you to become a great man."

But when Adoniram opened the book, his face fell. It was only the arithmetic used by the older boys in Master Dodge's school. Still, his father had praised him; and if there was anything puzzling in an arithmetic book he felt sure he would like it.

He did. He began frolicking in a sea of figures like a porpoise. His fame as a prodigious worker of problems even spread to Beverly. A man there sent him a puzzle with an offer of the fabulous sum of a dollar — more than his father earned in a day — for the solution. It proved to be far more difficult than the newspaper enigma, and the first day he got nowhere with it. But the next morning, when he was taking care of his little brother Elnathan, now about four years old, it came to him and he tasted triumph once more.

By the time he was ten and in grammar school his reputation for mathematics had extended into language — Greek and Latin — and his schoolmates called him "Virgil," or sometimes "Old Virgil Dug Up," in tribute to a shapeless hat he wore. Arithmetic and puzzle-solving had led to something else; for he was also learning navigation in a school kept by Captain Morton.

There was a school of navigation, kept by a retired sea captain, in nearly every seaport town. Nearly every family which had a son with a flair for figures thought at once of his learning navigation and becoming supercargo, mate, master, and perhaps eventually owner of his own vessels. It was a time when men commanded ships in their twenties and retired well-to-do in their thirties. It was an age of navigation. Nathaniel Bowditch, father of modern navigation, was himself a native of Salem; and in 1799, his fame as a navigator already a legend though he was still only twenty-six, he published the first American edition of *The Practical Navigator*. Adoniram was in his eleventh year then. Whether his ambitious father intended a career at sea for his son, it is impossible to say. Certainly the thought must have crossed his mind. Wenham may have been a slowly declining country village, but nearby Beverly and Salem, with their combined populations now passing twelve thousand, were enjoying the most dazzling prosperity ever seen in New England.

Jaunting the few short miles to Salem, as they must have done often, Adoniram and his father could not have gone far through Beverly's streets before unmistakable evidences of wealth began to appear everywhere.

Long before they crossed over the toll bridge to Salem, the tall ships' masts with their spidery rigging could be seen tickling the sky out of every cove — here and there groups of two or three masts, each marking a ship close at hand near the toll bridge; and on the horizon beyond the Neck a concentration as thick as the pickets in a fence, outlining Salem Harbor itself.

The wealth was visible in the form of the lordly homes of the merchants and sea captains being built on the tree-shaded streets near the swampy Common with its five as yet undrained ponds. Wealth showed in the crepe shawls from Canton, the silks and satins from Smyrna and Turkey worn by the women of the merchant and seafaring families. In the homes of the well-to-do — and the Reverend Mr. Judson and his son were welcome in many of them — it appeared in the carved teak, the jade and coral, the fragile porcelain from China, and even in the parrots, brilliant in harlequin green, red and yellow, jabbering a medley of the world's tongues.

For the wealth not merely could be seen, it also could be heard.

It was voiced not only by the parrots and songbirds brought in cages from the islands of the seven seas to warble their exotic songs in Salem's windows all year long. It was beaten out everywhere along the waterfront by the thump of the calkers' mauls. As Adoniram and his father walked along the harbor shore from Derby Wharf at one end to Crowninshield's wharf, nearest the harbor mouth, at the other, wealth sang out in the chanties of the men straining at the windlasses. When they paused to greet acquaintances, wealth told its story in heart-quickening tales of boys who went to sea at twelve or fourteen, soon thought nothing of circumnavigating the globe, spoke of Hong Kong as if it were a day's sail from Gloucester, and commanded their own ships before they were old enough to vote.

The wealth could even be smelled. The sea was redolent of it. The harbor air by the wharves reeked of it in the haunting aromas of the spices, the ginger and pepper and sandalwood disgorged from the capacious holds of the tall-masted ships that had loaded on the Java Coast, Canton, the Malay Islands and Singapore. To a poor country minister and his wide-eyed young son, Salem Harbor must have seemed like a cornucopia from which poured all the riches of the Orient.

Could it have been the Reverend Manasseh Cutler who had suggested to Adoniram's father that the boy learn navigation? His parish of Hamilton was next door to Wenham on the north. He knew Mr. Judson and could hardly have failed to know of the son.

The ministry had not kept Cutler from a career of adventure. Yale graduate of the class of 1765, he had been pastor at Hamilton from 1771 — when it was called "Ipswich Hamlet" — but his pastorate never interfered with his being a chaplain in the Revolutionary Army, with his forming the Ohio Company and leading settlers into the Far West — where he helped establish Marietta, Ohio — or later with his serving in Congress. Tall and portly, addicted to black velvet suits with silk stockings and silver knee and shoe buckles, he had a daring, unconventional mind that ranged through every field of learning. He practiced medicine, inoculated for smallpox, measured the distance of the stars with sextant and telescope, studied Jupiter's moons, made botanical investigations, and did a good deal of work with the microscope — then an almost unheard-of instrument of science.

Did he encourage the father's ambitions? Who knows? But with men like Cutler almost next door, and prosperity like Salem's almost as close, and with a son to whom the complexities of navigations were scarcely more than child's play, what golden dreams may have shimmered in the father's head?

If he had such dreams, they were to fade. For once more he was approaching the end of his pastorate. The reasons, so far as we can glimpse them in the minutes of the town meetings and the church records which Mr. Judson kept in his own handwriting, involve a baffling mixture of his failing health, his need for money, overlapping authority between church and town with regard to the support of the pastor, and his own rigid character.

In June of 1799, Mr. Judson asked the church for permission to give up preaching for three or four weeks "to ride for health." The church refused; whereupon Mr. Judson asked to be dismissed from his pastorate. This request was likewise refused.

At the same time, Mr. Judson had a matter to take up with the town. It was the town which paid his salary, as established by vote, and his salary had not been increased since he first settled in Wenham. The original ninety-five pounds was now paid in United States currency and had been determined as $316.66 a year. But dollars had fallen in value, so that although the needs of his three children were increasing as they grew older, the money he received bought less and less.

Unfortunately for Mr. Judson, the town's prosperity was declining too, and as a consequence its citizens were becoming more tax-conscious. A good many voters were not members of the church; and the abolition of the "halfway covenant" had probably discouraged some from trying to join. When the town met in July to decide what to do about "making up the Depreciation" of his salary, and learned from Deacon Stephen Dodge and Captain Samuell Blanchard that he wanted a permanent increase or his dismissal, the voters reacted to the ultimatum by agreeing unanimously not to make any addition to his salary at all, *either* permanently or yearly.

This left Mr. Judson no choice but to ask again for his dismissal, which he did in August, two days before Adoniram's eleventh birthday. The church refused it a second time, unanimously. But his health was failing so badly that a few days later he told the congregation after Sunday service that he must go to Saratoga Springs to recover, or be given a dismissal at once. Forced thus, the church voted to wait until he returned to decide the whole matter.

He was away six weeks. He had been back in Wenham only a

few days when he renewed his request to be dismissed. Once again he was denied, but in the confusion the meeting chose a committee by unanimous vote to agree upon dismissal terms. When the church met again to hear the report, the members rejected it, saying they wanted the minister to remain. They asked for another town meeting to consider the depreciation of money, and in addition voted as a church to give Mr. Judson five pounds a year in place of the undependable contributions, plus twelve loads of wood and an annual vacation of four or five weeks, provided that the town would vote a satisfactory increase in his legal salary. This the town refused to do. Instead, town and church finally agreed on the same day in October to grant the minister the dismissal he had requested so many times. The town did, however, agree to pay the cost of the ecclesiastical council which was to meet at the inn of Patty Lewis and ratify the terms of the separation. The council duly met on October 22, 1799, Manasseh Cutler being one of the members, and ratified the agreement so tortuously arrived at. And in the fellowship engendered by the good food and the many bowls of punch and glasses of wine which were customarily consumed at public expense at such meetings, the reverend members inscribed a curious sentence in the record of their findings:

*And while they bear testimony of their respect for Mr. Judson & esteem for his character, they cannot refrain from expressing their appreciation of the spirit, which the town has discovered toward him, & the liberality & candor which appeared to the gentlemen who conducted the business before the Council in the town's behalf.* Were they thanking the taxpayers of Wenham for their generous entertainment? Or were they saying that the Reverend Mr. Judson's inflexibility made him hard to get along with?

We do not know. We do know that the boy Adoniram was old enough to follow what was going on, and to draw his own conclusions from his father's example. And of those conclusions, one was: NEVER COMPROMISE.

## CHAPTER IV

# Braintree, Plymouth and Brown
## [ *1800–1807* ]

SO, in that fall of 1799, ended the Judsons' life in Wenham. The following spring found the family in Braintree, a few miles south of Boston.

It was an uncertain time. As the father's health improved, he made shift to support his family by any means at hand. Early in July the Massachusetts Home Missionary Society employed him as a missionary to the "interior parts of Vermont." During the three months he spent in Vermont he gave some forty sermons, and his employers paid him one hundred and eight dollars — about a third of a year's salary in Wenham.

He may have made other missionary journeys, and he probably filled in at neighboring churches from time to time. On at least one occasion he may have tried his hand at business, for an Adoniram Judson is mentioned as having conveyed to Wilson Marsh a patent for dyeing coach laces blue, a transaction in which this Mr. Judson acted as agent for a Noah Pond. Coach lace was a kind of brightly colored woven band, two or three inches wide, which was used as trimming for the upholstery of coaches; and at this time Wilson Marsh operated a flourishing establishment for its manufacture in Quincy, Braintree's neighbor town to the north.

In this new and unsettled existence, how fared the boy Adoniram? The Wenham parsonage had meant security and home from his fourth to his eleventh year. The move must have shaken him, but though he had his reputation to make over again, he still enjoyed his mother's love, his father's faith, and the admiration of Abby and Elnathan. Nevertheless, thrown on his own resources in a strange neighborhood, he must have found his main occupation in books and study even more than ever.

As for ambition, that flame never flickered. His father, looking for compensation in a time of depression, would certainly have seen to that. The way from Braintree to Quincy led past the unpretentious house of John Adams — farmer, lawyer, diplomat, and now in 1800 President of the United States. If Mr. Judson ever walked with his son along that dusty road on the way to see Mr. Marsh about the coach lace patent, he could not have failed to point out the house to Adoniram and to draw the moral. Adoniram Judson the younger had just as much native ability as John Adams at the same age and just as good a start. He was capable of becoming as great a man. And he would. He *must*.

But the Judsons were to live only two years in Braintree; for even as they left Wenham events were in the making in Plymouth which would result in the offer of a pastorate to Mr. Judson. Once again the cause was the old liberal–conservative controversy.

As the year 1800 opened Dr. James Kendall had become pastor of the Congregational Church of Plymouth. He was one of the liberals and, as it turned out, a very large minority of his congregation objected vigorously to his liberalism. Such feeling arose that in the fall of 1801 eighteen men and thirty-four women — one less than half the membership of the church — withdrew. At the end of March, 1802, their number now grown to one hundred and fifty-four, they incorporated as the Third Congregational Church of Plymouth and immediately began to erect a church edifice on the west side of Plymouth's Training Green, on the hill slope overlooking the harbor east of Town Brook.

They wasted no time in calling Mr. Judson. He was formally installed on the twelfth of May, and moved his family to Plymouth on the twenty-second. Two years to the day from their removal to Braintree righteousness had triumphed.

In the early 1800's Plymouth had a population of about thirty-five hundred. It was by far the largest town in which the Judson family had lived, but the section Mr. Judson chose for a home was still unpeopled.

The built-up area tended to cluster along the highway which led out onto Cape Cod, or between the highway and the harbor, west

of Town Brook and near Leyden Street, the first street laid out by
the Pilgrims in the Plymouth Colony, which ran straight back from
the harbor and up a hill called "Burial Hill" or "Fort Hill." On top
of this hill the Pilgrims had placed their first fort, and its outlines
were visible when the Judsons moved to the town. Later the hill
was used for the town burial ground. Many years later, when
Adoniram's sister Abigail was laid to rest there beside her mother,
the diggers of her grave were to discover part of the old Pilgrim
fort's guardhouse, the location of which had been forgotten for
more than two centuries.

But the Judsons did not settle on this side of Town Brook. East
of the brook, in the direction of the new church and the Training
Green, the land rose upward into what was then known as "Watson's Hill." Earlier it had been called "Mill Hill," and even earlier,
"Strawberry Hill." On this hill the Indian Chief Massasoit had
camped with his followers in April, 1621, while he sent his emissaries
Samoset and Squanto across Town Brook to notify the Pilgrims of
his presence. Here came Winslow to remain as hostage while the
great sachem visited the little settlement and made the treaty with
the Pilgrims which secured peace to them and protection to the
Indians.

Watson's Hill was still farm land when Mr. Judson bought land
on the seaward slope for a house and garden. The house he built
looked down to the harbor. A crude road in front of it, scarcely
more than a wagon track, became known as "the way to the new
meeting house." Later, it was called "the way to Mr. Judson's
house"; still later, "Judson Street"; and today, "Pleasant Street." The
house still stands — Number 17 Pleasant Street.

In time Mr. Judson was to buy more land around his house.
Eventually, as Plymouth grew, he divided it into house lots, which
he sold. The money, along with what other funds he could spare
from time to time, he invested in the stock of banks in the vicinity
of Boston. Dividends were high by today's standards. The stocks
increased in value. Mr. Judson was never afterwards to be wholly
dependent upon his ministerial salary, and was to die in comparative
affluence for a minister who never had a large church.

But this was in the future and was to have little to do with

Adoniram. He was nearly fourteen when the family moved to Plymouth. Once more life took on stability and security, in the pattern of Wenham. But the boy had learned that solidity of place and position are not essential to existence. Any half-formed ambitions in his mind — or his father's — of becoming a navigator and captain had been left behind in Wenham. There was little in Plymouth to encourage them. As a port, it lacked the splendor of Salem. Its ships were numerous but smaller, engaged in the duller pursuits of coastwise trade and cod fishing, and rows of flakes on which cod were cured gave out their pungent aroma along the shore. Its seamen knew the haunts of cod and the price of molasses in the small harbors of the Caribbean, but not the teeming waterfront life of Singapore, Canton and Bombay, or the tangy scents of coffee and of pepper.

His destiny now, Adoniram felt, was to become an orator, a poet, or a statesman — another John Adams, perhaps. But something connected with books and learning, something involving moving people's minds and hearts rather than grubby trade, something that would win him praise and fame and make his name ring down the ages.

Then, with the family scarcely settled in Plymouth, he fell ill — critically, nearly fatally ill. For a long time it was a question whether he would live or die. When it became clear he would live, he had ahead of him more than a year of convalescence.

Bookish and intellectualized as he was becoming, he had nevertheless always been active physically. He had liked to walk for hours — Abby and Elnathan sometimes tagging along. He had thrown himself into work and play with restless energy. He had been outward-looking rather than self-centered; even his vague ambitions always included others with him as their leader.

Now, lying in bed for months with nothing to do, he became introspective. He began to think of different things, peculiar things, strangely frightening things, thoughts that cast a new, lurid ominous light on his ambitions.

Suppose he became the most famous, most idolized man in the country. What difference could that make to him when he was dead? He had read about the great men of the past. Caesar, Virgil,

Cicero, Demosthenes — their names were known, they were praised, but they did not know it, for they were only dust.

Slowly, another thought came to him as he lay under the expansive counterpane. It was not new, but it came to him in a new way, with a new force. There were two worlds, two lives, for each person: this one — brief, narrow, finite; and the hereafter — eternal, limitless, infinite. Fame, to mean anything, should go with one into the next world, where one could enjoy it perpetually.

But that fame, he thought, came only from goodness, holiness, religion. He began to modify his ambitions. Perhaps, he mused, he would like to become a famous minister in charge of a wealthy city church — a great Boston church, for example, where he could expound his sermons to a thousand or more fashionably dressed gentlemen and ladies who would hang on every word as he stood in the pulpit above them. He would have praise and fame, and not only in this world.

As he toyed with this pleasing prospect, half smiling as he imagined the sea of admiring faces staring up at him from the crowded pews, he began to be aware of a feeling of uneasiness. Without realizing how it happened, he found himself comparing this minister with an obscure country pastor, humbly striving only to bring his congregation and himself to God, without any thought of self. The minister in whose place he had imagined himself was really no better than any other ambitious man, anxious only for fame. What would the judgment be on him in the next world? If he achieved heaven, he would certainly not achieve fame in heaven. It would be the obscure country pastor whose fame would ring out there through eternity, even though he were never heard of here. The world was wrong about its heroes. The world was wrong in its judgments. The fame of the unknown country pastor was really the greater — so much greater that any worldly accomplishment shrank into insignificance. This was the only fame that triumphed over the grave.

Suddenly through his mind words rang out so powerfully that he all but heard them spoken: "Not unto us, not unto us, but to Thy name be the glory." And with the words such a dreadful shock of realization that he almost sat bolt upright in bed.

He had always wanted to be truly religious. He had been learning the lessons of religion since he first understood words. Yet how could he be religious and accomplish any ambition in this world?

There was a terrible contradiction here. For a moment, in a flash of inner anguish, he saw that he did not really want to be a Christian at all, for being a Christian stood in the way of his being a great man. Yet his father, a Christian, and the very image of the obscure country pastor, had predicted that he would be a great man, had encouraged Adoniram's ambitions; and, ever since Adoniram could remember, he had set himself to fulfill his father's prediction.

The contradiction was insoluble. Dimly he must have sensed it involved something in his father as well as in himself. The only way to get rid of it was to force it quickly down, out of thought. Yet for that one brief moment the insight was so vivid and painful that he would remember it to the end of his life.

As he recovered, Adoniram's unpleasant introspections were buried in the routine of study. He had lost a year of schooling. The next year he made it up and gained a year besides, so that by his sixteenth birthday in 1804 he was ready to enter college.

Though a graduate of Yale himself, Adoniram's father did not select Yale for his son, perhaps because New Haven was too far from Plymouth. Yet Harvard, only fifty miles away at Cambridge, was out of the question on account of its lax theology. Instead, Mr. Judson decided on Rhode Island College at Providence. Providence was no farther from Plymouth to the south than Cambridge was to the north; and in doctrine, Mr. Judson felt, it was as sound as Yale. He knew the views of its president, Asa Messer, and on the whole approved of them. True, it was nominally a Baptist school, but Mr. Judson felt himself closer to most of the opinions of the Baptists than to those of the liberal Congregationalist faction; and in any case three times as many of its graduates had become Congregational ministers as had become Baptist, and Congregationalists were represented among its trustees. As he turned the matter over in his mind, Mr. Judson felt Adoniram would be safe enough at Rhode Island College.

Adoniram entered college just six days after his sixteenth birthday. He could not have stood out particularly as he made his first appearance on the unimpressive campus, a rough ungraded field about eight acres in size, walled with stone on three sides, fenced with wood in front, enclosing a few dusty shade trees, their dark green leaves drooping in August's heat. A slender lad of no more than medium height, he was not distinguished in physique. A girl might have glanced a second time at his curly chestnut hair, and perhaps sensed unusual vitality in the elasticity of his step and in the warm brilliance of his ready smile. But she might also have decided his nose was a little too large for even masculine good looks. His clothing was of distinctly inexpensive material. Although scrupulously neat and clean, it had seen plenty of wear. Before being finally discarded, it would be repaired again and again with the sewing kit Adoniram's mother had foresightedly packed with his belongings — for she had taught him to sew long ago.

By superficial standards, he should not have attracted any particular attention. Yet the fact is that, without wealth, physical distinction or established reputation to pave the way in advance, Adoniram began to make an impression at once — not only on the faculty but on his classmates, and soon, through the acquaintances he formed, even on the young ladies of Providence.

It began when he was admitted. On examination it appeared that he was already so well grounded in such subjects as Latin, Greek, mathematics, geography, and astronomy, which together with logic, oratory, rhetoric, and moral philosophy were the backbone of the curriculum, that there was no reason why he should have to take the studies of the Freshman year. Instead he was allowed to enter the Sophomore class.

His professors became aware of him almost instantly. Always perfectly prepared, always self-possessed, he never even hesitated in recitations, let alone ever failing. By the end of the school year (the college having changed its name, shortly after Adoniram entered, to "Brown University" — in honor of Nicholas Brown, merchant prince, who had just given it the first of several magnificent gifts) President Messer felt it incumbent on himself to write Adoniram's father about his son: ". . . and this, I can assure you, is not by way of complaint. A uniform propriety of conduct, as well as an intense application to study, distinguishes his character. Your expectations of him, however sanguine, must certainly be gratified. I most heartily congratulate you, my dear sir, on that charming prospect which you have exhibited in this very amiable and promising son; and I most heartily pray that the Father of mercies may make him now, while a youth, a son in his spiritual family and give him an earnest of the inheritance of the saints in light."

Mr. Judson's heart must have swelled with pride as he read this glowing praise. But pleased as he was, he was not surprised. Adoniram was only turning out to be what he had always predicted and always hoped for.

But Adoniram did not make a favorable impression on his faculty alone. Brown had less than a hundred and fifty students who lived, dined, studied, and attended classes and chapel in the large four-storied "college edifice" now known as University Hall. They discovered at once that he was the opposite of a narrow bookworm and that, in spite of being a minister's son, he had very little interest in the twice-weekly meetings of the Praying Society. Instead, he was high-spirited, irrepressibly gay, obliging, always easy to get along with. The student body at Brown in Adoniram's years there included a number of men who were to distinguish themselves in later life: future Congressmen; a Justice of the Massachusetts Supreme Court; a Governor of New York, Senator, Secretary of War and Secretary of State. But even among these men he stood out.

One future Congressman, Adoniram's classmate John Bailey, his keenest scholastic rival, quickly became one of his two or three closest friends. Bailey proposed him for the Philermenian Society, which, with its membership limited to forty-five, played the role of a fraternity of today but devoted its meetings to debates, speeches and its members' literary efforts.

An even closer friend, however, and one who influenced him more, was a member of the class ahead of Adoniram's. In after years, his name was charitably disguised as "E——," but he was almost certainly Jacob Eames of Belfast, Maine, "amiable, talented, witty, extremely agreeable in person and manners, but a confirmed Deist. A very strong friendship sprang up between the two young men, founded on similar tastes and sympathies; and Judson soon became, at least professedly, as great an unbeliever as his friend."

Proud as he was of his son's scholastic accomplishments, if Adoniram's father had even suspected he was dabbling in Deism he would have ridden posthaste to Providence and removed him from Brown at once. Liberal Congregationalism was anathema. Unitarianism and Universalism were unspeakable. But Deism . . . ! Mr. Judson's creed was founded on a strict construction of the Scriptures, aided by logic. It was a creed with a hell of flame as well as a heaven of bliss. The Deist rejected all revealed religion — the Bible, New Testament and Old, no less than the words of Mohammed and Buddha held to be sacred by their followers. All the Deist admitted was the existence of a personal God. Voltaire had been a Deist. Tom Paine had been a Deist. Benjamin Franklin had been a Deist. But so had the monsters of the French Revolution. The trials of Job multiplied ten times over would have been as flea bites compared to the feelings of Mr. Judson if he had known his cherished son admitted himself a Deist.

But he did not. In the bliss of ignorance, the father read and reread Asa Messer's congratulatory letter and flattered himself that Adoniram was turning out precisely as he had always hoped.

Meanwhile, Adoniram and Jacob Eames and John Bailey and their friends studied, attended parties in the homes of Providence's young ladies, walked together, talked together, and played together. But of all his friends, Eames had the ascendancy. Together they discussed what they would do with their lives. Sometimes they favored law, because it could lead to Congress, to the Senate, even to the Presidency. Sometimes they favored literature. America needed a literature of its own. They could become the Shakespeares, the Ben Jonsons, of the New World; write great plays, see them performed, consort with the interesting denizens of the stage, the actors — yes, and the actresses, too. But the ministry was never even considered. Fame was tangible — in this world, here and now, achievable. Where and when were heaven and hell?

As easily as this, the whole structure of the belief so carefully indoctrinated in Adoniram by his father collapsed like a house of cards. Or was belief, sown and nurtured in infancy, more like a plant with deep roots penetrating far into the very foundations of personality, involving forces never to appear to memory or awareness?

At any rate, the youth Adoniram felt a sense of relief. Perhaps he felt logic had a sharp edge, like a scythe. Wielded by the confident

Jacob Eames it leveled the dark tangled growth of the old creed and let the sun shine in. Now everything was so much simpler. Fame was the goal, ambition the spur. This his father had taught him. Now he could pursue the goal unfettered.

Perhaps something else was satisfied: an unacknowledged wish to surpass his father, to conquer, yet to win his approval. In his new, more logical belief he surpassed the Reverend Adoniram Judson. Most certainly he defeated him. Fame for the son was the father's deepest wish. Its pursuit was approved.

But there were uneasy flickers of guilt. Rejecting the father's God was rejecting the father. Something quivered with fear, something linked with childish memory and emotion, at the thought of that stern man's disapproval. Fortunately, it was not necessary to mention one's new beliefs at home. If that did not resolve the inner conflict, at least it deferred the outer one. Meanwhile he concentrated on his immediate goal: to be first in his class, valedictorian. This his father wanted; Adoniram himself wanted it. Together they had looked forward to it. He deliberately worked for it. There had been an obstacle: his Senior year he had had to teach six weeks in Plymouth to earn money for his support. Nevertheless, he succeeded. No sooner did he learn he had won the honor than he hurried to his room and wrote:

> Dear Father,
>     I have got it.
>         Your affectionate son,
>             A. J.

As he sealed the note, he realized all at once how his flushed, almost wildly elated expression might seem to his classmates. Bailey, his closest friend since Jacob Eames had left the year before, had raced him neck and neck to be first in class. Bailey had lost. Bailey would think Adoniram was exulting over him, glorying in his defeat! So would the other members of the Philermenian Society. But try as he would, he could not put on an air of indifference; the joy showed through too plainly.

Opening his door just a trifle, he peered down the hall, watching for a moment when no one was in sight. When he was sure it was deserted, he slipped rapidly down the stairs of the college building, and made his way to the post office by a roundabout route. By the time he returned he was ready to receive congratulations with just the proper expression of pleasure for himself and sorrow for his competitor.

The commencement exercises were held September 2, 1807. Their length must have made them something of an ordeal for the audience — except, perhaps, for proud parents like Adoniram's father and mother. Eighteen of the twenty-eight students in the graduating class gave orations. Most of the addresses were on the conventional subjects of the time: "Mental Preparation"; "The Dignity of Man"; "Literary Excellence"; "The Durability of the Christian Religion"; "The Rising Glory of America."

The last speaker, in the position of highest honor, was Adoniram. By the time his turn came the perspiring auditors must have been nearly stupefied by the interminable torrent of words. Perhaps even his father did not pay too much attention to precisely what his son said. And the son had too much tact to say precisely what he thought. But there was a hint in the title by which his part was listed on the program:

18. *An Oration on Free Enquiry; with the Valedictory Addresses.*
. . . ADONIRAM JUDSON.

CHAPTER V

# Revolt

[ *New York: 1807–1808* ]

THUS, at nineteen, Adoniram was ready to begin the work of his life. But as yet he had no idea what it would be.

Lacking any better plan, he opened the "Plymouth Independent Academy" within two weeks of graduation, probably keeping his classes in the family house on Pleasant Street. His spare time he used to write a textbook, which he finished in February under the title *Elements of English Grammar.* He sent the manuscript to President Messer and Calvin Park, one of his instructors. They replied approvingly, "It exhibits a fresh instance of the ingenious literary enterprise and perseverance of the author; and should you decide to give it to the public, it will, we hope, meet, as its merits, a generous patronage." He found a publisher for the book, Cushing and Lincoln, of Boston, and immediately went to work on another, *The Young Lady's Arithmetic,* which he completed toward the end of July.

As he surveyed his accomplishments that summer of 1808 he might have felt a good deal of satisfaction. Here he was, less than twenty and a year out of college, the author of two textbooks. Nevertheless, he was dissatisfied. His work seemed nothing but a way to occupy the time.

Worse, he was living a lie. Every day he dutifully took part in family worship. Sundays he faithfully attended church. No one, least of all his father and mother, suspected his real beliefs. But his private creed did not deny ethics and morality, nor condone dishonesty. Living as he did, he could not help feeling a hypocrite every time he knelt at family prayers.

Every week he grew more restless. What kind of career was writing grammars and young ladies' arithmetics? What kind of life was it to drill the Plymouth children whose parents sent them to his academy?

REVOLT                    37

Unhappily he remembered the ambitions he had shared with Jacob Eames only a few years ago. What had happened to them? Were they nothing but dreams?

That summer, with *The Young Lady's Arithmetic* done, he finally came to a decision. He would leave home. He would go to New York. He would become acquainted with the people of the theater. He would learn to write for the stage.

He knew that to his father and mother New York was the most sinful of American cities, and the theater the ultimate in depravity. In a way he was too much a product of their teaching to disagree with them. But, to a twenty-year-old philosophical Deist like himself, the immorality of the people of the stage had to be balanced against the morality and grandeur of great tragedies; and to write the tragedies he must learn the requirements of the stage where it flourished best. After all, perhaps actresses and actors were not so *very* immoral. His parents took too narrow a view of many things. Most likely they took too narrow a view of the people of the theater as well.

Just the same, caution kept him from telling them exactly what he had in mind. When he closed his academy on August 9 — his twentieth birthday — he merely said he planned to travel for a while and see something of the world. He thought he would visit his Uncle Ephraim, pastor of the church at Sheffield, some hundred and fifty miles westward. Since he would be so far west, he might go on and see Albany. The newly invented steamboat, *Clermont*, had been in service for a year. Perhaps he might take that to New York, just to see what it was like, and broaden himself by looking at some of the sights of the city.

His parents reacted precisely as if he had casually announced his decision to take a little trip to the moon.

At first, they were incredulous. Then, when they realized that Adoniram was determined, they displayed a sort of horrified amazement. What was wrong, his mother asked, with the pleasant family circle in Plymouth? Why, demanded his father, had he suddenly decided to interrupt a promising career? Adoniram had no answer. They could not realize he had come to the point where he must throw off their rule, no matter how benevolent, and act and think for himself. He could not explain it. And why should he have to?

As he restlessly listened to their remonstrances, unreasoning anger began to rise in him. His father — unyielding, unperceptive to the nuances of feeling in others — finally goaded him too far. Why, asked the Reverend Mr. Judson, did not Adoniram study to become a minister, if he had found that teaching was not to his taste?

A minister? All at once Adoniram's resentment boiled over. Furiously, he flung out the truth. His father and mother froze with horror as Adoniram's words struck their startled ears.

The God of the Third Church of Plymouth was not his God, Adoniram told them. He could not believe that the Bible was anything but the work of men — any more than were the Koran or the sacred writings of Buddha — great as its principles might be. Even Jesus . . . He was certainly the son of man, but almost as certainly not the Son of God except in the sense that all men are.

Mr. Judson was outraged. What had got into the boy? He had felt sure that at Brown, of all places, no harm would be done to his son's soul. Certainly these pernicious vaporizings did not come from any of the faculty. They must have been picked up from some fellow student infected with the noisome Jacobinism blowing over from France these years. If so, a few solid arguments should set the boy right.

Swallowing his anger, Mr. Judson set himself to reason with Adoniram. Very shortly he realized with dismay that every argument he advanced was being met by two better ones. Not for nothing had Adoniram been valedictorian of his class. Exposing the fallacies in his father's syllogisms was child's play. Point by point, with crushing finality, he demolished every thesis his father set out to prove. By nightfall, Adoniram was completely master of the field. So far as logic and evidence went, Mr. Judson had to concede that Adoniram had everything in his favor. Mr. Judson was beaten. He still knew he was right, but he could not prove it. He lapsed into grim, impotent silence.

Adoniram might have gone to bed flushed with triumph had his mother not possessed other, more deadly, weapons: tears, prayers, and expostulations. Weeping, she pursued him from room to room. How could he do this to his mother? If he loved her, how could he consent to fry in hell for eternity, while his mother and father enjoyed heaven? How could she enjoy heaven knowing her

son was in hell? She used no logic. She simply assumed that, through
some perverseness of his own, her beloved Adoniram chose the
devil against God, hell against heaven, and wounding her feelings
against making her happy.

When, finally, she saw that Adoniram withstood her, she turned
to prayers. Wherever he turned, he saw her bowed in prayer and
heard her lifting her voice brokenly, sobbing, pleading with God to
change the heart of her wayward son and save him from damnation.

For Adoniram it was a little hell. He endured it for six days until,
on the fifteenth of August, mounted on a horse his father gave him
as part of his inheritance, he rode westward down the steep grade
of Pleasant Street, crossed Town Brook, and slowly jogged on
toward Boston, Worcester and Sheffield.

He had won his freedom, but he was not entirely happy with it.
He passed over the broad Connecticut River at the village of
Springfield and presently found himself among the mountains, green
in August, rising around him like the huge combers of the sea. It
was a kind of country he had never seen before. As he thought of
the new life ahead, his spirits began to soar with the hills; yet he
could not quite throw off a certain uneasiness.

At Sheffield his Uncle Ephraim, now an old man of seventy,
received him kindly, but Adoniram stayed at the parsonage only
overnight. In the morning, leaving his horse in his uncle's care, he
pressed on over the hills to Albany. There he took passage on the
*Clermont* for New York.

The trip down the river was so much of a success that he always
remembered it afterward with pleasure. As the little craft churned
along, its paddle wheels thrashing and its stack belching thick
clouds of wood smoke, Adoniram savored the thrill of being a
passenger on the first successful steamboat. Even the Berkshires had
not prepared him for the grandeur of the Hudson Valley. He never
forgot beetling Bear Mountain, all but overhanging the deck as the
*Clermont* threaded her way through a river narrowing to a few
hundred yards; nor the lakelike expanse of the Tappan Zee —
haunted at times, so it was said, by an old Dutch wraith ship; nor
the towering rampart of the Palisades. He struck up casual acquaintance with a few of the men leaning idly along the rail. They
must have pointed out to him the vast manor of the Van Rensselaers,

its extent measured not in acres but in scores of miles, its wealth not by farms but by the cities flourishing on its land. Perhaps some of them told him the legends of the river — perhaps of the goblin who guarded the Donderberg, Thunder Mountain, to whom river vessels lowered their peaks as they sailed by. "There's where Major André was captured," one of them, a veteran of the Revolution, might have commented, pointing with his cigar at the Tarrytown shore. "There's where they rowed him across the river. And over there, on the opposite shore, out of sight beyond the cliffs, is where they tried and hanged him." And a few miles farther, "And down below there, see there. That's the Harlem River, going off to the left. That point's the upper end of Manhattan Island. Our troops skedaddled out of there upriver when the British drove them off that high land. And down there . . . 'way, 'way down — can't hardly see it yet . . . that's New York, down on the end of the island."

They called him "Mr. Johnson." Perhaps he mumbled his name when someone asked for it. Perhaps the clanking machinery and puffing steam muffled it. With some intuitive caution, he let the error stand.

Covered with cinders and smoke grime, he stepped off the *Clermont*, heart pounding with excitement, and made off over the cobbled streets for the theaters he had been dreaming of. Who knows how his enthusiasm pictured them? He may have expected to see brilliant temples of pleasure peopled with thespians almost more handsome, more witty, more talented than human.

If so, he was disappointed. It was true that commerce was in process of making New York more populous and prosperous than either Boston or Philadelphia and its arts were beginning to flourish as never before on the continent. Only two years before, the play of a boy even younger than Adoniram — young John Howard Payne — had been produced, and he had even acted successfully though briefly. His family had promptly packed him off to Union College in Schenectady, from which he was to return, within six months of Adoniram's arrival in the city, to act and write plays again with astounding success, though the future would remember him mainly for his haunting song, "Home, Sweet Home."

But Payne came from one of New York's best families. All doors were open to him as they were to such young men-about-town as

Washington Irving. Then, as now, the city was cold to obscure young men. And a young man of twenty with nothing to recommend him but a wish to learn how to write for the stage could not expect to be received with open arms.

Worse, Adoniram had arrived in one of the quietest months of a rather poor theatrical year. Only a few theaters were open. Most of the entertainment consisted of variety: Pepin and Breschard's circus, which had come down from Boston; sleight of hand, magic and tumbling acts (livened, to be sure, with a three-act farce, *The Doctor's Courtship*) at the Lyceum. There were a few benefits, but well-known players were earning even less than the six dollars or so they were accustomed to make weekly in better years. By comparison, the Reverend Mr. Judson's salary was munificent.

The prospects were poor for a young stranger. But Adoniram persisted, and in a few days he succeeded in attaching himself to a shabby little band of strolling players who were trying their prospects where they could outside the city. For a few weeks he roamed with them, living, as he said later, "a reckless, vagabond life, finding lodgings where we could, and bilking the landlord where we found opportunity — in other words running up a score, and then decamping without paying the reckoning."

For some, the life might have been fascinating. For Adoniram it was the opposite of his anticipations. If there was a better theater somewhere, more like his dreams, capable of opening a road to the fulfillment of his ambitions, he did not know where it was or how to find it.

Disgusted, heartsick, he left without notice one night, and, nursing his disappointment, made his way back to his uncle's home in Sheffield.

The experience in New York had left Adoniram without a plan. Unless he wanted to go home, he could think of nothing better than procuring his horse from his uncle and continuing to wander.

But he was uneasy. What should he strive for now? He felt aimless. He had expected to find a more honest, freer world, swelling with fresh, brilliant thought and companionship. But the world he *did* find was a tawdry world of bombast and fustian. Its honesty was a kind of thieves' honor. By contrast, his father's character,

with all its obstinate wrongheadedness, stood out in simple grandeur.
His father could be mistaken — was mistaken, in fact — but he was
honest granite clear through.

In this bewildered mood Adoniram returned to Ephraim Judson's
parsonage. His uncle was away and a young minister, as yet without
a regular charge, was taking his place. But it was too late in the day
to ride on, so Adoniram decided to spend the night at the parsonage.

The two young men — close enough to the same age to talk as
equals — spent several hours in conversation. Adoniram was struck
by the fact that, although his host was as pious as his father, there
was a warmth, "a solemn but gentle earnestness," in his speech which
kindled an answering warmth in the heart. To be a devoted minister
it was not necessary, it seemed, to be austere and dictatorial like
the Reverend Mr. Judson.

Adoniram rode away in the morning deeply impressed. Perhaps
the young minister would never find the fame Adoniram was looking for, but neither would he experience the pain of Adoniram's
inner conflict. He was at peace with himself.

These were Adoniram's thoughts as he rode on, still trending
away from Plymouth. September's frosts were already dappling
the green mountainsides with flecks of red, but Adoniram scarcely
noticed them. He was absorbed in trying to understand how this
man, not much older than he himself, could apparently be without
ambition and yet have such inner tranquillity.

As night drew on he found himself passing through a small village. Finding the local inn, he stabled his horse and asked the innkeeper for a room. The house was nearly full, said the landlord
apologetically. But he had one next to a young man who was
critically ill, perhaps dying. He might be disturbed, but . . . ? No,
said Adoniram, still wrapped in his own thoughts, he would not let
a few noises next door deny him a night's rest. After giving him
something to eat, the landlord lighted Adoniram to this room and
left him. Without further ado, Adoniram got into bed, and waited
for sleep to come.

But though the night was still, he could not sleep. In the next
room beyond the partition he could hear sounds, not very loud;
footsteps coming and going; a board creaking; low voices; a groan
or gasp. These did not disturb him unduly — not even the realiza-

tion that a man might be dying. Death was a commonplace in Adoniram's New England. It might come to anyone, at any age.

What disturbed him was the thought that the man in the next room might not be prepared for death. Was he, himself? A confusing coil of speculation unwound itself as he lay half dreaming, half waking, while the autumn chill stole down from the mountains and crept through every crack and cranny of the house. He wondered how he himself would face death. His father would welcome it as a door opening outward to immortal glory. So much his creed had done for him. But to Adoniram the son, the freethinker, the Deist, the infidel, lying huddled under the covers, death was an exit, not an entrance. It was a door to an empty pit, to darkness darker than night, at best to extinction, at worst to — what? On this matter his philosophy was silent. It had no answer but "Who knows?"

He had always been neat and well groomed. His mother had taught him to be fastidious. He cared for his own person. But he must die, and the grave was a cold, dark place. His flesh crawled. Was the wet earthy mold and the motionless body, the slow dissolution of muscle and tendon, the slower crumbling of bone, the immense weight of soil — was this all, through the endless centuries? What of that part of Adoniram Judson he thought of as "I"? Did it go out like the flame of a candle? Or did it, too, stay in the ground with the flesh?

There was terror in these fantastically unwinding ideas. But as they presented themselves, another part of himself jeered. *Midnight fancies!* that part said scornfully. What a skin-deep thing this freethinking philosophy of Adoniram Judson, valedictorian, scholar, teacher, ambitious man, must be! What would the classmates at Brown say to these terrors of the night, who thought of him as bold in thought? Above all, what would Eames say — Eames the clearheaded, skeptical, witty, talented? He imagined Eames's laughter, and felt shame.

When Adoniram woke the sun was streaming in the window. His apprehensions had vanished with the darkness. He could hardly believe he had given in to such weakness. He dressed quickly and ran downstairs, looking for the innkeeper. It was past time to have breakfast, pay his reckoning, saddle his horse and be on his way.

He found his host, asked for the bill, and — perhaps noticing the man somber-faced — asked casually whether the young man in the next room was better. "He is dead," was the answer.

"Dead?" Adoniram was taken aback. There was a heavy finality to the word. For an instant, some of his fear of the night made itself felt once more. Adoniram stammered out the few conventional phrases common to humanity when death takes someone nearby, and asked the inevitable question: "Do you know who he was?"

"Oh yes. Young man from the college in Providence. Name was Eames, Jacob Eames."

How he got through the next few hours Adoniram was never able to remember.

All he recalled afterwards was that he did not try to leave the inn until some hours had passed. Whether he looked on Eames's body, whether he made himself known as Eames's friend, whether any of Eames's relatives or family were in the village, whether he wept — on all this he was always silent.

Later, however, he found himself on the road, continuing his journey, without being sure how he came to be there. He was aware that one word was tolling in his mind like a bell: the word "Lost!"

Lost. In death, Jacob Eames was lost — utterly, irrevocably lost. Lost to his friends, to the world, to the future. Lost as a puff of smoke is lost in the infinity of air. If Eames's own views were true, neither his life nor his death had any meaning. The coincidence of his dying on the other side of a partition from Adoniram, in a remote country inn, was simply a meaningless incident in a plan too huge and impersonal to take account of individuals.

But suppose Eames had been mistaken? Suppose the Scriptures were literally true and a personal God real? Then Jacob Eames was already lost in a most desperate sense. For already, this moment, Eames knew his error — too late for repentance. Knowing his mistake, regretting it with a bitterness which no living human could ever possibly imagine, he was experiencing already the unimaginable torments of the flames of hell — any chance of remedy, of going back, of correcting, lost, eternally lost.

Thus the pattern in Adoniram's shocked mind. It was the night-thoughts back again, but in a more dreadful form. The road was an ordinary country road, barely more than a trail, dusty and warm in the September sun. The horse ambled quietly, almost unguided, the saddle leather squeaking as always. But there was an indefinable menace everywhere. Even the flaming reds against the thick evergreens on the hillside suggested hungry tongues of hell's flame licking through the forest cover from under the granite beneath.

For that hell should open in that country inn and snatch Jacob Eames, his dearest friend and guide, from the next bed — this could not, simply could not, be pure coincidence.

Adoniram knew his father's God very well. He was omniscient. He knew everything. He was omnipotent. He had all power. He could foresee where Adoniram would be that night, could foresee his leaving New York when and why he did. He could foresee that Jacob Eames would be where he was, fall sick, die, be damned.

More: being All-Powerful, this He must have done with a purpose, for He could have arranged matters otherwise.

This God of the Bible, Adoniram had been taught, was an angry God, a vindictive God. But He was a just God. He could be a loving God. And He gave ample warning. If This was the real God, it was no mere coincidence that Adoniram had fallen in among rogues and left, disgusted. It was no coincidence that the pious young man had been at his uncle Ephraim's house to converse with him. It was no coincidence that Adoniram had spent this particular night at this particular inn, thinking those particular thoughts. He had been warned, amply warned.

*Was* This the real God? If so, He had a purpose for Adoniram, which Adoniram must learn to read. In his very bones, all at once, logic or no logic, Adoniram was imbued with the feeling that the God of the Bible was the real God. And Adoniram was filled with despair and dread. For Deist logic and evidence said "No."

Suddenly he reined in his horse. Without realizing it, he had been continuing the tour he had planned originally. He straightened in the saddle for a moment of decision. Yes, he must find out about this, once and for all. He turned the horse in the road, spurred it to a faster pace, and headed back in the direction from which he had come — homeward.

Toward Plymouth.

## CHAPTER VI

# The Dedication

*[ Andover: 1808 ]*

ADONIRAM reined his horse at the house in Plymouth on September 22, 1808. His journey had lasted only a little more than five weeks, but in that five weeks what had begun as the throwing off of parental control, a natural preliminary to manhood, had turned into a soul-shaking inner convulsion. He was in mortal fear for his own soul.

On his return his parents at last became fully aware of the gravity of their son's inner crisis but they were unable to help him. His intuitions and feelings — all those deep unconscious conceptions instilled in infancy — urged him to accept his father's creed. But his mind, that keen instrument sharpened by careful training from childhood through college, would not be satisfied. It said that until incontrovertible evidence provided the facts, and logic came forth with the reasoning, Adoniram Judson could not be a wholehearted Christian.

His father had already shot his bolt. Since he could not even imagine how anyone could question the underlying premises of Christianity, he knew he was not equipped to deal with Adoniram's dilemma. Adoniram's mother and sister had the same weapons of tears and prayers they had used before — but using them only intensified Adoniram's agony. For Adoniram, faith must depend on more.

For a few days everyone in the parsonage was involved in one way or another with Adoniram's ordeal, except, perhaps Elnathan. At fourteen, he dutifully did the chores, but for the rest he must have been out of it. One suspects it was hard for him to see why the others were so upset. Quietly, perhaps observing with something like distaste, he may now have begun to form the resolutions that

eventually took him into an unusual channel for a Judson — medicine, and the Navy.

At this juncture, two visitors came to call on Adoniram's father.
They were Dr. Moses Stuart and Dr. Edward Dorr Griffin, both
leading figures among the conservative faction of Congregationalism. Dr. Stuart, not yet thirty, was already pastor of the important
First Church of New Haven. Dr. Griffin, about ten years older, held
the equally important pastorate of the First Presbyterian Church
of Newark, New Jersey. Like the Reverend Mr. Judson, both
were Yale graduates, and both had studied theology at New
Haven.

The subject they came to discuss was a new theological seminary
in which they had agreed to be professors. With Harvard in the
hands of the liberals, the orthodox needed their own divinity school.
Such a school had been incorporated a year ago. Now it was ready
to open. It was to be located on the premises of Phillips Academy
in Andover, some twenty-five miles northwest of Boston. Three
wealthy merchants — John Norris of Salem, and William Bartlet
and Moses Brown of Newburyport — had given forty thousand
dollars toward it. Samuel Abbot of Andover had donated twenty
thousand dollars for a professorship of Christian Theology. The
Phillips family of Andover, founders of the Academy, had erected
a suitable building.

The Reverend Mr. Judson had been intensely interested in the
progress of the new seminary since its conception, but just now he
had a more immediate motive for welcoming the visitors with open
arms. Perhaps men of their eminence could help his son, as he
could not.

Adoniram made an instant impression on these two divines. His
personality was ingratiating, yet without false humility. His mind
was of the finest order. He already knew more theology than many
theological students. He was open to conviction. He understood
that he must undergo inner regeneration before he could look
forward to faith and personal salvation. But clearly this was not to
be accomplished in a few hours of argument. The very qualities that
made the boy so worth saving made him hard to save. Yet the
visitors felt almost at once that if he could find conviction he could

become a minister such as had not been seen since the days of Whitefield and Jonathan Edwards.

After some discussion, they suggested that Adoniram enroll in the new seminary, where he would have the materials he needed to study to make up his own mind, and the counsel of some of the best theologians in the country. Adoniram resisted without actually declining, and they went away without learning his decision.

Within a day or so Adoniram received an offer to become an assistant teacher in a private academy in Boston. He accepted, and left for Boston only a week after having returned to Plymouth. But he carried his torment with him.

Hardly had he begun his new duties when he came across an old theological work, *The Fourfold State*, by Thomas Boston. At another time it might not have made much impression on him, but now only this little push was necessary. Almost at once he decided to enter the seminary as Dr. Stuart and Dr. Griffin had advised, in order to look there for the inner certainty he felt he needed so desperately.

He entered Andover Theological Seminary on the twelfth of October. He made no profession of religious belief, and was enrolled as a special student — not as a candidate for the ministry. As at Brown, he was admitted into the studies of the second year, thanks to his excellent academic background.

The village in which Adoniram now found himself was so isolated, in spite of its comparative nearness to Boston, that it could almost be called cloistered. The mail came three times a week. The recipient of a letter paid twenty-five cents for it. A newspaper was seldom seen unless someone brought one from Boston.

It was a pious place. A Sunday traveler, no matter what his reason for being on the road, could expect arrest and a fine. All work in the village ended at sunset on Saturday. From then until sunrise Monday the normal routine of life stopped. The only sounds were the sound of the church bells; the only traffic that of going to church and returning; the only preparation of meals, the placing of cold dishes on the table; the only reading, the Scriptures, or printed sermons, or the Shorter Catechism.

There was a low hill or ridge on the Academy grounds, a few

hundred yards to the east of the main road into Andover, which the students dubbed "Pisgah," or "Zion." At the foot of it the seminary's main building, Phillips Hall, had been erected just before Adoniram arrived, and here he was assigned a room. Like the college building at Brown, it was without ornament, spare, of red brick with a slate roof. One room was set aside as a chapel, another for a reading room, and thirty rooms were used for dormitory purposes. The Hall stood on the border of a huckleberry lot which flooded in heavy rains so that students and professors had to cross on stepping stones. At these times, the fields and meadows looked like shallow lakes.

Life at the seminary had a Spartan simplicity. The students heated their rooms with firewood they chopped themselves and drew water in pitchers from nearby wells. But this was no hardship for Adoniram. He was used to it. And living was cheap. There was no tuition. Rent was two to four dollars a year. The only other major expense was food, which was supplied by Mrs. Silence Smith, who had been licensed by the trustees' "Committee of Exigencies" to keep boarders in a low, brown, two story cottage nearby.

The members of the faculty lived like country ministers anywhere in New England, hoeing their own gardens, milking their own cows, and cutting their own hay. When Adoniram arrived, however, there were only two professors — Eliphalet Pearson, Professor of Sacred Literature; and Leonard Woods, Abbot Professor of Christian Theology. Dr. Pearson, who was about the age of Adoniram's father, was to serve for only a year before being succeeded by Moses Stuart, whom Adoniram already had met in Plymouth. Pearson had been at Andover earlier, as the first principal of Phillips Academy; but for the twenty years from 1786 to 1806 he had been Professor of Hebrew and Oriental Languages at Harvard. Woods was much younger, in his middle thirties, and before he came to Andover had been pastor for ten years at West Newbury, a dozen miles or so to the east of Andover.

So far as Adoniram was concerned, however, the two-man faculty served as well as a score. Languages had always interested him. Besides Greek and Latin he already knew some Hebrew. Now, under Dr. Pearson, he began to read sacred literature in the original. At the same time he began to thrash out his theological doubts with

Professor Woods, who turned out to be fully his match as a dialectician.

Soon he was completely engrossed in his new life of plain living and high thinking. Part of the day he spent in his room translating and working on theological problems. Part he spent with the two professors. Another part he spent alone, walking in a wooded grove behind the seminary building, reflecting on the meaning of what he was learning.

November came. The grove was a less pleasant place, perhaps, than it had been in October. The ground was wet with fall rain, the weather raw; only a few lonely leaves lingered on the bare boughs. But with the trees bare, he could see farther. And as he walked thoughtfully through the grove, he found that he could see farther into his problems, too. He began to suspect he had not seen the forest for the trees, nor the trees for the leaves. That month his doubts began to leave, little by little. He underwent no sudden conversion, felt no blinding flash of insight. But he was able to note that he "began to entertain a hope of having received the regenerating influences of the Holy Spirit."

On the second day of December — a day he never forgot — he "made a solemn dedication of himself to God."

With the issue settled and himself at peace, he devoted himself with a single mind to his studies. The next summer he joined the church at Plymouth, to the unrelieved joy of his father, mother, and Abby. From this time on he was literally a new man. "He banished forever those dreams of literary and political ambition in which he had formerly indulged, and simply asked himself, How shall I so order my future being as best to please God?"

## CHAPTER VII

# Embassy to Ava — The Decision
## [ *1809* ]

ADONIRAM had banished his old dreams of literary and political ambition, but had he banished ambition itself? Urges implanted in childhood, beyond earliest memories, sometimes persist in unrecognized forms when we are grown. Age as we will, beneath the wrinkling skin we still remain all the persons we were. Infant, child and youth still live within us, without our knowledge or will, never giving up their deep purposes. One way blocked, they seek another, like the shoots of a plant in a dark cellar twisting and reaching toward the tiniest crack of light.

With one kind of ambition, Adoniram was done for good and all. In June of 1809, about the time he joined his father's church, he was offered a tutorship at Brown. A year before he would have snapped at the opportunity. Now he declined. Whatever his destiny, he was sure it did not lie in college or university. Nevertheless, he still felt as always that he was marked for something out of the ordinary: not merely something greater than other men achieved, but something different, something distinctive. It was the feeling that had been planted in him when he learned to read at the age of three, and his father had taken him in his lap and told him for the first time that he would surely be a great man.

But how could he reconcile ambition with the service of God? His present course led to a pulpit, nothing more, no matter in how great a church. And had he not felt a sudden flash of insight as a boy, when he lay sick in Plymouth, that the fame of an obscure country pastor would resound longer and louder in heaven than that of the eminent divine in a fine city church? Unconsciously he was casting about for a direction to his life, watching for a sign.

The sign appeared in September, when he had completed his first year at Andover. That month he came across a printed copy of a sermon which had aroused a great deal of interest in America. It was entitled "The Star in the East," and had been preached by a Dr. Claudius Buchanan not long before in the parish church in Bristol, England. Buchanan belonged to the evangelical school of the Church of England and had spent many years in India as a chaplain for the East India Company. He had taken for his text the part of the second chapter of Matthew which reads, "For we have seen his star in the east, and are come to worship him." Buchanan recounted how the Gospel had been brought to India, and how it had progressed. He emphasized that the time was ripe to spread Christianity among Eastern people by a greater effort than any up to this time. Most interesting to Adoniram, he told about the work of the beloved German missionary Schwartz, who had spent nearly fifty years teaching the Gospel to the Indian heathen.

As Adoniram, sitting alone in his little room, read Buchanan's stirring account with growing fascination, the stories of other pioneers must have risen to his mind. As long ago as 1715 Bartholomeus Ziegenbalg had fashioned the New Testament into the Tamil language of India. William Carey, an English cobbler, had made his way to India and within Adoniram's own lifetime established a mission center in Serampore, a few miles above Calcutta, where in 1800 he had brought out the Gospel of St. Matthew in Bengali. Americans knew a great deal about Carey's Baptist Serampore group, for Captain Benjamin Wickes, who carried Carey's co-workers Marsh and Ward to India in 1799, had arrived in Philadelphia in 1805 and told the story so appealingly that Protestant ministers of every denomination had raised several thousand dollars to aid the Serampore missionaries.

In Canton, Robert Morrison, masquerading as a mercantile clerk and interpreter, was translating the Bible into Chinese, with death waiting if the real nature of what he and his Chinese helpers were doing should be discovered by the government.

And only two years before, in 1807, as Adoniram surely knew, Morrison had been in Boston arranging passage for China because the East India Company had refused to take a missionary of any kind to the Orient. Morrison's mission had been approved by such prominent men as Mr. Madison, then Secretary of State, soon to become President. Adoniram could hardly have missed hearing of Morrison's stout reply when the owner of the ship on which he was to sail had commented skeptically, "And so, Mr. Morrison, you really expect to make an impression on the idolatry of the great Chinese empire." To which the missionary had made his now oft-repeated rejoinder: "No, sir; I expect God will."

But none of these missionaries had been Americans. New England had sent missions to the "red men" in the West and to the sparsely settled regions west of the Hudson. In 1800 Adoniram's own father had made that summer missionary journey to "the interior parts of Vermont." The northern seacoast states teemed with missionary societies and "mite" and "cent" societies to support endeavors such as these. But no American, so far as Adoniram knew, had even thought of going out of North America, and no organization existed in the country to support American foreign missionaries.

All at once his imagination kindled. An amazing, a brilliant, a dazzling prospect appeared to him. Why should not *he* be a foreign missionary to one of these remote parts of the world as yet un-reached by the Gospel? He would be the first Congregational foreign missionary — the first American, the very first!

Everything in his life had prepared him for the idea. A career as the first American foreign missionary curiously combined his many conflicting ambitions. Fame, eminence, humility, self-sacrifice, obscurity, adventure, uniqueness, the service of God — it had all of these.

No work in the ministry could be more useful. Dark souls by the million were waiting to learn about the Gospel, the only key to salvation. Did not Jeremiah say, "O earth, earth, earth, hear the word of the Lord"? And Matthew, "Go ye therefore, and teach all nations, baptizing them in the name of the Father, and of the Son and of the Holy Ghost"? Had not Hopkins, spiritual mentor of Adoniram's father, written of the time when "Christianity shall spread over the whole world . . . forming men to a high degree of universal benevolence and disinterested affection . . . uniting all mankind into one happy family, teaching them to love each other as brethren, each seeking and rejoicing in the public good and in the happiness of individuals"?

And did not all foreign missionaries have to be translators? How could the natives read the Gospel unless it were put into their own tongue? And who had more aptitude for languages than Adoniram Judson?

And there may have been other motives, not so self-evident. A foreign missionary automatically removed himself from the acrimonious religious controversy of the time that had embroiled his father so often. Adoniram, so far as he knew, was free of doubt concerning his creed. But might not it be a relief to sidestep metaphysical hairsplitting for the straightforward job of translating the Scriptures just as they stood and conveying them to a heathen people? Not only that, but in what other career could he both defy his father and obey him; be like him, but unlike; follow, yet surpass? But thoughts such as these, if they came to him at all, he must have put hastily away in the glorious conception of the idea as a whole.

"For some days," Adoniram wrote years later, "I was unable to attend to the studies of my class, and spent my time in wondering at my past stupidity, depicting the most romantic scenes in missionary life, and roving about the college rooms declaiming on the subject of missions." He even talked rather wildly about offering himself to the London Missionary Society at once, since there was no American organization able to send him.

His enthusiasm kindled no answering flame whatever in the other students. His ideas were "condemned by all and not infrequently ridiculed and reproached." Under this deluge of cold water he began keeping his thoughts a little more to himself. Meanwhile, he "devoured with great greediness every scrap of information concerning Eastern countries." In this pursuit he presently came across a book entitled *An Account of an Embassy to the Kingdom of Ava*. It had been written by Michael Symes, a British army officer who had been sent in 1795 by the Governor General of India to the mysterious empire of Burma. It began provocatively, "There are no countries on the habitable globe, where the arts of civilized life are understood, of which we have so limited a knowledge, as those that lie between the British possessions in India and the empire of Burma."

Much of the book was given over to long accounts of past wars and Symes's fruitless negotiations with the Burman court. But through this dull matter one could glimpse bright reflections of a strange, colorful, feudal empire, populous and rich, which had no counterpart on the globe.

Its people were civilized. They could read and write, and had an extensive literature along with so overweening a national pride that, "Like the Sovereign of China, his Majesty of Ava acknowledges no equal; indeed it is the fixed principle of all nations eastward of Bengal, to consider foreign ministers as suppliants come to solicit protection, not as representatives who may demand redress; rather as vassals to render homage, than as persons vested with authority to treat on equal terms."

Everything about this sovereign was "Golden." To journey to see him was to be invited to "kneel at the Golden Feet." The King never heard anything; instead, the news "reached the Golden Ears." He was an absolute monarch who had not, so far, extended his sway over the rest of the world only because up to now he had hardly thought it worth the trouble. His courtiers and the wealthy wore long robes of flowered satin or velvet, reaching to the ankles, with a scarf flung over the shoulders. Their heads were covered with high velvet caps embroidered with flowers of gold. In their ears dangled solid gold earrings three inches long, shaped like speaking trumpets.

The nation was warlike and particularly well equipped with war vessels, some of which were a hundred feet long but no more than eight feet wide, each propelled by fifty to sixty oarsmen. These needlelike craft carried cannons in the bow, although grappling and hand-to-hand combat were the preferred battle procedures. As they darted away toward the enemy, their crews sang weird war songs.

The country contained incalculable riches — not only great forests of teak, so much desired by the English for building ships, but mines of gold and silver, rubies and sapphires, amethysts, garnets, chrysolite, jasper, and amber. It even had wells of a natural oil, earth oil, sometimes called "petroleum" by scientists, a nauseous liquid which was collected in barrels and used in lamps all over the kingdom. Symes, however, was scarcely interested enough in this useless substance to visit the wells himself.

The people were utterly pagan, wrote Symes. They worshiped Buddha and believed each person went through many cycles of existence, sometimes as a human, sometimes as an animal — a dog, a cat, even an insect. Yet — read Adoniram with special interest — His Majesty granted toleration to all sects. There was even one missionary, a Catholic, an Italian named Sangermano, whose "congregation consisted of the descendants of former Portuguese colonists, who, though numerous, are in general very poor."

What a prospect for a missionary! thought Adoniram as he turned the pages of Symes's book. Surely a people like this needed nothing but the true Word of God. Once it was brought to them, literate and civilized as they were, they would certainly seize on it. What other place on earth offered promise of such a harvest of souls? And no missionaries except Sangermano, who, since he was both a Catholic and a minister to Europeans rather than Burmans, hardly counted.

From this time on, Burma was much in Adoniram's thoughts. But he kept those thoughts to himself for the moment, not only because of the reception they could expect, but — more important — because although he had talked so glowingly in the seminary halls about missions, he had not yet quite made up his mind whether he really wanted to become a missionary.

He debated the problem with himself all through that fall of 1809. Christmas passed, and the New Year came. The snow lay thick on the ground. Then one day in February, coldest month of the year, a message came to him while he was walking in the grove. One can imagine him slowly pacing the snowy ground between the bare, spectral trees, his breath pluming in the frost, his mittened hands stuffed in his coat pockets. It may have been late in the afternoon with the pale sun low in the west and the first lights gleaming from under the eaves of Phillips Hall. He never recorded the day or the time of day. We know only that "It was during a solitary walk in the woods behind the college, while meditating and praying on the subject, and feeling half inclined to give it up, that the command of Christ, 'Go into all the world and preach the Gospel to every creature,' was presented to my mind with such clearness and power, that I came to a full decision, and though great difficulties appeared in my way, resolved to obey the command at all events."

Every urge, every experience from the beginning of his life, had brought its influence to this one focus.

From this time on, he never doubted his destiny.

## CHAPTER VIII

# The Brethren; the American Board

## [ *1810* ]

HIS decision made, Adoniram went home to Plymouth for the winter vacation. He was, he believed, the first and only student at Andover dedicated to foreign missions. He saw no reason to expect anything but opposition from the professors and his fellows there. He probably expected something similar from his parents. Perhaps some obscure impulse in him welcomed the prospect. Certainly he had at last accomplished an apparently impossible feat: he had chosen the one course which his father would not approve, yet from which he could not withhold his approval. He had welded defiance and obedience into one inseparable whole.

He was welcomed warmly, as usual — perhaps even a little more warmly than in the past — and for a few days he kept his secret to himself, waiting for the best time to bring it up. Soon, however, he began to be aware that he was not the only one with a secret. His father, mother and sister were keeping something to themselves too.

They were seated around the fireplace one evening when Mr. Judson began to drop rather broad hints to the effect that something highly desirable was about to happen to Adoniram. Mrs. Judson and Abigail, with smiles and cryptic remarks, suggested that, whatever it was, it concerned his career and was something Adoniram would like very much indeed. In view of his own secret all this was disquieting. Growing more and more uneasy as he listened, Adoniram finally asked his father to explain directly what he was hinting at — adding, by way of warning, that he might have plans of his own which might interfere with what they had in mind.

Mr. Judson was undisturbed. He was positive that Adoniram would be overjoyed. Adoniram knew Dr. Griffin, of course, who with Dr. Stuart had influenced him to go to Andover, and who now was Adoniram's instructor in Sacred Rhetoric? Adoniram nodded impatiently. Well, continued Mr. Judson, Adoniram had heard that Dr. Griffin was about to become pastor of the Park Street Church in Boston — the largest church in Boston? And — this was the secret — he wanted Adoniram to be his assistant as soon as he graduated from the seminary. He had spoken to Mr. Judson about it this early to be sure Adoniram would not commit himself to anyone else!

Nothing could possibly have made Adoniram's father prouder. His mother, who had been almost unable to contain herself while her husband spoke, broke in with, "And you will be so near home!" Abigail followed. Dr. Griffin was sure, she said, that Adoniram was destined to become one of New England's great ministers. This assistantship would be the first step on the ladder! So the three talked, fairly exploding with joy.

Adoniram, meanwhile, was overcome with a feeling akin to horror. Every word they spoke was a blow on his heart. Although he had known he must hurt them with his own news, he had never expected to hurt them as he must now. For a few moments he was unable to speak at all. Then, his voice hoarse and shaking with emotion, he broke in on his sister's glowing description of his future with, "No, Abigail. I shall never live in Boston. I have much farther to go."

His vehemence stilled them. In broken phrases, he told them of his decision and how he had arrived at it. As its full meaning sank home, his mother and Abigail exchanged fearful glances. Their eyes filled with tears and they broke into uncontrollable sobbing. As soon as they could recover themselves a little, they flung their tearful arguments as they had once before, when he set forth for New York. Why should he throw himself away among ignorant savages who could never appreciate him, half a world from home? Think how much good he could do in Boston! There were souls to save in New England, too. And so on . . . To no avail.

Only Adoniram's father had nothing to say. As a minister, what arguments could he bring against *this* decision? He sat with a stony face in the rocker beside the fire, silently digesting the wreck of his hopes, in the bitterest moment of life.

The remainder of Adoniram's vacation was a tumult. His mother and Abigail persisted in believing that if they deluged him with enough entreaties and enough tears he would give in. The father kept his hands off. It was obvious, to him, that no power on earth could move Adoniram Judson once he had come to a decision.

Adoniram returned to Andover in an unhappy frame of mind. He had foreseen "great difficulties," but perhaps not any quite as great from his mother and sister. Now he steeled himself for even greater ones at Andover. Instead, to his surprise, he met encouragement from an unexpected quarter.

Unknown to Adoniram, at least four other students in the seminary had considered foreign missions even earlier than he had. They had heard Adoniram "declaiming on the subject of missions," but they had kept their own counsel for various reasons: reluctance to take the final plunge — uncertainty whether to go abroad or to the American West — or, possibly, a doubt of Adoniram's sincerity and determination.

One of the four was Samuel Newell, who had begun to think of becoming a missionary while still an undergraduate at Harvard. Another was Samuel Nott, who had arrived in Andover the previous November. After graduating from Union College at the age of twenty, he had studied theology with his father, a minister of Franklin, Connecticut. He had come to the conclusion that his future lay in missions about the time Adoniram had entered the seminary in 1808. And it was Samuel Nott who approached Adoniram first that spring. Although he had felt for more than a year that it was his duty to become a missionary, he had hesitated to commit himself. Now his doubts melted quickly under Adoniram's enthusiasm. Samuel Newell joined these two next. If either Nott or Newell had cherished any idea of missions on the American continent, Adoniram soon persuaded them that Asia was the best field. He had fixed his own eye on Burma, but there was room in Asia for an army of missionaries. The important thing was to translate intentions into action. All three were seniors. There was no time to waste if they hoped to set out for their stations as soon as possible after graduation.

The third and fourth missionary-minded students had dedicated themselves as long ago as 1806, as freshmen at Williams, at an extraordinary gathering which is still remembered as "the Haystack Meeting." Their names were James Richards and Samuel J. Mills. Mills, a modest, almost retiring youth with an enormous amount of quiet drive, had been the instigator. The son of a minister of Torringford, Connecticut, he had decided on a missionary career largely as a result of the influence of his mother, even before entering college. He arrived in Williamstown just at the beginning of a movement of religious revival among the students — part of a wider movement which swept through a good many New England colleges and academies about that time — and quickly became a leader in it.

One hot, humid Saturday afternoon in August of 1808, Samuel Mills led five students in a prayer meeting in a maple grove known as "Sloane's Meadow," between the college and the Hoosac River. They had scarcely assembled when a thunderstorm broke from the heavy clouds which had been piling in the west. The only shelter was a haystack in a clearing in the grove; they took refuge from the torrential rains under its overhanging sides. They began to discuss Asia, which they had been studying in geography, then a compulsory subject at Williams. Here was a vast empire still ignorant of Christianity. Only India was hearing anything of the Gospel, and that only what could be brought to the people in spite of the East India Company's opposition. While lightning flashed and thunder cracked overhead, four of the five enthusiastically approved a proposal "to send the Gospel to the pagans of Asia and to the disciples of Mohammed." It was Mills, one of them wrote, who "proposed to send the Gospel to that dark and heathen land, and said that we could do it if we would. 'Come,' said Mills. 'Let us make it the subject of prayer, under the haystack.' . . . We all prayed. . . . Mills made the last prayer. . . . He prayed that God would strike down the arm with the red artillery of heaven that should be raised against the Cross."

The Haystack Meeting led, two years later, to the formation of a society called "the Brethren," the very existence of which was kept secret for several years. Once again, Mills probably played the leading role in establishing it; and James Richards was one of those who signed its constitution, which stated: *The object of this society shall be to effect, in the persons of its members, a mission to the heathen.* . . . *Each member shall keep himself absolutely free from every engagement which, after his prayerful attention, and after consultation with his brethren, shall be deemed incompatible with the object of this society, and shall hold himself in readiness to go on a mission when and where duty may call.*

Richards had arrived in Andover the preceding September, just about the time Adoniram began vociferating about missions. Although he was older than Adoniram, as a newcomer to the seminary he may have felt hesitant about thrusting himself on an upperclassman. More likely, he was skeptical of such wild enthusiasm. He watched and listened, and wrote about what he saw and heard to some of the other Brethren from Williams. Gradually his skepticism thawed, but he still kept silence.

Mills had been studying theology at Yale. What he heard from Richards may have made him think he would be better off at Andover, for toward the end of December he wrote to another member of the Brethren, Gordon Hall, who was preaching at Woodbury, Connecticut, that he thought he would transfer to Andover within four or five weeks. "I heard previously of Mr. Judson. You say he thinks of offering himself as a missionary to the London Society, for the East Indies. What! Is England to support her own missionaries and ours likewise?. . . I do not like this dependence on another nation, especially when they have done so much and we nothing."

But Mills was delayed by the death of his mother at the end of the year. He did not arrive at Andover until late January or early February of 1810, about the time Adoniram made his final decision. With Richards and Edward Warren, a Middlebury graduate, Mills then made himself and his intentions known to Adoniram Judson. Organizer and, in a sense, a politician, Mills saw his new acquaintance's problem at once. It was all very well to say you were going to be a missionary in Asia. But who was going to send you? A foreign missionary movement would have to be created, and a foreign missionary organization. Judson was concerned only with going. How, and by whom, he was sent, he did not care.

Very well. Adoniram Judson, Samuel Nott and Samuel Newell

were the three seniors. Some means must be found for sending them at once. Samuel Mills, James Richards and Edward Warren would not graduate for two years. They must throw their efforts behind the three seniors, and somehow get them started on their way. That done, it would be easier for the rest.

As a preliminary, Adoniram was informed about the Brethren and inducted as a member, and steps were taken to get in touch with the other Brethren who had formed the same purpose.

In the spring, the six became seven with the arrival of another signer of the constitution of the Brethren, Luther Rice, who had graduated from Williams in 1810. He would not finish at the seminary for a full year and therefore joined Mills, Richards and Warren in the effort to find support for Judson and the other two seniors.

Through March and early April they discussed ways and means among themselves and with their professors. They consulted most with Dr. Griffin, who had resigned himself to losing Adoniram as his assistant in the Park Street Church. Adoniram still clung to his original idea of getting English support, and Dr. Griffin agreed to write on the students' behalf. But when, for some reason, he delayed, Adoniram wrote in April to Dr. Bogue of the London Missionary Society — "... wishing *myself* to receive a letter from you *immediately;*" he wanted to know "whether there is at present such a call for missionaries in India, Tartary, or any part of the *eastern* continent, as will induce the directors of the London Missionary Society to engage new missionaries."

It would be months before a reply could arrive from England. Meanwhile the students looked for ways to promote their project nearer home. They sought every opportunity to preach in nearby towns, and on these occasions always took pains to meet the most influential local clergymen and explain their purpose. Adoniram tried the press with a piece for The *Panoplist and Missionary Magazine United*, the conservatives' religious magazine. Titled "Concern for the Salvation of the Heathen," his article scornfully pointed to those church members who were content to let well enough alone: "How do Christians discharge the trust committed to them? . . . They let three fourths of the world sleep the sleep of death, ignorant of the simple truth that a Savior had died for them. Content if they can be useful in the little circle of their acquaintances, they quietly sit and see whole nations perish for lack of knowledge."

All this energetic work bore results. In the fall of 1809 Adoniram had been alone. Students and professors had thought him a wild man obsessed with a visionary scheme as impractical as perpetual motion. Six months later, in the spring of 1810, he was the leader among seven students acknowledged by everybody to be as good men as had ever studied for the ministry. Scorn had changed to respect. The visionary scheme had somehow begun to seem more practical. Other students began to wonder whether duty did not point to foreign-mission careers for themselves. Professors began to feel such selfless dedication deserved support.

That spring, the seven walked and talked often together in the woods behind Phillips Hall where Adoniram had made his solitary decision in February. The ice had melted from the quiet little pond in the grove, and dandelions and buttercups starred the green under foot. As they fervidly debated, they began to feel a hope that was not merely the optimism of spring. If they kept up their hard work a real opportunity must appear sooner or later.

The opportunity came late in June. On Sunday the twenty-fourth, Samuel Nott had delivered a sermon in the Second Church in Newburyport, that flourishing seaport town some eighteen miles east of Andover. The regular pastor of the church was Dr. Samuel Spring, one of New England's most influential conservatives. Dr. Spring was a member of the Board of Visitors of the seminary. Together with Dr. Woods he had drawn up its official creed. His son Gardiner was one of Adoniram's closest friends and classmates at Andover, and from Gardiner, a warm supporter of the seven, though one with no intention of becoming a missionary himself, he had heard a good deal about the missionary project, all of it favorable. Samuel Spring himself had been interested in missions for years. In 1806 he had delivered a powerful sermon on the claims of the heathen to salvation at the General Assembly in Philadelphia, a sermon that was remembered for years. He was a man who liked bold projects and bold men. In 1775, only four years out of Princeton, he had been chaplain of Benedict Arnold's corps of the Revolutionary Army on its historic expedition through the wilderness of northern New York toward Quebec. He knew from experience that often the most formidable obstacles give way to vigorous attack by undaunted men.

The day after Nott's sermon in his church, Spring rode in company with Nott to Andover, where he had an appointment. Nott could never hope for a better chance to explain the object of the seven, nor a better listener. And the time was golden. On Wednesday of that week the General Association of Massachusetts Proper, the newly organized association of the state's evangelical Congregationalists, was to open its annual meeting at Bradford, halfway between Newburyport and Andover, on the Merrimack River road. Dr. Spring was riding to Andover to attend a sort of preconvention caucus which had been arranged by Dr. Griffin. If the growing missionary movement at Andover was to be brought up for action by New England Congregationalists, the meeting of the General Association was the place to do it. Another opportunity as good would not come for at least a year.

All this Nott must have realized with a thrill as the two jogged slowly along the river road, so engrossed in talk that they may hardly have noticed when their horses paused for minutes at a time to crop the rich grass by the roadside. When they reached the top of the long gentle grade that led to the seminary grounds, he must have bid a hasty good-by to Dr. Spring and hurried as fast as he could to Phillips Hall to tell Adoniram and the others what events were suddenly in the making.

The caucus was held that night in the parlor of Dr. Stuart's long white house. Drs. Griffin and Spring were there, of course, and Dr. Samuel Worcester, pastor of the renowned Tabernacle Church in Salem. Like Spring, Worcester was famous for a missionary sermon which he had delivered the previous year to the Massachusetts Missionary Society. Most of the others were ministers, but one layman was present, Jeremiah Evarts, a Yale graduate of the class of 1802 and a New Haven lawyer who had just moved to Charlestown, Massachusetts. He had brought along a classmate, the Reverend John Keep, a delegate to the convention, whom he had happened to meet on the road into Andover. It was Keep, attending by mere chance, who fifty years later gave his recollections of that night and thereby provided the only record.

To this group the students had been invited to state their case. They had selected Newell to be their spokesman. Slender, self-possessed, yet modest, he would make the best impression, they must have thought. Why they did not choose Adoniram it is hard to say. He was younger than the others, but only by a few years. They may have feared his tactlessness. When he drove hard he had a tendency to ignore the feelings of others. Mills, the organizer, probably ruled himself out. He knew as well as anyone that he was awkward and ungainly and had an "unelastic and croaking sort of voice."

Newell — probably trembling inwardly — briefly stated the purpose of the students, and the thoughts and feelings that had led up to it. He was received well, but his statement was only the opening gun. A long, searching questioning and discussion followed.

One of the older men, the Reverend Mr. Sanborn of Reading, was doubtful of the whole idea. He admitted that the young men had courage, but it seemed to him that their enthusiasm for foreign missionary service was simply blind infatuation. There was more work at home than they could do. Why leave it, for a wild goose chase to the other side of the world? And the proposal placed a serious responsibility on the older men. Most likely the expense could not be met. Were they willing to become responsible for the young men's actions in so momentous a matter? After all, how well did they know them? How firm were their principles?

Dr. Worcester answered Mr. Sanborn, "grouping the prominent facts" which had become familiar to everyone who had studied the problems of foreign missions and who knew the seven students. Dr. Griffin followed him with a "passionate appeal" for their proposal. So the discussion went. Mr. Evarts, when he had heard the various arguments, thought the facts justified action. Dr. Stuart believed the project was feasible. When it became clear that only Mr. Sanborn was doubtful — and that only on general principles — the Reverend Mr. Reynolds of Wilmington put a close to any further objections, by remarking significantly that "We had better not attempt to stop God." Finally the council agreed that if the students would place their proposal in writing they would be given an opportunity to submit it to the General Association.

Dismissed, the elated seven made their farewells and hurried out of Professor Stuart's parlor. Crossing the road and walking up the slope to the boxlike bulk of Phillips Hall, the lights of a few candles from the windows of late readers still glimmering in the night, they discussed who should write and present the proposal. Adoniram was the uanimous choice. Then they separated to their rooms, but perhaps not to sleep.

All day Tuesday Adoniram worked on the wording of the proposal, calling on the others for criticism and advice. When it was done, six of them signed their names at the bottom: Judson, Nott, Mills, Newell, Rice, and Richards. Together they took it over to Professor Stuart's house. The delegates found it satisfactory, but six names seemed too many even to the most optimistic. Financial support would be impossible. The Association would only be frightened. After some discussion, the names of Rice and Richards were dropped.

Early Wednesday morning the delegates began to leave for Bradford. Dr. Worcester had brought his chaise, and invited Dr. Spring to share it with him. It was a dull day with occasional sprinkles of rain. As the twinkling spokes of the chaise brushed the buttercups and daisies leaning into the road, the two ministers discussed the events of the past few days. It seemed obvious that if a foreign mission were to be anything but a pious hope, a foreign missionary organization had to be formed to popularize the idea, raise money, disburse it, select missionaries, assign them to stations, support them and supervise their activities.

One thought led to another. Before the chaise topped the rise sloping down to the little church on Bradford Common, the two ministers had worked out the complete plan of a society: its form, the number of members, and even its name — "The Board of Commissioners for Foreign Missions." With the addition of the single word "American" — so that it was to become familiarly known as "the American Board" — this was the organization which, when it came into being, was to father all Congregational foreign missionary activities for a century and more to come.

The next morning, Thursday, the twenty-eighth of June, the seven together walked to Bradford in the company of a few other students. Their "memorial," carefully copied out, was in Adoniram's custody, undoubtedly in the inside breast pocket of his best but somewhat shiny and threadbare black coat.

The meeting had been going on in one of the two classrooms of Bradford Academy since seven in the morning. At eleven it had been adjourned "for public worship at Haverhill," across the river. At two, it resumed in the First Church, a squarish, unpainted building without steeple or chimney which stood on the green a few steps from the Kimball Tavern. The scientist-promoter-politician, the Reverend Manasseh Cutler of Hamilton, known to Adoniram and his father from Wenham days, was moderator.

Cutler had served two terms in Congress since attending the Ecclesiastical Congress which approved the terms of dismissal of Adoniram's father from the Wenham Church in 1799. He was an old man now, with his great accomplishments behind him, but his tall, portly figure must have made an impressive sight, especially since he still clung to his favorite costume of black velvet suit and black silk stockings, with silver buckles at knee and shoe.

Cutler, however, was not alone in his old-fashioned garb, for the pastor of Bradford's First Church, familiarly known as "Parson Allen," affected very much the same fashion, and even insisted on wearing the old-style three-cornered hat. Parson Allen was one of the nine ministers who were present at the meeting as guests. They, together with the nineteen delegates, occupied the box pews on the main floor. The public occupied the gallery, which was crowded to capacity. To the residents of Bradford, a meeting such as that of the General Association of the Commonwealth was an affair to be long remembered.

And this Thursday afternoon, there was a reason for added interest. For when the delegates and honored guests entered, four young men entered with them and took their seats up front, side by side, their faces solemn and tense. For some time rumors had been circulating in Bradford that a new movement was growing in the theological seminary in nearby Andover. It was said that some of the students there wanted to become *foreign missionaries* — the first, it was said, from America!

Today, the word had leaked out: something momentous in connection with their purpose was expected to happen. As the onlookers in the gallery whispered to one another behind the backs of their hands, they said it certainly looked like it, for, look, those four young men are from the Seminary, and people say they are the leaders — especially that one there, that young slender fellow with the curly chestnut hair and the long nose, Mr. Judson, his name is.

So the whispers went, while the afternoon session opened with a long, dull account of the state of religion and churches in such uninteresting places as central and southern New Hampshire.

The whispers died down as the reports concluded. Maybe, decided the onlookers, they would hear something about those seminary students now. Yes, there was the imposing Dr. Cutler calling the attention of the General Association to the next item of business — a memorial to be presented by four of the theological students from the Seminary in Andover.

A hush fell as Adoniram stepped forward in front of the pulpit, coolly surveyed the delegates, guests and audience, a paper in his hand, and then with complete self-possession, began reading in a calm, clear, powerful voice. As soon as he opened his mouth the other three must have rejoiced inwardly that they had selected Adoniram to present the memorial, for it was instantly apparent that he had that rarest of attributes, a commanding stage presence.

"The undersigned," he read, "members of the Divinity College, respectfully request the attention of their reverend fathers, convened in the General Association at Bradford, to the following statement and inquiries. . . ."

To John Keep, who had been at the meeting at Professor Stuart's house, the memory of that scene was still vivid five decades later. Knowing what was to come, he recalled, "some of us held our breath."

"They beg leave to state," went on Adoniram, "that their minds have long been impressed with the duty and importance of personally attempting a mission to the heathen; that the impressions on their minds have induced a serious, and, they trust, a prayerful consideration of the subject in its various attitudes, particularly in relation to the probable success and the difficulties attending such an attempt; and that, after examining all the information which they can obtain, they consider themselves as devoted to this work for life, whenever God, in His providence, shall open the way."

A gasp, a barely perceptible indrawing of breath, came from the audience in the gallery. The rumors were true, then, that the young men were offering themselves as foreign missionaries!

"They now offer the following inquiries," continued Adoniram, "on which they solicit the opinion and advice of this Association: Whether, with their present views and feelings, they ought to renounce the object of missions, as either visionary or impracticable; if not, whether they ought to direct their attention to the Eastern or Western world; whether they may expect patronage and support from a missionary society in this country, or must commit themselves to the direction of a European society; and what preparatory measures they ought to take previous to actual engagement.

"The undersigned, feeling their youth and inexperience, look up to their fathers in the Church, and respectfully solicit their advice, direction, and prayers."

Adoniram paused for a moment, then slowly read the four names signed to the memorial: "Adoniram Judson, Jr.; Samuel Nott, Jr.; Samuel J. Mills; Samuel Newell." Without further words, he laid the paper on the baize-covered sacramental table in front of Moderator Cutler and resumed his seat. Not three minutes had elapsed between the time he had risen with the paper in his hand and the time he laid it on the table.

Now, one by one, each of the four rose, made a short personal statement telling why and how he had come to the conclusion that he must be a foreign missionary, and answered questions from the delegates. At this point the hush — by now a hush almost of awe — dissolved, as tears began to roll down the cheeks of the people in the audience, while some covered their faces with their hands and sobbed. The delegates themselves must have had difficulty maintaining their composure.

The Association took no action that session. A committee of

three was appointed to consider and report its recommendation the next day. Since two of the members were Samuel Spring and Samuel Worcester, who had the plan of a missionary organization already clear in their minds, and since the third — Mr. Hale, secretary of the meeting — could be expected to follow their lead, a favorable report was a foregone conclusion. By four the session was over and the convention adjourned for public worship.

The students, however, trudging under a dull sky back to Andover, were too inexperienced in the ways of conventions to realize that the issue was all but settled. In the recollections of Samuel Nott, they were "anxious and solemn in their aspect and spirit, wholly uncertain and perfectly unable to conjecture what action with regard to the memorial and themselves the Association would feel authorized to take."

Adoniram, his coolness in front of the meeting now vanished in the reaction, was even more abstracted than his companions. But he had a different reason.

For between the morning and the afternoon he had fallen in love.

## CHAPTER IX

# Nancy

*[ Ann Hasseltine: 1810 ]*

THAT noon Adoniram had been invited to dine at the home of Deacon John Hasseltine, who was boarding a number of the delegates during the convention. Hasseltine's big, comfortable house stood only a little west of the Academy grounds, looking northward across the Andover road toward the Merrimack River flowing in the valley below.

A table had been set in the west front room. As the guests filed in, urged by the hospitable deacon, Adoniram noticed a girl of about twenty bent over a huge pie which she was cutting into generous slices. Instantly he decided she was the most beautiful creature he had ever seen. Her jet-black curls, clear olive complexion and dark, lustrous eyes would have made her appearance striking in any case. But there was something about the irrepressible smile lurking on the full curve of her lips — a certain gay impertinence, almost, in her dancing eyes — that hinted a vivacity and even mischievousness, under the conventional demureness, that were new and attractive to Adoniram. He had never seen a girl like her.

He was anything but shy, yet when Parson Allen introduced him and she looked him full in the face, he was struck dumb. From then on he was extraordinarily aware of every move she made about the room as she served the guests, but he was unable to unglue his eyes from his plate. He could hardly make an intelligent reply when he was asked a question about the missionary movement at the Seminary. Perhaps, thought his questioners kindly, the young man was intimidated by the august gathering he was about to address. The truth was that, instead of thinking about the memorial in his pocket, he was preoccupied with the phrasing of a poem which kept composing itself, almost against his will, to this raven-haired beauty.

Her name was Ann Hasseltine, but people usually called her
"Nancy." She was the youngest of the deacon's four daughters.
She had heard of Adoniram Judson and the storm he had been stirring up in ecclesiastical circles, and had been curious to see what
he looked like. And now that she saw him she was disappointed.
He was fairly good-looking, of course, but perhaps a little too short
and slight. His nose was somewhat too prominent, although that
curly chestnut hair was rather attractive. And above all, where were
the wit and liveliness she had heard about? His replies were nothing
but abstracted monosyllables. Most of the time he spent staring
into his plate. When the meal was over and young Mr. Judson
mumbled his thanks and went out the door, she wondered why
everybody made such a fuss about him.

Later, hearing about the impression he made in church that afternoon, she may have changed her mind.

Nancy Hasseltine was a year and a half younger than Adoniram.
She had been born in Bradford December 22, 1789. With three
sisters and a brother ahead of her, she was the pet of the family.
She may have been a little spoiled. She certainly had a determination to get her own way. But she was so cheerful and lively that
it was hard to stay angry with her. She seemed to have no fear.
Punishments and restraints brought no reform, nothing but resent-
ful grief. When she was not underfoot, she would be gone no one
knew where until her exasperated mother would burst out, "Ann,
I hope one day you will be satisfied with rambling."

To her father she was a joy. He was amused by what neighbors
remembered for years as "her fertility in devising schemes for the
attainment of her wishes." He could not punish her even when at
sixteen she was seen in the unladylike activity of chasing thirteen-
year-old Rufus Anderson around the Academy grounds with a
stick. For Mr. Hasseltine was a man who liked to be gay himself,
and who liked to see other people gay. When he had built his
house at the upper end of the farm that sloped down to the Merrimack he had included a wing at the rear which had a spacious
second-floor room for entertainment, games and dancing. The
Hasseltine "dance hall," as everybody called it, immediately became
a social center for Bradford's youth, which was numerous and

lively. All the Hasseltine children attended Bradford Academy at one time or another, and all the boys and girls in the Academy — about eighty when Nancy was in her teens — attended the Hasseltine "dance hall." In no village for miles was there such fun and excitement. Bradford was a bright spot against the soberer, drabber pattern of Essex County rural life. Even the church was affected — even good Parson Allen, whose conservative garb matched the conservative Hopkinsianism he had learned studying his theology under Ephraim Judson, Adoniram's uncle. Though he took the most serious view of his Christian duties, he was less solemn than his sermons. It is written that, "It was not an uncommon thing for Parson Allen to call for his deacon to go and spend the evening at the dance hall." But then, Parson Allen's vivacious daughter Betsey was a student at the Academy herself, and a good friend of the Hasseltine girls.

Of course, some disapproved. Even Parson Allen came under attack from certain quarters. One anonymous pamphlet, published in nearby Essex but inspired in Haverhill across the river, accused him of "doctrines of Arians and Socinians which are infinitely below the true standards of gospel and morality." Worse, he had, it was averred, at a *meeting of ministers*, "zealously advocated the cause of frolicing and dancing!" In fact, "In seasons past, Mr. A has attended frolicings and dancings with his young people, not only till nine o'clock, and ten o'clock, and eleven o'clock, and twelve o'clock at night, but even till one o'clock in the morning."

Nancy was a good student and an avid reader, but, as she later wrote remorsefully, by her teens study was running a poor second to entertainment. "I soon began to attend balls and parties of pleasure and found my mind completely occupied with what I daily heard were 'innocent amusements.' . . . I was surrounded with associates, wild and volatile like myself, and often thought myself one of the happiest creatures on earth." Of course, she had been carefully taught by her mother to pray, not to lie, not to steal, not to disobey her parents. If she met these requirements, she believed, "I should, at death, escape that dreadful hell, the thought of which filled me with alarm and terror." So, like the good girl she was, she always said her prayers night and morning and left off playing on Sunday, "not doubting but what such a course of conduct would ensure my salvation." In her teens, however, she began to backslide. She stopped saying her prayers and reading her Bible when she returned at night from a party. At times her conscience disturbed her, but she consoled herself "by thinking, that as I was old enough to attend balls, I was surely too old to say prayers."

This was Nancy Hasseltine to the age of fifteen. As her friends said, "Where Ann is, no one can be gloomy or unhappy." To Nancy and her friends there seemed no reason why this pleasant existence should ever change.

In May of 1805, however, when Nancy was fifteen — and five years before Adoniram met her — a new preceptor came to take charge of Bradford Academy. His name was Abraham Burham. The son of a farmer of Dunbarton, New Hampshire, he had achieved his education by grinding toil and rigid self-denial. He was near thirty when he graduated from Dartmouth in 1804 and even more mature than his years. He was determined to become a minister. To accumulate money he not only taught at Bradford but used the vacations to teach in Concord, New Hampshire. Until he could begin his theological studies he looked upon his preceptorship as an opportunity to guide his students into religious experience as preparation for a Christian life. He was an unusually good teacher, but he considered this aim fully as important as secular instruction.

Burnham's influence soon began to be felt by the students, Nancy among them. At first the effect was so subtle, however, that she was not aware of what was happening to her. It first manifested itself one Sunday morning when she was dressing for church. On her dresser lay a copy of Hannah More's popular *Strictures on Female Education*. As she idly opened the book one italicized sentence caught her eye: "*She that liveth in pleasure, is dead while she liveth.*" The line jumped out at her so startlingly that she felt as if an invisible power had brought it to her attention. Though the effect of the warning wore off after a while, she did not forget it. A few months later, reading Bunyan's *Pilgrim's Progress* as "a Sabbath book" she was struck by the final impression it left, "that Christian, because he adhered to the narrow path, was carried safely through all his trials, and at last admitted into heaven."

This time Nancy promptly went to her room and prayed for help in leading a religious life. But after the prayer she had no more idea than before what to do to be saved. She finally decided that the correct conduct was to stay away from parties "and be reserved and serious in the presence of other scholars."

But lighthearted Nancy Hasseltine was incapable of keeping any such resolution. The very next day she was invited to a party, refused, invited to another, decided the second was really only a family gathering, and went to it. "Dancing was soon introduced; my religious plans were forgotten; I joined with the rest — was one of the gayest of the gay — and thought no more of the new life I had just begun."

Then when she returned home late that night, her conscience began to reproach her with breaking her "most solemn resolutions." Knowing full well she would break them again on the slightest temptation, she was afraid to make any more. She decided that since she could not reform, she might as well try to suppress her conscience. "From December, 1805, to April, 1806, I scarcely spent a rational hour. My studies were slightly attended to, and my time was mostly occupied by preparing my dress, and in contriving amusements for the evening, which portion of my time was wholly spent in vanity and trifling. I so far surpassed my friends in gaiety and mirth, that some of them were apprehensive, that I had but a short time to continue in my career of folly, and should suddenly be cut off."

But her conscience insisted on asserting itself. The more feverish her activity, and the more successful she was in denying it during the day, the more it filled her with anxiety and foreboding during the quiet moments of the night.

Meanwhile, under Mr. Burnham's stimulus a religious revival was beginning to occur in the town. That spring Nancy began to attend the meetings. She felt torn apart by her inner conflict. She did not see how she could be a Christian "in the midst of my gay companions," but she did not want to give them up. Her behavior was as contradictory as her feelings. At the meetings she would sit in the most remote corner of the room so that no one could see her tears. Yet afterwards she would pretend a lightness of heart she did not feel.

Such a masquerade could not be kept up forever. In a little while she had "lost all relish for amusements." She could not evade facing the fact, as it appeared to her, that she "must obtain a new heart, or perish forever."

Mr. Burnham often visited the Hasseltine home. No house in Bradford was more hospitable, and probably no other — with four charming daughters ranging in age from sixteen to twenty-four — offered a greater attraction to a thirty-year-old bachelor. On one of these evenings the discussion turned to the manner in which the Holy Spirit works on the hearts of sinners. This was a subject Nancy had never thought about. One thing Satan does, Mr. Burnham remarked, is tempt us "to conceal our feelings from others, lest our conviction should increase."

All at once Nancy saw how this statement applied to her. Quietly she left the room and went into the garden, where she began to weep uncontrollably. She felt that she was a captive of Satan, who was leading her wherever he wanted; yet she still was not willing to have any of her friends know that she was considering religion seriously.

A week later Nancy agreed to pay a visit, with several other Bradford girls, to a former schoolmate in another town. At the last moment she made some excuse and instead visited an aunt who lived a few miles away and was reputed to be strongly religious. She found her aunt "reading a religious magazine. I was determined she should not know the state of my mind, though I secretly hoped, that she would tell me something of hers."

Presently the aunt asked Nancy to read to her. She began, but in a moment broke down, buried her face in her hands, and burst into tears. She could no longer hide what was in her mind. Between sobs, she confessed her agony to her aunt. Her aunt told her to follow the feelings in her heart before it was too late — for if she "trifled with impressions which were evidently made by the Holy Spirit," she "should be left to hardness of heart and blindness of mind."

Having made her confession at last, Nancy's spirits began to rise. "I felt resolved to give up every thing, and seek to be reconciled to God. That fear, which I had ever felt, that others would know I was serious, now vanished away, and I was willing that the whole universe should know that I felt myself to be a lost and perishing sinner."

For the next two or three weeks she secluded herself in her room "reading and crying for mercy." To her surprise and resentment, she felt worse at the end than when she began. She began to blame God for not giving her peace of mind, and, now that she thought of it, found some additional things to blame Him for. "I could not endure the thought that he was a sovereign God, and had a right to call one and leave another to perish." Not only did she think God cruel, but she hated Him for being so utterly pure and holy. The whole idea of such a God filled her with aversion, "and I felt, that if admitted into heaven, with the feelings I then had, I should be as miserable as I could be in hell."

After a few days in this hostile frame of mind, however, her feelings began to alter as she considered the character of Jesus. She began to think that "God could be just, in saving sinners through him." Reading Bellamy's *True Religion*, she came to accept God's hatred as a hatred of sin rather than of sinners, and love for "the good of beings in general." She realized that she was beginning to have feelings and desires which were new to her and gradually had a hope that she "had passed from death unto life."

In a short time she had changed completely. "I earnestly strove to avoid sinning, not merely because I was afraid of hell, but because I feared to displease God, and grieve his Holy Spirit. I attended to my studies in school, with far different feelings and different motives, from what I had ever done before. I felt my obligations to improve all I had to the glory of God; and since he in his providence had favoured me with advantages for improving my mind, I felt that I should be like the slothful servant if I neglected them. I, therefore, diligently employed all my hours in school, in acquiring useful knowledge, and spent my evenings and part of the night in spiritual enjoyment."

Nancy's conversion had its effect in the family. Her father, who had never had much use for what he called "experimental piety," began to listen more attentively to Mr. Burnham. One night that summer, the Bradford legend goes, he crossed the field toward the house and through a window saw Nancy kneeling in her room, in tears, praying. Suddenly he was shaken by fear of what could become of him if even his youngest daughter, his most dearly beloved, found herself in tears when she approached God. He turned and in the darkness walked out across the farm to a big oak tree. Throwing himself on the ground beneath its broad branches, he "poured out his soul in an agony of prayer."

Thus the legend. It is a fact that on the eleventh of August, 1806, the month of the Haystack Meeting at Williams, John Hasseltine and his wife joined the Bradford church, and Nancy and her twenty-year-old brother John were baptized. A month later Nancy was admitted to the church — but not John; the day before, he had been lost at sea, though none of the family could have known it for some time. The same Sunday that Nancy joined the church, her sister Mary was baptized; and by spring of the following year Rebecca and Abigail, too, had entered the fold.

With her conversion, Nancy quickly put on maturity. That winter she studied harder than ever before in her life. In the spring she began to teach between terms. She opened her first school, probably in Bradford, with prayer, and noted in her journal, from the majesty of her seventeen years, that "The little creatures seemed astonished at such a beginning."

During the next few years she taught schools in a number of nearby towns — at Haverhill, across the river; and at Newbury. Her sister Rebecca took a school at Byfield, not far from Bradford, and Nancy spent a term there with her. And at some time she kept a school in Salem.

In Salem she may have lived with her intimate friend Lydia Kimball, whose father Eliphalet had moved from Bradford some years earlier and established a store on Essex Street where he sold "European and India goods," including cottons, flannels, broadcloths, satins, muffs and tippets, silk gloves, and miscellaneous notions.

At the Kimball home she must have met sea captains and shipowners. Certainly she must have seen their ships at the wharves along Derby Street, and watched the towering white sails move grandly out past Baker's Island and Big and Little Misery. Perhaps she had fleeting wishes she could be a man and sail to the far places she heard of. But, so far as she knew, her destiny lay in Essex County, in teaching and, eventually, marriage.

Perhaps she wished she could marry a minister, as her sister Rebecca did early in 1810 when she became the third wife of the scholarly Joseph Emerson, pastor of the Dane Street Church in Beverly. In the spring of 1810 Nancy visited the Emersons more than once, and conceived a real admiration for the kindly, stoop-shouldered preacher.

But of what was in her mind with regard to these matters we know nothing.

We know only that on June 28, 1810, aged twenty-one, Nancy Hasseltine was at her home in Bradford; and that at noon on that day Adoniram Judson saw her serving dinner and promptly fell in love.

## CHAPTER X

# A Wild, Romantic Undertaking

## [ *1810* ]

ADONIRAM did not mention Nancy Hasseltine when he wrote to his mother and father the next day. Instead, he confined himself to a businesslike account of his letter to Dr. Bogue in England and the memorial he had presented in Bradford. As he wrote, he realized that he did not yet know the decision of the General Association and put the letter aside unfinished.

At Bradford, meanwhile, the committee of three had made its report at the first session of the Association, which opened at seven in the morning. The committee agreed that the students deserved support, and recommended "That there be instituted, by this General Association, a Board of Commissioners for Foreign Missions, for the purpose of devising ways and means, and adopting and prosecuting measures, for promoting the spread of the Gospel in foreign lands." They recommended further that the students put "themselves under the patronage and direction of the Board of Commissioners for Foreign Missions, humbly to wait the openings and guidance of Providence in respect to their great and excellent design."

Adoniram was not one humbly to wait the openings and guidance of Providence. When he resumed the letter to his parents nearly two weeks after setting it aside, he told them that a missionary board was to be established, but added impatiently, "I have not heard the *precise* object of these commissioners, nor when they are to meet." The students wanted to promote missions as actively as possible in the United States, but for themselves they wanted no action taken which would prevent their "soliciting British aid." So long as they were sent on a mission soon, they did not care too much who sent them.

He told his parents that the students had a noteworthy addition — Gordon Hall, another Williams graduate. Hall, a friend of Mills, had been preaching in Woodbury, Connecticut. The congregation had just offered him a permanent appointment at six hundred dollars a year. While Hall was considering the offer, his interest in missions became known to Adoniram, through Mills, and Adoniram wrote to him. Hall immediately left for Andover to investigate. He had been in Andover only a few days when he declined the call from Woodbury and enrolled at the seminary with the class of 1811, in order to prepare himself for foreign missionary work. "He is sensible, judicious, learned, pious," wrote Adoniram; "has been preaching nearly a year, and quite united the Woodbury people. There are now four of us who are ready to start, at three months' warning, for any part of the world — Hall, Newell, Nott, and myself. There are at least four others in the junior class who are ready to support the mission wherever it shall be established."

He himself was preparing in every way he could for his future work. When he preached in the neighboring towns he seldom even used notes. "I hardly think that I shall write any more sermons. Why should I spend my time in attempting the correctnesses and elegancies of English literature, who expect to spend my days in talking to savages in vulgar style?" His health was good, except that his eyes troubled him so that he could not study at night — a common consequence of reading by candlelight. For several months he had been systematically hardening himself with deep-breathing exercises, a daily cold water sponge bath, and long walks.

Of Nancy Hasseltine he made no mention, but there might have been a warm reflection of his feelings in his concern for his sister Abigail, who had not yet joined the church in Plymouth: "I think sometimes that A. is all alone at Plymouth. There is a Friend, whose friendship, if she would secure it, would never leave her alone."

Meanwhile, he himself was losing no time trying to secure the friendship of Nancy. One month from the day he met her he formally "commenced an acquaintanceship" with her, which meant that he formally declared his intentions as a suitor. This he did in a letter, and tradition declares that for several days she did not reply to it. Its contents were an open secret within the Hasseltine family, however, so much so that one of her sisters finally threatened to answer the letter herself if Nancy delayed any longer.

Her reply was not encouraging, but neither was it a flat rejection. Evading the issue, she wrote that her parents would have to consent before she could even consider Adoniram. Privately, she speculated in her journal whether she would be able to commit herself "entirely to God, to be disposed of, according to his pleasure," and decided, "Yes, I feel willing to be placed in this situation, in which I can do most good, *though it were to carry the Gospel to the distant, benighted heathen.*"

Adoniram promptly sat down at his table and wrote to Nancy's father urging . . .

I have now to ask, whether you can consent to part with your daughter early next spring, to see her no more in this world; whether you can consent to her departure, and her subjection to the hardships and sufferings of a missionary life; whether you can consent to her exposure to the dangers of the ocean; to the fatal influence of the southern climate of India; to every kind of want and distress; to degradation, insult, persecution, and perhaps a violent death. Can you consent to all this, for the sake of him who left his heavenly home, and died for her and for you; for the sake of perishing, immortal souls; for the sake of Zion, and the glory of God? Can you consent to all this, in hope of soon meeting your daughter in the world of glory, with the crown of righteousness, brightened with the acclamations of praise which shall redound to her Saviour from heathens saved, through her means, from eternal woe and despair?"

It was a letter that must have made John Hasseltine's eyes pop nearly out of his head. One would have expected him to agree with the father of a friend of Nancy's — one of the numerous Kimball clan — who, when he heard that young Judson was paying court to Nancy Hasseltine, declared stoutly that he would tie his own daughter to the bedpost rather than let her go on such a harebrained venture.

John Hasseltine took no such action. With many misgivings, he left it to Nancy to make up her own mind. Whatever her choice, she had his blessing — but let her consider carefully before taking an irrevocable action. Nancy's mother had little to add to this advice. She hoped Nancy would not go. But she would not withhold her consent. Thrown back on herself, Nancy did not know what to do. She was beginning to love Adoniram — what woman could withstand such a combination of impetuosity and tenderness? — and there must have been something irresistibly appealing about sharing his adventures in far places. But the hazards were appalling. Surely she would have children, she must have reflected. What of them? But on the other hand, how better could she serve God?

Torn this way and that, Nancy went to Beverly for advice early in September. Besides Rebecca, her sister Abigail was there now, teaching. She may have wanted Mr. Emerson's counsel even more than that of her sisters. In spite of his mildness and a vein of gentle humor that endeared him to everyone, he was anything but soft; and on occasion he could be devastatingly frank.

When Nancy revealed her hopes and doubts to him, he told her that the issue was not as complicated as she thought: if she really loved Adoniram and wanted to submit herself to the Lord, there could be no better way of serving His will.

Encouraged, she wrote confidentially to Lydia Kimball in Salem:

> I feel willing, and expect, if nothing in providence prevents, to spend my days in this world in heathen lands. Yes, Lydia, I have about come to the determination to give up all my comforts and enjoyments here, sacrifice my affection to relatives and friends, and go where God, in his providence, shall see fit to place me.

Possibly, like Adoniram, she was getting some enjoyment out of dramatizing her choice. But she could not admit, even to herself, that love for Adoniram had very much to do with it. She emphasized to Lydia, "Nor were my determinations formed in consequence of an attachment to an earthly object; but with a sense of obligations to God, and with a full conviction of its being a call in providence, and consequently my duty."

Perhaps so. At least, whether love or a sense of duty came first, on her return to Bradford she was almost ready to tell Adoniram she would be his wife.

Adoniram graduated from the seminary the twenty-fourth of

September, about the time she returned from Beverly; but he stayed on in Andover, preaching wherever he could and seeing Nancy often. More verbal and more objective, man-fashion, about his love than Nancy, he wrote to Nott that fall: "I have done nothing scarcely since I saw you, beside . . . riding about the country with Nancy. Pretty preparation, this article, for a missionary life — isn't it?"

There was little else to do. The fifth of the month (the same day Brown awarded him the degree of Master of Arts) the Board of Commissioners, now coming to be known as the "American Board," had met in Farmington, Connecticut. Its deliberations produced little but advice to the missionary candidates "to pursue their studies until further information relative to the missionary field be obtained, and the finances of the institution will justify the appointment."

Occupied with his courtship, Adoniram for once did not fret at the delay. Mary Hasseltine remembered him as he was then, "in the ardor of his first love. It may literally be said that he was a man of one idea, and that was, love, to Jesus, and a desire to manifest it in all its varied forms. Yet he was by nature ardent, impetuous, and ambitious, with the most unshaken confidence in his own judgment, irrespective of the advice of his elders."

How long could a woman resist such a wooer?

Precisely when she said "Yes" is not recorded; but by mid-October nearly everyone in Bradford seemed to know that Nancy Hasseltine was going to marry Adoniram Judson and go to the Orient with him. Opinions were divided.

Some were like that of the Bradford matron who accosted an acquaintance on the street one day with, "I hear that Miss Hasseltine is going to India. Why does she go?"

The acquaintance replied mildly, "Why — she thinks it her duty. Would you not go if you thought it your duty?"

The opinion of the conservative half of Bradford sounded in the emphatic response: "But I would *not* think it my duty."

Others felt like seventeen-year-old Harriet Atwood, who lived across the river in Haverhill. She was a close friend of Nancy's and had admired her since they had first met as students at Bradford Academy more than four years before.

Like Nancy, Harriet had been caught up in the religious revival of 1806. She had been preoccupied with religion ever since, but not in Nancy's vigorous way. Slender, frail, of a family prone to the tuberculosis which had killed her father two years before, she lived much more within herself.

When Harriet heard the news from Nancy's own lips she confided in astonishment to her diary:

"A female friend called upon us this morning. She informed me of her determination to quit her native land, to endure the sufferings of a Christian amongst heathen nations — to spend her days in India's sultry clime — How did this news affect my heart! Is she willing to do all this for God; and shall I refuse to lend my little aid, in a land where divine revelation has shed its clearest rays?"

In her secret heart, however, Nancy still sometimes found her determination undermined by fears:

"Jesus is faithful; his promises are precious. Were it not for these considerations, I should, with my present prospects, sink down in despair, especially as no female has, to my knowledge, ever left the shores of America to spend her life among the heathen; nor do I yet know, that I shall have a single female companion. But God is my witness, that I have not dared to decline the offer that has been made me, though so many are ready to call it 'a wild, romantic undertaking.'"

As it turned out, however, Adoniram and Nancy were to be parted for nearly a year before the "wild, romantic undertaking" could begin.

The American Board had appointed Samuel Spring, Samuel Worcester, and the layman William Bartlet as a "Prudential Committee" to find means of supporting the missionaries. By December the fund-raising operations of the committee were exactly where they had been in September — which was nowhere. The Committee finally decided, rather desperately, that some joint arrangement might possibly be worked out with the London Missionary Society — the Prudential Committee to provide the missionaries, whom it would certify as of suitable character and qualifications, the Londoners to provide the funds, or at least most of the funds.

On Christmas Day of 1810, Adoniram, Newell, Nott and Gordon Hall appeared before the committee to go through the formality of examination and certification. This done, Adoniram was chosen as a representative of the American Board, to lay the proposal before the London Missionary Society. He was to sail on the first day of January, 1811 — a week hence — on the ship *Packet*, bound from Boston to Liverpool.

The committee was so lacking in money, however, that it could not even pay its representative's passage. But Adoniram was able to raise a few hundred dollars from Mr. Bartlet and Mr. Norris, two of the seminary benefactors; and the committee promised to make up his expenses when he returned to the United States. He was supplied with a letter of instructions and a letter to the Reverend George Burder of the London Missionary Society. His instructions were explicit.

First, he was to find out what arrangements could be made for the American and London organizations to work together, and particularly whether the London society would support the missionaries for a while without insisting they be permanently and wholly under London's control. Or, if the London group felt the mission should be supported partly by the Americans and partly by the British, who should have the control? These matters were to be Adoniram's primary concern.

Second, he was to find out as much as he could about the various fields of endeavor for missionaries, the preparation necessary, and the correct method of carrying out missions.

With so short a time to prepare for departure, Adoniram had few opportunities to see Nancy, but from his room in Phillips Hall he poured out his heart in letters — one on the thirtieth of December, one on the thirty-first, and one (the *Packet* having been delayed in sailing) on New Year's Day.

The first two were a mixture of affectionate chattiness and somewhat gloomy philosophy (the latter probably engendered by the fact that he had a cold). But in his letter of New Year's morning he rose to magnificence:

It is with the utmost sincerity, and with my whole heart, that I wish you, my love, a happy new year. May it be a year in which your walk will be close with God; your frame calm and serene; and the road that leads you to the Lamb marked with purer light. May it be a year in which you will have more largely the spirit of Christ, be praised above sublunary things, and be willing to be disposed of in this world just as God shall please. As every moment of the year will bring you nearer to the end of your pilgrimage, may it bring you nearer to God, and find you more prepared to hail the messenger of death as a deliverer and friend. And now, since I have begun to wish, I will go on. May this be the year in which you change your name; in which you take final leave of your relatives and native land; in which you will cross the wide ocean, and dwell on the other side of the world, among a heathen people.

When Adoniram had finished the letter, with speculation about how next New Year's Day he and Nancy might wish each other a happy new year "in the uncouth dialect of Hindostan or Burmah," he folded it, and arranged for its posting. Then he made his way to Boston to await the sailing of the *Packet*.

## CHAPTER XI

# France and England
## [ *1811* ]

THE *Packet,* a British vessel, did not leave Boston harbor until the eleventh of January, 1811. Besides Adoniram she carried only two passengers, a couple of Spanish merchants. With England and France at war, and the United States on the verge of war with both, passenger travel was light.

For some days the voyage was uneventful. Then one morning the sails of a strange craft loomed over the horizon. They belonged to a French privateer with the awe-inspiring name of *L'Invincible Napoléon.* The *Packet* was a fair prize.

The officers, passengers and crew of the *Packet* were carried on board *L'Invincible Napoléon.* The two Spanish merchants, who spoke French and were obviously men of substance, were well treated and given a cabin. Adoniram was not so fortunate. French was not one of the languages he knew, and his unimpressive black clothing did not suggest to French naval officers that he was anyone of importance. Along with the crew of the *Packet* he was unceremoniously thrust down into the hold of the Frenchman. The hold was dark, dirty and overcrowded. Presently a typical January storm blew up and the men below became seasick, Adoniram among them. In a short time the hold became a revolting mess.

This was one experience for which Adoniram had not been prepared. His cleanliness and dislike for dirt were almost obsessive. He had never known anything but kindness, or at least a decent respect for his person. Now he wallowed in filth and received the same harsh treatment as the rest of the *Packet's* crew. In all his worst dreams of missionary life he had never conceived of anything as repulsive and degrading as this. The ship's doctor visited the hold every day. Adoniram tried to make his plight known to him, but without French he got nowhere.

Dismally, he began to think of home — of Nancy, of Bradford, of his family in Plymouth, even of Dr. Griffin's rejected offer of a post in the Park Street Church in Boston. He had turned his back on all of them. Now, between homesickness and seasickness, he began to wonder whether he had chosen the right vocation after all.

At the very depth of his despair, however, a new thought came to him. Perhaps God was giving him a foretaste of missionary life to test his faith and determination. Supporting himself on his knees as well as he could in the pitching hold, he prayed for strength to withstand his weakness. After a while he felt a little better, and fumbled around in the dark until he could lay hands upon his Hebrew Bible. When he had it, he found a place where a faint light fell, enough to read by, and began to amuse himself by translating the Hebrew into Latin.

One day while he was thus busy translating, the ship's doctor came upon him during his rounds. The doctor picked up the Bible curiously, and examined it in the better light near the gangway. An educated man, he recognized it, and, returning to Adoniram, asked him a question in Latin. Latin turned out to be an effective means of communication. Mentally thanking his stars, we may suppose, that he had once been called "Old Virgil Dug Up," Adoniram explained who he was and why he had been aboard the *Packet*. With quick sympathy for the young divine, who was obviously of his class, though so different from a French curé, the doctor arranged for Adoniram to be removed from the hold at once. Before sundown he was assigned a berth in a cabin, and thenceforth he took his meals at the captain's table with the officers and the two Spanish businessmen.

With the run of the ship and facilities for keeping clean, Adoniram found the rest of the voyage pleasanter. From the deck he witnessed one momentarily exciting event, when *L'Invincible Napoléon* was sighted by a bigger and better-gunned British brig. But the French vessel was a faster sailer, and any hopes Adoniram had of getting to England by a second capture were disappointed.

Eventually the privateer touched at Le Passage in Spain, where she landed the two Spaniards.

But Adoniram, educated man or not, was carried to Bayonne and herded to prison at gunpoint with the crew of the *Packet*.

By now Adoniram's spirits had rebounded to their usual vigorous level. On the march to prison he vented his indignation with shouts in his few words of French to crowds lining the streets. His complaints merely convulsed the onlookers with laughter. It occurred to him that some of them might understand English, and undaunted he began a violent diatribe "against oppression and this one act in particular."

The power of Adoniram's voice had been famous in Andover, and his outburst in English disturbed the guards. They tried to stop him with threatening gestures, but he noticed that no one actually struck him and raised his voice even higher, to the increasing hilarity of the crowd. But a moment later, a voice called from the crowd in a familiar American accent: "Lower your voice!" Adoniram obeyed at once. "I was only clamoring for a listener," he explained, and in a few hasty words told how he came to be where he was.

The voice belonged to a Philadelphian — an officer of one of the many American ships trying to pierce the English blockade — who promised to try to help him. "But you better go quietly now," he cautioned. "Like a lamb," promised Adoniram, "now that I've got what I wanted."

The prison was an improvement over the ship's hold mainly in that it did not pitch or roll. The prisoners were confined in a huge, dark, underground dungeon, damp and chilly, lighted dimly by a single feeble lamp hung from a central stone column. The beds consisted of piles of straw strewn on the floor along the walls.

When they were safely immured in this vast communal cell, Adoniram began impatiently pacing up and down, waiting for his rescuer. After some hours the cell door grated open and the Philadelphian, shrouded in an immense military cloak, was admitted by the jailer. Adoniram had been leaning against the central pillar when his friend entered. Now, avoiding any appearance of impatience and without giving any sign of recognition, he moved directly underneath the lamp.

Ignoring Adoniram, the American walked over to the pillar and lifted the lamp from its bracket, saying, "Let me see if I know any of these fellows." Lamp in hand, he walked away from Adoniram, inspecting each of the men who lay huddled in their piles of straw.

When he had gone once around the room, he pretended to give up in disgust. "No, no friend of mine," he muttered, and returned the lamp to its bracket over Adoniram's head. In the same movement, he swung his cloak around Adoniram.

Crouched under the cloak, half-blinded by its enveloping yards of fabric, Adoniram crept to the cell door on his companion's heels, doing his best to keep in step. The Philadelphian was an extremely tall man, the cloak as voluminous as a tent, and the room dim. Even so, however, the most unobservant turnkey could hardly have failed to notice that the visitor not only had become much bulkier but had acquired two extra legs.

But the American knew the magic needed for making extra legs invisible. As the cell door swung open, he slipped some money into the jailer's waiting palm. He gave more to the guard who opened the outside gate of the prison. Thus, the Philadelphian striding ahead, Adoniram hunched behind under the cloak, they passed beyond the walls of the prison. Outside, the Philadelphian swept the cloak off Adoniram's shoulder, commanded brusquely, "Now, run!" and led him at a full gallop to the wharf, where he concealed him aboard an American ship. The next night Adoniram spent in the attic of a shipbuilder. A few days later, he was provided with parole papers, and from then on was free to walk at large.

He found a boarding place with an American woman who had spent most of her life in France. Here he stayed for six weeks. She knew he was a minister, but he concealed his occupation from others, "as he thought it would interfere with a plan he had of learning as much as possible of the real state of French society" — which sounds remarkably similar to his earlier passing as "Mr. Johnson" in New York.

As a layman he "attended various places of amusement with his fellow boarders, pleading his ignorance of the language and customs of the country as an excuse for acting the spectator merely; and in general giving such evasive replies as enabled him to act his part without attracting undue attention."

"Places of amusement" was a polite understatement. Bayonne, like Marseilles, teemed with the ragtag and bobtail of a Europe convulsed by a generation of revolution and war. The diversions available for visiting mariners were an open secret, and tales about the entertainment provided for American shipmasters were whispered behind discreet palms for generations by their descendants.

Finally, however, revulsion overcame his curiosity. "The last place of amusement he visited was a masked ball; and here his strong feelings quite overcame his caution, and he burst forth in his real character. He declared to his somewhat startled companions that he did not believe the infernal regions could furnish more complete specimens of depravity than he there beheld."

He did not stop here, but went on — in English — to enumerate "many of the evils which infidelity had brought upon France and upon the world, and then showed the only way of escape from these evils — the despised, but truly ennobling religion of Jesus Christ." Carried away, he spoke louder and louder until he attracted a good-sized audience. Most of the guests, not understanding his language, thought his performance was part of the show. But a fair number, though their faces were concealed by masks, showed by their behavior that they understood, and were stung as he voiced his disgust at the behavior of men who were undoubtedly Americans in disguise.

Shortly afterwards, Adoniram left Bayonne for Paris — according to one account, in a military carriage with some of the officers of Napoleon's suite. In Paris he spent some time with them before finally receiving a safe-conduct for England, and is said to have visited with them places similar to those he had seen in Bayonne. True or not, his involuntary stay in Bayonne certainly opened his eyes to a kind of existence scarcely dreamed of in sedate New England. He considered the experience invaluable for a missionary, and all the rest of his life "regarded his detention in France as a very important, and, indeed, necessary part of his preparation for the duties which afterwards devolved upon him."

Important or not, the French episode was irrelevant to his real purpose. It was May when he finally arrived in England, four months after sailing from Boston, and called on the directors of the London Missionary Society. It was a good time to seek decisions. The annual meeting of the society was about to begin. He was able to attend it knowing that he could receive prompt answers to his requests.

The directors had already received Dr. Worcester's letter on behalf of the Board's Prudential Committee. Now they read Adoniram's letter of instructions and other documents he brought, and immediately delegated a committee to explore the matter more thoroughly and report to them without delay.

Under the kindly but realistic questioning of this committee, Adoniram realized what a weak proposal the Board had given him. As the English committee said: "Mr. Judson is able to offer very little encouragement as to pecuniary assistance. The zeal for missionary effort seems to have been excited chiefly, if not entirely, among those who have only their personal services to offer." With even reasonable prospects of raising money at home, he would never have been sent to England. Yet his elders in the United States had instructed him to learn whether "you and your brethren can be supported in missionary service for any time by the London funds, without committing yourself wholly and finally to the direction of the London society; or whether it may be in any case consistent for the mission to be supported partly by them and partly by us; and if so, under whose direction it must be held." Behind these words, it was obvious that the Americans were asking for joint control of a mission without offering joint support. Joint control, the Londoners knew, was impracticable from opposite sides of the Atlantic; without the inducement of joint support, the mere suggestion was ridiculous.

The motive of the Americans was plain — at least, it must have seemed so to Adoniram. He was learning in London that the London society was planning to spend ten thousand pounds on missions during the coming year. It had a generation of experience in its field. His own superiors had been unable to raise even his passage money to England; they had no experience at all. Yet now they had the effrontery to ask to share without contributing. His hot temper must have flared when he thought of the humiliating position in which he had been placed. What was the American missionary movement? It was himself, and a handful of students in Andover. What had the American Board done? Nothing but stand in the way of his original idea of a year ago of offering his own services to the London Missionary Society. Thus he must have reasoned.

Under these circumstances, Adoniram felt absolved of any ob-

ligations to the American Board and promptly offered himself to
the London society. He also offered Newell, Nott and Hall — with
only two stipulations. He asked that all four be kept together and
used in forming a new mission station. And, thinking of Nancy
and knowing that the other three had come to believe it would be
best to marry before going abroad, he asked that the new missionaries be permitted to take their wives. About the matter of
wives, the members of the committee were dubious, but finally
agreed. As to the whole group forming one station, there was more
doubt. In view of the well-known antagonism of the East India
Company to missionaries, the committee felt it would be best for
two to go to one station and two to another. But even here the door
was not closed completely. Accordingly, the committee recommended to the directors that the four "be accepted as missionaries,
to be employed by this society in India."

The arrangement was conditional, of course. Newell, Nott and
Hall might not agree to it. Or the American Board might suddenly
find funds. In fact, word had just come that Mrs. Norris, who with
her husband had helped finance Adoniram's passage, had died and
left a large sum of money for missions.

Thus, thought Adoniram triumphantly to himself, whether it
came about one way or another, the accomplishment of the first
foreign mission by Americans was assured. And this was what he
had come for.

His main business accomplished, he spent the rest of his time in
England visiting the missionary seminary in Gosport, where he
learned all he could from its leader, the aged and experienced Dr.
Bogue. Occasionally he took part in church services here and there,
and "his voice surprised those who saw his slight frame." In one
of the London churches, where he read a hymn, the minister remarked to the congregation, after explaining that the young man
was to be a missionary: "And if his faith is proportioned to his voice,
he will drive the devil from all India!"

Altogether, Adoniram spent six weeks in England. On the eighteenth of June he went on board the ship *Augustus* at Gravesend,
and on August seventh sailed into New York Harbor. He had been
away from home a little more than eight months, but he was sure
that the news he brought was worth it.

## CHAPTER XII

# The Formal and Solemn Reprimand

## [ *1811* ]

BEFORE leaving for home from New York, Adoniram had an old wrong to set right. He had never forgotten the landlords he once helped cheat out of food and lodgings, when he had traveled with the strolling players three years before. Now he repeated the stops of that tour and paid up his debts. His conscience was clearer when he finally took the stage to Boston and home.

At Andover and Bradford he caught up with the news. The report of Mrs. Norris's bequest to missions was true, he learned. When she died in March, while Adoniram was in France, it was found that her will gave thirty thousand dollars to the American Board, more than enough to enable four missionaries and their wives to establish a mission station anywhere in the world. Some of the other heirs had tied up the estate in litigation, and the money was not immediately available; but there seemed little doubt that it would be released eventually, as it was well known that both John Norris and his wife had long been firm believers in missions.

In fact, when Samuel Spring had called on Mr. Norris in Salem as long ago as 1806 with his proposal for a theological seminary, Norris had been cool because he wanted to give money directly to missions. After talking the matter over with his wife, however, he had changed his mind, and the next morning told Spring: "My wife tells me that this plan for a theological school and the missionary enterprise is the same thing. We must raise up the ministers if we would have the men to go out as missionaries." Forthwith he went to the bank and drew out ten thousand dollars in silver money which he gave for the proposed seminary because, as he said, he "never heard that *paper* money was given to the temple."

Mr. Norris had died without seeing his missionary dreams realized, but his wife had not forgotten them. His gifts, her payment of part of Adoniram's expenses to England, and this bequest were devoted to the same end. With thirty thousand dollars in sight, Adoniram and Samuel Nott felt sure that it would not be necessary to take advantage of the London Missionary Society's offer.

On his return, Adoniram had no opportunity to discuss the meaning of the Norris bequest with Samuel Newell and Gordon Hall. They were not in Andover, but had gone to Philadelphia in June to spend the summer and the following winter studying medicine, wisely thinking that medical skill might be nearly as valuable to a missionary as knowledge of the Bible. In so doing they were setting a precedent for what eventually became a distinct type of work, that of the medical missionary.

Before leaving for Philadelphia, however, Newell had become engaged to Nancy's youthful friend Harriet Atwood of Haverhill. To Nancy this was even better news than the fact that the mission had become a certainty. It meant that she would not be the only woman to go with the group. Better still, her companion would be someone she had known since girlhood.

The romance had begun even before Adoniram had left for England — in fact, only two days after Nancy had told Harriet she planned to marry Adoniram.

A mutual friend had brought Newell to the Atwood homestead in Haverhill. The two introverts, both serious and introspective, shy and frail, found much in common. Within a week Newell had called again, and Harriet was confiding to her diary: "If such a man, who has devoted himself to the service of the gospel, has determined to labor in the most difficult part of the vineyard and is willing to renounce his earthly happiness for the interest of religion; if *he* doubts his possessing love of God — what shall *I* say of *myself?*"

Newell lacked Adoniram's impetuosity. It was not until spring, some six months later, that Harriet received a certain letter. "I broke the seal, and what were my emotions, when I read the name of ——. This was not a long-wished-for letter, — no, it was a long-dreaded one, which, I was conscious, would involve me in doubts, anxiety, and distress. Nor were the contents such as I might answer at a *distant* period; they required an *immediate* answer. And now what shall I say? How shall I decide this *important*, this *interesting* question? — Shall I consent to leave forever the *Parent* of my youth; the *friends* of my life; the dear scenes of my childhood, and my native country; and go to a land of strangers, 'not knowing the things that shall befal me there'?"

Harriet's father, Moses Atwood, had died a few years before. She took the problem to her mother, perhaps hoping her mother would say no. Mrs. Atwood would certainly have been justified in refusing to allow Harriet to marry Newell. She was not even seventeen, hardly old enough to know her own mind in the judgment of most people. She was subject to sick headaches. Tuberculosis ran in the family, and had carried away both her father and an uncle. On the other hand, Mrs. Atwood had nine children. She must have seen advantages in marrying one of them off to a minister, most desired of husbands, even though this minister was bound on such a dangerous venture. And after all, competent Nancy Hasseltine would be with her. After much anguish and many prayers, she finally told her daughter, as Harriet wrote to a friend, "If a conviction of duty, and love to the souls of the perishing heathen, lead you to India, as much as I love you, Harriet, I can only say *Go*."

Forced, like Nancy, to make her own decision, Harriet spent most of May hesitating. Newell refused to influence her. One of her chief fears was whether she had the strength to bear up under the hardships of a missionary life. On this one matter he repeated what a friend had told him, "A little slender woman may endure losses and suffering as cheerfully and resolutely as an apostle." Perhaps this was all the encouragement she needed. At the end of May, shortly before Newell left for Philadelphia, she gave her consent, though with many misgivings.

To Adoniram, once more riding about the countryside near Bradford with Nancy, and preaching in country churches Sundays, all this seemed good news. The closer they drew to the day of leaving the more their spirits rose.

On the eighteenth of September there was to be a meeting of the Board, in Worcester. To this Adoniram and Samuel Nott rode in optimistic mood. At last, they were sure, they would receive the Board's blessing and be sent on their way without further ado.

If this is what they thought, they were due for a shock.

The Board took up their business of the first day in the form of a report by the Prudential Committee on Adoniram's trip to England. In its report, the committee placed in the record all the correspondence between its secretary, Samuel Worcester, and George Burder, secretary of the London Missionary Society, including its letter of instructions to Adoniram, and Burder's final reply which Adoniram had carried home with him.

It was clear, said the committee, that the English had made no direct reply to the questions it wanted answered. Instead, the English expressed willingness to take Adoniram and his colleagues under their wing, and were willing to receive funds from the Americans, but this was as far as they could cooperate. The direction must remain in English hands.

This was only reasonable, believed the committee. The English organization expected to spend ten thousand pounds during the coming year, and already had allotted all of it. The cost of maintaining four American missionaries would be only six hundred pounds. If the Americans could not supply even this much, why should they enjoy any control? Particularly as they had no experience in operating missions and the English had a vast amount?

But, thought the committee, it would be shameful to resign its own four missionaries to the London Society for lack of a mere six hundred pounds, when Mrs. Norris's thirty thousand dollars would be available soon, and another fourteen hundred dollars had already been given by others. It urged, therefore, that the four be kept under the Board's control and that strenuous efforts be made to raise the money immediately.

Some of the leading members of the Board were apathetic. Its President was John Treadwell, fourth Governor of Connecticut. Another leading member, William Bartlet, one of the few whose princely gifts had helped found Andover Theological Seminary, had advanced some of the money which had sent Adoniram to England. But although he was now one of the three members of the Prudential Committee (the other two being Spring and Worcester) he shared with Treadwell the conservative merchant's point of view. Both felt that for the moment the best policy was a cautious do-nothing policy. The Embargo resulting from the war between

England and France had all but paralyzed American maritime trade. For two or three years business had been practically at a standstill. To men like Treadwell and Bartlet it seemed a poor time to take on the support of four missionaries and their wives, and undertake to raise the money to get them to the Orient and keep them there. Treadwell, now in his late sixties, felt particularly strong on the subject.

Adoniram and Nott felt just the opposite. They felt it was now or never. A war with England seemed imminent. It might come any time, possibly within a few months. If it did, they might not be able to get away for years. Time was of the essence. They must be sent at once, they urged — in a few weeks, if possible.

This argument had merely annoyed the laymen on the Board. They pooh-poohed the idea of imminent war. Treadwell even pledged his word that there would be no war at all.

At this point Adoniram, backed by Nott, made up his mind to force matters to a decision. Both told the Board quite frankly that if the American Board did not send them as missionaries they would go anyway, under the auspices of London — by the first available ship. Adoniram was especially emphatic. He stated his position so bluntly that it was virtually an ultimatum.

Tempers flared at once. Who was this brash young man, to lay down the law to his elders? Some members of the Board were already incensed because he had not followed his instructions. He had all but begged the London Society to ditch the sponsors who had sent him to England and take him under their own wing. On his return, he had not even given the Board a report in writing. Now he had the audacity to present them with a flat "take it or leave it." By the end of the first day's session some were all for dismissing Adoniram on the spot.

By the second day, however, feelings had cooled — thanks largely to Dr. Spring's diplomacy in dealing with the most irritated of the older men. As Adoniram knew, Spring loved him as if he were his own son. Now he came to his defense by pointing out to his fellow members that the trait which had precipitated the squabble was Adoniram's excess of self-reliance — and it was precisely this characteristic which would make him of greatest value as a missionary

47776

in a strange country, among strange people where he would have no one to depend on but himself.

And after all, he pointed out as he smoothed down various ruffled feelings, with the Norris bequest in prospect the Board could make commitments that would have seemed foolhardy a year ago. Everyone knew of the bequest. What would be thought if the Board did not send missionaries abroad at once, beginning with the men who had started the whole movement and made it practicable by volunteering themselves?

Dr. Spring's labors had their effect. On the second day the Board officially appointed Adoniram, Newell, Nott and Hall as its missionaries. But Adoniram's behavior was not overlooked, for at the same time Dr. Spring delivered to him, in the name of the Board, a rebuke which in later years became known as a "formal and solemn reprimand." Particularly because it came from Spring, it moved Adoniram deeply. He was well aware of his impetuousness and self-will, admitted it freely, and promised, almost in tears, to do better in the future.

Duly the Board's decision was inscribed in the records:

"That this Board did not advise Messrs. Adoniram Judson, Jr., and Samuel Nott, Jr., to place themselves at present under the direction of the London Missionary Society, but to wait the further intimations of Providence relative to our means of furnishing them with the requisite support in the proposed foreign mission.

"Messrs. Adoniram Judson, Jr., Samuel Nott, Jr., Samuel Newell, and Gordon Hall were appointed missionaries to labor under the direction of this board in Asia, either in the Burman Empire, or in Surat, or in Prince of Wales Island, or elsewhere, as in view of the Prudential Committee, Providence shall open by the most favorable door."

By a later vote the salaries of the missionaries were established — $666.66 a year if married, $444.45 if unmarried, with an amount for outfitting equal to a year's salary, and an additional appropriation for all the missionaries of three hundred dollars for books.

Elated, Adoniram rode back to Andover with Nott, "formal and solemn reprimand" already forgotten — so completely forgotten, in fact, that when he was reminded of it some years later he denied that it had ever been given. His memory of it, and of another he was to receive in about a month, was not to return until he was much older, wiser, and humbler.

But reproofs always rolled off him like water off a duck's back. He had got what he wanted. Now there remained only the actual preparations for departure, the raising of money, and the finding of a ship.

CHAPTER XIII

# The Ordination

### [ 1812 ]

IF he stopped off at Andover at all on the way back from Worcester, Adoniram may have spent no more than a few hours there before hurrying on to Bradford and Nancy with the news that they would be sailing soon. He probably spent the week end at the Hasseltine house, for on Sunday the twenty-second he preached at the church in Rowley, some five or six miles southeast of Bradford near the seacoast. Perhaps Nancy rode with him — it would have been a pleasant early morning ride — and listened with pride to his sermon. Most of the theological students had preached in the Rowley church at one time or another for the past year — Nott, Newell, Hall and Rice as well as Adoniram. Deacon Joshua Jewett was always one of their auditors, and although they did not know it, he faithfully noted in his journal who preached and the text. This day he thought Adoniram "preached well," as he had done the previous Sunday and the Sunday before that.

Meanwhile 1811 was flaming into autumn, and Adoniram and Nancy were increasingly conscious that they might be seeing the change of New England's seasons for the last time. They fretted to go, but they felt, too, the sadness of looking at faces and scenes they would never see again. It was a kind of dying. They looked forward to a glorious immortality but they regretted leaving all the dear familiar things they had always known.

But time ran on and no ship to India could be found. New York was already under British blockade. John Treadwell to the contrary, it was obvious to everyone else that war with England was close at hand. As the shriveled leaves fell and the land dissolved in the rains preceding the first snowstorms, a sense of urgency grew in the missionaries. A ship *must* be sailing, and it *must* be found.

December came, its first day a Sunday, and Adoniram preached once more in Rowley — "well," according to Deacon Jewett. The year 1812 opened and still nothing had been learned about a ship. By now a third of the four missionaries was engaged to marry — Samuel Nott. His wife was to be Roxana Peck, whom he had known since childhood. Roxana had written to Harriet Atwood, suggesting that they study "some new language in order to acquire an eastern language with greater facility." Harriet replied in January with a lengthy letter welcoming Roxana to "those 'dear selected few' who will be my only associates, through the little remnant of my life." But as to the languages, she and Newell had come to the conclusion that it was impracticable because they might be sailing in as soon as three months.

It was to be much less than that. Late in January, 1812, Hall and Newell appeared unexpectedly in Andover. They had dropped their medical studies and hurried up from Philadelphia with word that the ship *Harmony*, Captain Brown, was to sail from that port for Calcutta in about two weeks, by special permission of the federal government, and would take the missionaries.

The news was electrifying. All at once everyone realized that everything remained to be done with no time in which to do it. The Prudential Committee, meeting in Newburyport on the twenty-seventh of January, was suddenly faced with the matter of money. The only funds in hand amounted to five hundred dollars, although another twelve hundred were in sight. It would cost at least four times that much to outfit and send the missionaries out for a year, even on a dangerously modest budget. Opportunities for communication with the East would be few after war broke out. The missionaries might easily be stranded overseas unless they had at least a year's supply of money with them when they sailed.

But so far as the committee could see, it would be impossible to send the missionaries out with a full year's salary in advance. It finally recommended that they go without their wives; or, if they would not do that, that they accept half a year's salary, trusting that the other half could be forwarded later to India. If this could not be done, two of them should look to the London Missionary Society for support, to work under its auspices.

These decisions probably reflected the feelings of Mr. Bartlet of the Prudential Committee. But Dr. Worcester, who together with Samuel Spring made up the remainder of the committee, had a more daring heart. It was his Tabernacle Church in Salem which had been chosen as the place to hold the ordination ceremonies, which were to be on the sixth of February, the last day which would permit the missionaries to reach Philadelphia in time for the *Harmony's* sailing. Dr. Worcester never stopped preparations for a moment. He coolly borrowed money right and left in the name of the Prudential Committee. He even frightened bold Dr. Spring, who demurred one day, "Brother Worcester, I fear you are going too fast. I doubt if we shall have the means to pay the sum which we must borrow."

"There is money enough in the churches," asserted Worcester.

"I know that very well," replied Spring. "But how can you get at it?"

"The Lord has the key," Worcester affirmed calmly, and went on with a fine disregard for obstacles.

All at once a fifth candidate for the mission expedition presented himself and applied to the Prudential Committee for appointment. He was Luther Rice, a big man of boundless energy, a fine public speaker, quick with a jest, and an accomplished musician.

Rice would have applied long before, but the girl to whom he was engaged had been unwilling to share a missionary life with him. He had waited patiently, hoping she would change her mind. When he saw that she would not, he felt free to apply to go alone. But the Prudential Committee was having trouble enough. The most it could do was agree to appoint him if he could raise his own passage money. He had six days in which to do it. Caution and timidity — or, as some said, discretion — were not among Rice's characteristics. He promptly set off on a whirlwind horseback tour through New England to get the money wherever he could.

During that same hectic week, news came of another sailing for Calcutta, this one from Salem. It was learned that Pickering Dodge, owner of the brig *Caravan*, had just received permission from the government to let her go. She could carry three or four passengers, and her sailing date was tentatively set for February 10, four days after the ordination.

The Prudential Committee immediately decided to have half of the missionaries go on the *Caravan*, to lessen the "general risk," of which there was no question, what with the danger of capture added to the normal hazards of a voyage halfway around the world.

As news of the missionaries' imminent departure spread, public interest quickened. Long ocean voyages were an old story to Salem, but always with home and a fat profit to be anticipated at the end of a year or two. The missionaries, however, were making a one-way trip. They planned never to return. They had martyrdom to anticipate, with the only possible profits the glory of their souls and the salvation of a few heathen. They included women, too — and so young! One of them was only seventeen! *What selflessness!* said some. *What folly!* said others.

Meanwhile the indefatigable Dr. Worcester fanned the interest in every way he could, including announcements in the *Salem Gazette* and the *Essex Register:*

### MISSIONARY ORDINATION

Next Thursday, February 6, by appointment of the *Prudential Committee* of the *American Board of Commissioners for Foreign Missions, Messrs. Adoniram Judson, Samuel Newell, Samuel Nott,* and *Gordon Hall,* are to be set apart by a solemn ordination as Christian Missionaries to carry the Gospel of Salvation to the Heathen. The public exercises are to be holden at the Tabernacle in this town, and to commence at eleven o'clock A.M. A Collection will be made on the occasion in aid of the Missionaries, which, to embrace a very unexpected opportunity for conveyance to India, is now fitting out with all possible dispatch.

SAMUEL WORCESTER
*Clerk of the Prudential Committee*

Dr. William Bentley of the East Church in Salem saw the announcement. It was he who had rejoiced in his private journal when Adoniram's father had left Malden and Wenham. A good man, a liberal man, and that rarity in respectable circles in Salem, a Jeffersonian, he hated the conservative theology with all his heart. Now he noted: "The Hopkinsians give notice that they have four candidates for their Missions to be ordained in the Tabernacle this week, who are to go immediately to India. . . . We learn nothing favorable to their talents or experience. It is said that Pickering Dodge, Merchant of Salem, gives them a passage to India at 3 hundred dollars each and some of them carry their wives."

Thus Dr. Bentley. But a great many felt differently. The daring of the project caught their imagination and their sympathies. From all directions contributions began to come in — a trickle at first, then a torrent, and at the end a very flood.

While all this activity went on, Nancy Hasseltine in Bradford and Harriet Atwood in Haverhill were busily preparing for their weddings and the voyage. Adoniram went to Plymouth to say good-by to his father and mother, his sister and brother.

It is not hard to imagine the lamentations with which Mrs. Judson and Abigail contemplated farewell, nor the heavy heart with which Reverend Mr. Judson contemplated his son's departure. With Adoniram would go all his hopes, all his ambitions, for his favorite son, the one in whom he had meant to witness the triumph he had forsworn for himself.

And, bitterest of ironies, the boy was throwing himself away for the very cause the father himself preached. By his own creed his mouth was stopped. He could say not a word in opposition. The two Adonirams were more alike than they knew. When it came to belief, neither counted the cost. Neither could compromise.

Adoniram left Plymouth early in the morning of February 3, a Monday. He had a peculiar horror of farewells — perhaps because of the unhappy emotions associated with his previous departures — so he slipped away while the family still slept.

Only his brother Elnathan, now eighteen, rode with him to Boston. Adoniram knew that Elnathan had never professed religion. At some point along the way, the two dismounted from their horses and knelt on the snow-covered ground beside the road. Here Adoniram prayed fervently for the soul of his younger brother. In Boston they shook hands and parted, to see each other only once again.

Adoniram probably stayed in Boston overnight and went on alone to Bradford the next morning. There had been a heavy rain in the night; but during the day, as his horse plodded northward, fresh-falling snow blanketed the muddy roads.

On Wednesday, February 5, 1812, a dull warm day, Adoniram and Nancy were married by Parson Allen in the west room of Deacon Hasseltine's house — the very room where they had first met.

The same day, the two attended a great meeting in the church in Haverhill. The church was jammed to the rafters with onlookers. Some were merely curious to see the first American foreign missionaries in person. But to most, the occasion was a heart-wrenching farewell to two girls they had seen grow up almost as members of their own families.

Parson Allen delivered the sermon. The good old minister had known the two since their infancy. Many times, visiting the Hasseltine "dance hall," he had seen them whirling about, flushed and happy, enjoying themselves without a thought of what life would bring. He spoke to them, therefore, before the packed throng as if he were a loving father.

"My dear children," he told them, "you are now engaged in the best of causes. It is that cause for which Jesus the Son of God came into the world and suffered and died. You literally forsake father and mother, brothers and sisters, for the sake of Christ and the promotion of His Kingdom."

He had some special advice to them, as women and wives, concerning their duty to heathen women. To convert these women "will be your business, my dear children, to whom your husbands can have but little, or no access. Go then, and do all in your power to enlighten their minds, and bring them to the knowledge of the truth. . . . Teach them to realize that they are not an inferior race of creatures, but stand upon a par with men. Teach them that they have immortal souls; and are no longer to burn themselves in the same fire, with the bodies of their departed husbands."

He had words for the girls' parents, too, and for the congregation. But at the end of his discourse he turned again to Nancy and Harriet and concluded in a voice nearly breaking: "To the care of the great Head of the church I now commit them. To His grave I also resign you all. May He gather you together in one. And may you all return and come to Zion with a song, and with shouts of everlasting glory."

This was the end of the service except for the hymn before the

benediction, which Parson Allen had composed especially for the
occasion. People wept unashamedly as they sang:

> Go, ye heralds of salvation;
> Go, and preach in heathen lands;
> Publish loud to every nation,
> What the Lord of life commands.
> Go, ye sisters, their companions,
> Soothe their cares, and wipe their tears,
> Angels shall in bright battalions
> Guard your steps and guard your fears.
>
> Landed safe in distant regions,
> Tell the Burmans JESUS died;
> Tell them Satan and his legions,
> Bow to him they crucified.
> Far beyond the mighty Ganges,
> When vast floods beyond us roll,
> Think how widely Jesus ranges
> Nations wide from pole to pole.
>
> While from heathen nations blended
> Light and peace within shall rise;
> When your days on earth are ended,
> Christ receive you to the skies.
> To his grace we now resign you,
> To him only you belong;
> You with every christian Hindoo,
> Join at last th' angelic throng.

But this meeting at Haverhill was only a preliminary neighborhood gathering compared to the much greater one held in Salem
the next day at which the missionaries were ordained. The night of
the fifth a heavy snow had fallen. The morning of the sixth dawned
clear and cold — one of the coldest days of the year — so that as
people walked to the huge white Tabernacle Church their feet
creaked on the fresh crisp snow. They had come from many places
— from Boston, Bradford, Rowley, Andover, Wenham, Beverly,
Gloucester, Manchester, Haverhill, and Newburyport. They had
come in sleighs, on horseback, and afoot. Some brought their chil-

dren, so that they might be able to boast the rest of their lives that they had seen the ordination of the first American foreign missionaries. A delegation of boys from Phillips Academy at Andover and another of students from the Theological Seminary had started long before dawn, in order to be able to trudge the full sixteen miles to Salem over the drifted roads and still get to the Tabernacle Church before ceremonies opened at eleven in the morning.

The huge Tabernacle, a barnlike structure with a tent-shaped roof, could hardly contain all the people. Some thought they numbered as many as two thousand — fifteen hundred at the very least. The auditorium was so packed that "the aisles could be traced only by the ridges or seams made by the people standing." The platform around the high white pulpit was completely filled by members of the ecclesiastical council and various dignitaries, both clerical and lay.

In the very front of this immense gathering, facing the high pulpit, sat the five candidates on a hard wooden settee — Nancy, resplendent in a new scoop bonnet, just behind them in the aisle seat of the foremost box pew.

Her thoughts might not have all been on the ordination. That morning her husband had given her proof of his aversion to formal partings. He had hurried her away from Bradford before dawn without allowing her to take leave of anyone. This time, however, his stratagem had been discovered, and the newlyweds had been called back after they had already gone a short distance and made to shake hands all round. Adoniram's action had created a peculiar impression, not entirely favorable. From time to time during the service Nancy may have wondered why her husband was sometimes so regardless of the feelings of others, and how she could change him. But these thoughts must have been lost in the rising tension of the ceremonies.

No foreign missionaries had ever been ordained in America, and, lacking any traditional procedure, the general form used in the ordination of any Congregational minister was followed.

Onlookers are always stirred in some degree by an ordination, for it is the rite which dedicates the minister to the service of God, sets him aside from his fellow men, and admits him into the consecrated brotherhood of the ministry. But this ordination in the Tabernacle was charged with unusual, almost unbearable emotion. It was noticeable even during the routine of the missionaries' examination by the ecclesiastical council in respect to "their Christian knowledge and piety, and their motives in offering themselves as missionaries to the heathen." It was even more noticeable when — probably after some of the "appropriate music," which next day's *Salem Gazette* reported "was performed at proper intervals" on a "bass viol" — Dr. Griffin began the introductory prayer.

To Adoniram, there must have been a special poignancy in seeing Dr. Griffin as one of the ordaining ministers. He had been Adoniram's mentor at the theological seminary. Now he was pastor of Boston's Park Street Church — where Adoniram could have been assistant pastor at this very moment if he had wished. But all five of the presiding ministers were closely associated with the missionary movement in one way or another. There was Dr. Woods, who had taught Adoniram as Abbot Professor of Christian Theology. If Dr. Griffin represented Adoniram's rejected opportunities, Dr. Woods might have represented Adoniram's conversion from infidelity. And there was Jedediah Morse, pastor of the First Church in Charlestown. He represented both Andover Theological Seminary and the American Board, as trustee of one and member of the other. As for the remaining two, Samuel Spring and Samuel Worcester, they might be said to represent the mission itself, for those two had literally invented the American Board and had done more than anyone else to bring a mission under American auspices actually into being.

To the audience, however, another feeling began to well up as soon as Dr. Griffin began the prayer. The auditorium fell into a hush "as still as death," as one eyewitness remembered it; for by accident or design, everything said and done from then on conveyed the spirit of *farewell*. The audience realized it was seeing the five men being bid a farewell that in some respects approached that bade at the edge of a grave in the prospect of an eventual resurrection.

Dr. Woods made this increasingly clear during the sermon following the introductory prayer, when, speaking directly to the five, he said: "Dear young men, I will not break your hearts and my own, by dwelling on the affecting circumstances of this parting scene." Later, he spoke of seeing them again "at the glorious appear-

ing of the Son of God, and those whom their labors may rescue
from pagan darkness, at his right hand." And he closed: "With this
joyful anticipation, I do, my dear friends, cheerfully and most affectionately, bid you, farewell!"

The most impressive part of an ordination — and, in a way, its
soul — is the "laying on of hands" as a prayer of consecration is
said. When the time for it came, the five missionaries and the audience knelt. Nancy, if the traditional representations are correct,
slipped out into the aisle and knelt there by the front corner of the
pew, almost beside the missionaries. Each of the ordaining ministers
stood before one of the five and placed both hands on his head as
Dr. Morse gave the consecrating prayer.

The moment was too much for the audience. "An irresistible
sighing and weeping" broke out. It had been heard before, but from
now on "The entire wrapt congregation seemed moved as the
trees of the wood are moved by a mighty wind. Pent-up emotion
could no longer be restrained."

Dr. Spring gave the charge to the newly ordained missionaries.
He pointed out that "no enterprise comparable to this has been embraced by the American Church. All others retire before it, like
stars before the rising sun." But in nearly everything he said, though
it was nominally the statement to the five of their duties and responsibilities, sounded that same haunting note of farewell.

Even Samuel Worcester, receiving them into the brotherhood of
the ministry by giving them "the right hand of fellowship," returned to the same theme: "By the solemnities of this day, you,
Messrs. Judson, Nott, Newell, Hall, and Rice, are publicly set aside
for the service of God in the Gospel of his Son, among the Heathen.
With reference, therefore, to this momentous service, we, who are
still to labor in the same Gospel here at home, in the presence of
God, angels and men, now give to you, dear Brethren, the right
hand of fellowship. . . . Go, carry to the poor Heathen the good
news of pardon, peace and eternal life. Tell them of the God whom
we adore; of the Saviour in whom we trust; of the glorious immortality for which we hope. . . . We are not insensible to the
sacrifices which you make, or to the dangers and sufferings to which
you are devoted. You stand this day 'a spectacle to God, to angels,
and to man.' You are in the act of leaving parents, and friends, and

country. . . . But, dear Brethren, we shall have you in the tenderest remembrance, and shall not cease to make mention of you in our prayers."

There was more. Ministers and orators never feared to take sufficient time to make their points, in those days. But Dr. Worcester's conclusion expressed the general feeling:

"You are but the precursors of many, who shall follow you in this arduous, glorious exercise; for the Gospel shall be preached to all nations, and all people shall see the Salvation of God.

"Beloved Brethren, be of good courage; go in peace; and may the Lord God of the holy apostles and prophets go with you. We commend you to him, and to the word of his grace; and devoutly pray, that in the day of the Lord Jesus, we may have the happiness to see you present many of the Heathen before the throne of his glory with exceeding joy. Amen."

It was early in the afternoon, when, after a concluding prayer by Dr. Spring, the services ended. Most of the onlookers were so moved that they would describe the events they had witnessed to their dying day. Meanwhile, they had to make their way home through the bitter cold. One of them, Ephraim Newton, a theological student who had to walk all the way back to Andover, wrote two days later that he was still badly way-worn. Another, William Goodell, a student at the Academy who later went himself as a missionary to Turkey, became so exhausted and chilled that, at nightfall, still some distance from Andover, he fell and would have frozen to death had not a group of returning theological students found him. By taking turns carrying him, they managed to get him to a house on the outskirts of Andover, where a mattress and blankets could be spread for him in front of a roaring fire.

While these hundreds were streaming home over the drifted streets and roads, Adoniram and Nancy went to Beverly to stay with her sister Rebecca and her husband in the parsonage of the Dane Street Church until the *Caravan* should sail — in about four days, it was hoped. Abigail, another of Nancy's sisters, came down from Bradford to help out and be company. The Reverend Joseph Emerson was seldom home, however. He was out — everywhere — feverishly trying to collect money for the missionaries.

For that matter, everyone was feverishly active. The morning after the ordination, Adoniram made a brief trip to Boston to say a final good-by to his sister Abby and his brother — the last time the brothers ever saw each other. The next day, the eighth, Samuel Nott and Roxana Peck were married and left for Philadelphia with Hall and Rice, for the sailing of the *Harmony*. Sunday evening, the ninth, there was another huge meeting in the Tabernacle, nominally the ordinary Sunday evening service, but in fact a second farewell service. But so many were the meetings these days that this one was scarcely remembered afterward.

Somewhere in these crowded days Samuel Newell and Harriett Atwood found time to be married in the big white Atwood house in Haverhill. An old, gnarled apple tree grew in the yard beside the house. Harriet had seen it bloom that spring, but now its branches were bare. As she looked at it, she may have reflected sadly that she would never see an apple tree bloom again.

But there was little time for reflections like these. There was too much to do in the few days remaining until the *Caravan* should sail.

## CHAPTER XIV

# The Embarkation

## [ *1812* ]

MEANWHILE, money was flooding in. The American Board's treasury had contained twelve hundred dollars the morning of the ordination. The collection taken there had added two hundred and twenty. But this was only the beginning. Everywhere ministers and laymen were soliciting gifts. At Andover, nearly the whole student body, as well as the professors, asked money at every door for miles around. The appeal was irresistible. Even people who disbelieved in missions gave. One night when Nancy and Adoniram were seated with the Emersons around the fire in the parsonage in Beverly, the front door was opened, a heavy object thrown in, and the door closed with a bang. Mr. Emerson peered outside, but could see no sign of the intruder. In the living room, the occupants picked up the object and examined it. It was a purse. The tag attached read, "For Mr. Judson's private use." Inside was fifty dollars in coin.

Before the *Caravan* and *Harmony* actually sailed, more than six thousand dollars had been collected. And besides money, there were other gifts — clothing, and even food, including so much New England gingerbread that the missionaries were still eating it three months later.

But the thrill of sympathetic enthusiasm that ran through the countryside was not felt by everyone. One "prominent citizen of Haverhill" expressed the minority point of view in a letter which he wrote the twelfth of February to a friend in Lisbon, Portugal:

> I can think of nothing interesting to add. I will just observe that religious enthusiasm still continues to prevail here. Believe me, unaccountable as it may appear to you, that what I am about to repeat to you is true. A daughter of the late Moses

Atwood, deceased, by name of Harriet, and a young Miss Hazeltine, of the Hazeltine family of Bradford, young (about seventeen or eighteen years old), and totally inexperienced in the school of human nature, are about to embark with their companions (to whom they have but yesterday allied themselves by marriage) — yes, *I say that these four foolish and inexperienced young people are about to embark, and will actually sail to the far-distant shores of Hindoostan, and marvellous to tell, to teach that numerous and ancient people the right way to heaven!*

But if there were carpers, Nancy and Adoniram at Beverly, and Harriet and Samuel staying with Isaac Newell in Salem, did not mind. They were too busy, too excited, and too happy — the Judsons with their usual buoyancy, the Newells in their own "more sober and contemplative way."

It proved impossible to load the *Caravan* in time to sail on the tenth. She lay at the end of Crowninshield's Wharf — closest to the sea of all Salem's wharves — until the thirteenth. But even after she had been taken out into the middle of the harbor, she rode idly at anchor while more cargo was put aboard. As the last Salem ship, in all probability, to sail for the Orient until after the expected war, her owner and master were determined to cram her with everything her ninety-foot length and two-hundred-and-sixty-seven-ton burden could contain.

Meanwhile, Adoniram, Newell, Nancy and Harriet became acquainted with her captain, Augustine Heard, as they paid constant visits aboard with their friends to inspect their cabins and supervise the stowing of what Heard called "tangible evidence of the good will of their friends in the shape of boxes of all sizes . . . containing almost everything that is conducive to comfort on a voyage."

Heard, a native of Ipswich, was only twenty-seven — not much older than the missionaries — and this voyage was to be his first command, an unusually important one in view of the circumstances and the cargo. But Pickering Dodge, the *Caravan's* owner, had full confidence in the young captain. Even-tempered, courteous, com-

petent, he had a cool daring which was to become a legend in
Essex County.

His ship carried valuable freight — goods amounting in value to
some forty thousand dollars, and another forty thousand in specie
and bills of exchange. In addition he had accepted, with his usual
amiability, a host of personal commissions. He carried two thousand
silver dollars for his father and the same amount in paper. Numerous
female relatives and retired sea captains from Ipswich had given
him sums from twenty to a hundred dollars each. Three of the
Francis children had presented him with a dollar apiece, for him
to invest for them in Calcutta.

Besides all this, he was laden with lists of things to buy for friends
and relations — Salem's equivalent of asking a neighbor to pick up a
small item while passing the corner grocery. For Henry Pickering,
he was to buy a Sanskrit Bible. For others he was to buy cashmere
and camel's-hair shawls, two large "palompons" for the covering
of a large bed, a netting covering for a bed, some lengths of "Mull
Mull" or cobweb muslin, straw carpets, red carnelian necklaces, pots
of preserved ginger and articles of all sorts too numerous to mention.

The deck of the *Caravan* presented a peculiar appearance. It was
covered with coops and pens full of cackling chickens and
squealing pigs — fresh meat for the long voyage. Concerning this
seagoing barnyard and other matters, Pickering Dodge kept up a
barrage of advice in the form of letters: " . . . the yellow corn is
for the fowls, the old white corn for the hogs." The missionaries
were to dine in the cabin. "I hope you will find them pleasant companions, give a fresh dish once a week or oftener, if practicable,
and puddings, rice, etc.: be as careful as possible of the water, as
your ship's company is large and considerable live stock to subsist,
but hope you will be fortunate enough to catch some near the line,
avoid Speaking to any Vessel on your outward or homeward
voyage."

The general confusion of loading, of animals and fowls, of missionaries and their friends coming on board and leaving, of Pickering Dodge's old seafaring acquaintances and of last-minute changes
in rigging was compounded by almost hourly changes in weather
and wind, both of which had to be suitable for clearing the harbor.

By the thirteenth, when the *Caravan* was moved out into the harbor, Adoniram and Nancy had moved from Joseph Emerson's parsonage in Beverly to the Salem home of the drygoods merchant Eliphalet Kimball, whose daughter Lydia had been Nancy's close friend and schoolmate in Bradford, in order to be closer at hand when it should finally be time to embark. But still the *Caravan* was delayed. The fourteenth and fifteenth were wet and stormy. The sixteenth, a Sunday, continued wet and stormy, and Adoniram and Nancy went back to the Emersons' in Beverly. On the seventeenth a tremendous snowstorm fell, "almost burying the town in snow."

Early in the morning of the eighteenth — a bleak, cold day — they returned to the Kimball house in Salem. By now, excellent arrangements to see that the missionaries got on board at the proper time had been made by two young men in Salem. The two had taken particular interest in the missionaries, had done a good deal to collect money, and ever since the ordination had neglected their own work to form a sort of volunteer executive staff. One of them was Israel W. Putnam, who had spent two years with Newell at Harvard before transferring to Dartmouth to graduate with the class of 1809. At this time he was studying law with Judge Samuel Putnam in Salem, but very shortly was to enter Andover Theological Seminary, graduate in 1814, and enjoy a distinguished career as a minister and a trustee of Dartmouth. The other was S. B. Ingersoll, who had been a sea captain, had been converted and left the sea, and was eventually to become a minister at Shrewsbury.

Putnam had made the Newells his particular responsibility, Ingersoll the Judsons.

Adoniram and Nancy had been at the Kimball house only a few hours when word came suddenly from Captain Heard that they should go aboard the *Caravan* as soon as possible. A fair wind had sprung up from the west and he wanted to sail out on the full tide that very afternoon.

Adoniram and Nancy had been in high spirits all along, but this news threw them into a fever of exhilaration. Adoniram immediately repacked their just-unpacked personal luggage, flinging all sorts of articles into the nearest handy containers, and carried them in a sleigh to Crowninshield's Wharf.

When he returned he found the Kimball house filled with friends, chattering and laughing in excitement, shedding farewell tears, and bemoaning the fact that Mr. Kimball, not expecting the sailing to be so soon, had gone to Boston that morning on business. In fact, no one had expected it to be this day. Dr. Worcester, that tower of strength, was out of town on American Board business. Even Joseph Emerson was away soliciting money and there was no way of reaching him.

From Adoniram's point of view, with his aversion to formal partings, this was all to the good. Without a word to anyone, he slipped quietly out of the house, walked alone down the snowy street to the wharf, found a boat, and went on board the *Caravan*. Here he waited for Nancy.

In the Kimball house, the discovery that Adoniram had stolen away caused a good deal of disappointed surprise. Nancy was distressed, but she must have remembered that his stealthy leaving was only a repetition of what she had witnessed in Bradford the morning of the ordination. At any rate, there was no lack of conveyance. Ingersoll, by previous understanding with Adoniram, had procured a sleigh as soon as he learned of the sailing, and driven at once to the Kimball house. Here he bundled the last of the luggage, Nancy, and four of the ladies into the sleigh and hurried them down to the wharf, where they met the Newells, who had been conveyed by Putnam.

It was a blustering day — no time for lengthy farewells, with that icy west wind knifing down the length of the harbor. The customhouse boat was waiting. There were a few brief words of love and blessing while the luggage was hurriedly stowed in the boat. Nancy, Harriet and Newell were helped down into it. Putnam and Ingersoll followed, with such others as could crowd in.

The men at the oars shoved the heavily laden boat out from the wharf and began to row toward the *Caravan*. The watchers on the wharf — their numbers growing as more people heard of the sailing and hastened to the harbor — saw it rise and fall, shrinking smaller and smaller as it passed over the steely water until it reached the side of the brig. Some turned away now, but a group of the hardiest remained on the cold exposed end of the wharf, stamping their feet and blowing on their freezing fingers.

Darkness came, and still the *Caravan* did not sail. The few still remaining on the wharf began to think of their warm dinners and the roaring fires in their living rooms. By twos and threes they turned away and made their way to their homes, perhaps pausing now and then to look back at the lights gleaming across the black water from the *Caravan's* portholes.

On board the *Caravan*, meanwhile, there had been a change of plan. For in spite of Captain Heard's determination to sail that afternoon, the wind had died and he had been forced to give up the attempt. He decided to try again with the next tide, early in the morning.

At dark, the visitors who had been lingering on board with the missionaries returned to their homes ashore, but Ingersoll and Putnam offered to spend the night on the ship and make company for the Judsons and Newells, who were "much pleased." After a while even Captain Heard went on shore, and the four missionaries and the two visitors had the brig nearly to themselves.

They made a gay time of it. As Putnam wrote: "The evening was spent in pleasant conversation, and singing from one of the old singing books; and although everything *external* wore a dismal aspect" — and it certainly must have, on a cold February night in the middle of the harbor with the waves slapping the sides of the hull — "yet *in the cabin*, where we were with the missionaries, singing and praying, there was a perfect contrast. All was cheerfulness and even joy."

But some of the joy may have been a little forced. Nancy confided to her journal later that night that she "had so long anticipated the trying scene of parting, that I have found it more tolerable than I had feared."

Still my heart bleeds. O America, my native land, must I leave thee? Must I leave thee, Bradford, my dear native town, where I spent the pleasant years of childhood; where I learned to lisp the name of my mother; . . . where I learnt the endearments of friendship, and tasted all the happiness this world can afford; where I learnt also to value a Saviour's blood, and to count all things but loss, in comparison with the knowledge of him? . . . Farewell, happy, happy scenes, — but never no, never to be forgotten.

Captain Heard returned to the *Caravan* before dawn. The tide was full and a west wind had sprung up, fair enough to give a reasonable chance of clearing the northern end of Cape Cod. The weather remained clear and cold. A little after sunrise the brig left the harbor. Six or eight miles out, clear of the Miseries and Baker's Island, Ingersoll and Putnam went over the side with the pilot and dropped into the little pilot boat. Adoniram, Nancy, Samuel Newell and Harriet leaned over the rail waving as the pilot boat swung aside and began to drop astern.

The four watched longingly as the sails of the pilot boat filled and she came about to return to the harbor. In a little while she vanished, and there was nothing to see but the dark coastline streaked with the white of snow. Soon that, too, melted out of sight, and the *Caravan* was rising and falling in the swells of the open sea. Shivering in the piercing wind, the missionaries turned away from the rail and went below.

The next landfall would be India.

# PART TWO
# The Dangerous Voyage
## [ *1812–1826* ]

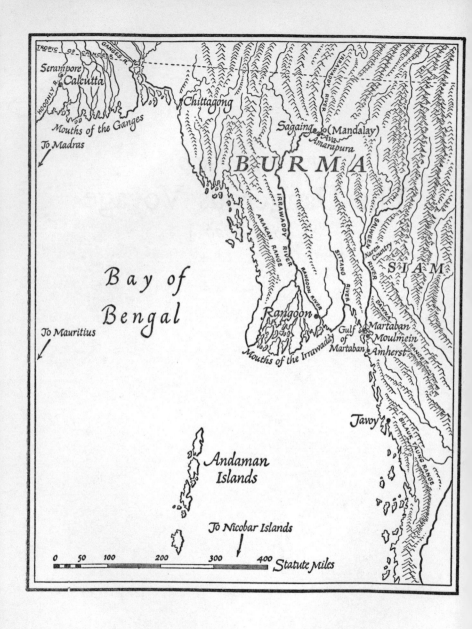

TROPIC OF CANCER
GANGES R.
Serampore
Calcutta
HOOGHLY R.
Mouths of the Ganges
To Madras

Chittagong

IRRAWADDY RIVER
Sagaing
(Mandalay)
Ava
Amarapura

B U R M A

ARAKAN RANGE
IRRAWADDY RIVER
RANGOON RIVER
SITTANG RIVER
SALWEEN RIVER
Karen Country
DWNA
S I A M

Bay of
Bengal

To Mauritius

Rangoon

Gulf of Martaban
Mouths of the Irrawaddy
Martaban
Moulmein
Amherst

ANGANDA RANGE

Tavoy
BILAUK TAUNG RANGE

Andaman
Islands

To Nicobar Islands

0   50   100       200        300        400   Statute Miles

## CHAPTER I

# India

## [ *1812* ]

THE *Caravan* was not long out of sight of land before Harriet and Nancy became aware of something unpleasant about the rise and fall of the vessel on the open ocean. Within a few hours both were seasick. Probably their husbands were, too, but they did not record their sensations in their journals.

Harriet was completely incapacitated for several days. Nancy was more fortunate. The first night she "had many distressing apprehensions of death," and "felt unwilling to die on the sea, not so much on account of my state after death, as the dreadfulness of perishing amid the waves." But she was less sick than she had expected, "no worse, through the whole, than if I had taken a gentle emetic." Meanwhile, five days out, the *Caravan* scared everybody by springing a bad leak and nearly sinking in spite of the efforts of all hands at the pumps, until the hole was finally located and stopped. After a week or so, however, all four of the passengers began to enjoy the voyage.

Captain Heard and his officers and crew treated their passengers with great kindness and respect. The first Sunday at sea, bad weather and sickness had prevented any formal observance of the day. But the next Sunday — March 1, 1812 — the passengers suggested to him that worship be held in the cabin. Heard agreed at once, and from then on he and at least two of his officers joined in regular Sabbath services every week.

The Christian behavior aboard the *Caravan* went so far that Nancy noted with wonderment, "I have not heard the least profane language since I have been on board the vessel. This is very uncommon." Even when the ship had seemed to be sinking, there had been no language stronger than the Captain's cool observation that only the hand of Providence could save them.

As the long days passed, the weather became warmer. There was little to do but read. Evenings were spent in "religious conversation." Occasionally the monotony was broken by the sighting of a ship. Sometimes they could even see the men on deck, but Captain Heard faithfully obeyed his orders not to speak to any vessel.

For a while the missionaries had poor appetites. "Everything tasted differently from what it does on land," wrote Nancy, "and those things I was the most fond of at home, I loathed the most here." Finally they decided the trouble was lack of exercise.

They tried walking, but the cluttered decks lacked room. Then someone thought of skipping rope, and for hours every day the two couples diligently skipped. Finally it occurred to them that dancing was just as good exercise and more fun. From then on they danced long and often, and health and appetite returned — although through the whole voyage Harriet remained finicky about her diet and never could stomach coffee or tea without milk.

But Harriet had a reason. She was pregnant and looked forward to the birth of her baby about November. It would be born, she supposed, in India or Burma. Perhaps she would have no help but that which her husband could give her.

Meanwhile, the four young people found a good deal of enjoyment in their long honeymoon. Nancy thought Adoniram "one of the kindest, most faithful and affectionate of husbands." Harriet echoed her: "My dear mother, unite with me in praising God for one of the best of husbands. Oh what would have been my wretchedness, had I found Mr. N. a cold, inattentive partner. But he is *all* I could wish him to be."

Presently the *Caravan* entered the torrid zone. The missionaries discovered the invigorating effects of a bath in salt water; following her first, Harriet noted that it "has refreshed me much. I think I shall bathe regularly every other day." Even so, they were often "lethargic. . . . While my dear mother, brothers and sisters are probably shivering over a large fire, I am sitting with the window and door open, covered with sweat. Brother and sister Judson are asleep on one bed, Mr. N. lounging on another, while I am writing."

This was their life as the *Caravan* slowly crossed the infinity of ocean. Buoying up their spirits was their faith in God and their belief in their mission; and, almost equally, the richness of the love each husband found in his wife, and each wife in her husband. But there were moments of nostalgia, too. "We often look the way where Captain H. tells us Haverhill lies. But alas! a *vast* ocean and the blue sky is all we can see."

By the first of May they had crossed the Equator and run into cold, rainy weather as they began to round the Cape of Good Hope. On this day Harriet summed up her feelings:

> I care not how soon we reach Calcutta, and are placed in a still room, with a bowl of milk and a loaf of Indian bread. I can hardly think of this simple fare without exclaiming, oh, what a luxury. — I have been so weary of the excessive rocking of the vessel, and the almost intolerable smell after the rain, that I have done little more than lounge on the bed for several days. But I have been blest with excellent spirits, and today have been running about the deck, and *dancing* in our room for *exercise*, as well as ever. What do some females do, who have unkind husbands in sickness? Among the many signal favors I am daily receiving from God, one of the greatest is a most affectionate partner. With him, my days pass cheerfully away — happy in the consciousness of loving and being beloved. With him contented would I live, and contented I would die. This, my mother, is the language of your Harriet's heart.

Meanwhile Adoniram had involved himself in a theological inquiry which was showing unexpected results.

In Andover he had begun a translation of the New Testament from the Greek, which he continued on board ship. Along toward April he became interested in the Greek word which is usually translated as "baptism." Adoniram had been baptized as an infant in the Congregational way, by the sprinkling of a few drops of water on his head. But as he conned the New Testament he could find no indication that anyone mentioned there had ever been baptized by sprinkling. In every case in which it was described, baptism had been performed in a river, and the people baptized actually went down into the water. Studying the word itself, he could not find that it was ever used to mean anything but immersion.

More than once he spoke to Nancy of his discovery. Of course, he was a staunch orthodox Congregationalist, but he admitted to

her with some chagrin that in this case, at least, it looked as if the
Baptists were right and the Congregationalists wrong. No matter
how he stretched the sense, he could not see how any impartial
person could ever make that Greek word mean "sprinkling."

As a missionary, he was disturbed, because his instructions from
the American Board told him to baptize "credible believers and
their households." Naturally, only the "credible believers" were
to be admitted into church membership, but their "households"
could and must be baptized. In New England this would have
meant their infant children. In the Orient, it would also mean
adult sons and daughters and probably servants as well, since the
believers would probably never have heard of Christ until Adoniram told them. This was much different from baptizing newborn
children of church members, one by one as they came along, New
England fashion. What would the thirty-year-old still-pagan son of
a newly admitted church member think of being baptized? Would
he consent? If he did, what good would baptism do if he remained
an unbeliever?

Adoniram had another reason for concern. He carried with
him a letter from Dr. Worcester to Dr. Carey and the missionaries
at Serampore, outside Calcutta, asking them to give the Americans
their advice and aid. The Serampore missionaries were Baptists, and
as such baptized only believers, not their children and servants. With
them, the ceremony was inseparable from personal conversion; in
Adoniram's words, "the initiating ordinance of the church."

The Baptists and orthodox Congregationalists of New England
had always been on friendly terms. In fact, Adoniram had met Dr.
Lucius Bolles, pastor of the First Baptist Church of Salem, before
the departure of the *Caravan*, and had urged that American Baptists
follow the example of British Baptists in forming a missionary organization. But Adoniram was not so sure about his relation with
the Serampore Baptists. If they attacked the Congregational position on baptism, how could he defend it? He feared much more,
however, the dilemma in which he would find himself if natives
asked him to explain the difference! They might even conclude
there were two competing religions, each calling itself Christian —
and thus find it easier to resist conversion.

With his usual vigor Adoniram plunged into a study of the matter.

Finally he came to the conclusion that baptism of infants and un-converted members of a household, as Congregationalists performed it, grew out of the way church membership was acquired in the Old Testament, as illustrated by the case of Abraham. Abraham's male descendants and servants were automatically members of the church from birth. They did not have to join it by an act of individual choice, because the church consisted of the whole people. They left it only by being "cut off from the people." But in the *New* Testament, the basis of Christianity, so far as he could see, the membership of a church was restricted to the individuals "who gave credible evidence of being disciples of Christ." Baptism was mentioned "always in connection with believing."

But this was the Baptist position! It worried him. He began saying to Nancy, "I am *afraid* the Baptists may be in the right."

It worried Nancy even more. She did not feel the point was vital, but she was afraid that if he kept on this way her uncompromising Adoniram might come to believe that the Baptists were right in other things. *Then* where would they be? But although she never hesitated to argue with him, she must have learned by now that she was wasting her breath. He continued to worry the subject and it continued to worry him.

Meanwhile the *Caravan* was approaching India. By early June Captain Heard thought they were within a hundred miles of Ceylon. Warm torrential gales blew from the shore. But by now even Harriet was hardened: "I know not how it is; but I hear the thunder roll; — see the lightning flash; — and the waves threatening to swallow up the vessel; — and yet remain unmoved."

The missionaries began to pack up their belongings. Adoniram dropped his preoccupation with baptism, much to Nancy's relief. The first visitors came from land — two birds and a butterfly. And the next day, the twelfth of June, "after seeing nothing but sky and water for *one hundred and fourteen days*, we this morning heard the joyful exclamation of 'land, land!' It is the coast of Orissa, about twenty miles from us."

The first day all they could make out were "the towering mountains of Golconda," but the following morning they were close enough to shore to distinguish trees, which they delightedly assured each other must be orange and palm trees. They spoke to two vessels and were happy to hear the sound of a new voice. At nightfall Captain Heard anchored in the dangerous, shallow Bay of Bengal until he could secure a pilot.

In this bay vessels had been known to wait for a pilot as long as ten days, but the *Caravan* was lucky. A vessel turned up the next morning with the English pilot, his leadsman, an English lad, and a Hindu servant. They all came on board, but the missionaries had eyes for nothing but the Hindu, the first they had ever seen. He was a small man, perhaps twenty years old, of "a dark copper color," wearing "calico trousers and a white cotton short gown." He was a Mohammedan, and Harriet thought his countenance expressed "the most perfect apathy and indolence." She doubted whether "he had force enough to engage in any employment." Nancy agreed: "He looks as feminine as you can imagine. What an alteration would a belief in Christianity make in such a degraded creature."

If the Hindu lacked energy, the pilot had enough for ten. Until dusk he guided the *Caravan* through the intricate lanes between the shoals, seeming to propel her largely by the force of his blistering oaths.

At nightfall the brig came to anchor, but not for long. One of a series of heavy seas rolled the vessel until water flooded the missionaries' quarters. Another snapped the anchor cable, and the *Caravan* began to drift dangerously with wave and tide in the shallow waters. The rest of the night the *Caravan* was kept slowly under way, the pilot's cursing reaching new heights as he navigated by guess in the dark. Nancy was unable to catch a wink "in consequence of the continual noise, and profane language on deck. The captain has never used any profane language since we have been with him; but the pilot, much more than we ever heard before."

As the sun rose and the *Caravan* entered the calmer waters of the Ganges delta, the pilot carefully (and perhaps less profanely now that he had the vessel safely out of the dangerous Bay) guided her between the little islands until he had her moving up the Hooghly River, one of the mouths of the Ganges, toward Calcutta.

With land almost within touch after so many months at sea, the missionaries spent most of the morning running from rail to rail pointing out new wonders to each other or dashing below deck to describe them in letters. The exotic sights on shore — and the delicious fragrances drifting to the ship — fulfilled all their expectations of India. Nancy had never "witnessed nor read anything so delightful as the present scene":

On each side of the Hoogli, where we are now sailing, are the Hindoo cottages, as thick together as the houses in our seaports. They are very small, and in the form of hay-stacks, without either chimney or windows. They are situated in the midst of trees, which hang over them, and appear truly romantick. The grass and fields of rice are perfectly green, and herds of cattle are everywhere feeding on the banks of the river, and the natives are scattered about, differently employed. Some are fishing, some driving the team, and many are sitting indolently on the banks of the river. The pagodas we have passed are much larger than the houses.

Harriet, perhaps thinking of the child she expected to bear among these people, liked especially the natives "walking with fruit and umbrellas in their hands, with the little tawny children around them." There was no sign here of the hardships she had anticipated. All in all, she decided, "this is the most delightful *trial*, I ever had." About noon some natives came aboard the ship — the Hindu crew of a port-boat which visited the *Caravan* to pick up mail. To Harriet's slightly shocked surprise, they "were *naked*, except a piece of cotton cloth wrapped around their middle." But they had "much more interesting countenances than the Hindoo we have now on board. They appeared active, talkative, and as though capable of acquiring a knowledge of the Christian religion, if instructed. Their hair is black — some had it shaved off the fore part of the head, and tied in a bunch behind; that of the others, was all turned back."

The pastoral river banks gave way to something entirely different when they reached Calcutta and docked that afternoon at about three. It was the largest and "by far the most elegant" city, with its blocks of white-painted brick buildings, any of them had ever seen. The masts of ships palisaded the shore for miles, and the wharves and waterfront streets swarmed with hundreds of natives who flocked "thick as bees" around the ships, keeping up a "continual chattering" in Bengali. The two women were "almost stunned with the noise."

But there was compensation: fresh food from shore, sent by a friend of Captain Heard's — exotic delicacies new to them, such as pineapples and bananas (the latter tasting like "a rich pear"); and, most delicious of all, what Harriet had dreamed of all the months on the ocean, *milk* with *fresh bread!*

With these viands Nancy and Harriet regaled themselves in a cabin. Adoniram and Samuel, meanwhile, went ashore with Captain Heard to comply with the first obligation laid on every visitor to the East India Company's domain — that of reporting to the police station.

On the way they were able to secure a little firsthand information about Burma through some of Captain Heard's acquaintances. Nearly all they knew came from Symes's book, the one Adoniram had read in Andover. Few Salem ships had visited Burma since Captain John Gibaut's unfortunate experience with the *Astra* in 1793, nearly twenty years before. Gibaut's ship had been commandeered as soon as he entered Pegu, near Rangoon, and taken up the Irrawaddy. Although he had finally managed to get her back, he had found nothing in the way of trade; only some curiosities which he had deposited in Salem's East India Museum. A year later Captain Hodges had taken aboard a good deal of gum lacquer in Burma, but on his return had found no one to buy it. After these two experiences, Salem ships had left Burma strictly alone.

Now Adoniram and Newell learned that it was the unhappy experience of Gibaut and Hodges, rather than Symes's glowing account, which most nearly represented the true Burma. Symes, in his ignorance of Burmese customs, had not realized that, instead of being treated as a distinguished visitor, he had actually been led about with subtle mockery, and dealt a succession of calculated insults in the guise of compliments. The Burmese court had silently rocked with laughter during his whole mission.

Ava had no intention of dealing with the West, and no conception of English power. Two missions to Burma had failed, although Dr. Carey's son Felix still hung on at Rangoon. The fact was, any inhabitant of Burma — even of a border seaport such as Rangoon — lived at the mercy of a despotic governor. Everything depended on his whim. Officialdom was unspeakably corrupt. Treaties meant nothing. The Burmese had no conception of trade, and only contempt for foreigners. Missionaries would have to live like rats in holes, unable to teach the Gospel, exposed to arbitrary torture or execution if discovered. For a man, life would be difficult; for a woman, impossible.

Captain Heard's friends, shaking their heads gravely, warned the American newcomers to put any thought of a Burmese mission out of their heads. Let them go back to America, or anywhere else in the world — but forget Burma.

With this unsettling news in their heads Adoniram and Newell soberly made their way through the bustling streets, crowded with dark-hued humanity and hurrying carriages, to the police station. A bored, unfriendly clerk questioned them. Did Mr. Judson and Mr. Newell have permission from the Court of Directors of the Company to live in India? No; they were Americans, with no purpose but the conversion of heathen. They had intended to stop in Calcutta only until they could find a ship to Burma; but judging from what they had just learned, they might have to ask to stay in India a little longer than they had intended.

It was most unlikely, said the clerk, that they would be permitted to remain. That would be decided by the authorities. Meanwhile, he would give them a certificate showing that they had complied with regulations by reporting.

Leaving the police station with their certificates, they made one more call before returning to the ship — this one on William Carey, dean of the Serampore group, pioneer of the English Baptist missionaries, to whom Adoniram had a letter written by Dr. Worcester asking for any help he could give.

Carey spent as much time in Calcutta, now, as in Serampore. The Government, disapproving his mission but recognizing his attainments, had made him professor of Oriental languages at the college at Fort William, and given him a good salary and a huge stone house. He had accepted, in order to use his position to gain toleration for Serampore and his colleagues Marshman and Ward.

Something like this he told them as they talked in his high-ceilinged second-floor study. Studying the quiet, elderly man, small of stature and unpretentious in appearance, they could sense his immense determination. They knew he had arrived at this lordly house from a poverty-stricken beginning as an all-but-illiterate cobbler in his native England. He had entered India as superintendent of an indigo plantation, had succeeded, and had finally been able to emerge in his true role as missionary. His translation of the Gospel into Bengali had been a great accomplishment. Now his knowledge of Oriental languages was second to no one's.

Carey painted a discouraging picture of the Americans' prospects in either Burma or India. Really, Burma they might as well put out of their minds. It was true that his son Felix had been there four years now, but he was the only one — of four missionaries, representing two separate missionary societies — who had been able to stay; and that, probably, was because he had married a Burmese woman of European extraction and so enjoyed some small amount of official favor. Burma itself was an anarchic despotism embroiled in a fierce war with Siam. Enemy raids, the tyranny of the government and the constant rebellion of the tax-burdened people made life so uncertain that a man never knew, when he woke in the morning, whether he would be allowed to live until night. Religious toleration was unknown; the viceroy in Rangoon had not the faintest idea that the missionaries had come to convert the natives — he thought they were in Burma to minister to the few Europeans in Rangoon. This was why every missionary effort so far had got nowhere. Pritchett and Brain, who had been sent by the London Missionary Society, had failed. Brain had died in Burma, and Pritchett had given up and gone to Vizagapatam. Chater, Carey's son Felix's colleague, had given up, too, and gone to Ceylon. But he was in Calcutta now, and could give them firsthand information. As for Felix, he himself said that he could do nothing but translate the Scriptures, and this he could do as well in Serampore, if he brought a Burmese scholar with him.

But if prospects were dismal in Burma, Carey told them, for Americans they were equally dismal in India. Even the Serampore missionaries, native-born English subjects, found great difficulty in remaining. The fact was, the East India Company was using any means in its power to discourage missionary activities. The Company did not want the natives to learn Western ideas — particularly the subversive revolutionary ideas of the Gospel. They could lead to unrest, disturbances, even revolt. Meanwhile, Carey would do what he could to help Mr. Judson and Mr. Newell remain. But he could promise nothing. And with this cold comfort, after being introduced by him to his colleagues Marshman and Ward, who happened to be in the city, Adoniram and Newell returned to the *Caravan*.

The next day, leaving Nancy and Harriet still on board, they set out with Captain Heard once more for the police station. They had no sooner arrived than they received another sample of what they might expect from the East India Company. Mr. Martyn, chief of the police force, promptly gave Captain Heard a dressing down for bringing missionaries to India without permission and without notifying the government.

It turned out that the Calcutta newspapers had published their names as missionaries and passengers on the *Caravan* but the clerk had failed to give their papers of yesterday to the chief police magistrate. It took some time to straighten out the confusion and lay the blame on the clerk, where it belonged. But the incident did nothing to improve their standing with the police. Mr. Martyn was more than doubtful whether they would be allowed to stay in India.

That night was to be the last the missionaries spent aboard the *Caravan*. The next afternoon they had two offers of accommodations ashore — one from Captain Heard, who had just succeeded in renting a house for himself, and one from Dr. Carey. Captain Heard's invitation touched them; it was one more example of his unfailing courtesy and kindness — but they felt they had no right to continue being a burden on him; and, after all, their future, they hoped, lay with men like those of the Serampore group. Late that afternoon, with profuse thanks to the master of the *Caravan*, they left the ship.

By now Adoniram and Samuel Newell were familiar with the way to Dr. Carey's house. But to Nancy and Harriet, who had not yet set foot on shore, everything was strange and a little frightening. Each of the wives traveled in a palanquin carried by natives. The bustle in the streets, the noisy native crowds, the babel of unknown tongues, the rushing English carriages — nothing was like Salem or Boston. They began to understand why "no English lady is here seen walking the streets." Adoniram had set out for Dr. Carey's house on foot. The men who trotted off with Nancy's palanquin went so fast that she soon lost sight of him. For a few panicky moments she wondered where she was being taken, until all at once her bearers came to a stop and set the conveyance down, next to Harriet's, in front of a stone house so large that to her wondering eyes it looked like a palace.

It was the first Calcutta house Nancy and Harriet had entered. They stared with awe at the immense rooms with their twenty-foot-high ceilings. One of those rooms could hold almost a whole house of the Bradford and Haverhill variety. Nothing was like the homes they knew. There were no fireplaces or chimneys anywhere. Instead, huge glassless windows opened from room to room to let the air circulate freely.

And the servants! They were everywhere, in obsequious hordes. Apparently no white person in India ever lifted a finger to perform any household task. There were too many servants. They were in each other's way. It was embarrassing, but there was no help for it, work; For instance, one servant will sweep a room; but no per- "for their religion will not permit them to do but one kind of suasion will be sufficient to make him dust the things."

They liked Dr. Carey, who greeted them in his study. He had an invitation for them on his own account, and a special one from the Marshmans and Wards, to stay at the Serampore mission until Rice, Hall and the Notts should arrive in the *Harmony*.

It is not hard to imagine the pride (and perhaps the amusement) with which Adoniram and Newell showed their awed wives the sights in the vicinity of Dr. Carey's house. That evening they attended services in the English Episcopal Church and Nancy was delighted to hear the organ play her old favorite tune "Bangor." The tune and the service were familiar, but there was an oriental touch — the immense fans called punkahs ("punkies," as she spelled it), which hung inside the church and were operated from the outside by natives pulling ropes. She could not keep her eyes off the majestically swaying "punkies."

And the next morning she saw her first mission school, almost next door to Dr. Carey's house. It had nearly two hundred students, both boys and girls, mostly casteless natives and children of Portuguese parentage. And she saw a wedding procession, with a bridegroom only ten years old riding in a palanquin — her first sight of child marriage.

That afternoon, when it was time to leave the ship permanently, the Judsons and Newells wrote to Captain Heard expressing their overflowing thanks and appreciation for all he had done for them. Ruefully they added, "We wish that we could make some suitable return for your goodness, but as this is far out of our power, we can only express our feelings." All four signed the letter. Then they stepped aboard a boat for the fifteen-mile upriver trip to Serampore.

The Serampore mission, where they were met at the waterside by Marshman and Ward, was a revelation. It was a complete, almost self-contained community. The dwellings consisted of four roomy stone buildings commanding a beautiful view of the river. Dr. Carey's wife, who was seriously ill, occupied one building with her husband when he was not in Calcutta. The Marshmans lived in one, and the Wards in the third. In the fourth, "the common house," the Judsons and Newells were each provided with "two large spacious rooms, with every convenience we could wish."

The Americans' four rooms took up only a fraction of the space in the building. Besides the visitors' apartments, it contained a dining hall capable of seating a hundred or more, "a large elegant chapel, and two large libraries."

In addition to the four houses, there were numerous outbuildings — including a cookhouse, and even a factory for making paper. Until a few months before there had been still another building housing a printing plant where Gospels translated by the missionaries and tracts written by them had been printed, but this had been destroyed by fire and not yet rebuilt.

The Americans had never seen such a garden as the mission had. It was beautifully cared for and it covered acres. Everything seemed to grow in it — fruit trees, vegetables, flowers, plants of all kinds — some familiar, but many unknown. Nancy, who had grown up on a farm, thought it "as far superior to any in America, as the best garden in America is to a common farmer's." But even she could not fully appreciate what it really was. Dr. Carey had a passion for horticulture almost equal to his passion for translation. For a score of years he had been acquiring specimens through correspondence with naturalists all over the world. At this time he had well over four hundred species of plants growing, and botanists knew, if others did not, that the garden at Serampore was one of the finest in existence.

In this delightful place the four Americans quickly fell into a pleasantly busy routine. For the two women it must have been particularly enjoyable because they had no housework. That was all done by the armies of servants, each inflexibly devoted to his one allotted task.

Nearly every hour had its appointed occupation, which was marked by the ringing of a bell — the first one at five in the morning, to wake the boys for school. Mrs. Marshman also kept a school for European young ladies and the children of the mission families, in which she taught needlework, embroidery, useful arts and languages. The language study was anything but superficial: "Mrs. Marshman's eldest daughter, fourteen years of age," noted Nancy, "reads and writes Bengalee and English; and has advanced some way in Latin, Greek and Hebrew." There were also various meetings of a religious character going on nearly all day, from morning prayers to explanations of the Scriptures. Sundays were given over wholly to religion. There was a service in English in the evening. Adoniram watched the Bengali services with special interest; this was what he hoped to be doing soon himself. Meanwhile, he had to content himself with preaching at the evening service in English.

But the Americans did not wholly lose themselves in the activities in the mission. They were taken "in a budgerow (a boat with a little room in it, cushions on each side, and Venetian blinds) . . . to see the worship of the Hindoo god, Juggernaut, a few miles from Serampore." The idol "was only a lump of wood, his face painted with large black eyes, and a large red mouth," but they took him "out of the pagoda, and bathed him in the water of the Ganges, which they consider sacred. They bathed themselves in the river — repeated long forms of prayer — counted their fingers — poured muddy water down their children's throats, and such like foolish, superstitious ceremonies." Watching this spectacle with horrified fascination, Adoniram, Nancy, Newell and Harriet realized "more than ever the blessedness — the superior excellence of the Christian religion."

Their serenity at Serampore was shattered abruptly on the first of July, when Adoniram and Newell were summoned to the police station at Calcutta. Here an order was read to them requiring them to leave Calcutta at once and return to America on the *Caravan*. Captain Heard was told he would receive no port clearance until he gave security that he would take the missionaries home with him. As it happened, he was not planning to leave Calcutta for some time, but the order added one more annoyance to his already numerous troubles. He had found that bills could not be negotiated on any terms on account of the fear of war between England and the United States. (Actually, war had been declared in June but the news had not yet reached Calcutta.) Besides, his cargo was in poor condition and sales very difficult.

The Judsons and Newells were sorry for Captain Heard, but there seemed nothing they could do except draw up a petition to Lord Minto, the Governor General, explaining that they had no intention of settling in Bengal or India. All they wanted was permission to stay in Calcutta until the *Harmony* should arrive. After that, the whole party would make haste to go somewhere else.

The petition had a little effect. The fifteenth of July they were summoned again to police headquarters and told formally that they could not attempt a mission in any British dominion or the territory of any British ally, including Java and all the eastern islands; but if they could prove they were going still farther, they would not be required to return to America aboard the *Caravan*. By an ironic chance they were at the police station to receive this order when the Reverend Mr. Thomason, an East India Company chaplain, gave Newell five hundred rupees, which had been collected by friends of missions in Calcutta.

But where could they go?

They had finally put Burma out of their thoughts, for about that country they had learned a good deal more that was unpromising. Chater had repeated that in Burma they would be under both a king and local governors who were absolute despots and that governmental corruption was unbelievable. — And the laws were the bloodiest on earth: the commonest punishments were beheading, crucifixion, and "pouring melted lead in small quantities down the throat," and these were inflicted for such minor offenses as chewing opium or drinking spirits. Recently, added Dr. Carey, a Burmese commander had ordered five hundred of his men to be buried alive merely because they were recruits sent to him by an officer whom he disliked. Even Felix had been having trouble. Along with the other English in Rangoon he had had to take refuge from a general massacre in an English man-of-war lying in the river. The viceroy had demanded Felix, his wife and child, of the captain; but the captain had refused until he received a written guarantee that they would be protected. Later, a number of the rich residents of Rangoon had bribed the viceroy with large sums of money for permission to leave. Harriet summed up the sentiments of all of them when she remarked: "We cannot feel that we are called in Providence to go to Burmah. Every account we have from that savage, barbarous nation, confirms us in our opinion, that the way is not prepared for the spread of the Gospel there." And even if these objections had not applied, Felix Carey was a Baptist. How could Congregationalists establish a joint mission with Baptists?

But China was equally inaccessible. Morrison, the one missionary there, was employed as an interpreter at Macao and was known only in that capacity. The penalty for introducing Christianity there was death.

They considered Arabia, Turkey or Persia; but Mohammedan intolerance effectively ruled out those countries.

Their friends in Calcutta now advised them to give up the Orient, and to return to America to become missionaries to the Western Indians in the savage Mississippi country, or to go to the wilds of Ohio, Tennessee or Arkansas. But this they would not do — perhaps partly for dread of returning ingloriously by the same ship on which they had departed amidst so many prayers and plaudits.

*But where, where, could they go?* they inquired frantically. *They must know soon.* Captain Heard wanted to leave Calcutta in August, and as matters stood he could not go without the missionaries.

Then, a few days later, the skies brightened.

Dr. Marshman, who had been soliciting everyone he knew in Calcutta officialdom, returned to Serampore with the good news that a secretary of the Company named Rickets had told him unofficially that he would arrange to give the *Caravan* port clearance without the Americans if they would promise solemnly to leave the East India Company's territory by some other ship. Thus they might be able to stay until the *Harmony* arrived, and a door might even open for them to go to "Isle of France," or to Madagascar. Isle of France (Mauritius or Île de France), although under British control, was not Company territory.

This concession looked even better at the end of a week, when a letter arrived from the *Harmony* passengers, who had arrived at Isle of France and reported that the governor was friendly to missions. He would like to see a missionary both on Isle of France and Madagascar, and had even written to the London Missionary Society asking for one.

Armed with the letter, Adoniram and Newell immediately went to Calcutta to see whether official permission would be given them to go to Isle of France. The next day Newell returned to Serampore to tell Nancy and Harriet that permission had been granted and a ship was sailing in four days — the *Col. Gillespie*, commanded by Captain Chimminant, "a serious man." But he would not take passengers. Adoniram was remaining in Calcutta to try to change Chimminant's mind.

The following morning, a Wednesday, Adoniram returned to Serampore in great excitement. After much persuasion Chimminant had agreed to carry two of the missionaries, but no more.

He would sail Saturday. Who should go?

It took little discussion to decide that the Newells should sail with Chimminant. Harriet expected her baby in less than three months. If she had to travel by sea, she had better get it over with as quickly as possible in order to have the baby on land.

There was no time to lose. The Newells began packing. They were short of money — the price of the passage alone was six hundred rupees — but Dr. Carey gave Newell a letter of credit to a commercial house in Isle of France, which he could use until funds from the American Board could catch up with him.

The next morning, after many farewells — tearful on the part of Harriet and Nancy — the Newells stepped aboard a budgerow and, escorted by Adoniram, went down the river to Calcutta.

The thoughts in Harriet's mind must have echoed in the minds of the others. She and her husband would miss their friends on the *Harmony*. Perhaps, if the *Harmony* missionaries decided to establish a station in some distant part of the world, they might never meet again. Worst of all was the thought that Harriet was leaving on a long, dangerous voyage late in her pregnancy "without *one single* female acquaintance." But there was no help for it.

As it turned out, the *Col. Gillespie* did not sail until Tuesday, the fourth of August. The days before had been filled with a thousand tasks: the purchase of an infinite number of little necessities remembered at the last moment; teas, lunches and dinners with a host of well-meaning acquaintances whose kindly but energy-consuming invitations it might have been wiser to refuse. By the time the ship drew out into the river, Harriet was completely exhausted.

Perhaps she had not employed the best of judgment in trying to do so much — but she was only eighteen. And her next birthday was to be her last.

## CHAPTER II

# Exile
## [ *1812* ]

A MR. ROLT of Calcutta invited Adoniram and Nancy to stay in his house until they could find a ship on which to follow the Newells. They accepted his invitation and moved from Serampore about the time the *Col. Gillespie* sailed.

Rolt had married the widow of an English Baptist missionary and in the room Adoniram and Nancy occupied there was a fair-sized library which contained a good many books dealing with baptism. This was fortunate: whether the word "baptism" meant sprinkling in infancy or immersion by voluntary decision at the age of discretion was a question that had been occupying Adoniram more and more. The Serampore missionaries had no idea of his thoughts on the subject; aware of their role as hosts, they had carefully avoided even mentioning any of the doctrinal differences between the two denominations. If they influenced him at all, it was unconsciously, through their personalities, especially that of the modest Carey, who in ability and accomplishments stood head and shoulders above any man Adoniram had ever met.

At any rate, with a fine library in his room and nothing in particular to do but await the *Harmony*, Adoniram seized the opportunity to study the question thoroughly and settle it in his mind for once and all. Nancy was alarmed. "I tried to have him give it up, and rest satisfied in his old sentiments, and frequently told him if he became a Baptist, *I would not*. He, however, said he felt it his duty to examine closely a subject on which he felt so many doubts," and ". . . determined to read candidly and prayerfully, and to hold fast, or embrace the truth, however mortifying, however great the sacrifice."

In self-defense, Nancy began to explore the Bible herself. Surely, it said *something* in favor of infant baptism. For two or three days she pored over it, comparing the Old Testament with the New, trying to find some foundation for the Congregational practice which she had accepted all her life. With growing dismay she had to admit that she could find nothing; and by now, under Adoniram's influence, she had become convinced that the issue was much more than a mere matter of form, regardless of which viewpoint was right.

It was at this juncture, four days after the departure of the Newells, that the *Harmony* arrived with Gordon Hall, Luther Rice, and Samuel and Roxana Nott.

It was a happy reunion. The four men had not seen each other since the ordination at the Tabernacle seven months before, and Nancy was pleased to have an American woman again for a companion. But there was no doubt from the first that Adoniram was preoccupied with some disturbing thought. Within a few hours he told at least Nott what was in his mind, and soon all the missionaries were discussing it.

The newcomers immediately raised one problem which had never occurred to Adoniram and Nancy. How could they make one joint mission if their party included two competitive — as they saw it — denominations? It would be impossible. Nancy was horrified: "If he should renounce his former sentiments, he must offend his friends at home, hazard his reputation, and, what is still more trying, be separated from his missionary associates."

But there was no use arguing with Adoniram. Within a few weeks she had to admit that "Mr. J. feels convinced from Scripture, that he has never been baptized, and that he cannot conscientiously administer baptism to infants. This change of sentiment must necessarily produce a separation. As we are perfectly united with our brethren in every other respect, and are much attached to them, it is inexpressibly painful to leave them, and go alone to a separate station."

As to herself, she was still spending hours in their room in Mr. Rolt's house poring over the Gospel and leafing through the many tomes in the library: "But I . . . must acknowledge that the face of Scripture does favour the Baptist sentiments. I intend to persevere in examining the subject, and hope that I shall be disposed to embrace the truth, whatever it may be. It is painfully mortifying to my natural feelings, to think seriously of renouncing a system which I have been taught from infancy to believe and respect, and embrace one which I have been taught to despise. O that the Spirit of God may enlighten and direct my mind — may prevent my retaining an old error, or embracing a new one!"

Poor Nancy! The prospect was worse than "painfully mortifying." It was terrifying. There was little in Mr. Rolt's spacious high-ceilinged house with its many obsequious servants to make her feel at home. Wherever she went, indoors as a white lady of leisure, or riding in a palanquin through the medley of races, costumes and tongues, in the bustling streets, she felt a stranger. Feeling more and more that she was about to cut every tie with home and be cast without support in this alien world, her thoughts turned with ever greater longing to familiar Bradford. "Grief for the deprivation of my friends, I love to indulge; and I find every such indulgence binds them more closely to my heart. Can I forget thee, O my country! Can I forget the scenes of childhood; and the more endearing scenes of riper years? Can I forget the parental roof, sisters, companions, and associates of my life? No, never! Never, till this pulse ceases to beat, this heart to feel."

But there was no help for it. Within a few more days Adoniram's sentiments crystallized. He must be baptized and become a Baptist. Nancy, after a little longer struggle, decided that she agreed with him. At the end of August he wrote a letter for both of them to Serampore, stating their conviction "that *the immersion of a professing believer is the only Christian baptism.* In these exercises I have not been alone. Mrs. Judson has been engaged in a similar examination, and has come to the same conclusion. Feeling, therefore, that we are in an unbaptized state, we wish to profess our faith in Christ by being baptized in obedience to his sacred commands."

Adoniram's letter came as a complete surprise to the Serampore missionaries. In one way the situation it created was not altogether to their liking. American Congregationalists might feel that they had seduced the Americans to Baptist ideas. But any momentary feelings of embarrassment were soon forgotten in the realization of the opportunity thus unexpectedly presented to American Baptists. As Marshman wrote to the Reverend Dr. Baldwin, pastor of the Second Baptist Church in Boston, whose writings had played a large part in Adoniram's conversion, it seemed "as though Providence itself were raising up this young man, that you might at least partake of the zeal of our Congregational missionary brethren around you. I would wish, then, that you should share in the glorious work, by supporting him. . . . After God has given you a missionary of your own nation, faith, and order without the help or knowledge of man, let me entreat you, and Dr. Messer, and brethren Bolles and Moriarty, humbly to accept the gift."

Adoniram, too, wrote to Dr. Baldwin and to Dr. Bolles, pastor of Salem's First Baptist Church, whom he had met before sailing. Now he reminded him that, at that time, "I suggested the formation of a society among the Baptists in America for the support of foreign missions. . . . Little did I then expect to be personally concerned in such an attempt."

Writing letters was all Adoniram could do for the present. What with the war, it would be months before the Congregationalists could know that their first American foreign missionary was now a Baptist, or the Baptists that they had a foreign missionary without their choice or expectation. Funds, location of a mission, support, organization — all these hung in air. But Adoniram had never concerned himself over such matters. He was satisfied that Baptism was the only correct creed. He had a burning determination to convert the heathen himself. For the rest, let others worry.

Adoniram and Nancy were baptized by immersion on September 6, 1812. The ceremony was performed by Ward in the Lal Bazar Chapel in Calcutta. "Thus," wrote Nancy, ". . . we are confirmed Baptists, not because we wanted to be, but because truth compelled us to be. We have endeavored to count the cost, and be prepared for the many severe trials resulting from this change of sentiment. We anticipate the loss of reputation, and of the affection and esteem of many of our American friends. But the most trying circumstance attending this change, and that which has caused us most pain, is the separation which must take place between us and our dear missionary associates . . . We feel that we are alone in the world, with no real friend but each other, no one on whom we can depend but God."

Their new status brought them to a fresh consideration of where they could go. By now Samuel and Harriet Newell should be nearly at Isle of France. The Notts, Hall and Rice, with a mission to Madagascar in mind, were planning to follow by the first available ship. A few days after their arrival in Calcutta they had been ordered, like the Newells and Judsons earlier, to leave aboard the ship on which they had come; but the Government had given them permission to go to Isle of France if they could find transportation. Adoniram and Nancy had permission to go to Isle of France too. But how could they, now that they were Baptists?

They considered other possibilities: Amboina, in the Spice Islands; Japan; Persia; South America. Adoniram had even begun to study Portuguese in case . . .

But in spite of all its drawbacks, it was Burma that still drew Judson. Since he had first read Symes's *Embassy to Ava* in his room in Andover, he had never quite been able to get that strange country out of his head. What caught his fancy as much as anything was the fact that the Bible had never been translated into Burmese. In Calcutta it was generally believed that Burma had a population of seventeen million — more than twice that of the United States. There would have to be a Burmese Bible before Burma could become Christian. Adoniram wanted to be the one to provide it: not simply one pioneer among many — but the *first* to give the Scriptures to a great nation.

Once more he began making inquiries, writing to Chater at Ceylon. In September Felix Carey arrived in Calcutta from Rangoon. Adoniram immediately cultivated his acquaintance. Felix was much taken with Adoniram and wanted the Judsons to return with him. He had made some beginnings with translation but would be glad to resign the work to a man as well qualified as Adoniram.

In October, however, Adoniram and Nancy gave up the idea. There were just too many difficulties. Even Felix retained his precarious foothold only through having a native wife and acting more as a Burmese government employee than as a missionary. For two Americans it would be all but impossible where, as Nancy put it, their "lives would depend on the caprice of a monarch."

Reluctantly, they finally settled on Java. "It presents a wide field for missionary labors, and no Missionary is there. We have spoken for a passage; and unless some new prospects open up of getting into the Burman empire, it is probable we shall go to Java if government will permit. There is some prospect of brother Rice's going with us, which we consider as a great favour in Providence, as we expected to go alone."

For Rice, too, was undergoing a change of sentiments. When he first arrived in Calcutta, Adoniram and Nancy had believed he was more hostile to Baptist views than anyone else aboard the *Harmony*. This impression had got about because some English Baptist missionaries had made the voyage with the Americans, and several rather heated discussions of baptism had taken place, Rice being the most vigorous defender of the Congregationalist position. In reality, his vociferousness had been prompted by his own inward doubts, some of which dated back to his undergraduate days at Williams.

Soon after Adoniram and Nancy were baptized, Rice came to stay with them at Mr. Rolt's house. Still using attack to conceal his secret intent, he tried again and again to draw Adoniram into an argument about baptism. Adoniram refused. He merely advised Rice to study the Bible. If he wanted Adoniram's further views, let him read the sermon Adoniram had preached late in September in the Lal Bazar Chapel, which Dr. Carey had pronounced the best sermon on baptism he had ever heard.

Rice followed Adoniram's advice. One morning in late October he even called on Dr. Carey before he was out of bed to ask to look at his Greek Testament. From some of Rice's questions, Carey "began to suspect that he was enquiring." Before long, the suspicion was confirmed. On Sunday, the first of November, Rice was baptized, and the three — Adoniram, Nancy and Rice — immediately began planning a joint mission.

Meanwhile, Samuel and Roxana Nott and Gordon Hall had been having troubles of their own. After receiving permission to go to Isle of France, they had been delayed for more than a month by sickness. Recovered, they engaged passage in mid-September on the ship *Adele*, but the sailing was delayed day after day into October.

About this time someone told them they might be able to secure permission to go to Ceylon. Inquiring at the police station, they were told they would have no difficulty, and on the strength of this assurance cancelled their arrangements for the *Adele* and began to look for a ship to Ceylon. It did not take them many days to find out that no ship was sailing for Ceylon, and probably none would until a large convoy set out for there in January. But by now the *Adele* had left. What were they to do?

A new piece of news which came to them about this time made them change their plans once more. They heard that a new governor, Sir Evan Nepean, had arrived in Bombay. He was a vice president of the British and Foreign Bible Society and known to be a friend to missions. Why not, they asked themselves, go to Bombay and start a mission there? Early in November they found a ship for Bombay: the *Commerce*, Captain Arbuthnot; they applied to the police for a pass to sail on it, received it, and promptly began to move their baggage aboard.

Unfortunately, they did not realize that a pass from the police to go on the *Commerce* was not the "general passport" they thought it. Worse, their many changes of plan had aroused the suspicion of the government. Bureaucracy made no distinction between Messrs. Nott and Hall, Congregationalists, and Messrs. Judson and Rice, Baptists. They were all Americans, all missionaries. They had sworn they intended to take the first ship to Isle of France; but instead, for months they had been reserving passage on one ship after another, bound every which way. At best, the officials suspected, the Americans were using all these subterfuges to remain in India. At worst — who knew? Perhaps they were spies. At any rate, people who so muddled up the orderly channels of procedure ought to be treated like spies. So reasoned officialdom, and, annoyed, promptly put down its foot.

A fleet was about to leave Calcutta for England. On the seventeenth of November Nott and Hall were handed a peremptory order to go in the fleet to England. The Judsons and Rice were included, and the names of all the missionaries were printed in the Calcutta papers as "passengers to England."

Nott and Hall, who for weeks had been acting independently of Adoniram and Rice, frantically tried to bring their plight to the personal attention of Lord Minto. But the officials would not even transmit their petition to Lord Minto — because it concerned a matter which would first have to appear before the Privy Council, and by the time the Council met next the fleet would be days at sea, presumably with the missionaries on board. Government was grandly (officially) unconcerned about the whole matter. Nott and Hall, who saw themselves against their will winding up their mission on English soil together with Adoniram and Rice, the very people from whom they were trying to separate, were desperate.

It was desperation which suggested an expedient. After all, they *did* have a pass from the police to go on board the *Commerce*. It had not been revoked. Their baggage was on the ship, Captain Arbuthnot had reported them as passengers and had received port clearance. Why not simply embark on the *Commerce* and stay there? If they got away, well and good. If not — then they went to England with the fleet, as the government intended. Captain Arbuthnot had no objection to trying it. *His* papers were all in order and whatever happened was no fault of his.

On November twentieth Nott, his wife and Hall went aboard the *Commerce*. So far as the authorities were concerned they simply dropped out of sight. Furious government officials searched the city for them. But somehow the police overlooked the *Commerce;* perhaps not entirely by accident: then as today one department sometimes worked at cross-purposes with another.

Adoniram, Nancy and Luther Rice, meanwhile, were not having so much luck. Adoniram and Rice had been called to the police station to receive their orders to go with the fleet. When they left, a petty officer was detailed to accompany them to Mr. Rolt's house, and when they arrived there he told them not to leave it without permission.

But Adoniram and Rice were the last men on earth to obey any order that conflicted with their intentions. It did not take them long to find out that a ship named *La Belle Créole* was leaving for Isle of France in two days. They had no particular desire to go there, but at least it was not England, and the Company's authority did not extend there. The only difficulty was their lack of a pass to sail with the ship, such as the Notts and Hall had to go on the *Commerce*. They applied to Mr. Martyn, the chief police magistrate. But Mr. Martyn had been having altogether too much trouble with American missionaries lately. One group — or were they part of the same group? — had already vanished and were not to be found anywhere, perhaps as a result of some ill-advised issuance of a police pass. He refused to issue any passes.

Denied a pass, they explained their problem to the captain of the *Créole*. Would he, they asked, take them on board without one? The captain, no more a lover of the authorities than many others in Calcutta, replied that he would be neutral. There was his ship. They might do as they pleased.

This was enough for Adoniram and Rice. But how were they going to get aboard the ship without being seen? Here Mr. Rolt lent a hand. The dockyards were always closed and the gates locked at night. Opening the gates without permission was a serious offense. Nevertheless, through influence (and perhaps a little money in the proper places) Mr. Rolt arranged for Nancy, Adoniram and Rice to be passed through the gates at midnight on the twenty-first of November. That night they stole out of his house, coolies hired by Rolt carrying their baggage, and went through the gate to the *Créole*. The next morning, a Sunday, the ship began to move down the river and they congratulated themselves that they had got away safely — even ahead of the *Commerce*, which remained tied up at the dock, the Notts and Gordon Hall still aboard, hoping the police would not find them.

Sunday the *Créole* sailed undisturbed down the Hooghly, and the three missionaries began to become acquainted with the other passengers, of whom there were four besides the captain's wife, none of them, judging by the way they ignored the Sabbath, in the least religious. By Monday the fugitives must have begun to feel that they were out of the grasp of the East India Company.

If they did, they were deluding themselves. Late that night, an hour or so after midnight, the *Créole* was hailed and stopped. Hastily dressing, they left their cabin to find out what had happened. They soon learned that the news was as bad as possible. The pilot had just been handed a dispatch from Calcutta commanding him to anchor and wait for further instructions, "as passengers were on board who had been ordered to England."

The three immediately held a conference with the captain. There was no question what the order portended. Soon, perhaps tomorrow, the police would appear and search the ship. If the missionaries were found they would be taken off and sent back to Calcutta, and England. They must get off the ship before the search began.

There was an English tavern on shore about a mile from where the ship was anchored. Adoniram and Rice decided to hide there until the search was over. Securing a small rowboat, they put into it some of their cases and bundles and went ashore. Nancy, on the captain's advice, decided to stay on the ship with the baggage. He was sure that her presence aboard would make no difference "even should an officer be sent to search the vessel." Perhaps, banking on interbureau rivalry in Calcutta, he felt that the police would only see as much as they had to see. If the two men were absent, they would pay no attention to Nancy.

All the next day Adoniram and Rice remained in the tavern while Nancy fretted aboard the idly rocking *Créole*. That evening a boat brought a note from the ship's owner in Calcutta. It added nothing to what they already knew — the *Créole* must remain at anchor until it was known whether "there were persons on board which the captain had been forbidden to receive." The pilot, anxious to help, sent back to the owner a certificate to the effect that no such persons were on the ship, and a list of the passengers. But the government had gone so far now that no one really expected his efforts to have any result.

Later that evening Nancy decided to go to the tavern herself. She was given the use of the pilot boat, with its crew of six natives, and rowed across the dark, quiet waters to shore.

At the tavern she told the news of the day and evening to her husband and Rice. As they discussed what it meant, it became plain to all of them that they could never hope to stay on the ship without an official pass. Someone would have to go back to Calcutta and try once more. Rice was chosen, and he left that night. Adoniram and Nancy remained at the tavern. Late the next day he returned with empty hands. The police flatly refused to issue a pass. Moreover, by now the owner of the *Créole* was angry at them for delaying the sailing of his ship, which they had caused to idle at anchor in the Hooghly for three full days. He washed his hands of the whole affair. From now on let the missionaries take care of themselves.

The owner's feelings were implemented in the morning by a note

from the captain. The *Créole* had just received permission to leave
— but not with the missionaries. They must remove their baggage
from the ship at once.

Despairingly the three considered what they could do. Whatever happened, they were resolved not to allow themselves to be
taken back to Calcutta. They had heard that at Fultah, sixteen miles
farther down the river, there was another tavern kept by an Englishman, and they decided to try their luck there. But how would they
get their baggage? Adoniram and Rice both felt it would be dangerous for them to go back to the ship. Nancy would have to take
care of it herself.

On Nancy's return to the *Créole* she realized at once that the
little pilot boat, overcrowded already with its crew of six and one
passenger, could never carry all the baggage. Would the captain,
she begged, let it stay on board as far as Fultah? There she could
find a boat big enough to move it to shore. The patient captain
agreed, and even gave her permission to stay on the ship herself as
far as Fultah.

Again she returned to shore in the pilot boat to inform the two
men of the new plan. With Nancy and the baggage taken care of,
at least for a while, they devised a fresh expedient. Rice would go
back to Calcutta and try to get a passage for them to Ceylon. Meanwhile Adoniram would row down the river to Fultah in the little
boat with their hand luggage.

But while they were discussing all this in the tavern, a strong
wind had sprung up. The *Créole's* captain had taken advantage of
it and hoisted sail, so when the missionaries stepped outside to the
riverbank the ship was almost out of sight downstream. Fortunately
the pilot boat was still waiting for Nancy; she sprang into it and
ordered the crew to hurry after the ship. The next hour or so was
as terrifying as any in her experience. The sun was scorching bright;
she suffered from the lack of an umbrella and the wind-whipped
water was dangerously rough for the little boat. In order to make
better speed the native crew "hoisted a large sail, which every now
and then would almost tip the boat on one side," until Nancy expected sail, mast, boat, natives and herself to overturn. She could
not help showing her fear. But in order to comfort her the crew
"would constantly repeat, 'Cutcho pho, anna sahib; cutcha pho,

anna.' The meaning, 'Never fear, Madam; never fear.'" After a while they caught up with the ship, and Nancy was helped aboard in time to assemble the missionaries' possessions for removal.

When the *Créole* reached Fultah the wind was still strong; the ship merely checked speed enough to let Nancy get aboard the pilot boat again, alone. But once landed at Fultah, she was able to hire a large boat which she sent in pursuit of the baggage on the *Créole*, which continued to move rapidly down the river.

Then, "I entered the tavern, a *stranger*, a *female*, and *unprotected*. I called for a room and sat down to reflect on my disconsolate situation. I had nothing with me but a few rupees. I did not know that the boat which I sent after the vessel would overtake it, and if it did, whether it would ever return with our baggage; neither did I know where Mr. J. was, or when he would come, or with what treatment I should meet at the tavern. I thought of *home*, and said to myself, *These are some of the trials attendant on missionary life, and which I anticipated*."

She might have felt worse if she had known that while she was in the tavern the *Commerce*, carrying Gordon Hall and Samuel and Roxana Nott, overtook and passed the *Créole*, and that though her American passengers had learned that Nancy was alone on shore, they could not stop. There was nothing they could do for her. Soon the *Commerce* was far down the river, moving with wind and tide, Bombay-bound.

Fortunately, Nancy did not have long to wait. In a few hours Adoniram appeared as they had arranged beforehand, in the little skiff, with their hand luggage; and toward nightfall, the large boat Nancy had sent after the *Créole* appeared from the other direction with the heavy baggage. Now at least they were together; and they had their baggage.

But what should they do next? They would be marooned on shore unless Rice had better luck in Calcutta than before. Should they give up and go back to Calcutta? Never! . . . While there was any expedient untried. Adoniram sounded out the landlord, a friendly-looking fellow. Could he help them get a passage to Ceylon? The landlord was encouraging. A friend of his, he said, was in command of a ship bound for Madras; it was expected down-river the next day. He would speak to his friend. He was sure passage could be arranged.

Madras, on the Coromandel Coast, was more than two thirds of the way to Ceylon. If they could get as far as Madras they could surely secure passage to Ceylon somehow; so with incorrigible optimism they went to bed, their hopes higher than they had been for more than a week.

The Madras ship dropped anchor in front of the tavern on the third day, and the landlord went on board to see the captain. By this time Rice had rejoined them. He had been unable to do anything in Calcutta. It looked as if the landlord's friend offered their last hope. But even this failed them. The landlord soon returned with word that the captain could not take them to Madras.

By now it was late in the afternoon. The three talked it over. There was still one hope. Perhaps, if they went on board themselves after supper, by cajolery, pleas, tears or money they could somehow persuade the ship's master to take them.

With this resolve they sat down to eat. And at this juncture, as they always believed, Providence took a hand. The meal was just being served when a letter was brought in.

We hastily opened it, and, to our great surprise and joy, in it was a *pass* from the magistrate for us to go on board the *Créole*, the vessel we had left. Who procured this pass for us, or in what way, we are still ignorant; we could only view the hand of God, and wonder.

All at once, everything had changed.

But had it? Their elation turned to disappointment as they realized that the pass might have arrived too late to be of any use. For the *Créole* had vanished down-river three days ago and more than likely was already at sea. Was there any possibility of catching up with her? There might be one they learned. Seventy miles below Fultah was the port of Saugur, where vessels often anchored for a few days to make last-minute preparations before striking out into the Bay of Bengal. The *Créole* might possibly — just possibly — still be there. It was the only chance left to them.

The baggage was still in the large boat which had brought it from the ship. Hastily the three finished their meal, paid their bill, and in the darkness set out for Saugur, against the tide.

It was a most dreary night for me [wrote Nancy] but Mr. J. slept the greater part of the night. The next day we had a favorable wind, and before night reached Saugur where were many ships at anchor, and among the rest we had the happiness to find the *Créole*. She had been anchored there two days, waiting for some of the ship's crew. I never enjoyed a sweeter moment in my life, than when I was sure we were in sight of the *Créole*.

CHAPTER III

# Rangoon

[ *1813* ]

IT was an exhausted trio of missionaries who climbed wearily aboard *La Belle Créole* as she lay at anchor at Saugur. For several days, while the ship made up her crew, hoisted sail, and struck out across the Bay of Bengal for the Indian Ocean, they did little but rest. Nancy confessed to such "an uncommon degree of slothfulness and inactivity" that she even "enjoyed religion but little."

Eventually they roused themselves, but if they had hoped to hold religious services aboard, as on the *Caravan*, they were soon disappointed. Nobody but themselves was in the least interested in religion. The passengers even profaned the Sabbath by playing cards and chess on deck and amusing themselves with "trifling conversation" — behavior the missionaries found "very trying," but New England Sunday laws did not obtain aboard and there was nothing they could do to prevent it. In fact, Nancy was a little taken aback to realize that although the passengers' manner was respectful, they probably privately considered the missionaries "superstitious, unsocial creatures." She was more used to passing that judgment on others than to having it applied to herself. But she consoled herself with the thought that to be a missionary it was necessary to "take those methods which make us appear contemptible in the eyes of the men of this world."

Under the circumstances the three kept to themselves a good deal, occupying their time by studying French, which they expected to need in Isle of France, as they called Mauritius. They held private worship in their own quarters every evening and twice on Sundays.

The *Créole* made rather a slow voyage of it. There were light winds, in which the ship could but barely drift, then contrary winds and occasional rough weather. Adoniram, alternately optimistic and depressed, must have wondered in his gloomier moods whether their mission would ever begin. Were they doomed to sail the Seven Seas forever, in the character of evangelistic Flying Dutchmen, fated always to be sailing toward the place of their mission but never permitted to reach it? These gloomy thoughts of Adoniram's were of a piece with those of Nancy's, when she gave way to a peculiar form of self-criticism: "I find my nature shrinks from the idea of being shipwrecked and sunk amid the waves. This shows me how unlike I am to those holy martyrs, who rejoiced to meet death, even in the most horrid forms." Most of the time, however, they were in high spirits, rejoicing in their youth and good health, in the mission they had chosen, and in their love for each other. Both, by the nature of their creed, were given to feeling that they were unworthy to serve God. If they had possessed all the virtues of all the saints, they would still have felt guilt on this score. But they felt no guilt and made no apologies for their passion. To Adoniram, earthly love, bodily love, was almost a part of love for God. Its delights and satisfactions, were, so to speak, a foretaste of the ineffable delights of heaven, which no mortal on earth could even imagine except in some such manner. And Nancy was sure Adoniram was, "in every respect, the most calculated to make me happy and useful, of all the persons I have ever seen."

Eventually the voyage came to an end, when the *Créole* sailed into the harbor of Port Louis, Isle of France, late on Saturday, January 17, 1813. They had been at sea seven weeks, and away from Salem eleven months.

It was good to see land again. Even better, to both Adoniram and Rice, but especially to Nancy, was the prospect of meeting the Newells once more. Nothing, she felt, not even a change of denomination, could separate her from Harriet. And there was the baby. It — boy or girl? she wondered — must be about two months old by now. She longed to see the infant, pure New England in blood, born in this remote island set in the middle of an ocean so far from the home of its ancestors.

But the ship had scarcely dropped anchor when a boat from shore came alongside with stunning news.

Harriet was dead. The baby was dead.

This was all they could learn from the men in the boat. Questions brought no particulars, merely the statement that both were dead.

Dismayed, shocked, they talked late in the cabin that night, fruitlessly conjecturing much. Nancy, after her first tears, began to feel an anger against Providence itself that she had never experienced before. "O death," she wrote bitterly, "thou destroyer of domestick felicity, could not this wide world afford victims sufficient to satisfy thy cravings, without entering the family of a solitary few, whose comfort and happiness depended much on the society of each other?" But as she reflected she grew more resigned: "But thou hast only executed the commission of a higher power. Thou hast come, clothed in thy usual garb, thou wast sent by a kind Father, to release his child from toil and pain. Be still, and know that God has done it."

The next morning, Sunday, Newell came on board the *Créole*, disconsolate, brokenhearted. He was too distraught on that visit to give more than a few fragmentary hints of how Harriet died. Later, little by little, they learned the whole story.

Harriet, having worn herself out with that multitude of last-minute tasks even before boarding the *Gillespie* in Calcutta, had taken to bed with a fever about the time the ship sailed. She was up in a week, but a few weeks later she was attacked "with severe pains in the stomach and bowels, the disease of the country."

All this time the *Gillespie* was being driven about the Bay of Bengal by contrary winds, making little progress toward its destination. Along the Coromandel Coast it sprang a leak which became so bad that the captain had to put in for repairs at the small town of Coringa, south of Vizagapatam.

Harriet was taken ashore there. By the time the *Gillespie* set out again — a matter of some two weeks — she had apparently made a full recovery. But the delay meant that they were still at sea, more than two months after leaving Calcutta, when, on the eighth of October — two days before her nineteenth birthday — she gave birth to a baby girl — "on the cabin floor with no other attendant but my dear Mr. Newell."

The Newells' joy in their new daughter was to be pitifully short. A day or so later both mother and child were exposed to a violent storm which drenched and chilled everyone aboard. Harriet and the baby caught cold; the baby's cold turned into pneumonia, and five days after birth she died in her mother's arms.

Grief, exhaustion, exposure and sickness quickly did their work on Harriet. She lost strength rapidly. Soon both she and Newell recognized the symptoms of tuberculosis. Remembering her father's wasting and death, knowing that several other relatives had died of the same disease, she was convinced from the beginning that she must die. Newell was more optimistic and insisted that she would recover once they were on land again; but she told him to give up any such hope and help her prepare herself for death.

Early in November the *Gillespie* dropped anchor at Port Louis and Harriet was taken ashore to a small house Newell had rented. He found two physicians to care for her, but they could do nothing. Little by little she wasted away. By the middle of November, even Newell gave up hope. On the thirtieth, about four in the afternoon, her eyesight failed, and in an hour or so, she died. The next day Newell buried her in the shade of an evergreen tree in a secluded corner of the Port Louis cemetery.

These were the bare facts of Harriet's sickness and death. In them Newell found one consolation — the firm expectation he had shared with her that the two would be reunited in heaven. From the beginning, except for a few days following the baby's death, Harriet had never doubted that she was on the way to a better world than the one she was leaving. She looked forward to it, all but gloried in the prospect, and expressed no fears and no regrets except that of being parted temporarily from her husband.

For more than a week after the arrival of the *Créole* at Port Louis, the missionaries did little. Bereavement and the lonely weeks on the island had sapped Newell's initiative. Adoniram, Rice and Nancy, too, momentarily lost heart. They did what they could to console Newell, but they needed consoling themselves.

The grim, unromantic reality of the task they had undertaken was beginning to reveal itself. At Andover and in Salem they had talked about difficulties and dangers and probable martyrdom, but their departure had been, in a certain sense, almost festive, surrounded as it had been by the atmosphere of drama which always envelops the first volunteers at the start of a long war, before the big battles and the long casualty lists. Now had occurred the first skirmishes and the first casualties. It had not turned out the way they had expected. It was hard to see the glory in such deaths as Harriet's and her baby's.

Here they were, four of them, a full year after leaving Salem, on an island where none of them had ever intended to go. They were three Baptists and one Congregationalist, who had begun as four Congregationalists. They had given up hope of going to their original destination, Burma. The East India Company seemed intent on hounding them out of any other possible place.

And always, and always again, their thoughts reverted to Harriet, the youngest of them all. The accident of contrary winds, a leaky ship, drenching in a storm at sea, a cold, pneumonia, tuberculosis — where was the purpose of Providence in this mean, unfair, sneaky, even vindictive, attack on a young mother and her newborn baby?

Was the purpose to chasten them, or to fortify them for the trials ahead? If so, the method was a strange one. More of this, and there might not even be a mission. Newell was a broken man, the heart gone out of him. Rice was ill from another of the recurrent attacks of liver trouble which he had first experienced in Calcutta. Nancy knew herself to be pregnant. Thinking of what had happened to Harriet she wrote gloomily, "I am left behind, still to endure the trials of a missionary life. O that this severe dispensation may be sanctified to my soul and that I may be prepared to follow my dear departed sister." Only Adoniram continued in his usual good health, but even he, those first days in Port Louis, felt uncertain what to do.

Gradually, however, they roused themselves and began to investigate the prospects for a mission. Governor Farquhar turned out to be friendly, casually remarking that he had received orders from Bengal to "have an eye on those American missionaries," but so far as he was concerned they were free to go anywhere on the island.

The trouble with Isle of France, however, was not the governor but the fact that there was really nowhere to work except in the Port Louis army barracks and hospital; there the missionaries preached to the soldiers and patients, but that was not their idea of a mission. Most of the population consisted of slaves, and the slaveowners would not permit religious instruction. That such instruction was needed there was no question — and probably even more needed among the owners, whose inhumanity was sometimes almost incredible, than it was among the slaves.

To this need an episode Nancy described to her sisters bore ample testimony:

> Last night I heard a considerable noise in the yard in which we live, connected with another family. We went to the door and saw a female slave with her hands tied behind her, and her mistress beating her with a club, in a most dreadful manner. My blood ran cold within me, and I could quietly see it no longer. I went up to the mistress and in broken French, asked her to stop, and what her servant had done.

When Nancy learned that the slave had recently tried to run off, she talked to the woman appeasingly "till her anger appeared to be abated, and she concluded her punishment with flinging the club she had in her hands at the poor creature's head, which made the blood run down on her garment."

> . . . The slave continued with her hands tied behind her all night. They were untied this morning, and she spent the day in labour, which made me conclude she would be punished no more.
>
> But this evening I saw a large chain brought into the yard, with a ring at one end, just large enough to go around her neck. On this ring were fixed two pieces of iron about an inch wide and four inches long, which would come on each side of her face to prevent her eating. The chain was as large and heavy as an ox chain, and reached from her neck to the ground. The ring was fastened with a lock and key. The poor creature stood trembling while they were preparing to put the chain on her. The mistress' rage again rekindled at seeing her, and she began beating her again, as the night before. I went to her again, and begged that she would stop. She did, but so full of anger that she could hardly speak. When she had become a little calm, I asked her if she could not forgive her servant. I told her that her servant was very bad, but that she would be very good to forgive her. She made me to understand that she would forgive her, because *I* had asked her; but she would

not have her servant to think it was out of any favour to her. She told her slave that she forgave her, because I requested it. The slave came, knelt and kissed my feet, and said, 'Mercy, madam — mercy madam,' meaning, Thank you madam. I could scarcely forbear weeping at her gratitude . . . How happy are the inhabitants of New England, who witness no such scenes of cruelty, and where every servant has his freedom as well as his master.

But the slaveowners, and the slave population of Isle of France, were unreachable. The other possibility considered, Madagascar, was also out of the question, for another — and more practical — reason: there, the natives were accustomed to imprisoning or killing all visitors. The missionaries would have to choose some other place; but even to get to one they would have first to go back to India.

Newell now decided to try to rejoin his fellow Congregationalists. Adoniram had brought him letters from Nott and Hall, but it was not clear whether they had meant to settle in Ceylon or go on to Bombay. Newell decided to try Ceylon first, and on February 24, 1813, five weeks after the arrival of the *Créole*, he said good-by to Adoniram, Nancy and Rice, and sailed on a Portuguese brig, the *Generoso Almeida*, which was expected to touch at Point de Galle, Ceylon, on its way to Bombay.

Meanwhile Rice's liver trouble was growing worse. Soon it became apparent that he would have to find a better climate or he could expect to follow Harriet shortly. Why should he not, decided Adoniram and Rice, kill two birds with one stone by going to America to promote a Baptist missionary movement while being treated for the liver complaint? The news that there were American Baptist missionaries in the east must have reached the United States by now.

No sooner said than done. On account of the war, no ships were sailing directly for the United States; but in March one touched at Port Louis which was bound for San Salvador. From there it would be an easy journey to any United States port. Rice promptly took passage, and sailed about the middle of March.

Rice's departure left Adoniram and Nancy "entirely alone — no one remaining friend in this part of the world," as she remarked to her journal.

In a way, this was exactly what Adoniram wanted. He had always liked to do things on his own. At Andover he had come to his missionary decision alone. The others had joined him, not he them. He could work with groups on occasion, and enjoyed the company of others, but there was an intense individualism in him — a liking for the lonely way, the pioneer's trail-blazing, perhaps stemming from his father's insistence on his personal destiny — that made him prefer solitary effort. It was this, in part, which may have led him to become a Baptist in spite of any possible obligations of honor to his Congregationalist supporters, regardless of whether his decision would harm the welfare of the group of which he was one.

Now, with Rice gone, Adoniram could go with Nancy where and as he pleased, with no one to consider but the two of them.

Nancy, perhaps, had different feelings. She was keenly aware of her need for help and companionship when the time should come for her to bear her child. She had already undergone two or three short sieges of illness in Port Louis. But if she lacked Adoniram's disregard for others, she had something of his spirit of independence. And she had him. She had accepted the unalterable facts, and now joined with him in considering a destination.

They finally settled on Penang, in the Straits of Malacca. But no ship ever sailed there from Port Louis! They first would have to go to Madras — taking their chances again with the East India Company — and try there to discover a vessel bound for Penang. It was simple to find a Madras-bound ship, the *Countess of Harcourt*.

Before they sailed from Isle of France, Nancy paid a visit — her only one, on account of the cemetery's remoteness — to Harriet's grave under its evergreen tree.

> The visit revived many painful, solemn feelings. But a little while ago, she was with us on board ship, and joined us daily in prayer and praise. Now her body is crumbling to dust, in a land of strangers.

But Harriet's spirit, Nancy was sure, was already in heaven, and she consoled herself by thinking "that Jesus has himself entered the grave, and opened a path to eternal glory. He is with his disciples when they enter the gloomy passage. He was with my dear departed sister. O may he be with me."

On the seventh of May, 1814, the two embarked on the *Countess of Harcourt*, and on the fourth of June arrived at Madras. They received a warm welcome from Mr. and Mrs. Loveless, two English missionaries stationed there, and from many other people in the city, but they saw quickly that Madras would be another Calcutta. The attitude of the East India Company was hardening. Their presence was already reported to the police, who had forwarded an account of their arrival to the supreme government in Bengal. It would be merely a matter of time before an order came for deportation to England. Anxiously Adoniram haunted the vessels in the Madras roads looking for one going to Penang; but days went by without success. In desperation he began to look for a ship leaving for anywhere — he did not care where, so long as it sailed before that dreaded deportation order could arrive. He found only one, "a crazy old vessel," a Portuguese ship named *Georgiana*.

But *Georgiana* was bound for *Rangoon*, in *Burma!*

He told Nancy what he had learned. They could go to Burma in the *Georgiana* and begin their mission, or they could go to England in custody and vegetate until a better opportunity offered, if one ever did. There was no other choice.

Nancy and Adoniram had come to regard a mission to Burma "with feelings of horror," but it was beginning to seem almost as if their destiny were linked in some strange way with that terrible Golden Kingdom. Was it really chance that had brought Adoniram to read Symes's *Embassy to Ava* at Andover — the one book about Burma that painted the land in bright colors? In Calcutta, everything they heard about Burma had been bad; yet Felix Carey, a Baptist, had been able at least to stay there; and presently they had become Baptists — so that no objection to a joint mission existed any more. In fact, Felix had wanted them to return to Rangoon with him. And now, in Madras, only one vessel was leaving, and it was bound *for Burma*. Could this be nothing but chance? Or could Providence be suggesting gently, subtly, that if they really meant to be missionaries, Burma, with all its dangers and horrors, was the place they were meant to go?

They talked it over with the Lovelesses and their other friends in Madras. Everyone had the same opinion: *Stay away from Burma.* Let yourselves be taken to England. Lose a few years. For the sake

of yourselves, for the child you are to have, for the sake of your
mission, a few years lost are better than losing all to no purpose in
the living hell of Burma.

This argument did not convince Adoniram. He felt that they
should at least try Burma, to find out whether a mission could exist
there. Rangoon was a seaport on a river; foreign ships called there
often. A few Europeans had managed to remain; perhaps the Judsons could. But if they found no profit in a mission, they could
surely leave and still try Penang or the Malay Islands later.

Nancy agreed. They should at least attempt, with Felix Carey, a
mission among "a people who have never heard the sound of the
Gospel, or read, in their own language, of the love of Christ."

. . . The poor Burmans are entirely destitute of those con-
solations and joys which constitute our happiness; and why
should we be unwilling to part with a few fleeting, inconsid-
erable comforts, for the sake of making them sharers with us in
joys exalted as heaven, durable as eternity! We cannot expect
to do much, in such a rough, uncultivated field; yet, if we may
be instrumental in removing some of the rubbish, and preparing
the way for others, it will be a sufficient reward. I have been
accustomed to view this field of labor, with dread and terror;
but I now feel perfectly willing to make it my home the rest
of my life.

Thus they decided. And, as Adoniram remarked, "dissuaded by
all our friends at Madras, we commended ourselves to God, and
embarked the 22d of June."

With Nancy's pregnancy so far advanced, they did take a few
practical measures before sailing. Because it was altogether possible, even probable, that her baby would be born aboard the
*Georgiana*, Nancy employed a European woman to go with her as
servant and nurse — a fine, strapping woman, the picture of health.
She went on board the ship a few days early to make things comfortable for Nancy. But no sooner had Nancy and Adoniram entered the ship themselves, just as it was about to sail, than "she fell
on the floor, apparently in a fit. We made every possible effort
to recover her, but she gasped a few times and died."

There was no time to find another servant, and the *Georgiana* sailed out into the Bay of Bengal with Nancy stricken with shock and the heavy exertions she had made to try to save the woman's life. The ship was small and dirty, the winds strong and the waters rough. Even lying in a bunk called for hard effort.

They had been at sea like this only a few days when Nancy went into labor. Like Harriet she had "no physician, no attendant but Mr. Judson." The baby was born dead. For a while it looked as if Nancy, growing more and more exhausted from the continual tossing of the ship, would have to be buried in the waters of the Bay after her baby.

To make things worse, the ill-smelling, cranky *Georgiana* could not be held on her course. Her captain had headed her southeastward for the Nicobar Islands, above the upper tip of Sumatra, some hundreds of miles south of Rangoon, where he intended to take in a cargo of coconuts. Instead the ship was driven farther north, "into a dangerous strait, between the Little and Great Andamans, two savage coasts, where the captain had never been before, and where if we had been cast ashore, we should, according to all accounts, have been killed and eaten by the natives."

But great as the danger was, the mishap brought relief, perhaps life, to Nancy. The strait was filled with reefs, black fanglike rocks which came so close to the surface that the horrified watchers on deck could actually see them, but the water was still as a millpond and Nancy could rest. For once, the *Georgiana* behaved well and the captain was able to thread her successfully through the reefs. On the eastern side of the Islands, in the Andaman Sea, the ship found favorable winds from the south, and the captain, giving up any intention of getting coconuts, let the ship sail with the winds as they "gently wafted us forward to Rangoon."

Thursday, July 13, 1813, three weeks out of Madras, the *Georgiana* found the entrance of the Rangoon River, one of the Irrawaddy's many mouths.

Adoniram stayed on deck as the ship passed the Burmese watchboat a few miles up the river, picked up a pilot, and moved slowly on up the broad stream.

His first sight of Burma consisted of low, swampy land bordered, at the water's edge, by tall reeds and brushwood. It was not prepossessing, nothing like the cultivated, populous country along the

Hooghly below Calcutta. The river itself was magnificent, fully three quarters of a mile wide, with no shoals and ample depth for any ship. But there was something menacing about the steamy, silent lowlands sluggishly slithering out of the water, something less indolent than threatening, like a snake waiting motionless for the time to strike. He felt a curious unease, which communicated itself to Nancy when he went below to tell her what he saw.

As the *Georgiana* moved slowly upstream during the day, Adoniram saw that the country was not without people — for they passed miserable little fishing villages huddled along the banks here and there, and there were boats on the river — but the same impression of desolation persisted. But this was border country, Adoniram may have consoled himself; for years armies and rebels had passed and repassed over it, crushing out nearly all life and destroying men's work. Perhaps Rangoon would be better.

Later that day he caught his first sight of the city itself, in the form of a distant glint of gold flashing above the trees of the jungle in the late afternoon sun. The glint rose higher and higher as the ship approached, seeming to climb out of the horizon, until it revealed itself as a towering, pointed, glowing spire.

Adoniram had heard of that spire. It was the tremendous golden Shwe Dagon Pagoda, one of the wonders of the world.

The Shwe Dagon was the prime object of veneration in Burma. It had been erected little by little through generation after generation to enshrine certain holy relics which had been sealed up for centuries in a vault underneath. The three Buddhas who preceded the great Buddha, the Gautama, were represented in that vault by the staff of one, the water filter of another, and a piece of the robe of the third. And, holiest of all, with these relics were eight hairs from the head of the great Buddha himself.

No wonder the shining cupola of the pagoda, towering nearly four hundred feet into the air, was religiously overlaid with pure gold every three years. No wonder pilgrims by the tens of thousands came to worship at it during the great annual festival held there every spring.

But Adoniram had seen pagodas before. To him, this was simply a bigger, more lavish one, though its very size and magnificence amply foretold the difficulty of the task ahead of him.

He was more interested in the city; and soon, as the pagoda towered higher and higher ahead, he saw it — a disappointing huddle of thatched bamboo and teak houses, extending perhaps a mile along the river, cut by stagnant muddy creeks, almost like canals, which ran back from the shore, each giving off a perceptible reek of decay. Rangoon was certainly no Calcutta. It was a dirty, bedraggled overgrown village of ten thousand people at most, surrounding a square fortlike enclosure close to the riverbank, a quarter of a mile or so to the side, which seemed to protect the heart of the city.

Just below it, next to a few huts, three wharves with cranes for landing goods projected into the river. The middle one was surmounted by a kind of fort with portholes for ten or a dozen cannon. The whole suggested a garrison town, always half expecting a siege, and always at least partly prepared.

It was dusk when the *Georgiana* dropped anchor near the wharves. Adoniram knew where the mission house was — in fact, he could see it bulking large over the buildings near it outside the city walls, and he was at once determined to take a look at it. But he did not stay on shore long, nor did he even go very close to the house. Everything looked "so dark, and cheerless, and unpromising," that he soon returned to the ship and Nancy, to tell her what he had seen.

Still exhausted and sick, still suffering the anguish of losing her child, Nancy had lost her usual optimism. She could read Adoniram's impressions on his gloomy face and hear them in the tone of his voice. They alone were enough to describe Rangoon.

It was the unhappiest evening they had ever spent. At last they had arrived at the destination Adoniram had aimed at for three years, the place he had dreamed of, the goal of his ambition; and they had never regretted anything more in their lives.

But they must make the best of it. All they could do, with despair in their hearts, was commend themselves to the disposal of God in the hope of a speedy transition — which seemed all too likely — "to that peaceful region where the wicked cease from troubling and the weary are at rest." In this distressed mood they finally fell into troubled sleep.

## CHAPTER IV

# Burma

## [ *1813–1814* ]

THEY felt better the next morning as they prepared to go ashore in the bright sunshine. Nancy, still too weak to walk, had to be carried. On the dock, there was a good deal of discussion over how to convey her through the city. Finally an armchair was found. Two bamboo poles were thrust through it to make an improvised open palanquin. Four Burmese men, their long, skirtlike waistcloths knotted up in front to free their bare brown legs, each picked up an end of a pole, rested it on a shoulder, and started off, Adoniram walking beside.

By now Adoniram and Nancy were familiar with Oriental cities. But one like Rangoon they had never seen. Calcutta and Madras showed the influence of their English rulers everywhere. Rangoon was unalloyed Burman through and through. Its streets, narrow and dirty, were hardly more than alleys, the best paved crudely with worn brick. The houses were mostly ramshackle bamboo huts.

The city bristled with pagodas. They were everywhere. One whole street, the one leading to the great Shwe Dagon, which towered, glittering magnificently, over them all, was lined with pagodas. The pagoda bells, hung with umbrella-like canopies at the spires' tops, tinkled and clanged in every key as they swung in the wind.

The streets swarmed with humanity, talking, arguing, laughing and yelling in what was a perfect jargon to Adoniram and Nancy. Children, smoking cigars like their elders, naked as Adam and Eve except for the bright bracelets and necklaces and bangles they wore on arms, necks and ankles, were underfoot everywhere. Leprous beggars, sometimes with a whole hand or foot eaten off, pleaded for alms on the corners. Here and there a saffron-robed priest plodded along the street holding out his begging-bowl, his eyes modestly averted from the glances of the gaily dressed women.

A little way into the city, the carriers set Nancy's chair down for a rest in the shade. Immediately a crowd gathered to inspect that incredible rarity, an Englishwoman. Burmans were anything but shy, the women even bolder than the men. In a few minutes numerous women were close about her, exclaiming loudly over her pale skin, her peculiar clothing, her shoes, speculating about her personal habits and even fingering the fabric of her dress.

Weak and sick, Nancy had kept her head down and her face hidden. In a moment the curious women, gay as so many butterflies in their gauzy crimson silk petticoats, bright scarfs and gold earplugs, some with flowers in their oiled, knotted black hair, were actually pressing up against her in order to stoop and look under her bonnet. Seeing brown face after face peering up at her, she suddenly lifted her head, looked up at the women, and smiled.

At once the whole multitude burst into loud laughter. Nancy and Adoniram glanced at each other, amused. Rangoon might not be prepossessing, but they were already beginning to like the childlike frankness of its people.

In a moment the bearers picked up Nancy's chair to the accompaniment of a shout of applause from the crowd and trotted off with her to the customhouse, which proved to be "a small open shed, in which were seated on mats several natives, who were the customhouse officers."

The Burmese customs inspection was nothing if not thorough. Every box and bale in every ship had to be brought ashore, where one tenth of its contents was set aside for the king. Every trunk of every traveler had to be opened and each item in it taken out, examined, appraised, criticized, and sometimes handled so much as to be damaged. The person of each traveler was searched — not so much for fear anyone carried contraband as to satisfy the curiosity of the customs inspectors as to what strangers carried in their pockets and clothing. And after all, there *might* be something forbidden which, to be overlooked, would call for a huge bribe instead of a smaller one.

The men searched Adoniram from the skin out and a woman searched Nancy only a little less thoroughly. The searchers found nothing that would demand a larger than ordinary gift. Of course the next day, when the newcomers' trunks and boxes were brought on land, might prove more promising. After the search the Judsons were free to go to the mission house.

The mission house was "the largest and handsomest house in all Rangoon," a substantial structure of teak, the inside left unfinished with the beams and joists showing. Here Mrs. Carey — Felix was in Ava vaccinating some of the younger members of the royal family — reigned capably over the servants who cared for the house and the two-year-old Carey boy.

The daughter of Christian parents of Portuguese descent, Mrs. Carey had been born in Burma and grown up in the country. She knew little English, but the warmth of her welcome and her evident efforts to make them comfortable bespoke her good nature even more than her few halting phrases of English. Her presence relieved the missionaries of housekeeping details and freed them for their primary task of learning the language and the people.

Within a few days Adoniram found a teacher. He was a Hindu scholar of such great tolerance that in spite of his caste he would sit in a chair with the Judsons, eat with them, and even teach Nancy the Burmese language along with Adoniram. This last he was unwilling to do at first, "appearing to feel that it was rather beneath him to instruct a female, as the females here are held in the lowest estimation. But when he saw I was determined to persevere, and that Mr. Judson was as desirous that he should instruct me as himself, he was more attentive."

The learning proved unexpectedly difficult. Neither Nancy nor Adoniram knew a word of the teacher's language; he knew not a word of theirs. After all three sat smilingly helpless for a while, Adoniram finally hit on an expedient. He would point to an object in the room. The teacher, catching the idea, would name it in Burmese, and Adoniram and Nancy would repeat it after him. In this way they began to learn the names of common things around the house such as foods, trees, and plants. But it was slow work, although they each spent twelve hours a day studying.

As soon as they had a few words by ear, they began to study the written language, which consisted of what looked like a long series of circles and parts of circles written on palm leaves, the Burmese equivalent of paper. They found it easier to write than they had anticipated, but reading seemed hopeless. Neither Adoniram nor Nancy could see in it any grammatical structure resembling any language they had ever studied. The Burmese even seemed to think in a different way from Europeans. And worst of all, the written language had no punctuation, not even any separation between words. Paragraphs, sentences, words and letters — all ran together in one unbroken line without capitals or commas.

They had learned in a few weeks a little French to get along with, but they saw it might take them years to acquire even that much Burmese. And with no dictionary, no grammar except a beginning of one by Felix Carey, no interpreter, when would they ever, they wondered despairingly, know enough to express the abstract ideas of Christianity? Nevertheless, they persevered and progressed a little: a great deal, thought their teacher, though to themselves they admitted "we can hardly perceive that we make any advance."

Meanwhile they were becoming acquainted with Burmese life. It was completely unlike New England's — even very little like that of India. There was "no bread, butter, cheese, potatoes, nor scarcely anything that we have been in the habit of eating." There were almost no such meats as beef, mutton or pork, because the slaughter of animals for food was forbidden. Only animals that sickened and died could be eaten, or those that occasionally died by "accident." Instead, Adoniram and Nancy had mostly rice "and curried fowl, and fowls stewed with cucumbers," foods to which they quickly took a liking.

They were distressed by the poverty they saw:

The country presents a rich, beautiful appearance, everywhere covered with vegetation, and if cultivated, would be one of the finest in the world. But the poor natives have no inducement to labor or raise anything, as it would probably be taken from them by their oppressive rulers. Many of them live on leaves and vegetables that grow spontaneously, and some actually die with hunger. Everything is extremely high, therefore many are induced to steal whatever comes their way. There are constant robberies and murders committed; scarcely a night but houses are broken open and things stolen.

Yet the people were attractive. Although even babies smoked cigars and the women chewed betel until their mouths dripped scarlet and their teeth turned black, hardly anyone used alcohol or opium. Although life was insecure and officialdom cruel and corrupt, the Burmese had no caste system like that in India. The people had a remarkable spirit of independence and frankness. Women were not slaves to their husbands — in fact, they were lively, spirited, and even quarrelsome to a degree seen nowhere else in Asia. But personal honesty was almost unknown. "Lying is so common and universal among them, that they say, 'We cannot live without telling lies.' "

The crowded streets and bazaars were breathtakingly colorful. The small, turbaned men took intense pride in the length of their hair, which they wore knotted up on the top of the head. The lobes of their ears, like those of the women, were bored with huge holes in which they inserted plugs of gold the size of a finger. Precious stones were set into the ends of the earplugs of the wealthy. The poor often had no gold earplugs, but occasionally could be seen carrying cigars in the holes instead. The men's blue-tattooed bodies were covered above the waist with a sort of loose white vest, which could be tied together by dangling strings in front. Underneath they sometimes wore a sort of vest.

But the most spectacular color in the men's costume flamed in their waistcloths, the "patso," a huge piece of fabric eight yards long which covered them from waist to heel, knotted up in front of each leg like flowing trousers, with one dangling end flung over the shoulder. These were invariably of silk, in soft colors, sometimes in checks, sometimes in zigzag stripes shading from pale lemon to deep crimson.

The women, diminutive compared to a New Englander like Nancy, combed their straight, oiled black hair away from their temples, and arranged it in a flower-decorated knot on top of the head somewhat in the manner of the men. Above the waist they wore a light tunic of thin goldsprigged or black lace or yellow gauze, and over it a light scarf, silk handkerchief or small shawl. Their skirts, or petticoats — it was hard for a Westerner to know what to call them — were of bright silk with a top of crimson gathered in folds around the breast and a broad contrasting border at the bottom.

They loaded themselves with ear ornaments, necklaces and rings. In a country without banks or safe places to keep wealth, most people wore their treasures as adornment.

Although by European standards the dress of the women was somewhat immodest, it was so beautiful that Nancy fell in love with it at once and in time was to wear it habitually herself. But she could never get used to the customary sandals, which were always left at the door on entering any building, so, although above the ankles she eventually came to be attired like a Burmese woman, her footwear was always the sturdy black product of her native Massachusetts.

As for the children, up to seven or eight they wore nothing but necklaces, bracelets and anklets on their bodies and carried cigars in their teeth. When they were older, they put on the same clothing as their elders.

There was no English society in Rangoon at all. The only Europeans who could speak English were a few Frenchmen. Nancy regretted that their wives spoke only French so that there was no "female in all Burma with whom I can converse." But the lack made her study Burmese that much harder.

And Burmese still offered its difficulties. Once her teacher told her that when he died he would go to her country. She shook her head and told him he would not, but he merely laughed and insisted that he would. "I did not understand the language sufficiently," she confessed in frustration, "to tell him where he would go, or how he could be saved."

But if they could not yet discuss religion, they were fast learning the words and phrases of every day. After four or five months Adoniram felt confident enough of his command of the language to pay a call on the viceroy Mya-day-men, ruler of the city. Since life and death hung on the viceroy's favor, it was important to win his friendship.

The effort was a complete failure. The viceroy, wrapt in the consciousness of his own and Burma's greatness, reported Nancy, "scarcely deigned to look at him, as English*men* are no uncommon sight in this country."

But an English*woman* was "quite a curiosity." Nancy decided to exploit the fact by visiting the viceroy's wife. Her favor was nearly as valuable as that of the viceroy himself, and it was well known that a small present would secure nearly anything from her.

One day, accompanied by one of the Frenchwomen who often visited the viceroy's wife, she made her call.

When we first arrived at the government house, she was not up; consequently we had to wait some time. But the inferior wives of the viceroy diverted us much by their curiosity in minutely examining everything we had on, and by trying on our gloves, bonnets, etc.

At last her highness made her appearance, dressed richly in Burmese fashion, with a long silver pipe at her mouth, smoking. At her appearance, all the other wives took their seats at a respectful distance, and sat in a crouching position, without speaking.

She received me very politely, took me by the hand, seated me upon a mat, and herself by me. She excused herself for not coming in earlier, saying she was unwell. One of the women brought her a bunch of flowers, of which she took several, and ornamented her cap. She was very inquisitive whether I had a husband and children; whether I was my husband's first wife; meaning by this, whether I was the highest among them, supposing that my husband, like the Burmans, had many wives; and whether I intended tarrying long in the country.

When the viceroy came in, I really trembled, for I never before beheld such a savage-looking creature. His long robe and enormous spear not a little increased my dread. He spoke to me, however, very condescendingly, and asked if I would drink some rum or wine. When I arose to go, her highness again took my hand, told me she was happy to see me; that I must come to see her every day, for I was like a sister to her. She led me to the door, and I made my *salaam*, and departed.

Presently Felix Carey returned from Ava. To his father he wrote enthusiastically, "They are just cut out for this mission. I thought so, as soon as I first met them. In six months Mr. Judson has a splendid grasp of the language, and is the very colleague I wanted." But Felix was already in the process of ceasing to be a missionary. Ava had offered him a position in government service. He had nearly decided to accept, but first he wanted to go to Calcutta to consult with his father and others. In a few weeks he sailed down the river, leaving Nancy and Adoniram once more to their own devices.

Soon after his departure the Judsons decided to move out of the mission house to a house inside the city walls. By now they knew the language well enough to get along by themselves, and the mission was too isolated, they felt. Within the crowded city they could make themselves better acquainted with the people. Also, the bands of robbers roving the countryside were becoming bolder and more numerous every day.

They moved early in January of 1814, two years after the ordination in Salem, and barely a week later congratulated themselves on their good judgment when an armed band of fifteen or twenty robbers attacked and looted a house almost next door to the mission house, stabbing the owner. To deter a repetition, the viceroy had seven thieves executed as an object lesson. "They were tied up by the hands and feet and then left with their bowels hanging out. They are to remain a spectacle to others for three days, and then [be] buried."

A little later they attended the funeral of an upper class Burman. There was an immense, disorderly procession which included a parade of elephants, and a great distribution of money, gifts and food at the place where the corpse was burned. A local governor had attended the funeral. On his way home "a man on a sudden started up, and, with one stroke, severed his head from his body." The assassin turned out to be the victim's chief steward. Under torture he confessed that he had planned to seize his master's property after the murder, and with it go to the king and buy the governor's office. "He was afterwards treated in the most cruel manner, having most of his bones broken, and left to languish out his miserable existence in a prison, in chains. He lived five or six days in this terrible condition. All who were concerned with him were punished in various ways. The immense property of this governor goes to the king, as he left no children, although several wives remain."

They had been living in the city three months when one Sunday in March . . .

We came out to the mission house that we might enjoy the Sabbath in a more quiet way. We had but just arrived, when one of the servants informed us that there was a fire near the town. We hastened to the place whence the fire proceeded, and beheld several houses in flames, in a range which led directly to the city; and as we saw no exertions to extinguish it, we concluded the whole place would be destroyed.

We set off immediately for our house in town, that we might remove our furniture and things that were there; but when we came to the town gate, it was shut. The poor people, in their fright, had shut the gate, ignorantly imagining they could shut the fire out, although the walls and gates were made entirely of wood. After waiting, however, for some time, the gate was opened, and we removed in safety all our things into the mission house.

The fire continued to rage all day, and swept away almost all the houses, walls, gates, etc. We felt grateful to God that not a hair of our heads was injured; and that, while thousands of families were deprived of a shelter from the burning sun, we had a comfortable house and the necessaries of life.

They stayed on in the mission house with Mrs. Carey. They must have felt a little reluctant to add to her burdens, for by now she had a small baby besides her three-year-old son, but there was no help for it.

Felix Carey returned from Calcutta the next month. He had finally decided to give up his missionary career and enter the service of King Bodawpaya. In August, the Careys said farewell to the Judsons and moved out of the mission house. Their goods, their servants, and themselves were embarked aboard a government brig, and thus one day they sailed upriver for the capital, and out of the lives of Adoniram and Nancy.

The two saw the Careys go with mingled feelings. They regretted being left "alone in this great house, and almost alone as it respects the world." But Felix Carey had added no strength to the mission. He might do more good for them as an official at Ava, at the source of power, than he had ever done in Rangoon as a missionary.

At any rate, the Careys' departure marked the end of the missionary apprenticeship of Adoniram and Nancy. From now on they could depend on no one but themselves. They were their own masters. And they were keenly aware that the burden of the conversion of Burma lay upon them alone.

## CHAPTER V

# Little Roger
## [ *1814–1816* ]

As it happened, Adoniram and Nancy were never to see the Careys again. When only a few miles up the river, the Careys' brig overturned in a squall. Felix, along with a few of the men-servants, managed to reach shore alive, but not before he had seen his wife, baby and little son drown in front of his eyes in spite of his frantic efforts to save them. So poor were communications (after the accident Felix had continued on upriver alone) that the Judsons did not learn of the tragedy for two weeks. Meanwhile, they had established themselves in a routine which was to continue for years. Nancy described it:

> Could you look into a large open room, which we call a verandah, you would see Mr. Judson bent over his table, covered with Burman books, with his teacher at his side, a venerable looking man, in his sixtieth year, with a cloth wrapped around his middle, and a handkerchief over his head. They talk and chatter all day long, with hardly any cessation.
>
> My mornings are busily employed in giving directions to the servants, providing food for the family, etc. I have many more interruptions than Mr. Judson, as I have the entire management of the family. This I took on myself, for the sake of Mr. Judson's attending more closely to the study of the language; yet I have found, by a year's experience, that it is the most direct way I could have taken to acquire the language; as I am frequently obliged to speak Burman all day. I can talk and understand others better than Mr. Judson, though he knows more about the nature and construction of the language.

It was true: Nancy *was* more at home with the day-to-day speech of Burma. But Adoniram consoled himself with the realization that he was laying a foundation which would eventually make it possible for any European to learn Burmese and — most important — bring the Bible to the Burmese people in their own tongue.

In fact, he had undertaken several tasks simultaneously, any one of them formidable. One was the making of a Burmese grammar. Along with the grammar he was gradually accumulating a word-list, the embryo of a dictionary.

The growing word-list had already revealed a peculiar problem. Burmese itself almost completely lacked any words for the kind of ethical and abstract ideas which made up the core of New Testament Christianity. The best educated men employed some such terms, but they were not natively Burmese. They had been adapted from Pali, a language related to Sanskrit and the Indo-European tongues, which was used a good deal by the learned men of Burma.

For Buddhism had been brought to Burma in Pali nearly two thousand years ago, and the sacred writings taught by Burmese priests were still essentially in Pali, as was the form of the written language, although the speech of the people was very much like Chinese. Pali was partly a dead language by now, but it looked to Adoniram as if he would have to draw on it for a good many words and somehow transplant them into Burmese in order to make his ideas understood by the people. Promptly he set about making a Pali grammar and word-list.

At the same time he began testing his conception by beginning a tentative translation of one of the books of the New Testament, the Gospel of Matthew.

Months passed. Adoniram worked with his teacher all day on Pali and Burmese word-lists and grammars and translation, only interrupted when Nancy summoned him out to deal with an emergency, such as a cobra in the garden or an invasion by one of the numerous kinds of pests — bats, giant cockroaches, beetles, spiders, lizards, rats and bedbugs — which infested the houses of Rangoon. Nancy spent her mornings directing the household — thereby increasing her already enviable fluency in the popular speech — her afternoons in study with Adoniram and the teacher.

Sometimes they broke the monotony with early morning walks around the huddled, steaming and smelly, but interesting city. Regularly they bathed in one of the many tree-lined artificial ponds called by English-speaking people "tanks." They looked at the saffron-robed priests shuffling along the dusty streets, inspected the fantastic ornamentation of the Shwe Dagon pagoda, almost a city of lace in stone, and listened to the continuous tinkling, clanking cacophony of the temple bells.

They were beginning to make acquaintances. Soon they were spending "whole evenings very pleasantly in conversing with our Burman friends."

A new viceroy came to Rangoon, one "much beloved and respected by the people," unlike his fierce predecessor Mya-day-men, from whom everyone shrank as he stalked about with his long spear. The new viceroy actually visited the mission house and told Nancy and Adoniram they must call on him often. He was an old man, with many concubines and at least twenty or thirty children. His principal wife took a great liking to Nancy, and they became good friends — so much so that at one great party the viceroy gave for the English and French in Rangoon she asked Nancy to dance "in the English way" for the guests. Fortunately, Nancy now knew enough of the language to explain that as the wife of a priest she could not dance. This satisfied the Burmese. They understood that priests and their wives were a special sort of people, bound by their own rules.

But the better Adoniram and Nancy came to know the Burmese, the more they realized that even a lifetime was too short for more than the beginning of a mission. Although they were now fluent enough to talk fairly easily about ordinary subjects . . .

We find the subject of religion by far the most difficult, on account of the want of religious terms in their language. They have not the least idea of a God who is eternal — without beginning or end. All their deities have been through the several grades of creatures, from a fowl to a deity. When their deities take heaven, as they express it, they cease to exist, which according to their ideas, is the highest state of perfection. It is now two thousand years since Gaudama [Gautama], their last deity, entered on his state of perfection; and though he now ceases to exist, they still worship a hair of his head, which is enshrined in an enormous pagoda, to which the Burmans go every eighth day. They know of no other atonements for sin, than offerings to their priests and their pagodas. You cannot imagine how very difficult it is to give them any idea of the true God and the way of salvation by Christ, since their present ideas of deity are so very low.

Still they had to do it somehow, so they persevered. Yet at times they felt terribly alone. They had received no word whatever from America, or, in particular, from Rice. Whether American Baptists would undertake to support them, they had not the faintest idea. Their only visitors from outside, occasional sea captains from England, could tell them nothing.

So matters stood at the beginning of 1815, when they had lived in Rangoon a year and a half.

Then Nancy fell sick with one of those wasting diseases so common in the Orient. There were no doctors in Rangoon, and Adoniram's few medical books gave them no idea of what the ailment was or how to cure it. For a while they hoped Nancy would get better by herself, but instead she slowly grew weaker. And she believed she might be pregnant again.

There was only one thing to do, they decided. She must take the first ship for Madras, where there were good doctors. Adoniram took it for granted that he would go with her, but Nancy refused. She would not permit him to interrupt his studies for the many months she might be away.

Reluctantly, Adoniram agreed. But he insisted that she at least take a woman servant with her. This might be difficult, on account of a Burmese law which forbade any native woman to leave the country; but they decided to approach the friendly old viceroy with a small gift — "which is customary when a favour is asked" — and ask. To their surprise, he granted their petition immediately.

Nancy sailed late in January and returned, feeling much better, in the middle of April after a stay of six weeks in Madras. She brought with her Emily Van Someren, an orphan girl seven years old, whom she had agreed to bring up as one of the family. Perhaps Nancy thought of Emily as a companion for the baby she knew she would have early in the fall of the year. Emily was to spend the next seven years as a member of the household before returning to Madras. Beyond the bare mention of her coming to live with Adoniram and Nancy we know little about her.

They spent the summer quietly. They were acquiring the language rapidly now, enough to begin to talk to the people about religion, thanks partly to a new teacher — the fourth since their arrival in Burma — who proved to be an unusually learned man, a former priest who had lived "at the Golden Feet," in the capital, and who, remembering the dismissal of his three predecessors, was unusually anxious to please Adoniram.

But their efforts at conversion were unsuccessful. The people had a religion already. Before they could accept a new one they had to reject the old one. When Adoniram told the men about Jesus' atonement for their sins they replied politely that "their minds were stiff." When Nancy spoke to the women, they said, "Your religion is good for you, ours for us. You will be rewarded for your good deeds in your way — we in our way."

Once their hopes were raised "by the serious attention" of a son of the viceroy, who had been sent to them to learn English. During his year of study with Nancy and Adoniram he "at times appeared solemn and inquisitive."

But in the summer of 1815, the father was replaced by the same much-feared spear-stalker, Mya-day-men, who had been viceroy when Adoniram and Nancy first arrived in Rangoon. And when the father "lost his office" the son "of course lost his sense of dignity, mixed with his servants, and lost, we fear, most of his seriousness."

Even a Mr. Babasheen, "an aged Armenian, in high office under government," was a disappointment. He was a Christian by birth and had a Bible in his own language. Surely, thought Adoniram, it would be possible to show him the merits of Baptism. But Babasheen insisted that Adoniram's church, the Armenian church and the Roman Catholic church were really all the same thing, with their common root in the Bible. Adoniram tried to show him "that the Bible was indeed the same, but only those who adhered to it would be saved." But Babasheen merely replied, "You cannot speak the language fluently. When you can talk better, come and see me often, and I shall get wisdom."

But at least, Adoniram and Nancy consoled themselves, they were able to discuss religion a little. A year before they would not have been able to do even that much.

Soon they had heart-warming news. On the fifth of September came letters from America — the first direct words from home since Luther Rice had left them at Isle of France more than two years ago.

Nothing could have been more encouraging than the news in those precious letters. As soon as the New England Baptists had learned that the Judsons had been baptized, they had begun to form local societies for the support of the new missionaries. When he arrived in the United States Luther Rice had thrown himself into the work of forming more. Starting in the Southern states, he had soon organized Baptist missionary societies in nearly every state of the union. In May of 1814 a national missionary society had been established in Philadelphia under the name of "The General Missionary Convention of the Baptist Denomination in the United States of America for Foreign Missions." A Board of Managers had been elected, and the Reverend Dr. Thomas Baldwin of Boston made President, with the Reverend Dr. William Staughton of Philadelphia Corresponding Secretary. One of its first actions had been to appoint Adoniram its missionary. Rice was also appointed a missionary, but for the present placed in charge of setting up new missionary societies and raising funds in the United States.

Some months later the Managers had even accepted a new missionary, Mr. George H. Hough, a printer, who would be able to print anything Adoniram could put into Burmese. Hough and his wife Phebe were already preparing to sail for Calcutta.

For a few days Adoniram and Nancy neglected work to exult in this wonderful intelligence. They were not forgotten after all. They had support. Best of all, they would not be alone. Hough would more than double their effectiveness. With him at the press they could broadcast the main ideas of the Gospel all over Burma.

Their elation had hardly begun to cool when, six days after the arrival of the letters, Nancy's labor began. On the eleventh of September, 1815, with no attendant but Adoniram, she gave birth to a little boy, Roger Williams Judson.

The baby flourished from the start. He fed well, never cried

except when in pain, and to his doting mother and father seemed unusually sensitive to his surroundings. Nancy felt better than in
years, "almost in a new state of existence."

As if all this were not enough, when Roger was three weeks old
Adoniram had a conversation with a native Burman which led him
to believe that at last he was not so very far from being able to
replace Buddhism with Christianity in the heart of at least one
Burman.

The Burman was his teacher, who had been with him some
three months now, a man forty-seven years of age who had
proved to be "the most sensible, learned, and candid man that I
have ever found among the Burmans." His name would probably
be spelled today as U Aung Min, but Adoniram, spelling words
as they sounded to his ear and making his rules as he went along,
wrote it variously as Oungmen, Oo Oungmen, and Oo Oungmeng.

The conversation had begun one day when they were working
together at the book-piled study table on the veranda. Always
alert for an opportunity to bring up religion, Adoniram had remarked that a man they both knew had died. The teacher admitted
he had heard so. "His soul is lost, I think," said Adoniram.

"Why so?"

"He was not a disciple of Christ."

The teacher was skeptical. "How do you know that? You could
not see his soul."

"How do you know whether the root of the mango tree is
good?" Adoniram rejoined. "You cannot see it; but you can judge
by the fruit on its branches. Thus I know the man who died was
not a disciple of Christ, because his words and actions were not
such as to indicate the disciple."

"And so all who are not disciples of Christ are lost!" The teacher
was amazed.

"Yes, all, whether Burmans or foreigners."

"This is hard," answered the teacher, after digesting the idea a
little while.

"Yes, it is hard, indeed; otherwise I should not have come all this
way, and left parents and all, to tell you of Christ."

The teacher paused. Nothing in his experience or reading had
ever hinted a religion like this. Yet there was force in Adoniram's

last statement. After all, the teacher must have reflected, why *should* a man leave country and home except on a matter of desperate urgency? It must have been a strange moment: the young black-coated missionary, not yet thirty, facing the turbaned Burman, learned and wise, the latter beginning to grasp for the first time in his many years that here was a man — one of many white men, he knew — who believed with his whole heart in a future existence which involved perpetual punishment for one's beliefs on earth if they were wrong, but evidently something better if they were right. The thought led him to a question: "How is it that the disciples of Christ are so fortunate above all men?"

Adoniram sensed that he had made an impression. Cautiously he approached his real argument by asking a question which he knew could receive only one answer: "Are not all men sinners, and deserving of punishment in a future state?"

"Yes," the teacher admitted at once. "All must suffer, in some future state, for the sins they commit. The punishment follows the crime, as surely as the wheel of the car follows the footsteps of the ox."

This was Adoniram's opening. "Now, according to the Burman system," he said seriously, "there is no escape. According to the Christian system, there is. Jesus Christ has died in the place of sinners; has borne their sins, and now those who believe in him, and become his disciples, are released from the punishment they deserve. At death they are received into heaven, and are happy forever."

He had unveiled the heart of his doctrine: the innate sinfulness of man; the atonement of Jesus; the prospect of heaven instead of hell. It was too much for the teacher. "That I will never believe," he said firmly. "My mind is very stiff on this one point, namely, that all existence involves in itself principles of misery and destruction."

But at least, Adoniram must have thought to himself, studying the brown face of the learned Burman, now you know what I preach. Let us see, now, whether we can go at it another way. Aloud, he said, "Teacher, there are two evil futurities, and one good. A miserable future existence is evil, and annihilation or nigban [nikban] is an evil, a fearful evil. A happy future existence is alone good."

With this much the teacher could agree. "I admit that it is best, if it could be perpetual; but it cannot be. Whatever is, is liable to change, and misery, and destruction. Nikban — annihilation, nothingness — is the only permanent good, and that good has been attained by Gautama, the last deity."

"If there be no eternal being," replied Adoniram, "you cannot account for anything. Whence this world, and all that we see?"

"Fate," was the teacher's reply.

"Fate! The cause must always be equal to the effect." Adoniram raised the book-loaded study table slightly. "See, I raise this table. See, also, that ant under it: suppose I were invisible; would a wise man say the ant raised it? Now fate is not even an ant. Fate is a word, that is all. It is not an agent, not a thing. What is fate?"

"The fate of creatures is the influence which their good or bad deeds have on their future existence."

"But if influence be exerted, there must be an exerter. If there be a determination, there must be a determiner."

The teacher shook his head. "No. There is no determiner. There cannot be an eternal being."

"Consider this point," urged Adoniram. "It is a main point of true wisdom. Whenever there is an execution of a purpose, there must be an agent."

In short, Adoniram was saying, where there is an effect there must be a cause. But such a conception was not part of Burmese logic. Things happened. They did not have to have causes or effects. Fate was reasonless — at least, so it seemed the Oriental mind was trying to tell the Western mind.

The teacher said: "I must say that my mind is very decided and hard, and unless you tell me something more to the purpose, I shall never believe."

"Well, teacher," said Adoniram, "I wish you to believe, not for my profit, but for yours. I daily pray the true God to give you light, that you may believe. Whether you will ever believe in this world I do not know, but when you die I know you will believe what I now say. You will then appear before the God you now deny."

"I don't know that," politely rejoined the teacher.

Defeated, Adoniram turned to another matter, perhaps the very thing that had emboldened him to open the discussion. "I have heard," he said, "that one Burman many years ago embraced the Portuguese religion, and that he was your relation."

"He was a brother of my grandfather."

"At Ava, or here?"

"At Ava he became a Portuguese. Afterwards he went to a ship country with a ship priest, and returned to Ava."

"I have heard he was put to death for his religion."

"No, he was imprisoned and tortured by order of the Emperor. At last he escaped, fled to Rangoon, and afterwards to Bengal, where they say he died."

"Did any of his family join him?" asked Adoniram.

"None. All forsook him; and he wandered about, despised and rejected by all."

"Do you think that he was a decided Christian, and had got a new mind?"

"I think so," affirmed the teacher; "for when he was tortured, he held out."

"Did he ever talk with you about religion?"

"Yes," the teacher admitted.

"Why did you not listen to him?"

The question struck too close to home. The teacher replied non-committally, "I did not listen."

"Did you ever know any other Burman who changed his own for a foreign religion?"

"I have heard that there is one now in Rangoon, who became a Portuguese; but he keeps himself concealed, and I have never seen him."

Thus the conversation ended.

Adoniram was not discouraged. He had failed, but only because the idea of an inescapable linkage between cause and effect was foreign to the teacher. And, even more reason for hope, Burmans *had* become Christians. The teacher U Aung Min belonged to an important family. His very title "U" meant that he had position or prestige, or at least merited respect. His grandfather's brother must have moved in court circles in the capital. If he could be converted and hold to his faith under torture, others could. Burma had seemed a closed door. The door showed no signs of opening but Adoniram felt that it might, if he persevered. In this conversation he had pushed hard, and now he was sure he felt it give a little. Someday he would turn the key in the lock, the bolt would slide back, the door would swing wide on its hinges and he would open the way to the conversion of all Burma.

But the key was the language. He must study, and study, and study. He resolved to work harder than ever before.

The new year 1816 came and Adoniram continued to drive himself. Little Roger, who still flourished, was almost his only relaxation. The baby seemed to show an unusual desire to be with his parents. Sometimes when they went by his cradle without picking him up, "he would follow us with his eyes to the door, when they would fill with tears, and his countenance so expressive of grief, though perfectly silent, that it would force us back to him, which would cause his little heart to be as joyful as it had been before sorrowful."

He would lie for hours on a mat by his papa's study table, or by the side of his chair on the floor, if only he could see his face. When we had finished study or the business of the day, it was our exercise and amusement to carry him round the house or garden, and though we were alone, we felt not our solitude when he was with us.

The first baby of white parents born in Rangoon within living memory, Roger was the talk of the city as well as the pride of his parents. Once Nancy took him to the house of the viceroy's wife. The great lady was overcome with wonder. She placed him on the velvet cushion on which she usually sat herself and exclaimed admiringly over and over, "What a child! How white!" She played with the child so long that Nancy, thinking she was overstaying her welcome, rose to leave. But the woman insisted that she remain until the viceroy could see him.

When the viceroy came in, she showed him the child, saying, "Look, my lord, see what a child! Look at his feet! Look at his hands!" Even the ferocious Mya-day-men, stalking about with his long fierce spear, was impressed; he smiled at the baby Roger and admired his plump pink arms and legs before stalking out.

For six months Roger waxed fat and healthy. Then, in early March of 1816, Nancy began to notice that he was feverish and perspired heavily at night. Like any mother she was alarmed, but her fears quieted when she saw that his appetite continued good in the daytime and he seemed quite well. He even kept on gaining weight. She finally concluded that the baby had some childish ailment which would end when he cut his teeth.

Soon she almost forgot her worries about Roger in her concern for Adoniram. All at once he was attacked by severe headaches. His eyes hurt, and he became so weak that he could hardly stand. Reading, writing, or making any kind of effort caused such unbearable pain that he had to stop working. In a mood of depression he decided his missionary career was closing, and in the few moments when he felt well began to assemble his grammar and write a tract in Burmese to help his successor carry on without him.

So things went until the beginning of May — Adoniram sick and miserable most of the time, little Roger well enough during the day but feverish and sweating at night. Then one morning when Nancy lifted Roger from his cradle he was taken with a paroxysm of coughing which lasted half an hour. Within an hour or so he had developed a high fever. Both Nancy and Adoniram were alarmed. But when the fever abated the next day, they decided the attack had passed.

They were mistaken. The following morning, a Thursday, the cough and fever returned, worse than before. Something in his throat seemed to be choking him. His heavy breathing could be heard all over the house.

In all Rangoon the only person who knew anything about medicine was a Portuguese priest. They sent for him at once, but all he could give the baby was "a little rhubarb and gascoign powder," neither of which relieved the cough or the difficulty in breathing.

All through the night and the next day Roger continued the same while Nancy sat up, anguish in her heart, holding him. But the second night, about two in the morning, exhaustion overcame her and Adoniram, sick as he was, took the baby. "The little creature drank his milk with much eagerness (he was weaned) and Mr. Judson thought he was refreshed and would go to sleep. He laid him in his cradle — "he slept with ease for half an hour, when his breath stopped without a struggle, and he was gone!"

In that climate funerals could not be delayed. On the far side of the garden a circle of mango trees surrounded a little bamboo hut where Nancy was in the habit of writing letters home. Within the enclosure of trees a grave was dug beside the hut that very day, the fourth of May, and there, in the afternoon, Roger was buried while Adoniram and Nancy numbly watched in the company of forty or fifty Burmese and Portuguese acquaintances who tried to console them.

His death and interment occurred almost before they could feel grief. But in the next few days, as they put away the little evidences of his short life — the cradle, his clothing, the few toys — until the only tangible reminders were his absence and the fresh grave in the mango circle, their hearts began to bleed.

For more than a week they secluded themselves with their sorrow. Then the viceroy's wife paid them a visit of condolence accompanied by her whole retinue, numbering some two hundred people. She had heard the news only that day.

"Why did you not send me word, that I might have come to his funeral?" she exclaimed, smiting her breast.

Nancy explained that in her distress she never thought of it. The viceroy's wife comforted them as well as she could. She told them not to weep, and begged Adoniram not to let Roger's death affect his already poor health. Somehow her concern had its effect and began to restore them a little, enough so that Nancy could offer her "tea, sweetmeats and cakes, with which she appeared much pleased."

But her thoughtfulness did not stop there. A few days later she invited them to accompany her on a ride into the country, both for their health and, as she expressed it, that their minds might "become cool."

Nothing could have helped more to take their minds off their troubles than the outing the viceroy's wife provided.

For conveyance she sent them an elephant. When they had climbed into the magnificently decorated houselike howdah strapped on top of the elephant's back, the driver guided the huge beast to where they were to meet the viceroy's wife.

The party that set out on the ramble must have looked like a circus parade lost in the jungle. In front went the guard — "thirty men with guns and spears and red caps on their heads, which partly covered their shoulders." Two elephants followed, side by side. In the howdah of one rode Nancy and Adoniram. The howdah of the larger elephant was gilt. In this rode the viceroy's wife, "a tall, genteel female richly dressed in red and white silk."

Behind them followed three or four more elephants, carrying the viceroy's son and some of the higher government officials. And behind the elephants trailed the rest of the procession, which consisted of two or three hundred male and female retainers.

This was the party which proceeded on a three or four mile ramble through the dense jungle. "Sometimes the small trees were so near together, that our way was impassable, but by the elephant's breaking them down, which he did with the greatest ease at the word of the driver."

The route had been planned so that it ended in a garden of the viceroy's, a wildly beautiful spot full of luxuriant fruit trees of all kinds and varieties, growing untended as in nature. Here, in the shade of a huge banyan, mats were laid by the attendants and the hostess and her guests seated themselves.

Nothing [wrote Nancy] could exceed the endeavors of the Viceroy's wife to make our excursion agreeable — she gathered fruit and pared it; culled flowers and knotted them, and presented them with her own hands, which was a mark of her condescension. At dinner, she had her table spread by ours, nor did she refuse to partake of whatever we presented her.

We returned in the evening, fatigued with riding on the elephant, delighted with the view of the country and the hospitality of the Burmans, and dejected and depressed with their superstition and idolatry — their darkness and ignorance of the true God.

The ride *had* made them forget their grief for a while. But when they had returned to the mission house, and the elephant had departed, Nancy's glance fell on Roger's fresh grave in the circle of mango trees and she began to weep again bitterly.

Our hearts [she reflected, with a touch of resentment] were bound up in this child; we felt he was our earthly all, our only source of innocent recreation in this heathen land. But God saw it was necessary to remind us of our error, and to strip us of our only little all. O may it not be vain that he has done it. May we so improve it, that he will stay his hand and say, 'It is enough.' "

And, weeks later . . .

. . . When for a moment we realize what we once possessed . . . the wound opens and bleeds afresh. Yet we would still say, "Thy will be done."

CHAPTER VI

# Time Must Bring a Harvest

## [ *1816–1817* ]

ABOUT a month after Roger's death a sea captain named Kidd, "a pious man," came to live with the Judsons in the mission house. By this time Adoniram was suffering such pains in head and eyes that he could not even stand the sound of Nancy reading to him.

Kidd suggested that Adoniram try a voyage to Calcutta with him. Adoniram was on the point of accepting when letters came with the news that the Houghs were in Calcutta and about to leave for Rangoon. A printing press and types donated by the Serampore missionaries had already been shipped. He decided to wait.

The captain was in the habit of riding a horse for exercise, and persuaded Adoniram to try it. Although "this exercise was at first painful," Adoniram persisted and soon found he was growing better. After a while he bought a horse for himself and rode every morning before sunrise.

The summer passed. Nancy, perhaps partly to forget Roger by her activity, started a small school for little girls, and began to write a simple catechism in Burmese. The press and types arrived, but the Houghs were inexplicably delayed. Adoniram thought it would "probably be impossible to keep the press long in Rangoon. It will be ordered up to Java, as soon as the news of such a curiosity reaches the king's ears." If so, he conjectured hopefully, the press might be the means of letting the missionaries persuade the king to open all Burma to the propagation of the Gospel.

The Houghs with their two children did not arrive until the middle of October, 1816. They had left Calcutta late in June, but the ship proved to be unseaworthy and both captain and pilot drunkards who anchored opposite every tavern along the Hooghly and usually had to be carried back to the ship. After a few days of this, the alarmed Houghs returned to Calcutta to look for another ship. September was well along before they found one and made a fast, uneventful passage to Rangoon. But the misadventure had cost three months.

The Houghs immediately settled down in the mission house. To avoid the possibility of disputes each family had a certain number of the six rooms allotted to it for its own use. After the tedious work of passing the Houghs' possessions through customs, Adoniram and Hough sat down together and drew up a set of rules to govern their conduct and their relations with the mission and with each other. The Serampore missionaries had learned by painful experience the necessity of such rules, placed in writing and signed. Sooner or later missionaries were offered temporary appointments, usually by the government, which were often desirable for the good of the mission. These appointments were usually well paid; but they took the missionary from his regular duties. Where should the money go in such a case? Unless everything was understood and agreed to in advance, a good deal of heartburn could arise out of such a situation.

Therefore Adoniram and Hough agreed "to engage in no secular business, for the purpose of individual emolument; and not at all, unless, in the opinion of the brethren, the great object of the mission can be best promoted thereby." Any compensation or gifts of property were to be placed in the mission fund, "provided, that nothing in this article be construed to affect our private right to inheritances, or personal favours, not made in compensation of service."

All members of the mission family were to have an equal claim on the mission fund for support, "the claims of widows and orphans not to be, in the least, affected by the death of the head of their family." Appropriations were to be made by a majority vote of the missionaries involved in the compact.

After this agreement, the missionaries buckled down to work. A building was erected to house the press, and Hough studied the manuscript of Adoniram's Burmese grammar in order to learn enough about the language to begin printing. Adoniram continued his translation of Matthew during the day, and in the evenings met with Burmese men. Nancy continued with her school for Burmese girls, its numbers now swollen to twenty or thirty, and used the opportunities it gave to tell their mothers about Christianity. She also undertook a translation of the Old Testament book of Jonah, not because she considered it more important than other parts of the Bible, but because it was "easier to translate." Mrs. Hough took care of the children and applied herself to learning how to manage a Burmese household.

It was not necessary to know much about Burmese to begin printing, and Hough was ready within a few months. All he had to do was match the odd-looking strings of circles Adoniram had written with the appropriate circles in his fonts of Burmese type. For manuscript, he had the tract Adoniram had completed that summer.

In seven printed pages the tract attempted to outline what Christianity was and why the missionaries were preaching it. It began with the idea — startling to Burmans, as Adoniram knew — that: "There is one Being who exists eternally; who is exempt from sickness, old age, and death; who was, and is, and will be, without beginning, and without end. Besides this, the true God, there is no other God."

In a hundred words or so, the tract went on to tell the story of the creation, and of Adam and Eve and their transgression — on account of which they became subject to sickness and death, "and they became deserving of suffering, in . . . the dreadful punishment of hell." But after about four thousand years, God, moved with compassion, sent to earth Jesus, and the tract summarized His message. The true religion later spread into the East, and now to Burma a teacher of religion from America had arrived to proclaim the glad news. In a few hundred years, added Adoniram optimistically, "the religion of Christ will pervade the whole world; all quarrels and wars will cease, and all the tribes of men will be like a band of mutually loving brothers."

After defining a disciple of Christ as one who is inwardly reborn, the tract succinctly attacked the doctrine that one could achieve heaven merely by performing good works, for: "The unrenewed man, influenced by pride, hates the humbling religion of Jesus Christ.

When seized with alarm, he endeavors to perform meritorious deeds in order to make atonement for his sins, and obtain salvation. The renewed man, knowing surely that man, having sinned against God, and contracted great guilt, can not perform meritorious deeds, firmly fixes in his mind that it is on account of the God-man, Jesus Christ alone, that sin can be expiated, and the happiness of heaven obtained; and therefore, through supreme love to Jesus Christ, and a desire to do his will, endeavors to avoid evil deeds, and to perform good deeds only, according to the divine commands."

The last part of the tract consisted of the Commandments, and of these there were twenty-five instead of the familiar ten, for Adoniram wanted to include all the principal rules of conduct in the New Testament, including the one which distinguished Baptists from members of other denominations: "On becoming a disciple of Jesus Christ, receive baptism in water."

Such was the message. But Adoniram added a little more to explain his own position in Burma.

The teacher who composed this writing, seeing the great evil which is coming on the Burmans, left his own country from compassion, and from an immense distance has arrived, by ship, to this, the country of Burmah. He desires neither fame nor riches. Offering and gifts he seeks not. The disciples of Christ in his own country, moved with compassion for the Burmans, make offering sufficient for his use. He has no other motive but this: Being a disciple of Christ, and therefore seeking the good of others as his own, he has come, and is laboring that the Burmans may be saved from the dreadful punishment of hell, and enjoy the happiness of heaven.

In the year of Christ, 1816; in the Burman year, 1178; in the 967th day of the lord of the Saddan elephant, and master of the Sakyah weapon; and in the 33rd year of his reign; in the division Pashoo; on Tuesday, the 12th day of the wane of the moon Wahgoung, after the double beat, this writing, entitled *The Way to Heaven*, was finished. *May the reader obtain light. Amen.*

By early 1817 Hough had set the tract in type and printed a thousand copies. When he finished, he went to work on Nancy's catechism and after that on Adoniram's translation of Matthew.

But he could print much faster than Adoniram could write, and had plenty of time left over to see what went on around him in the mission and in the city. Though he printed faithfully, he was beginning to doubt whether either preaching or printing by themselves could move the hearts of the Burmans. Their laws, morals, customs, and the religion of the people, seemed too fixed to be changed. He wondered whether the Burmese could even understand Western ideas, so great were the differences in the two civilizations.

Along with the rest of the mission household he had attended the funeral of a Burman priest — a cremation attended with "loud shoutings, clapping of hands, the sound of drums, of tinkling and wind instruments, and a most disgusting exhibition of female dancing, but not weeping or wailing."

He had seen executions; in one case the disemboweling alive of some thieves who had been caught tunneling under a pagoda for the treasures beneath, in another the shooting of several criminals. He had seen the executioners shoot at one of these criminals four times and miss every time. "At every shot there was a loud peal of laughter from the surrounding spectators."

Everyone knew bribery was responsible for the misses. The man was the elder of two brothers who had asked pardon if they should be missed four times. The younger was killled by the second shot, the elder pardoned according to the agreement. For other crimes he had gone through the same experience twice before, and on each of those earlier occasions he had been missed six times successively. "He is now considered to be a wonderful man," wrote Hough in disgust, "and that a bullet cannot prove him mortal. . . . He is now raised to a *high* rank among the governor's attendants."

It was plain to Hough that "the Burmans are subtle, thievish, mercenary, addicted to robbery and fraud; truth and honesty are not known among them as virtues." Although they had "every motive, according to their religion, to practice good works, yet no people can be worse."

He had to admit that all the men could read, and that they constantly asked for "our holy books." But those "with whom brother Judson has conversed, since I have been here, appear inaccessible to truth. They sit unaffected, and go away unimpressed with what they have heard. They are unconvinced by arguments, and un-

moved by love; and the conversion of a Burman, or even the excitement of a thought toward the truth, must and will be a sovereign
act of Divine power."

Hough was too pessimistic. The first "sovereign act of Divine
power" occurred in the last month of the Burman year — "Tabaung"
to the Burmese, March to the Americans.

This month marked the climax of the nation's largest religious
festival. Preliminary celebrations of it began as early as January
and from then on the missionaries always found their ears "almost
stunned with the noise and confusion." Pilgrims from all over Burma
came by tens of thousands to worship day and night at the gold
Shwe Dagon pagoda with its eight precious hairs of the great
Gautama, the great Buddha himself, enshrined in sealed vaults far below its foundations. When they were not worshiping, the people were
watching the great processions led by the viceroy, and enjoying
"boxing, dancing, singing, theatrical exhibitions and fire-works."

It was about the time the festival began that Hough finished the
printing of Adoniram's tract. During the next few months copies
trickled, a few at a time, out of the mission house, carried by the
Burmans who had asked for the missionaries' "holy books." To
Hough, they may have seemed unaffected and unimpressed — as
most, probably, were — but they must have read the tracts, and
some of them must have passed their copies along to friends.

At any rate, one day in March, when the festival was at its height,
a Burman, followed by a servant, came up the steps of the mission
house veranda where Adoniram was studying with his teacher and
sat down beside him. He was well dressed, obviously a man of
considerable respectability. His name was Maung Yah.

Adoniram asked the question with which he always opened conversations with strange Burmans — where he came from. The man
gave a rather vague reply, and Adoniram began to think he was
a government official come "to enforce a trifling request, which,
in the morning, we had declined."

He was soon undeceived, however; for, after a few obligatory
politenesses, the man asked bluntly: "How long will it take me
to learn the religion of Jesus?"

Concealing his astonishment, Adoniram replied, "Such a question cannot be answered. If God gives light and wisdom, the religion of Jesus is soon learned. Without God, a man may study all his life long and make no progress. But how," he continued curiously, "came you to know anything of Jesus? Have you been here before?"

"No."

"Have you seen any writings concerning Jesus?"

"He is the Son of God," said the man, "who, pitying human creatures, came into this world and suffered death in their stead."

"Who is God?"

"He is a Being without beginning or end, Who is not subject to old age or death, but always is."

Instantly Adoniram recognized the wording of his own tract. An indescribable mixture of awe and exultation flooded over him. This was the first acknowledgment of the existence of an eternal God he had ever heard from the lips of a Burman. Without words he handed the man a copy of the tract and of Nancy's catechism. The man recognized both, and, leafing through them, read aloud here and there, remarking to his servant occasionally, "This is the true God. This is the right way."

Scenting a convert, Adoniram tried to tell the man more about Christianity, but he hardly listened. Unlike the other Burmans Adoniram had met, he had no interest in Adoniram's clothing or the peculiar customs and manners of the English. All he wanted was "more of this sort of writing."

Adoniram told him two or three times that he had finished no other book, but if the man could wait a few months he could give him a larger one which he was busy every day translating.

"But have you not a little of that book done, which you will graciously give me now?" the man insisted.

Finally Adoniram, thinking "that God's time was better than man's," folded and gave him the first two printed half-sheets, which contained the first five chapters on Matthew.

The man accepted them, immediately rose, nodded noncommittally to Adoniram's "Come again," and departed, followed by his servant.

Later that month Adoniram met one of his acquaintances "who

says, that he reads our books all the day, and shows them to all who call upon him." But nevertheless he never returned to the mission house and never asked for any more of Adoniram's writing.

In a few weeks Adoniram's first elation faded. But hope remained. The seed broadcast in the form of tracts and catechisms had sprouted at least once. Time must surely bring a harvest.

## CHAPTER VII

# Alarms and Excursions

## [ *1817–1818* ]

ADONIRAM finished his translation of Matthew in late May, 1817, and, while Hough printed it, began work on a Burmese dictionary. With the dictionary and the grammar he had already prepared, future missionaries should be able to learn the language and begin preaching without losing as much time as he himself had been forced to spend.

At best, Burmese was almost impossibly difficult for a Westerner. Although Hough could set it in type he sometimes wondered despairingly whether he would ever understand it, and all but decided it was useless for a man over thirty years old even to make the attempt. Once he suggested that the only way to make missionaries to Burma was to send teen-age boys over from New England and teach them the language while their minds still had the flexibility of youth.

Both men knew, of course, that Hough's idea was impracticable. More missionaries would arrive, and they would be grown men and women. Dynamic Rice, with his amazing persuasive powers, would be coming soon and certainly bring others with him. Adoniram could not know that, this very month, Rice had asked the mission board when it would let him go to Burma and that the board had told him his duty lay among American congregations for some time yet, in promoting foreign missions.

As a matter of fact, Rice was never to join the Burman mission or any other. But the same meeting of the board which had told Rice to stay home had accepted two young candidates for the mission, James Colman and Edward Wheelock, both of Boston. And Adoniram's father made a decision of his own. Adoniram's baptism four years earlier had forced him to reconsider his own position. Eventually that uncompromisingly honest old man came to the same conclusion his son had reached. At the age of sixty-seven, he resigned his pastorate in Plymouth and was baptized on the last day of August, 1817, by Dr. Baldwin in the Second Baptist Church of Boston, together with his wife and his daughter Abigail.

But news of these events could scarcely reach remote Rangoon in less than a year. Meanwhile Adoniram worked on the dictionary, Hough printed and studied the language, and Adoniram and Nancy talked about the Gospel and gave out tracts, catechisms and copies of the Matthew to curious inquirers.

But they made no converts. Several times that summer, Adoniram felt sure one or another of the Burmese men was beginning to take a serious view of Christianity; but every time he was disappointed.

Nancy had the same experience with the fifteen or twenty women with whom she met every Sunday. They would seem to accept what she told them but would not give up Buddhism. Some told her frankly they preferred spending eternity in hell with their families and ancestors to spending it in heaven by themselves.

Hough doubted whether any of the mission would live to see a Burman baptized. Some of his discouragement may have been due to his situation. He was in a distinctly subordinate position in the mission, partly because his usefulness was confined to the mechanical job of printing what Adoniram wrote, partly because Adoniram and Nancy were in the habit of doing what they thought right without even considering that anyone else might have another opinion. And Hough, recognizing their superior experience and command of the language, would have been diffident about expressing an opposing view. His wife was constantly occupied with the two children, and both the Houghs must have worried about the children's health in the dirt and heat of the tropics.

Adoniram was more dissatisfied than discouraged. He felt that the mission house was too isolated from the rest of Rangoon. He wished he could erect a small building — a "zayat," the Burmans would call it — on one of the busy main streets of the city where he could preach openly and attract more inquirers; but the expense put this out of the question for the present. The mission was already overdrawn on the account it kept with Serampore. More important, it was plain that the Burmans were still suspicious of the foreigner's religion and fearful of what might happen to them if they showed too much interest. Often Adoniram would sit on the verandah of the mission house animatedly discussing the Gospel with two or three Burmans who were mutual friends, only to see them fall silent and presently depart when a stranger appeared. Once his teacher was publicly threatened for helping a foreigner make subversive religious books. This threat came to nothing: the teacher replied that he merely taught the foreigner the language and had no concern with the foreigner's publications. He had strong connections in Ava, and in any case it was well known that his foreign pupil enjoyed the favor of the viceroy and the viceroy's wife, who continued to take Adoniram and Nancy on elephant rides.

Through the summer Adoniram considered plans for gaining more acceptance. He began to think of going to Ava and introducing the matter gradually and gently to the knowledge of the emperor:

> I am fully persuaded that he has never yet got the idea that an attempt is making to introduce a new religion among his slaves. How the idea will strike him it is impossible to foresee. He may be enraged, and order off the heads of all concerned. The urbanity, however, with which he treats all foreigners, and his known hatred of the present order of Boodhist priests, render such a supposition improbable. And if he should only be indifferent, should discover no hostility, especially if he should treat the missionaries with complacency, it would be a great point gained. No local government would dare to persecute the espousers of a new religion if it was known that they had friends at court.

The more Adoniram toyed with the thought, the better he liked it. Late in the year, with the dictionary nearly finished, he had all but decided to petition the viceroy for permission to go to Ava, when another possibility presented itself.

He had heard that in Chittagong there were a few Christian natives who had been converted by a Baptist mission which had existed there for a short time. Although Chittagong was in Bengal and under East India Company control, these converts belonged to the people known as "Mugs," Burmese-speaking natives of Arakan, a neighboring coastal province which had been conquered in 1784 by the same Burmese emperor Adoniram proposed to visit. To all intents and purposes these Baptist Mugs were Burmese, and Adoniram had long wished he had a few of them in Rangoon. Their mere presence would refute the stubbornly held Burman notion that Christianity was purely a white man's religion.

Chittagong was just a ten or twelve days' sail north of Rangoon, but ordinarily ships touched there only on their way to somewhere else. Opportunity for direct passage from Rangoon to Chittagong and speedy return in the same vessel almost never occurred. But in December Adoniram learned that the ship *Two Brothers* was about to make just such a round trip.

Adoniram decided he would never have a better opportunity to find one or two of the Arakanese Baptists and bring them back with him. He had worked so hard on the dictionary that he was showing signs of exhaustion. The voyage would refresh his health. Nancy and the Houghs could easily care for the mission during the few months he would be away. He boarded the *Two Brothers* on the twenty-fourth of December. Christmas Day she weighed anchor and began to drop down the river.

The voyage that followed was one he never forgot. No sooner was *Two Brothers* out of the river than Adoniram suffered a return of his old eye and head ailment and had to take to his bunk. As soon as the ship rounded Pagoda Point and headed northward for Chittagong, she was struck by headwinds in which she proved unmanageable. It took a whole month of beating back and forth in the dangerous waters to reach the coast of Arakan, and at that rate it would have taken months longer to reach Chittagong. The captain gave up, reversed his course to sail south for a few days, and finally headed westward across the Bay of Bengal for Madras, while Adoniram stood at the rail and bitterly "saw the summits of the mountains of Arracan [Arakan], the last indexes of my country, sinking in the horizon, and the ship stretching away to a distant part of India, which I had no wish to visit and where I had no object to obtain."

Madras proved as unattainable as Chittagong. *Two Brothers* made a quick passage across the Bay of Bengal, but on the Coromandel Coast ran into a combination of headwinds and offshore currents that kept her beating helplessly up and down, getting nowhere. The captain — incompetent, as Adoniram saw by now — optimistically decided he could make Masulipitam, north of Madras, in a few days. Once more wind and current kept him beating about the Bay until food and water gave out completely.

Adoniram came down with fever. Starving, thirsty and filthy — he had taken clothing for a two-week voyage and by now they had been at sea two months — he lay half dead in his bunk. Occasionally the ship met a native vessel and begged a few buckets of water and a bag of mouldy broken rice. Adoniram could not eat the rice and the water was not enough. It had to be rationed by spoonfuls and in his flaming fever he wanted gallons.

It was another month — twelve weeks in all from the time *Two Brothers* left Rangoon — before the ship dropped anchor in the mud a few miles off the beach of Masulipitam. When the captain asked Adoniram whether he would like to be taken ashore, he was so stuporous that the idea of land seemed only "a kind of dreamy illusion." Finally, however, he managed to pencil a note to "any English resident of Masulipitam" asking for a place to die on dry land.

Later one of the crew came below with word that a boat was on its way toward shore. Adoniram crawled feebly to the porthole and dragged himself up until he could see the boat, and in it the red coats of British soldiers and the white coats of Englishmen. Then he collapsed on the floor, tears streaming down his face. He thought he had never seen anything so like the faces of angels as the shocked faces of the Englishmen who entered his cabin to behold a haggard, dirty, unshaved scarecrow, so weak he had to be carried to shore.

He recovered his strength quickly in the house of one of the officers, who supplied him with clothing, food, and even a nurse; but for some time his eyes remained very weak. Meanwhile he learned that *Two Brothers* would unload her cargo at Masulipitam and would not sail for Rangoon for several months. His only chance was to go by land to Madras, some three hundred miles, and look for a ship there. He hired a palanquin and bearers and reached Madras on the eighth of April, only to find that no ship had sailed for Rangoon that year and probably none would for some months.

The next three months he stayed part of the time with his friends the Lovelesses, part with the Reverend Mr. Thomason of the East India Company, while he haunted the beach for a ship. It was late in July before he found one. This time, fortunately, the voyage was uneventful, and he heaved a sigh of relief when the vessel dropped anchor in the mouth of the Rangoon River on the second of August. He had been away more than seven months; he had never reached Chittagong; his quest had been an utter failure; but at least he was almost in sight of home.

But when the pilot who was to guide the ship up the river to Rangoon came aboard the next morning, he brought news that made Adoniram turn pale.

The mission had been broken up, said the pilot. The Houghs and Nancy had taken passage for Bengal. But at the last moment Nancy had refused to leave. She was waiting in the mission house for Adoniram. The Houghs were there too, but not through any wish of their own. Their ship had been detained as unfit for sea, and they were merely staying on until it should be ready to sail.

All that day Adoniram fretted as the ship slowly worked her way up the river under the pilot's guidance. When he saw the glowing golden spire of the Shwe Dagon slowly soar up from the green jungle horizon, he felt more apprehension than relief. His mind was filled with a single troubling thought: *What had happened to the mission?*

Nancy and Hough met him at the rickety wharf — Nancy resplendent in the colorful Burmese costume she affected, and fairly glowing with happy relief. In the intervals between the tedious formalities of passing his belongings through the customs they began to tell him what had happened; and before he went to bed in the mission house that night he had the whole story.

For a few weeks after Adoniram's departure things had gone on much as usual in the mission. The viceroy's wife had continued to invite the missionaries to go elephant riding at intervals, and had accepted from Nancy a copy of the tract, the catechism and the Matthew. Occasionally she had even permitted Nancy to talk to her "privately on the subject of religion." Nancy could not see that her efforts produced any effect, but all these evidences of favor from such a high quarter created a comfortable sense of serenity within the mission.

To add to the general air of good feeling, the Burman who had been Adoniram's first serious inquirer returned. This was the man who had wanted nothing but more of Adoniram's religious books. The man had not revisited the mission, he told Nancy, because he had been appointed governor of a cluster of villages on the Syriam River in the Pegu country east of Rangoon.

When Nancy asked him if he had become a Christian yet, he replied, "Not yet, but I am thinking and reading in order to become one. But I cannot yet destroy my old mind. When I see a handsome waistcloth or turban I still desire it. Tell the great teacher when he returns that I wish to see him, though I am not yet a disciple of Christ."

Nancy gave him the rest of the Matthew and distributed tracts and catechisms to his retinue. He told Nancy that he governed about a thousand houses. If Adoniram would honor his villages with a visit, he would call the people together to hear Adoniram preach.

Not all that happened was good, of course. Adoniram had been gone scarcely a month when Nancy heard that the leader of the Christian Mugs at Chittagong, the teacher of the others, had murdered the missionary de Bruyn. If the murderer was typical of the other "converts" there, they seemed not likely to prove much of an addition to the mission in Rangoon!

It was in March, however, about the time they were expecting Adoniram's return, that the mission's real troubles began. First, the viceroy and his friendly wife were ordered back to Ava and replaced by a man they did not know. He came without his wife, so Nancy had no way to gain a friendly ear in his court.

A little later a native boat arrived from Chittagong with word that neither Adoniram nor the *Two Brothers* had ever arrived there. About the same time Nancy received letters from friends in Bengal with word that the ship had not been reported anywhere. It was common knowledge that contrary winds in the Bay of Bengal could force ships to take all kinds of strange courses, but the news was dismaying just the same. Nancy stoutly refused to admit that Adoniram might have been lost at sea, but when her spirits were low — and they were, more and more, as the weeks passed — she could not suppress her fears.

In a few days another blow fell. An order was delivered to Hough, "couched in the most menacing language, to appear immediately at the court-house, to give an account of himself." No one in the mission had ever received an order anything like this, and it caused immediate consternation. Hough obeyed promptly, followed — at a safe distance — by some of the servants. They heard several of the government minor officials say that by royal command, directly from Ava, all foreign teachers were to be banished from Burma.

That day the officials merely made Hough give security for his appearance next morning, with the chilling threat that if he did not tell them everything about what he was doing in Burma "they would write with his heart's blood."

Adoniram's absence was never more regretted than that night. Hough could not appeal to the viceroy because he did not know the language. As a woman, Nancy could not appear at the viceroy's court. Nancy and the Houghs racked their brains half the night for some expedient, without success, before finally retiring for a few restless hours.

Hough spent the next two days, a Friday and a Saturday, at the courthouse answering thousands of questions concerning his activities in Rangoon, including how many suits of clothing he had and what were the names of his parents. While he fidgeted — he was denied food and water, and not even permitted to leave the room to relieve himself — all his answers were written down with grave formality.

By the second night both Nancy and Hough were convinced there was a hidden purpose under the questioning. From what they knew of Burma, it was not hard to guess: Hough's inquisitors were merely harassing him in order to extract a large bribe, because they felt sure that in Adoniram's absence the missionaries would not be able to take their case before the viceroy personally. Nancy had seen the viceroy perform his duties, and she knew that only important cases were brought to his attention — and, even those, privately. She felt certain that the viceroy had no idea what was being done to Hough.

Now they knew the purpose of the rapacious officials. But how could they thwart them? Sunday morning brought the answer. That morning, just as another summons arrived from the courthouse, Nancy's teacher came to the house. Nancy, Hough and the teacher took counsel together and presently concocted a petition, which the teacher wrote down, respectfully "stating the grievances to which Mr. Hough had been subject, and the present order for his appearing, in public, on our *sacred day* — and requesting that it might be the pleasure of his highness that those molestations should cease."

Nancy and Hough took the petition to the government building, where the viceroy was holding audience. They had no sooner entered the outer court of the building than the viceroy, seated in the midst of his officers, caught sight of them. Nancy held up the petition. The governor called them in and had a secretary read the petition.

As he listened, the viceroy's face darkened with anger. At the end he turned to the official who had been most unpleasant to Hough, who happened to be sitting almost next to him, and asked coldly, "Why has the examination of this foreign teacher been prolonged in this way?"

The viceroy's voice was known as "the voice which issues life or death." At the moment, it sounded more like death. Blanching, the official began a lame explanation which the viceroy interrupted with a command — obeyed with alacrity — that Hough be molested no more, and never be called on his sacred day.

Later, they learned the reason for the original order. A royal decree had been issued for the banishment of all the Portuguese priests in Burma. There were only a few — three, thought Nancy — in Rangoon, but "to ascertain who they were, the viceroy had issued an order, that all the foreign priests should be summoned to the courthouse, not intending that any but the Portuguese should undergo an examination, farther than to ascertain that they were not Portuguese." In fact, the viceroy had no intention of carrying out the royal decree at all if he could avoid it, but the opportunity his order offered his subordinates to mulct the mission was too good to miss; and, like almost all Burmese officials in similar situations, they took advantage of it.

Although Hough had been vindicated this time the incident had a bad effect because it made plain to all Rangoon that white foreigners enjoyed a less privileged position than had been supposed. From then on, very few Burmans came to the mission. Even the women were afraid, and attendance at Nancy's Sunday "female meetings" suddenly dropped from more than thirty to a mere dozen. Everyone was uneasy, especially Hough, who as the only man felt only too keenly both his responsibilities and his inability to meet them.

At this moment, cholera broke out. There had never been an epidemic in Burma. Until the preceding year it had never been seen outside India, where it had smoldered in certain areas since time immemorial. Suddenly it blazed up in Rangoon and spread like one of the terrible conflagrations that periodically devastated the city from one end to the other. The inhabitants died like flies. No age was immune, no rank, no locality. Death drums boomed dully all day long from every quarter. There was something peculiarly terrifying in the tigerish way the sickness pounced on its victims. A man — or a woman, or a child — might rise hale and hearty in the morning, be seized by the most violent diarrhea and cramps at noon, collapse and literally shrivel during the afternoon, and be dead by night. It seemed to be utterly capricious in its choice of victims. It could select one person in a house, or all, or arbitrarily skip over a whole street.

Hysterical panic gripped the whole population. The people had never seen the disease before, could not understand it and had no idea of how to deal with it. They could only suppose "that some evil spirits had entered the city, and were continually traversing the streets, and from pure maliciousness, destroying the inhabitants."

If so, there was one way of dealing with malicious spirits: they could be frightened away by a tremendous noise. Therefore, after due announcement, signal cannons were fired off one day at the courthouse. Immediately every Burman in Rangoon fell to beating on his house with clubs or any kind of noisemaker available. No one failed. The people had been warned that the evil spirits would enter the house of those who did not make enough noise. For three successive nights the ear-splitting uproar continued, but the spirits were deaf and refused to part.

The cholera had begun in the middle of the hottest season of the year. It was not to subside until the rains came, months later.

As if Adoniram's absence, official disfavor and cholera were not enough for the harried occupants of the mission to bear, an alarming rumor began to circulate just as the epidemic was at its worst: that the English would soon invade Burma.

In sober fact, the rumor was not hard to believe. Relations between the English and Burmese governments had been uneasy for years. When the emperor had overrun the border provinces with fire and sword a generation ago, thousands of dispossessed people had fled in huge masses to the adjoining British areas. The emperor considered that these people belonged to him. His troops were constantly crossing into British territory to force them back into Burma, plundering and burning as they went. Inevitably they clashed with the British outposts from time to time. The British, their hands full in India, had so far taken a conciliatory attitude which the Burmese mistook for cowardly weakness, although as a matter of fact the English were slowly coming to feel they would eventually have to deal with the Burmese annoyance once and for all. But the situation had existed for a generation without open war, and people had grown accustomed to it. The current rumor seemed to have some basis, however. For months no ships had arrived in Rangoon from any British port. The few foreign captains still in the city were suddenly beginning to make ready to leave.

This war scare was the last straw for Hough. Never sure of himself in this unfriendly place, doubtful almost from the first of the prospects of converting the Burmese, he now lost confidence completely. Adoniram was probably dead. Only Providence had kept cholera from the mission family up to now, but the epidemic still raged. If war came — the signs pointed to it, in his opinion — Rangoon would be the first battleground. He decided it was his duty to remove his wife and children to the safety of Bengal.

He urged Nancy to accompany them, but she refused — she hardly knew why. Certainly the mission seemed to be accomplishing little. Inquirers seldom came. Her little school for the women had dwindled almost to the vanishing point. Nevertheless she delayed. Suppose, she thought, Adoniram *were* alive and returned to Rangoon — perhaps sick, even dying — to find the mission house deserted? He would need her. And if he returned to Rangoon even in good health, and she were in Bengal, how would they ever find each other again? So in spite of Hough, she clung obstinately on until late June. By then only one foreign ship still lay in the river and it was nearly ready to leave. Then at last, thinking heavy-hearted in her room through the hot nights, while the death drums beat and the lizards pattered on the ceiling, she finally decided to go with the Houghs. If war came and Adoniram were still alive, he would not be able to enter Rangoon in any case until peace. But she did not believe there would really be a war; and war or no war, she would have hazarded the consequences — if she had only felt sure Adoniram were still alive.

She went aboard the ship with the Houghs early in July. She had taken passage for Adoniram's teacher, so that Adoniram could continue his studies if she found him in Bengal. But at the last moment the teacher changed his mind. His defection nearly made her give up the voyage herself. But her baggage was on board and her passage paid; she stayed with the ship as it weighed anchor and dropped down the river.

At the mouth of the river, just before putting out to sea, the captain found that the ship was so improperly loaded that it would be too dangerous to take her out into the Bay of Bengal. There was nothing to do but put in at the last anchorage in the river and spend a few weeks shifting cargo.

This was all the excuse Nancy needed. She arranged to have her baggage removed from the ship and she herself was back in the mission house, "to the great joy of all the Burmans left on our premises," only a little more than a week after she had left it. No matter what the Houghs did, she now intended to stay where she was, keep on with her studies, "and leave the event to God."

She appreciated the wisdom of her decision when *Two Brothers* unexpectedly put in at Rangoon. As soon as she heard of the ship's arrival Nancy hurried to the captain and learned that Adoniram had disembarked at Masulipitam and gone on to Madras by land. At least he is alive, she thought with joy.

In another ten days the Houghs returned. Their ship had turned out to be so badly fitted that the sailing would have to be delayed for several weeks. They had scarcely settled down in the mission house when the best of all news came: Adoniram's ship was at the mouth of the river. He was nearly home!

Nancy had to share the news with someone. She flew to her

writing table and added to one of those long letters she was almost perpetually in the process of writing to her father and mother:

How will you rejoice with me, my dear parents, when I tell you, that I have this moment heard that Mr. Judson has arrived at the mouth of the river! This joyful intelligence more than compensates for the months of dejection and distress which his long absence has occasioned. Now, I feel ashamed of my repinings, my want of confidence in God, and resignation to his will. I have foolishly thought, because my trials were protracted, they would never end; or rather, that they would terminate in some dreadful event which would destroy all hope of the final success of the mission. But now, I trust, our prospects will again brighten, and cause us to forget this night of affliction, or to remember it as having been the means of preparing us for the reception of that greatest of blessings — the conversion of some of the Burmans.

## CHAPTER VIII

# The First Convert

## [ *1818–1819* ]

WITH Adoniram's return, the mission's troubles seemed to fade away. The war scare died. The cholera epidemic slowly passed. Even the Portuguese priests — a number of whom had been sent down to Rangoon from Ava — were allowed to stay. This last was the result of the viceroy's personal mediation with the emperor, which he made more effective with large presents to his ruler.

The order of banishment still stood on the books, but Adoniram hoped it would be removed in time. He was not overly fond of the priests; but if Catholics could be banished, so could Baptists — "and banishment, as the Burmans tell us, is no small thing — being attended with confiscation of all property, and such various abuses, as would make us deem ourselves happy to escape with our lives."

In spite of Adoniram's return and the improved outlook for the mission, however, Hough remained firm in his determination to remove to Calcutta. As the weeks dragged on and the ship was still not ready for sea, Adoniram tried to persuade him to stay. But Hough had had enough of Burma. The only way he could make himself useful to the mission was as a printer, and he could print Adoniram's manuscripts just as well in Calcutta as in Rangoon, and with more peace of mind.

However, the Houghs were still living in the mission house in the middle of September when two new missionaries arrived, Edward M. Wheelock and James Colman, each with his wife. Adoniram and Hough met them at the dock. And to the delighted Burmans, who collected in a huge crowd to watch, the sight of *four* new foreigners — *two* of them *women!* — in addition to the four they already knew, was something to remember.

To Adoniram, now thirty, and even more to the still older Hough, the new missionaries must have seemed incredibly youthful. Both were in their early twenties; both frail, intense and visionary. Wheelock, in fact, was only twenty-two and his wife Eliza twenty. He had been eighteen when, in 1814, stirred by Adoniram's example, he had decided on a missionary career.

The mission house had only six living rooms and a hall which was used as a chapel and meeting place. It was badly overcrowded now by the eight adults and three children — the Houghs' two and Emily Van Someren — but everyone accepted the situation with good nature.

Adoniram helped the newcomers through the usual searching customs examination, which took the better part of a week, and continued their induction into Burmese life by introducing the two men to the viceroy. The viceroy was unusually affable to the new missionaries squatting shoeless on a mat opposite him in the government house. Noticing their discomfort as they tried to imitate the Burmese manner of sitting with crossed legs, he even said to Adoniram, "Let them sit comfortable."

Part of his affability may have been due to the present the missionaries had brought for him — a small chest of carpenter's tools which Wheelock and Colman had bought in Calcutta for the use of the mission. Nothing like it had ever been seen in Rangoon; and Adoniram, knowing the viceroy would never be satisfied until he owned it, had decided the mission had better give it to him. When the heavy chest was placed before him he even deigned to arise from his cushion, open it himself, and examine the tools one by one — which he admired so much that he even called in one of his own carpenters to see the tools that white men used. With the interview off to this good start, Adoniram now told him that the new teachers had brought their women and wished to take shelter beneath his glory. "Let them stay, let them stay," the viceroy agreed. "And let your wife bring their wives so that I may see them all."

In a few days the two young men secured teachers and buckled down to learn the language while their wives, under Nancy's tutelage, began learning how to manage a Burmese household. In the years Nancy had been in Rangoon she had learned how to reproduce several New England foods. She churned a rather inferior kind of butter from the poor Burmese milk, and had discovered that the sour fruit of the trees growing in the mission garden made good tarts and preserves. Flour was more of a problem. Along with sugar and tea it had to be ordered from Bengal, but Ava wheat was even better, when it could be procured. If neither was available, which was usually the case, Nancy had learned to use pounded rice mixed with plantains, a banana-like fruit. But for the most part, the mission diet was what it had been in 1814 — curried fowl, rice, and vegetables. Eliza Wheelock, perhaps privately a little shocked, but disposed to be charitable in the maturity of her twenty years, noted that "a European, favoured with health and a good appetite, could, I think, live almost entirely upon the productions of the country."

Unfortunately, good health was just what Wheelock and Colman lacked. They had no more than settled down to their studies when both began to cough blood and show the dreaded signs of tuberculosis. Within a few days they had to give up studying and take to their beds. It began to look ominously as if the newcomers were fated to accomplish no more than disrupting the work of the mission until they found their graves.

The Houghs finally departed for Calcutta the first of November, taking the press and types with them, and it became possible to reassign the living space in the mission house. The Colmans, the Wheelocks and the Judsons each could take two rooms, one for sleeping, one for study or parlor.

The house had been designed for only two families, and as a consequence the Wheelocks' two rooms, in the middle of the building, were unconnected with each other, a circumstance which Mrs. Wheelock did not neglect to point out in a letter to the wife of Dr. Baldwin of the Second Church in Boston, secretary of the mission board — although she carefully added, "But we do not feel a disposition to murmur. O no! These two rooms in Rangoon are far more preferable to us than the most convenient and elegant edifice in America."

Adoniram and Nancy had innocently believed the Wheelocks

lucky to be "in the coolest and driest part of the house"; but the fact was, Eliza Wheelock had begun to conceive a dislike for Adoniram and Nancy which was to grow more intense as time went on. Her idealized conceptions of danger and hardship had not been fulfilled, whereas the real danger, even the probability, that her husband would die of tuberculosis, was so menacing that she could not admit it to anyone, herself least, if with her twenty years she could even grasp it. The hardships, equally unexpected, were two-fold: first the dull, laborious routine of caring for Wheelock in such inconvenient quarters; second, and greater, acceptance of the fact that she was not considered a heroine but merely another worker in the mission, necessarily subordinate to the older and infinitely more experienced Adoniram and Nancy.

Within a few months Colman grew better. By the beginning of 1819 he had nearly recovered his health; but Wheelock was worse and grew more feeble and emaciated every day. Adoniram and Nancy told Mrs. Wheelock that they feared her husband's illness could have only one outcome. She refused to believe them; their warning merely angered her. She already resented what seemed to her their dictatorial way of running the mission, and she reacted by making demands for foods, comforts and services which could not be supplied in Rangoon, let alone the mission.

It could well have been true that Adoniram and Nancy ran things with a high hand. The story of the "formal and solemn reprimand" administered Adoniram by Dr. Spring in late 1811 was still circulating in New England, with the embellishment that Adoniram had changed from Congregationalist to Baptist in Calcutta for revenge; and this very spring Adoniram had written a letter home denying that any reprimand had ever been given him — a denial which he retracted many years later with the admission that he had hardly noticed the reprimand because of his intense desire to have the American Board send him abroad. As for Nancy, from childhood she had been famous for her persistence and ingenuity in getting her own way.

Two such determined people, comparing their nearly six years in Burma with the newcomers' few months, were probably often a good deal less than tactful in reaching decisions concerning the mission. Hough had felt something of the sort, and it may have played a part in his removal to Calcutta. Eliza Wheelock resented it, and rebelled. But the Colmans, man and wife, understood and accepted it.

The work of the mission had been nearly at a standstill while both Wheelock and Colman lay ill. Now as Colman recovered Adoniram felt free to go ahead with his plan for preaching in some place where he could attract more attention than in the secluded mission house.

He had thought of a zayat before. Now he decided to build one, even though the mission could hardly afford the two hundred dollars or so it would cost, partly because he found himself able to buy cheaply a piece of property behind the mission garden which fronted on "Pagoda Road," some thirty or forty rods distant.

Pagoda Road was the main thoroughfare from the city to the Shwe Dagon pagoda. It will be remembered that it was literally lined with smaller pagodas, their bells tinkling day and night in dissonant chorus; many people lived along the road, and numerous worshipers passed along it every day. On the Burmese Sabbath, which came four times every month — at the change, the quarters, and the full of the moon — thousands thronged along it on their way to the Shwe Dagon, where they knelt prayerfully for hours with lowered heads, holding flowers or lighted tapers between extended palms. At the annual festivals, the thousands swelled to tens of thousands.

There were many zayats along Pagoda Road, some small, some large with roof over roof. They were really shelters where travelers could rest, men gather to talk or listen, and Buddhist lay teachers teach. They served a different purpose from the pagodas, which were special places for the saffron-robed priests, who left them only to carry their begging bowls through the streets. The zayats were reserved for the laity. The priests came there to teach and preach only on special occasions.

Adoniram and Nancy spent all their free time for a month superintending their zayat's construction. By the beginning of April the wide porch in front and the steps leading up to it were the only parts not complete.

It was a small hutlike building not quite thirty feet long and twenty feet wide, and the front ten feet of the length consisted of the thatched bamboo porch where Adoniram planned to sit and exhort passers-by. The enclosed part was one room made of white-washed boards with a large glassless window in each wall where the men could study and public worship could be held. Behind was a sort of entryway opening into the mission garden, where the women could study. Like all the buildings in Burma, it stood on posts about four feet above the ground.

As Adoniram and Nancy surveyed their Baptist zayat they had to admit it could not compare with the gorgeous Buddhist ones up and down the street, with their many roofs up-tilted at the gables, but they were proud of it. At last they had "a Christian meeting house, the first erected in this land of atheists." They decided to begin using it immediately, without waiting for the porch to be finished.

Adoniram held his first service there on Sunday, April 4, 1819. His congregation consisted principally of about fifteen adults whom he had been able to collect in the neighborhood. The service was also attended by numerous uninvited children, richly decked with necklaces, bracelets and anklets, but otherwise in their state of customary nudity. Very few of his audience had ever attended any kind of religious service, and they occupied themselves looking around, commenting loudly on the construction and appearance of the zayat, and discussing the manners and dress of the English teacher and each other. Afterwards Adoniram congratulated himself on having held their attention at least part of the time. A few days later he and Nancy went to a Buddhist service in a neighboring zayat to see what they could learn about Burmese congregations. Everything was as different as could be. The worshipers were seated on mats spread on the floor, the men on one side, the women on the other. When Adoniram and Nancy entered, some of the people said, "There come some wild foreigners." But when they sat down quietly and took off their shoes, they said, "No, they are not wild; they are civilized." And a few, who recognized Adoniram, added, "It is the English teacher." The preacher was seated in the center of the room on a low stand a little more than a foot high. He welcomed them . . .

"but on learning that I was a missionary, or, in their idiom, a religion-making teacher, his countenance fell, and he said no more."

The people now being convened, one appointed for the purpose called three times for silence and attention. Each one then took the flowers and leaves which had been previously distributed, and placing them between his fingers, raised them to his head, and in that respectful posture remained motionless until the service closed. This ceremony we of course declined.

When all things were properly adjusted, the preacher closed his eyes, and commenced the exercise, which consisted in repeating a portion from their sacred writings. His subject was the conversion of the two prime disciples of Gaudama, and their subsequent promotion and glory. His oratory I found to be entirely different from what we call oratory. At first he seems dull and monotonous; but presently his soft, mellifluous tones will their way into the heart, and lull the soul into that state of calmness and serenity which somewhat resembles the boasted perfection of their saints of old. His discourse continues about half an hour; and, at the close, the whole assembly burst out into a short prayer, after which all rose and retired.

Adoniram and Nancy, putting on their shoes and returning to the mission house, had to admit the Buddhist service had a decorum and even a beauty they had not achieved in their own zayat.

The next Sunday Adoniram tried again. More people came than the week before and they behaved with more order; but it seemed impossible to get their attention and hold it. Afterwards he confessed, "I never felt so deeply the *immense* difficulty of making a first impression on a heathen people."

Nevertheless, his audience grew slowly. Toward the end of the month, when the stairs leading from Pagoda Road were finished, he took to sitting on the porch every day and hailing passers with a "Ho! Everyone that thirsteth for knowledge!"

Soon the zayat had such a stream of visitors that Adoniram had no time for study. Some were openly, even virulently, hostile. The majority were half curious, half indifferent. But within a week a visitor came who aroused Adoniram's highest hopes.

The important visitor had walked in off the street one Friday, the last day of April, and for several hours had sat silently on the zayat veranda listening to Adoniram debate with various inquirers. His name was Maung Nau.[1] He was about thirty-five years old, poor, without family, a man who had to work hard for a living. There was nothing remarkable about his appearance or manner, and he seemed to have no special abilities. That first Friday Adoniram would scarcely have noticed him except for his attentiveness and for the fact that he was unusually reticent for a Burman.

Saturday he came again. This time he hesitantly asked a few questions. His manner was that of one sincerely looking for information, not leading the teacher on into one of those hair-splitting metaphysical arguments the Burmese men enjoyed so much.

Sunday he attended service, which was attended by about thirty people. By now Adoniram had come to think of him as "the quiet and modest Maung Nau." Maung Nau really listened. Of the others, Adoniram thought, "Very few paid much attention, or probably received any benefit."

Monday and Tuesday Maung Nau visited Adoniram several times and Adoniram realized that the man had "a teachable and humble spirit."

By Wednesday, the fifth of May, 1819, Adoniram was almost afraid to record the conclusion to which he was coming:

> I begin to think that the Grace of God has reached his heart. He expressed sentiments of repentence for his sins, and faith in the Saviour. The substance of his profession is, that from the darknesses, and uncleannesses, and sins of his whole life, he has found no other Saviour but Jesus Christ; nowhere else can he look for salvation; and therefore he proposes to adhere to Christ, and worship him all his life long.
>
> It seems almost too much to believe that God has begun to manifest his grace to the Burmans; but this day I could not resist the delightful conviction that this is really the case. PRAISE AND GLORY BE TO HIS NAME FOREVERMORE. *Amen*.

It was really happening. After six years, day by day Maung Nau grew in grace. At the next Sunday's worship in the zayat he openly

[1] *Maung* (or "Moung," as Adoniram often spelled it) is really a sort of title for "boy," or expresses the idea of "young."

professed himself a believer in Christ in the presence of at least thirty people.

Maung Nau worked for a timber merchant. Monday he had to leave on a trip for timber — probably teak, much prized for ship-building, which grew upriver, but he told Adoniram he hoped he could be baptized when he returned.

By now all the missionaries and their wives were excitedly talk-ing about Maung Nau. Even Wheelock, so low that it was obvious to everyone but Eliza Wheelock that he could not live many months, was interested. Nancy spent hours by his bed telling him all the details of the conversion of the first Burman, much to the annoyance of Eliza, who was beginning to cherish an irrational suspicion that the Judsons had some evil intention toward her husband.

No one had expected to see Maung Nau for several weeks, but he showed up in a few days. He had discovered the timber mer-chant to be untrustworthy, thrown up his job and abandoned the trip. He was not out of work long. The next week he was offered a job in Ava with a boat owner. Ava was several hundred miles up the river. If he took the job he would not see the missionaries for a long time, perhaps a year. He asked Adoniram what he should do. He did not want to go to Ava, but he had to have work.

The missionaries did not want him to go either, not while he was in his present interesting situation. If he were away for several months, there was no telling what might happen to his new convic-tion. On the other hand, they did not like to tell him to stay. After discussing the matter with Nancy and the Colmans, Adoniram finally invited Maung Nau to stay at the mission with the mission-aries. They would pay him ten ticals a month for making himself useful copying pamphlets, which they had no way of getting printed now that Hough was gone. When Maung Nau accepted, the missionaries heaved a sigh of relief. They were positive that a few days in the mission would make him fit for baptism.

They did. On the sixth of June, a Sunday, only a little more than a month after first appearing at the zayat, Maung Nau bashfully presented Adoniram with a letter. That evening, after communion, all the missionaries but the dying Wheelock assembled to listen to it. Adoniram translated it, aloud:

I, Maung Nau, the constant recipient of your excellent favor, approach your feet. Whereas my lords three have come to the country of Burmah, not for the purpose of trade, but to preach the religion of Jesus Christ, the Son of the eternal God, I, having heard and understood, am, with a joyful mind, filled with love.

I believe that the Divine Son, Jesus Christ, suffered death, in the place of men, to atone for their sins. Like a heavy laden man, I feel my sins are very many. The punishment of my sins I deserve to suffer. Since it is so, do you, Sirs, consider, that I, taking refuge in the merits of the Lord Jesus Christ, and receiving baptism, in order to become his disciple, shall dwell with yourselves, a band of brothers, in the happiness of heaven, and grant me the ordinance of baptism. It is through the grace of Christ that you, Sirs, have come by ship from one country and continent to another, and that we have met together. I pray my lords three that a suitable day may be appointed, and that I may receive the ordinance of baptism.

As it is only since I have met with you, Sirs, that I have known about the eternal God, I venture to pray that you will still unfold to me the religion of God, that my old disposition may be destroyed, and my new disposition improved.

No one in the mission doubted that Maung Nau had experienced the grace of God, and it was agreed that he should be baptized the following Sunday, after which he would be received into church fellowship. The "church" had consisted of six members — the two Judsons, the two Colmans and the two Wheelocks. Now it would number seven, but in the eyes of the other members the seventh was the most important. For the seventh would be the first Burman ever to become a Baptist.

As it happened, however, Maung Nau's baptism had to be deferred for three weeks. The cause was a crisis of state, the greatest in Burma in a generation.

From the mission's humble point of view the first omen appeared a few weeks after Maung Nau began attending the zayat. It took the form of a demand on the missionaries to pay a special head tax of forty-eight ticals of pure silver — about thirty dollars — for the servants in the household. Inquiring, Adoniram learned that it was a new tax being levied throughout the empire. Adoniram and Nancy went to the viceroy about it. He replied "that it was an extraordinary tax, and must be paid; but that we might be excused from paying it to the proper officer, and have the privilege of paying it to himself! We were, therefore, obliged to produce the money."

At the same time, attendance at the zayat suddenly fell off to nearly nothing — a result, surmised Adoniram, of distress at the tax. He was mistaken. It was a second omen of something far more serious.

A week later a parcel of letters and a box arrived for the missionaries from Bengal. It was no sooner out of the ship and on shore than the mission "received peremptory orders from the collector of the district to pay four hundred and fifty ticals of pure silver." This was about three hundred dollars, more than the zayat and its land had cost. To Adoniram and Nancy it looked like another attempt at extortion. But they were in a dilemma. Everything indicated that the demand came by the authority of the viceroy. He had insisted they pay the head tax a few days before. He had not been long in office and they did not know him well. How could they refuse? If they paid, there would be other demands and the mission would be unable to afford to stay in Rangoon. Such a big tax would make it worth while to go to Ava and protest to the emperor — but the viceroy would certainly deny Adoniram permission to make the trip.

There were two Englishmen in Rangoon who for reasons of their own had found it advisable long ago to leave India, become Burmese subjects, and enter the service of the emperor. One was named Rodgers, the other Gibson. Adoniram determined to appeal to them for help.

But with Rodgers, who had been in Burma nearly forty years, he got nowhere. That Englishman had spent years intriguing in court circles at Ava against a Spaniard named Lanciego, for the lucrative collectorship of Rangoon. In 1782 Rodgers had attacked the first mate of a ship on which he was fourth mate with a loaded cane — known in the East as a "Penang lawyer" — and left him for dead. He had fled the East India Company's territory and, after a year of wandering through Arakan, had made his way to Rangoon. He had married a Burman woman of Portuguese descent and had a child. Now, in spite of his Yorkshire accent, bright blue eyes, and tall European stature, he considered himself Burman, dressed in Burman fashion, and even trimmed his long gray beard in the Burmese style, thinned to one long tuft straggling goatlike from his chin. Taking up the case of the mission would not help him secure the collectorship, and therefore Adoniram's pleas had no effect on him.

Gibson, the other Englishman, although cool at first, was more friendly, and, thought Adoniram, more to be trusted. Gibson finally agreed to intercede with the viceroy, and the affair turned out as might have been expected. An underling of the Raywoon, who was second in command to the viceroy, had merely thought he saw a chance to make some easy money. The underling was reprimanded and the "tax" forgotten.

But the episode was disquieting. Apparently something mysterious was going on at Ava which was emboldening officials to make extortionary attempts, unusual even for Burma. A little later the mission was called on for still another tax, this one for fifteen ticals, which they finally escaped by paying half. Minor officials now visited the mission nearly every day with one kind of demand or another.

Slowly Adoniram became aware that all Rangoon was in an unprecedented state of confusion which had a curious undernote of apprehension. Shortly after Maung Nau presented his petition to be baptized, they learned the viceroy was preparing to leave for Ava. An immense multitude of boats was being collected just above the city to accommodate his huge retinue; evidently the viceroy's trip was to be made in the greatest pomp and state. This must be the reason for the confusion in Rangoon, thought Adoniram. At any rate, he decided it would be best to delay Maung Nau's baptism until things quieted down.

Late in June the viceroy left Rangoon to join the fleet of river boats. By now the city was "in the utmost anxiety and alarm," and the rumors about its cause had finally reached Adoniram.

Order after order has reached our viceroy to hasten his return to Ava, with all the troops under arms. Great news are whispered. Some say there is a rebellion; some say the king is sick, some that he is dead. But none dare say this plainly. It would be a crime of the first magnitude; for the "lord of land

and water" is called immortal. The eldest son of his eldest son (his father being dead) has long been declared the heir of the crown; but he has two very powerful uncles, who it is supposed, will contest his right; and in all probability the whole country will soon be a scene of anarchy and civil war.

The next day Adoniram neglected the zayat and was "out all morning, listening for news, uncertain whether a day or an hour will not plunge us into the greatest distress."

The whole place is sitting in sullen silence, expecting an explosion. About 10 o'clock, a royal dispatch-boat pulls up to the shore. An imperial mandate is produced. The crowds make way for the sacred messengers, and follow them to the high court, where the authorities of the place are assembled.

*Listen ye:* The immortal king, wearied, it would seem, with the fatigues of royalty, has gone up to amuse himself in the celestial regions. His grandson, the heir-apparent, is seated on the throne. The young monarch enjoins on all to remain quiet, and wait his imperial orders.

It appears that the Prince of Toung Oo, one of his uncles, has been executed, with his family and adherents, and the Prince of Pyee placed in confinement. There has probably been bloody work; but it seems, from what has transpired, that the business has been settled so expeditiously that the distant provinces will not feel the shock.

There had been bloody work indeed; but it was over and old King Bodawpaya dead two weeks before Adoniram heard of it. The new king's first act, according to the stories which later seeped into Bengal, was to have his brother, his brother's children, his brother's grandchildren and the rest of his brother's family sewn up in red sacks, as befitted royalty, and drowned. His uncle was strangled after his bones were crushed on the rack. One of the prime ministers, governor of the Western Provinces, met the same fate. Their property was confiscated and devoted to the support of the army.

Altogether, it was believed, some fourteen hundred members of the upper classes were put to death and some ten to fifteen thousand commoners. In this manner were newly ascended emperors of Burma in the habit of making certain that their reigns would be long, peaceful and serene.

The new ruler was named Bagyidaw. It was in the fourth week of his reign, on Sunday, June 27, 1819, that Maung Nau was baptized.

In the zayat, before the little congregation — there were several new faces this day, and it numbered somewhat more than thirty — Adoniram called Maung Nau before him, "read and commented on an appropriate portion of Scripture, asked him several questions concerning his *faith, hope* and *love*, and made the baptismal prayer."

The whole party then left the zayat and proceeded to a large pond nearby, on the bank of which stood a huge statue of Buddha. Here, with the Buddha benignly looking down on the scene, Adoniram led Maung Nau waist-deep into the dark water, immersed him, and received him into the Baptist faith, while a wondering crowd of gaily clad Burmans watched from the hill above.

One baptism was not much to show for six years of work. But as Adoniram and Maung Nau returned dripping to the mission house, followed by Nancy, the Colmans, and the rest of the company, he hoped: "O, may it prove the beginning of a series of baptisms in the Burman empire which shall continue in uninterrupted succession to the end of time!"

## CHAPTER IX

# Let Us Go to the Golden Feet

## [ *1819* ]

BY the end of that June in which Maung Nau was baptized there was no doubt in anyone's mind that Wheelock had only a few months to live. No doubt, that is, in any mind but Eliza Wheelock's. The weaker he grew, the more vehemently she denied that he was even seriously ill.

A confusing struggle began to be waged around him — for custody of his body, now mere skin and bones; and for his mind, now slowly losing its grip on reality.

On one side were the Colmans and Judsons, led by Nancy and Adoniram; on the other Eliza Wheelock. Each side strove for Wheelock's best interests, as they saw them.

Nancy tried to make him comfortable by exerting all her inventiveness to prepare for him foods he especially wanted. By some legerdemain she even managed to make him custards. His mind and soul she tried to ease with items of news about the progress of the mission. After Maung Nau's conversion she spent hours at a time by Wheelock's bed "interpreting to him the new learnt language of the convert, which highly interested the feelings of our dying brother."

But there was one duty more which the missionaries felt they owed Wheelock for the welfare of his soul. They felt strongly that they should talk with him on the subject of his coming death, to help prepare him for the transition which they were sure could not be far away. Such a service was customary with religious people in the America they knew. It was no more than Samuel Newell had done for Harriet in her last days in Isle of France.

Eliza Wheelock would have none of it. She seemed to feel that the other missionaries were plotting to steal her husband from her. Nancy's laboriously prepared foods, her interpretations of the talk of the Burmans who visited the mission, probably most of all her attitude that Wheelock was dying and must be prepared for the next world — all these, Eliza must have felt, were ways of excluding her. From this frame of mind it was only a step to her suspicion that the Judsons and Colmans — and even those strange dark-skinned natives with their unintelligible jabber — were arrayed against her, and were intent on some mysterious harm to Wheelock. She defended herself by keeping the missionaries out of Wheelock's room as much as she could. She voiced her suspicions to him and tried to persuade him that his only hope of safety was to take ship for Bengal.

At first he did not believe her. But eventually he became "so weak, and his mind in such a state of distraction, that he could hardly bear the noise of a person's walking across the room." His mind began to wander and he opposed his wife no longer. About the end of July or the beginning of August, she engaged passage on a ship anchored in the river fifteen miles below Rangoon and prepared for departure.

By now everyone in the mission was convinced that a sea voyage would only end Wheelock's life sooner. It was the worst season of the year for sea travel, and Wheelock had always suffered so badly from seasickness that he dreaded the ocean. Even getting to the ship would mean a long, uncomfortable trip down-river in a small open boat. Adoniram, Nancy, Colman and Mrs. Colman all remonstrated with Mrs. Wheelock by turns, and with Wheelock on the rare occasions they could see him. Eliza was adamant. As a last gesture, Nancy and Mrs. Colman offered to help her pack her trunks. She refused. Wheelock, in a moment of lucidity, accepted all the preserves they had in the mission to help improve the ship's poor fare, but for the rest the missionaries were permitted to do for the Wheelocks only what Mrs. Wheelock could not do for herself. This amounted to Adoniram's seeing their baggage through customs and procuring a boat, and Colman's accompanying them to the ship and seeing them on board.

It was not a pleasant way to part. The missionaries were heartsick to see Wheelock go to what they knew must be his death, but they must have heaved a sigh of relief when they saw the last of his wife.

The result they learned much later. It was what might have been expected. On the stormy waters of the Bay of Bengal, Wheelock became almost crazed by violent fever. On the thirteenth day of the passage, Mrs. Wheelock took a few moments to write a letter — thinking he was asleep. The writing table was so placed that her back was turned to his bed. Suddenly she heard the cabin door close and turned around to discover him gone. She ran after him, but it was too late. He had made his way to the deck and plunged into the sea. In the high wind it was impossible for the ship to attempt a rescue.

With the Wheelocks gone, the members of the mission resumed their routine. Colman made good progress in learning Burmese, although his health still did not permit him to do a full day's work. Nancy kept on with her female meetings and the supervision of the household. Her spare time she spent studying Siamese, an occupation she had begun more than a year before. She had translated the catechism, and Adoniram's tract and the Matthew into Siamese, and then for amusement a Siamese book into English — "an account of the incarnation of one of their deities, when he existed in the form of a great elephant." Adoniram continued with his days in the zayat.

The conversion of Maung Nau seemed to have given the mission an impetus. Rangoon's idle curiosity about the new religion had been satisfied. The inquirers who came now were genuinely interested in Christianity as a faith for themselves.

Some of them were people who had built huts in the unused parts of the mission yard, in the free and easy manner of the country, and had been living there for months. Building a bamboo hut was almost as simple as pitching a tent, and the ordinary Burmans were in the habit of setting up houses wherever they pleased and staying as long as they wanted.

One of these squatters was a young man named Maung Thahlah, who settled in the yard with his sister, Mah Baik, and her husband. One day when Adoniram happened to ask him "the state of his mind" he replied with considerable feeling that he knew he was a sinner and subject to future punishment, like all men. He was disturbed, because although according to Buddhism there was no hope of pardon, according to Adoniram there was, and a heaven, and a way of reaching it.

Adoniram began to explain Christianity to Maung Thahlah while Nancy did the same with his sister Mah Baik. Mah Baik, even more independent and quarrelsome than most Burmese women, presently fell by the wayside through her inability to control her temper. She tried hard to cultivate Christian humility, but a sharp word from one of the other women living in the compound was enough to touch her off. She would explode in rage and for an hour or so would enjoy the intoxication of unleashed wrath. Afterwards, like a repentant drunkard, she felt remorse. But with her, as with her native sisters, quarreling was like liquor to an alcoholic: she simply could not resist it.

But her brother Maung Thahlah was made of different stuff. He persevered and grew in grace. Adoniram was particularly interested in him because, although by no means a learned man, he was much better read and had greater natural ability than anyone else living in the mission yard. A few weeks after the departure of the Wheelocks Adoniram became convinced he was a convert.

Maung Byaay was another man who had moved into the mission yard with his family. Unlike most Burman men, he had achieved the age of fifty without learning to read or write until he had joined a class which Adoniram and Nancy taught in the main room of the zayat. Here, along with five or six others, each with a torch and blackboard, he laboriously formed the letters and repeated the sounds by rote — *kwa, kwar, kwe kwee, kwa kwoo,* and so on — from which the words were formed. To Adoniram, Maung Byaay had seemed at first "too legalistic and narrow, too set on good moral works alone to become a real Christian at heart." But this may have been due to an illiterate's exaggerated respect for the written word, for soon his mind began to open rapidly.

About this time a man named Maung Ing, a poor fisherman, also began visiting the mission, where he spent most of his time with Maung Thahlah. He told Maung Thahlah that "he had long been looking after the true religion, and was ready to wish he had been born a brute rather than to die in delusion and go to hell." His mother had married a Roman Catholic and been christened. His father had disappeared a long time ago, but Maung Ing had kept from childhood some vague memories of an eternal God. Under Maung Thahlah's influence these memories came to life. Soon he too was clearly on the way to adopting Christianity.

Maung Thahlah, Maung Byaay and Maung Ing, all three poor, all belonging to the lower classes like the baptized Maung Nau, appealed to Adoniram's heart. The winning of their souls, he knew, would be as pleasing to God as the soul of the emperor himself. But now there came to the zayat a man who interested Adoniram even more because he appealed to his mind.

His name was Maung Shway-gnong. He was a man of middle age, a teacher and scholar of considerable distinction in Rangoon, who was accompanied wherever he went by a group of adherents, like an itinerant Sophist of ancient Greece. He did, in fact, have something in common with the Sophists. To Adoniram he seemed "half deist and half skeptic, the first of the sort I have met with among the Burmans," although he bowed to convention by worshiping at the pagodas and conforming to "all the prevailing customs." Adoniram enjoyed Maung Shway-gnong more than any Burman he had ever met. "He is the most powerful reasoner," thought Adoniram, "I have yet met with in this country except my old teacher Oo Oungmen (now dead), and he is not at all inferior to him."

Soon the two men were spending whole days together at the zayat, surrounded by Maung Shway-gnong's followers. Their words dealt with theology and philosophy, but privately each one took as keen a pleasure in exploring the other's mind as in the discussion itself.

At first the scholar baffled Adoniram. He seemed to be "a complete Proteus in religion, and I never know where to find him. We went over a vast deal of ground, and ended where we began, in apparent incredulity." In a short time Adoniram learned, however, that caution played an important part in Maung Shway-gnong's verbal elusiveness. One night the two men talked so late that the Burman's adherents left and the two men were alone. Immediately Maung Shway-gnong's attitude changed. His half-ironic, skeptical manner dropped away. With some show of emotion he admitted that he had no inner knowledge of religion and asked Adoniram to teach him. And when he left he amazed and flattered Adoniram by prostrating himself in the obeisance called the *sheeko* — "an act of homage which a Burman never performs but to an acknowledged superior."

In one of their day-long discussions Adoniram finally found out why Maung Shway-gnong wanted to learn about Christianity:

> It appears that he accidently obtained the idea of an eternal Being about eight years ago; and it has been floating about in his mind, and disturbing his Buddhistic ideas ever since. When he heard of us, which was through one of his adherents, to whom I had given a tract, this idea received considerable confirmation; and today he has fully admitted the truth of this first grand principle. The latter part of the day we were chiefly employed in discussing the possibility and necessity of a divine revelation, and the evidence which proves that the writings of Jesus contain that revelation; and I think I may say that he is half inclined to admit all this. He is certainly a most interesting case. The way seems to be prepared in his mind for the special operation of divine grace."

All this represented progress — more than the mission had ever seen. But progress increased danger, because it meant that the purpose of the mission was becoming more widely known. Even during the reign of the priest-hating old King Bodawpaya, inquirers had warned Adoniram again and again that he could not hope to make many converts without the favor, or at least the acquiescence, of the lord of land and water in Ava. Fear of the royal displeasure hung over the people like a sword suspended by a hair. Every official strove to read the king's faintest mood as if his life depended on it — which it did. A frown could turn loose death preceded by unimaginable tortures on any Burman even remotely connected with the mission.

No one knew how the new king, Bagyidaw, would take the news that some of his slaves were deserting Gautama for Christ, but there were ominous signs. In that fall of 1819, following his accession to the throne, new pagodas began to be built in increasing numbers. There were rumors that Bagyidaw, unlike his predecessor, was encouraging the Buddhist priests. If so, Christians might soon expect persecution for heresy — or even, since Christianity was identified with alien countries, for subversion, espionage or treason.

The danger made Maung Thahlah and Maung Byaay hesitate to take the final step of asking for baptism. Maung Ing, when Adoniram asked him whether he loved Christ better than his own life, replied "very slowly and deliberately, 'When I meditate upon this religion, I know not what it is to love my own life.' "

But Maung Ing had to go off on a long fishing trip from which he might not return for months, and in Adoniram's opinion was not quite ready for baptism, although he was certainly a true believer. When it came to the final step of baptism Adoniram then, as always, insisted on far more preparation from Burman converts than any minister would ask of people in England or America. But he knew Burman Christians had to withstand pressures which an Englishman or American, safe in a friendly Christian environment, could not even imagine.

His good sense was vindicated one day that autumn when the viceroy rode by "on a huge elephant, attended by his guards and numerous suite, and, as he passed, eyed us very narrowly." An hour or so later two of his private secretaries visited the zayat with an order for Adoniram to show the viceroy how printing was done. Adoniram told them that the teacher who understood printing had gone to Bengal, taking the type with him, an answer which plainly displeased the secretaries.

The next day Adoniram managed to secure an audience with the viceroy, who seemed to accept his explanation without displeasure. But, the day after that, the viceroy rode again past the zayat and a little later sent a message that Adoniram should translate, and have printed, some historical writings about America. Adoniram evaded this order by promising to call on the viceroy at the first opportunity. When he called he begged off, by saying he was not familiar with the style of Burmese historical writing; and he gave the viceroy a copy of a tract as a specimen of the kind he was accustomed to printing. The viceroy handed the tract to a secretary to read, but after only a sentence stopped the reading with the cold remark: "This is the same as a writing I have already heard, and *I do not want that kind of writing.*"

A few weeks later, Adoniram became aware that Maung Shway-gnong was growing indifferent, if not antagonistic, to Christianity. He seemed to avoid any discussion of his personal beliefs, and even alone with Adoniram was "as crabbed as possible; sometimes a Berkeleian, sometimes a Humite or complete skeptic." Soon he stopped visiting the zayat altogether. Rangoon gossip told why.

For some time, the Buddhist priests and teachers had been watching the mission. The visits of Maung Shway-gnong had been reported to them.

At length one of the teachers, — known as "the Mangen teacher" — had arranged for it to be mentioned in the viceroy's hearing that Maung Shway-gnong had renounced his native religion. The viceroy had merely said, "Inquire further."

This was enough for Maung Shway-gnong. As soon as he heard of the incident he went to the informer to clear himself, and — remarked Adoniram with a mixture of sorrow and disgust — "I suppose, apologized, and explained, and flattered."

It was three weeks before Maung Shway-gnong returned to the mission. When he did, he denied that he had really recanted; and Adoniram hoped he had not. "But he is evidently falling off from the investigation of the Christian religion. He made but a short visit, and took leave, as soon as he could decently."

After the affair of Maung Shway-gnong, Adoniram thought it prudent to stay away from the zayat for a while. No native of Rangoon dared be seen in it, and, with the coming of one of the great annual festivals on the first of November, Pagoda Road would be thronged with immense crowds of Buddhist worshipers. The festival coincided with both the new king's coronation in Ava and his birthday. For a white foreigner to be seen in the zayat at such a time, propagating his subversive un-Burman, un-Buddhist notions, seemed foolhardy. Even Maung Thahlah and Maung Byaay, who had presented the missionaries with applications for baptism, were intimidated. They followed their applications with a request to be baptized "not absolutely in private, but about sunset, away from public observation." They had been searching the Scriptures, they said in their new petition, and could not find "that John and other baptizers administered baptism on any particular time, or day, or hour. We, therefore, venture to beg of the two teachers, that they will grant, that on the 6th day of the wane of the Tanzoungmong moon, at 6 o'clock at night, we may this once receive baptism at their hands."

Adoniram and Colman questioned the two hesitating disciples closely, with a suspicion that Maung Thahlah and Maung Byaay might want to behave as Buddhists in public and as Christians only in private. But they denied any such intention. If they were actually brought before the authorities and accused of heresy, "they could not think of denying their Saviour." Finally the missionaries agreed that the request was reasonable. It would not be the first time in history Christians had needed to be discreet about flaunting their beliefs.

Therefore, on Sunday, the seventh of November, 1819, the mission family had worship as usual — in the mission house, not the zayat. About half an hour before sunset, when service was over and the Burmese visitors had left, the two candidates presented themselves at the zayat with three or four friends. After a brief prayer, the little party proceeded as inconspicuously as possible to the pond overlooked by the huge image of Buddha where Maung Nau had been baptized. The sun had set and the still water was nearly dark. Here Maung Thahlah and Maung Byaay, the second and third converted Burmans, received baptism and afterwards quietly made their way back to the mission for communion.

That night Adoniram wrote sadly of the baptism:

No hymn of praise expressed the exultant feelings of joyous hearts. Stillness and solemnity pervaded the scene. We felt, on the banks of the water, as a little, feeble, solitary band. But perhaps some hovering angels took note of the event, with more interest than they witnessed the late coronation; perhaps Jesus looked down on us, pitied and forgave our weaknesses, and marked us for his own; perhaps, if we deny him not, he will acknowledge us another day, more publicly than we venture at present to acknowledge him.

After a week or so Adoniram appeared again at the zayat. But though the street was thronged and the weather at its finest, he passed whole days sitting on the veranda without a single visitor. He knew why.

We and our objects are now well known throughout Rangoon. None wish to call, as formerly, out of curiosity; and none dare to call from a principle of religious inquiry. And were not the leaders in ecclesiastical circles confident that we shall never succeed in making converts, I have no doubt we should meet with direct persecution and mistreatment.

In fact, that very day Adoniram and Nancy had undergone an unpleasant encounter with the Mangen teacher, their implacable enemy. The experience was not quite persecution, at least not as Adoniram understood the word, but it certainly fell in the category of malicious annoyance. Adoniram and Nancy both had horses by now and were in the habit of taking a ride early every morning to bathe in a mineral pond a few miles distant. Their way took them along one of the roads leading to the Shwe Dagon pagoda. Suddenly the Mangen teacher had stepped out from the side of the road and stopped them. He must have watched them for days to learn the route they usually followed. Emboldened by investiture with a little brief authority, he arrogantly forbade them to ride anywhere on the roads near the pagoda. If they attempted it again they should be well beaten.

Bewildered, they turned their horses home and proceeded to look into the matter. Sure enough, the viceroy had just issued an order — at the Mangen teacher's request — providing that thenceforth no one "wearing a hat, shoes, or umbrella, or mounted on a horse, shall approach within the sacred ground belonging to the great pagoda" —an area which included all the land for half a mile around the Shwe Dagon and every main road in the vicinity. As the missionaries were the only people in Rangoon who habitually rode horses and wore hats and shoes (they carried umbrellas, too, but so did some Burmans) and while doing these things traversed the roads near the pagoda on the way to their daily bath, there was no question that the order was aimed solely at them. No one in the mission house, or in Rangoon, for that matter, could possibly mistake its meaning. From now on they were to be subjected to every kind of petty harassment which the Mangen teacher and the priestly party could get the viceroy to permit.

There was only one way to stop it:

Our business must be fairly laid before the emperor. If he

frown upon us, all missionary attempts within his dominion will be out of the question. If he favour us, none of our enemies, during the continuance of his favour, can touch a hair of our heads.

Colman agreed, and toward the end of November the two began to make their preparations.

A trip to Ava was no light undertaking. The city was three hundred and fifty miles up the Irrawaddy, in the interior of the country. Only a handful of foreigners had ever been there. For most of the way the river was infested with pirates, the shores with dacoits — a class of robbers in India and Burma who plundered in armed bands.

There were other dangers, for the Golden Presence was the source of arbitrary power itself, wrapped around in layer on layer of intrigue and hence perilous even to approach. The dangers, however, were lessened by the fact that Adoniram had at least a few friends at court. Mr. Gibson and Mr. Rodgers were both in Ava. Rodgers could not be relied on, but Gibson had proved a friend in Rangoon and might again. More important, the old spear-carrying viceroy of Rangoon, Mya-day-men, he whose wife had done so much to console Nancy at the time of little Roger's death, was now the emperor's prime minister, the exalted Wungyi, highest in the kingdom next to the emperor himself.

Because of her close friendship with the Wungyi's wife, Nancy wanted to make the trip with Adoniram. But Adoniram refused. For a foreign missionary to prostrate himself at the Golden Feet with a petition asking toleration to propagate an alien religion among Burmans was revolutionary enough. For him to bring his wife to a court where no foreign woman had ever appeared would be too much.

And Adoniram and Colman were already having trouble enough deciding how to present themselves in suitable fashion. The emperor would have to be given a gift, they knew. But what could two poor missionaries give an Oriental emperor that could tempt him to look with favor on them?

They finally settled on a Bible, of which they had a magnificent copy in English, in six volumes. They had one of the many artisans in gold in the city cover the volumes with gold leaf and make a rich wrapper. It was the best they could do, and at least, they assured themselves, the gift would be both appropriate and unusual.

Another problem was what to wear when they were presented to the emperor. The ordinary black suit of the missionaries seemed all wrong. The saffron-yellow robe of the Buddhist priests would be in character but would convey a false impression. At length they each had made a white robe something like a surplice. The robes would distinguish them as religious teachers and the color would show they were not Buddhists.

They were well into their preparations when old Maung Shway-gnong paid the mission another visit. He no longer would go near the zayat, but he did not seem to be able to stay away from Adoniram. This time he spent hours raising hair-splitting objections, all of which Adoniram answered fully. Suddenly Maung Shway-gnong admitted that he did not believe a word of what he had been saying. He had merely been trying to test Adoniram and his religion.

"Do you think I would pay you the least attention if I found you could not answer all my questions and solve all my difficulties?" he said. He really did believe in God, in His son Jesus, and in the atonement. In short, he was a Christian at heart.

Adoniram was skeptical. "Do you believe all that is contained in the book of St. Matthew that I have given you? In particular, do you believe that the Son of God died on a cross?"

"Ah, you have caught me now," the old teacher admitted with some chagrin. "I believe that He suffered death. But I cannot admit He suffered the shameful death of the cross."

Adoniram, knowing Maung Shway-gnong, had expected the answer. It was difficult for a Burman, particularly a high-born scholar, to imagine a God who would permit His Son to undergo any kind of indignity. The whole idea was abhorrent. Adoniram pressed home its meaning: "Therefore you are not a disciple of Christ. A true disciple inquires not whether a fact is agreeable to his own reason, but whether it is in the book. His pride has yielded to the Divine testimony. Teacher, your pride is still unbroken. Break down your pride, and yield to the word of God."

Maung Shway-gnong stopped to think. Then he said: "As you utter those words I see my error. I have been trusting in my own reason, not in the word of God." Someone entered and he fell silent. When the intruder left after a little while, he said thoughtfully, "This day is different from all the days on which I have visited you. I see my error in trusting in my own reason; and I now believe the crucifixion of Christ, because it is contained in the Scripture."

They talked for a while at random and the conversation led to the uncertainty of life. Maung Shway-gnong had a new thought. "I think I shall not be lost even though I should die suddenly."

"Why?"

"Because I love Jesus Christ."

"Do you really love Him?"

"No one that really knows Him can help loving Him," said the old man with feeling; and so departed.

Maung Shway-gnong's visit was a welcome interlude in the labor of getting a boat. Adoniram hunted the river front for a week before he found one he wanted.

It had the typical needlelike lines of a Burman river boat. Although its length was forty feet, its width at the widest point was only six feet. Its pointed prow swept up and forward into the Viking-like dragon head most native craft carried. The stern took a similar leap upwards, but backwards, and terminated in a high, elaborately carved seat for the steersman, whose position of honorable responsibility was indicated by a large umbrella placed overhead for his protection.

Adoniram immediately employed workmen to lay down a light bamboo deck along the whole length of the boat. Aft, he had a tiny low-roofed cabin made where he and Colman could sleep. It was just high enough so the missionaries could crawl in and sit down, provided they kept their heads low.

When the work was well begun, he applied to the viceroy "for a pass to go up to the Golden Feet, and lift up our eyes to the Golden Face." The pass was granted at once, "in very polite terms."

Now there was no obstacle to their going to Ava. Nothing remained to be done but find a crew and depart.

## CHAPTER X

# Ava — and Failure

## [ *1819* ]

IT took Adoniram longer than he expected to outfit the boat and recruit a crew so that it was nearly two weeks after the pass was granted — December 21, 1819, the day before Nancy's thirtieth birthday — that they actually left Rangoon.

The departure was typically and colorfully Burmese. In addition to Nancy and Mrs. Colman (who had moved into the city from the more exposed mission house for the duration of their husbands' absence), the converts, the entire population of the mission compound, and a chattering crowd of the merely curious, thronged the wharf to see them off.

There were eighteen men aboard the boat: Adoniram, Colman, ten oarsmen, a steersman under the umbrella on the high platform aft, a "headsman" representing the government, two cooks — one for Adoniram and Colman and another, Maung Nau, for the crew — a Hindu washerman, and "an Englishman, who has been unfortunate all his life and wishes to try the service of his Burman majesty." The Englishman was in charge of the ship's armament, which consisted of an assortment of guns and blunderbusses.

The teacher Maung Shway-gnong was not among them. Adoniram had invited him to go along, but, torn by inner doubts, he had refused and had not visited the mission for several days. Now, however, as the chanting oarsmen dug their blades into the muddy, yellowish water and the long, narrow craft moved away from the wharf to the accompaniment of shouts and farewells, Adoniram caught sight of his tall figure among the crowd. When Maung Shway-gnong saw Adoniram had noticed him, he raised one hand to his head in a slow, dignified gesture of farewell, and in this position remained until the boat rounded a projecting point above the city which cut the wharf off from view.

Soon even the shining spires of the Shwe Dagon, bright in a fresh new covering of gold leaf, sank below the horizon and they were fairly up the Rangoon River on the way to its junction with the Irrawaddy at the head of the delta. In a few days they entered the broad Irrawaddy, and the low paddy fields of the delta gave way to upland plains covered with forests of mangoes, tamarinds, bananas and figs. Along the shore they passed occasional bamboo-and-thatch fishing villages, boats clustering around their rickety docks. And from the docks themselves, along with the fragrant scents of the forests, drifted the unforgettable odor of *ngapi* in the making — that pungent compound of spiced, partly decayed fish which was the national condiment of Burma.

The broad river itself, with its busy traffic of teak rafts, clumsy-sailed rice vessels, and a multitude of other craft, presented an almost gay spectacle. But Adoniram and Colman were aware of danger, too. One kind was the ever-present possibility of attack by the organized gangs of robbers and river pirates, the dacoits. The very first night above Rangoon they had tied up at a village where only a few days before dacoits had attacked a boat belonging to Mr. Gibson and killed the steersman and one of the crew. A week later, at a larger town, they met a detachment of soldiers pursuing a band of dacoits who had stormed a large boat, wounded and driven off its crew, and plundered it of goods worth some fifteen hundred ticals.

Another kind of danger was that of despotism, an anarchical, irresponsible despotism which knew no bounds. The deeper they went into the interior, the more they felt it and the more they saw it in the poverty of the villages cowering on the riverbanks in the middle of a landscape which promised nothing but abundance. These abject villages made a striking contrast to the ruins of ancient capitals of forgotten rulers — extending for acres and even miles along the shore where the upland plains gave way to rolling hill country and forested mountains slashed by wooded ravines. The ruins consisted of thousands of white stone pagodas, palaces and huge statues of Buddha; for every dynasty and almost every emperor of Burma had decreed a metropolis for itself in a new place along the river, leaving the old ones to the creeping vines, the monkeys and the tree rats.

One of these abandoned capitals was Prome, still something of a trading center. Another was Pagan, where, Adoniram had read, Buddhism had been proclaimed Burma's state religion eight centuries before. But others were completely uninhabited. In still others a handful of humans remained, their frail huts almost lost in the immense, confused expanses of crumbling masonry.

The farther northward they went, the less friendly were the people, the more frequent the warnings about pirates, but they were not actually molested until they had been on the river a month and were only four or five days below Ava.

Here, when they had anchored one evening under a little point of land, a large boat full of men suddenly swept from behind the point and headed straight for them at top speed. The missionaries' headman warned it off, but it kept coming. At the last moment, when the men in the attacking craft seemed almost ready to board the missionaries' vessel, the latter's headman fired a musket close over the men in the attacker. The shot had its effect. The men in the attacker called out to the missionaries' boat to leave off firing, and at the same moment the attacking boat itself sheered off sharply and fled away.

The incident gave them a sleepless night, but there were no further attacks and a few days later they were close to Ava and out of the dangerous part of the river.

On January 25, 1820, after a trip of a little more than a month, they drew up to the landing place, about four miles below the capital. Even from here Adoniram and Colman could see "the golden steeple of the palace, amid the glittering pagodas."

This was Ava, seat of the Golden Presence — that fabled Ava, heart of the mysterious golden empire of which Adoniram had read with kindling excitement in Symes's *Embassy to Ava*, so long ago in prim Andover: the book which had done so much to crystallize in him his decision to become a foreign missionary.

Actually, as he now knew, there were now two Avas — "Old Ava," seat of the preceding dynasty, and "New Ava," more usually known as Amarapura, a few miles farther upriver. The emperor lived in Amarapura, and it was below Amarapura that Adoniram's boat had anchored about noon, opposite Sagaing, a hamlet remarkable for its numberless pagodas. For Sagaing in its day had also been the seat of emperors.[1]

For the remainder of the day Adoniram and Colman busied themselves in various ways. Early next morning they set out to arrange an audience with the emperor.

Even before leaving Rangoon, Adoniram had intended to ask Mya-day-men to secure an audience. As a Wungyi, Mya-day-men was one of the four high Burmese officials who made up the Hlutdau, the great council of state, which discharged at the emperor's pleasure all the administrative, executive, legislative and judicial functions of the state. Only the four Atwinwuns who composed the emperor's privy council enjoyed comparable power; and it was always a matter of debate among Burmans whether Wungyis or Atwinwuns really had the higher rank.

Adoniram's acquaintance with Mya-day-men, it will be remembered, went all the way back to the time when he and Nancy, newcomers to Rangoon more than six years before, had paid him their respects as viceroy. Then, they had been frightened by the tall, stern old man stalking about his palace with his great spear. But during his later term as viceroy they had learned to know him better. His wife had become one of Nancy's closest Burmese friends since little Roger's death; and Mya-day-men himself, if not exactly a friend, certainly entertained friendly feelings toward the Judsons. Thus it was toward Mya-day-men's house in the walled city four miles away that Adoniram and Colman set their steps, followed by a little retinue consisting of Maung Nau and three or four of the boat's crew bearing gifts of valuable cloth.

On the way they stopped to see Mr. Gibson and Mr. Rodgers, who were living on the outskirts. Gibson, Adoniram hoped, might prove of real help to him. He was in favor at court and had not hesitated to stand up for the missionaries when the exorbitant demand for the "head tax" had been made on them at the time of the old emperor's death. Of Rodgers they did not expect much. He

[1] Today's Mandalay, second largest city in Burma, is just a few miles upriver from the two Avas of Adoniram's time.

had never been willing to intercede for them in the past and now was out of favor at court. But courtesy required that they at least pay him a call.

The city of Amarapura itself, containing the palaces and government buildings, occupied a square area enclosed by a wall about three-quarters of a mile on a side. A brick pagoda perhaps a hundred feet high stood on each corner. At the gate, Adoniram inquired for the location of Mya-day-men's house and was told by the keepers that it lay on the other side of the palace, a sprawling many-acred confusion of connected buildings with gilded roofs, surrounded by numberless pagodas. Around it were the elaborate houses of the high officials, each with its enclosure containing the dwellings, no more than ramshackle huts, of the servants and underlings. The hot season was still a month away and the air, although sunny, was dry and temperate, the unpaved streets dusty.

Mya-day-men softened into real warmth as he received Adoniram and his gift; and his wife, to whom Adoniram gave a less valuable one, had dozens of questions to ask about her friend Mrs. "Yoodthan" — as all the Burmese pronounced the name Judson. They were curious about Adoniram's purpose in visiting the capital; Adoniram was tactfully vague on that score. He merely said that he and Colman had made the journey in order to behold the Golden Face, and begged the severe old viceroy to secure him the privilege.

Mya-day-men was more than willing. He immediately told Maung Yo, one of his favorite officials, to arrange with the Atwinwun Maung Zah, one of the emperor's four privy councillors, for the interview. With so exalted a sponsor as Mya-day-men, Adoniram found his request fulfilled sooner than he expected. That evening Maung Yo called at the boat to tell the missionaries they would be conducted into the Golden Presence the very next day.

The night was an anxious one. The gentle, cradlelike rocking of their boat failed to lull them to sleep. All through the hours of darkness the two men lay wakefully in the cramped, thatched little cabin, sometimes preoccupied with their own thoughts, sometimes speculating in hushed voices on the reception they would meet on the morrow. At the first flush of dawn they rose, nervously set out the white surplice-like robes in which they intended to appear before the emperor, made a last inspection of the six volumes of the Bible on the covering of which they had spent so much money for gold leaf, and settled down to wait for Maung Yo.

He came when the sun was well up and conducted them to Mya-day-men's palace. Maung Nau and several members of the crew of the boat followed them, bearing the emperor's Bible and a gift for the Atwinwun Maung Zah. From Mya-day-men they learned that the emperor had been told they were in the city and had said, "Let them be introduced." These words from the Gold Lips seemed a good omen, and they felt a little more hopeful of success.

Presently Maung Yo, at the head of his numerous retinue, led them through the sun-baked street to the emperor's palace. After a long delay at the gate while official after official satisfied himself that their permits to enter were in order, they were ushered — after removing their shoes and leaving a present — into the Atwin-wun Maung Zah's columned reception chambers in the palace courtyard.

Though Maung Zah's huge audience hall, thronged with hundreds of retainers and suppliants, was really only a sort of anteroom to the royal quarters, to Adoniram and Colman it looked impressive enough for an emperor in its own right. Maung Zah was seated at one side on a low dais. Before him sat — or rather squatted — the several dozens of dignitaries whose affairs were worthy of the attention of a privy councillor of the ruler. They were arranged by rank, governors and sub-kings in front, others of less, though high, importance behind them. It was a tribute to Mya-day-men's influence that the two missionaries were seated a little in advance of even the front row.

Affably Maung Zah asked them what they wanted. Adoniram explained their purpose: they were, as the Burmese expressed it, propagators of religion who wished to present to the emperor their sacred books and a certain petition. The petition he handed to Maung Zah, who took it, read about half, and then, mildly inter-ested, asked a few questions about their religion which Adoniram answered as clearly, but as diplomatically, as he could.

Suddenly there was a stir in the audience hall. An official entered hurriedly and announced that the Golden Foot was about to ad-vance. The interview ended abruptly. Maung Zah scrambled to his feet and began to don the robes of state held for him by attendants, hastily explaining to Adoniram and Colman as he did so that if he were to present them to the emperor it would have to be now. The crowd, except for the two or three who were to enter the presence of royalty, dissolved as if by magic, leaving the two missionaries seated almost alone in front of the frantically dressing Atwinwun.

For a while the Atwinwun forgot them as he busied himself with his robes and put on his *tsalway*, the golden chain of office with its twelve highly ornamented strands, highest permitted to any subject but a prince of the blood, which had to be passed over his left shoulder and displayed so as to cross on his breast.

A courtier took advantage of the interval to speak to Adoniram. Today was an unfortunate day for their purpose, he told them, with the melancholy satisfaction of one who enjoys bringing bad tidings. This was the day of celebration of the Burman victory over the Cassays. The Golden Feet were advancing with the intention that the Golden Eyes might look upon a military display. An interruption in order to hear a petition concerning a foreign religion might not be viewed with favor by those Eyes.

Adoniram and Colman were digesting this news when Maung Zah completed arraying himself, and said to them, "How can you propagate religion in this empire? But come along," and hurried out of the room. With sinking hearts they followed him and Maung Yo through what seemed miles of splendid walks and corridors until they passed up a flight of stairs into a magnificent hall, so long as to seem nearly endless, every square inch of surface covered with gold, its lofty dome supported by hundreds of tall pillars.

Here they were led to an alcove or corner at one side and told to sit down. Next to them knelt Maung Zah, behind them Maung Yo and another of Mya-day-men's retainers. Now there was nothing to do but await the advance of the Golden Foot.

Adoniram employed the interval by looking around. They sat facing in the direction from which the emperor would appear. Since he would have to walk past them to reach the end which opened out on the parade grounds where the display was to take place, they were admirably placed to attract his attention.

The four of them were almost lost in the nearly empty room, which was so long it seemed all but endless; yet every square inch of visible surface was completely covered with gold leaf. Adoniram began to appreciate his presumption in petitioning a monarch who used such a room as a mere corridor. His fear grew as he realized how insignificant a gift his gold-covered Bible would seem to a ruler who saw nothing but gold wherever he turned his eyes. But it was too late for retreat now.

He had perhaps five minutes for such reflections. Then, without warning, every Burman in the room flung himself flat on the floor. From this position Maung Yo whispered to Adoniram that the Golden Feet had entered the room. The two missionaries did not prostrate themselves, but they did kneel, and, with their hands folded respectfully, waited to catch sight of the emperor.

The man who strode unattended toward them with "the proud gait and majesty of an Eastern monarch," although he had a "high aspect and commanding eye," was impressive on account of his rank rather than for stature or costume. He was about twenty-eight years old, short, just a little over five feet tall, and extremely bandy-legged. His expression was pleasant and good-humored but the appearance of his face was marred by a forehead which slanted sharply backward — an inherited peculiarity of the descendants of the emperor Alompra.

Around his legs and waist he wore a skirtlike checked silk cloth, the patso, of the bright scarlet reserved for royalty. His light jacket, the engyee, was of white muslin. Around his head he had knotted a handkerchief, turban-fashion, to hold his long hair. Although his attire was rich, the only thing about him that indicated royalty to Adoniram was the gold-sheathed sword he carried instead of a scepter.

As he drew near he caught sight of the two kneeling missionaries, the only people in the room who dared look at him and were not stretched flat on the floor. He stopped and turned partly toward Adoniram and Colman.

"Who are these?" he said.

Adoniram undertook to answer for himself. "The teachers, Great King," he replied in Burmese.

The king was surprised. "What, you speak Burman? . . . The priests that I heard of last night? When did you arrive?"

"Yesterday, Your Majesty."

The king was interested. He sat down on an elevated seat, his hand resting on the hilt of his sword, his eyes studying the two men in a not unfriendly way.

"Are you teachers of religion?" he inquired. When Adoniram assented he asked a dozen or so other questions: Were they like the Portuguese priests? Were they married? Why did they dress as they did? Adoniram replied briefly and respectfully each time until the king appeared satisfied.

All this time Maung Zah and the other high officials had been lying with their faces pressed to the floor. Now, when the king seemed to have no more questions to ask, Maung Zah raised his head enough to read the missionaries' petition.

The American teachers present themselves to receive the favor of the excellent king, the sovereign of land and sea [it began]. Hearing that, on account of the greatness of the royal power, the royal country was in a quiet and prosperous state, we arrived at the town of Rangoon, within the royal dominions, and having obtained leave from the governor of that town, to come up and behold the Golden Face, we have ascended, and reached the bottom of the Golden Feet.

In the great country of America [Maung Zah read on] we sustain the character of teachers and explainers of the contents of the sacred Scriptures of our religion. And since it is contained in those Scriptures, that, if we pass to other countries, and preach and propagate religion, great good will result, and both those who teach and those who receive the religion will be freed from future punishment, and enjoy, without decay or death, the eternal felicity of heaven — that royal permission be given, that we, taking refuge in the royal power, may preach our religion in these dominions, and that those who are pleased with our preaching, and wish to listen to and be guided by it, whether foreigners or Burmans, may be exempt from Government molestation, they present themselves to receive the favor of the excellent king, the sovereign of land and sea.

The king listened quietly. Then he stretched out his hand. Maung Zah crawled forward and presented the petition. His Majesty took it and deliberately read it through, from top to bottom. Meanwhile, Adoniram passed to Maung Zah a carefully abridged and edited copy of the tract which Adoniram had written four years before. When the king had finished the petition he silently returned it to Maung Zah, who now handed him the tract. Watching the king take the tract, Adoniram prayed inwardly with all the fervor of his heart, "Oh, have mercy on Burma! Have mercy on her king!"

But King Bagyidaw merely read the opening sentences: "There is one Being who exists eternally; who is exempt from sickness, old age, and death; who is, and was, and will be, without beginning and without end. Besides this, the true God, there is no other God . . . ." Then he opened his hand with indifference and let the paper fall to the floor. Maung Zah picked it up and returned it to Adoniram.

There was a moment of deathly silence. Maung Yo, with some courage for a courtier, made an attempt to save the situation by opening one of the volumes of the Bible and showing it to the king, but the monarch took no notice.

The missionaries' petition had been rejected.

Adoniram and Colman knelt in dejected silence as Maung Zah interpreted the king's decision: "Why do you ask for such permission? Have not the Portuguese, the English, the Moslems, and people of all other religions, full liberty to practice and worship according to their own customs? In regard to the objects of your petition, His Majesty gives no order. In regard to your sacred books, His Majesty has no use for them. Take them away."

Someone — probably Maung Yo — said that Colman had skill in medicine. The king ordered: "Let them proceed to the residence of my physician, the Portuguese priest. Let him examine whether they can be useful to me in that capacity, and report accordingly."

Then he rose, strode on without a backward look to the end of the hall overlooking the parade ground, threw himself down on a cushion, and began to watch the military display. This was all Adoniram and Colman had time to see. They were hurried unceremoniously out of the audience hall and led back to the house of Mya-day-men. The king had been cold to their mission. No one in the palace wanted to have anything more to do with them.

Even so, however, Maung Yo did what he could to make things easier for them by giving the Wungyi as favorable a report of their reception by His Majesty as he could without actually being untruthful. As Mya-day-men did not know precisely what they had asked for, their rejection did not seem as serious to him as Adoniram knew it was. The meeting was short. Afterwards, the two were hurried two miles through the hot, dusty streets to the Portuguese priest. It took him only a few minutes to learn that Colman had no magic art which would protect the king's health and make him live forever, and they were dismissed.

That afternoon they sat on the deck of the boat and discussed their rebuff. Was there any way of persuading the emperor to change his decision? If they saw Maung Zah at home could they gain at least a few concessions?

The next morning Gibson, who already knew what had happened, called on them. He agreed that if Maung Zah could be approached at his home there was at least a chance he might look on them more favorably. He took them to Maung Zah that afternoon. But the Burman was cold and distant, almost openly hostile. He would not even listen to Adoniram, and Gibson had to do most of the talking. Maung Zah made it plain that even petitioning for religious toleration for the Burmans had been an almost unpardonable offense.

Gibson, doggedly advancing every argument he could think of, finally pointed out that if the American missionaries could win royal favor, other foreigners would settle in Burma, and trade would improve. This was the only idea which seemed to affect Maung Zah at all. "Looking out from the cloud which covered his face, he vouchsafed to say, that if we would wait some time, he would endeavor to speak to his majesty about us."

Adoniram and Colman walked the four miles from Maung Zah's house to the boat in the moonlight. The miles of walking in the heat each day, the tension and the repeated discouragements, had so exhausted them that for once they threw themselves on their mattresses and fell asleep without even trying to think of any more expedients.

In the morning, however, they made one more attempt by sending a message requesting Gibson to ask Maung Zah whether they might advance their cause by remaining in the capital for several months. Gibson brought them Maung Zah's reply the next day. Maung Zah had said, "Tell them, that there is not the least possibility of obtaining the object stated in this paper, should they wait ever so long."

Furthermore, added Gibson, the emperor had decided to open war with Siam. He would have no time for the missionaries. In the fall he planned to march in person to Pegu, below Rangoon, to set up his campaign headquarters. If they saw him at all, it would have to be there. Gibson agreed to give Maung Zah a copy of the tract, but he had no hope that it would have any effect. They knew that if Gibson said their cause was hopeless, it was. With heavy hearts they decided to depart.

First, however, they paid a call on Mr. Rodgers, of course more out of courtesy than from any feeling that he could or would help. But he gave them one piece of information which told them why their effort had failed, and why, in all probability, any future efforts would fail.

Adoniram had heard from his old teacher, U Aung Min, of the one Burman who had become a Christian some fifteen years before and had been tortured for his belief. Rodgers, it now turned out, had witnessed the whole affair. The man, a teacher at Ava of important family and outstanding ability, had been converted by the Roman Catholics and sent to Rome for study. On his return his nephew, then a Thau-dau-sen, a secretary of the Atwinwuns, had denounced him for forswearing his country's religion. With the emperor's approval, the nephew had thrown his uncle into prison and had him tortured. When he would not recant he was beaten with an iron maul inch by inch from the feet to the breast. Rodgers had been present at this beating and had paid the executioners to strike as gently as possible.

But the man would not recant. To save him, some of the people close to the emperor told him the man was insane, and he was released. The Portuguese priests took him secretly out of the country and sent him to Bengal, where he ended his days. Since then, the priests had never tried to convert Burmans, but had confined their labors to their own congregations of descendants of the Portuguese mercenaries of old, who were permitted to be Christians by custom and law.

Up to this point little in the story told by Rodgers was new to Adoniram. He had learned most of it from U Aung Min long ago, and its lesson had not deterred him from trying to convert Burmans. But one thing Rodgers told him *was* new: The nephew, the Thau-dau-sen who had accused and tortured his uncle, was now an Atwin-wun himself, one of the four privy councillors to the king — and not only an Atwinwun, but the first, ahead of even Maung Zah, who had introduced the two Americans into the emperor's presence. With such a man having the imperial ear, Maung Zah could accomplish nothing for them even if he wished.

Worse still, went on Rodgers, the chief queen, the first of His Majesty's wives, was a fanatical Buddhist, and had acquired such power over the king that he was practically under her thumb. She had been daughter of a jailer, a member of the most degraded class in Burma. She was older than the king. Somehow, with incredible cunning and ruthlessness she had raised her status from mere concubine to first wife. Her suspiciousness and vindictiveness were well known in court circles. People whispered that she was a sorceress. How else could a woman of such origin rise to ascendancy over the ruler? But sorceress or not, said Rodgers, Adoniram and Colman must see the hopelessness of their mission.

Adoniram knew that Rodgers had reasons of his own, connected with his intrigue for power, to discourage Christian missionaries — or any white men, for that matter — from staying in Burma. But in this case he knew Rodgers was telling the truth.

Only the day after the king had rejected their petition, he had given a great feast in the palace for all the Buddhist priests in the surrounding villages. At the same time he had created a hundred new priests, some of them sons of noblemen.

The intent of the new ruler was plain. Against it Christian missionaries stood no chance at all, Adoniram and Colman agreed. Sadly they returned to their boat and the next day applied for a passport to leave the capital.

Getting the passport took five days of petitioning and bribery. During that time they learned that Maung Zah had read their tract and kept it, saying, "The doctrine and commands are very good — but it will be a long time before Burmans can be convinced there is a God and Saviour."

Gibson had even dared to mention them again to the emperor, but the emperor had merely laughed and replied, "What, they have come presuming to convert us to their religion! Let them leave our capital. We have no desire to receive their instructions. Perhaps they may find some of their countrymen in Rangoon who may be willing to listen to them."

The king's open contempt worried Gibson. He warned Adoniram and Colman that they had better secure a royal order protecting them against personal molestation. "Otherwise," he said, "as it will be notorious that you have solicited royal patronage and been refused, you will lie at the mercy of every ill-disposed person."

But an order like the one Gibson advised would cost several hundred ticals and they could not afford it. They would have to put their trust in the Lord.

No one could have been more discouraged than Adoniram when, on the sixth of February, their boat started down-river. They had spent much time and money, only to fail. Worse, they had staked all their future prospects on this one attempt to gain royal favor. In losing, they had not only failed to help their own cause, they had hurt it. The news would follow them — perhaps even precede them — down the river and it was not hard to imagine the effect it would have in Rangoon.

No wonder Adoniram wrote that day, just before the boat shoved off:

I could moralize half an hour on the apt resemblance, the beautiful congruity, between the desolate state of our feelings and the sandy barren surface of this miserable beach. But "'tis idle all." Let the beach and our sorrow go together. Something better will turn up tomorrow.

## CHAPTER XI
# Crisis
## [ *1819–1820* ]

MOVING with the current, the boat slipped downstream a good deal faster than it had gone up. But the prospect of a quick homecoming did not make Adoniram any happier when he thought of the news he carried. Ahead he saw nothing but the breakup of the mission, the dispersal of the few converts, their probable loss of faith, and the wiping out of all his efforts. Thus he was in one of his characteristic depressed moods when they tied up one night at Prome, a hundred miles or so above Rangoon.

The boat had been at the landing only a little while when he was pleasantly surprised by a greeting from a familiar voice. In a moment its owner stepped aboard — none other than Maung Shway-gnong, whom he had last seen standing on the wharf at Rangoon giving his dignified salute of farewell. The old man had just arrived to visit a friend who was seriously ill. He intended to stay in Prome only a few days. If Adoniram and Colman could wait, he would gladly return to Rangoon with them.

To Maung Shway-gnong Adoniram poured out the story of the rejection of his petition by the emperor, winding up with Mr. Rodgers's account of the Burman who was beaten with the iron maul. Adoniram was taken aback by the calmness with which Maung Shway-gnong received the news. He had expected the Burman to be disturbed and sympathetic. Instead he seemed almost indifferent.

Irritated, Adoniram lashed out. "It is not for you that we are concerned, but for those who have become disciples of Christ. When they are accused and persecuted, they cannot worship at the pagodas or recant before the Mangen teacher as you have done." His remark stung. Maung Shway-gnong began to defend his past conduct, but Adoniram interrupted: "Say nothing. One thing you know to be true — that when formerly accused, if you had not in some way or other satisfied the Mangen teacher, your life would not now be remaining in your body."

Maung Shway-gnong had no answer to this but that he was a new man now, regardless of the past. "If I must die," he said earnestly, "I shall die in a good cause. I know it is the cause of truth." And he repeated to Adoniram with a good deal of emphasis, "I believe in the eternal God, in His Son Jesus Christ, in the atonement which Christ has made, and in the writings of the apostles, as the true and only word of God."

He continued, "Perhaps you may not remember that during one of my last visits you told me that I was trusting in my own understanding rather than the divine word. From that time I have seen my error, and endeavored to renounce it. You explained to me also the evil of worshiping at pagodas, though I told you that my heart did not partake in the worship. Since you left Rangoon I have not lifted up my folded hands before a pagoda. It is true, I sometimes follow the crowd on days of worship in order to avoid persecution, but I walk up one side of the pagoda and walk down the other. Now you say that I am not a disciple. What lack I yet?"

These honest words convinced Adoniram that the old Burman's faith had really grown during the past month or so. But he insisted: "Teacher, you may be a disciple of Christ in heart, but you are not a full disciple. You have not faith and resolution enough to keep all the commands of Christ, particularly that which requires you to be baptized, though in the face of persecution and death. Consider the words of Jesus just before He returned to heaven: 'He that believeth and is baptized shall be saved.' "

To this Maung Shway-gnong made no reply. For some time he sat on the deck in silence, with an expression which, Adoniram knew, meant that he was considering deeply what he had just heard. After a few minutes Adoniram told him that the missionaries were thinking of leaving Rangoon. As soon as it became known that the emperor had all but prohibited any teaching of Christianity to Burmans, no Burman would dare to listen to the Gospel, much less accept it.

This news roused Maung Shway-gnong. "Say not so," he said.

"There are some who will investigate, notwithstanding; and rather than have you leave Rangoon, I will go myself to the Mangen teacher and have a public dispute. I know I can silence him."

"Yes," Adoniram replied, "you may have a tongue to silence *him* — but he has a pair of fetters and an iron maul to silence *you*. Remember that."

It was nine o'clock when Maung Shway-gnong left the boat. But Adoniram and Colman discussed the meaning of the conversation until midnight, and lay awake much later as the boat rocked gently on the dark water, wondering.

Could God have arranged this strange meeting as a sign that He would help them in their last extremity? The temple bells tinkling gently in the night breeze were a melodious reminder from the pagodas on shore of the power of Buddhism in Burma. But here had been Maung Shway-gnong, the teacher and skeptic, volunteering to defend Christianity publicly!

Perhaps God had chosen a few, like Maung Shway-gnong, whom He meant to call to their aid at the most dangerous moment. If this wild surmise were correct, the missionaries had no right to desert their disciples by removing the mission from Rangoon. But how could they endure seeing them in prison, in chains, under torture?

Perhaps they had better wait until they reached Rangoon. If the disciples stood firm and others were seriously inquiring, it might be a portent. At least, for the first time since that meeting with the emperor, they thought they saw a glimmer of hope. "But it was not like the soft beam of the moon, which kindly shines on the path of the benighted pilgrim, and guides him to a place of shelter. It was rather like the angry gleam of lightning which, while for a moment it illumines the landscape around, discloses the black magazine of heaven's artillery and threatens death to the unwary gazer."

They returned to Rangoon on February 18, 1820. They had been away almost exactly two months. A few days later, a Sunday evening, Adoniram called together his three converts Maung Nau, Maung Thahlah and Maung Byaay, and gave them a complete account of what had happened in Ava. He told them frankly that the trip had been a complete failure and that from now on Christian Burmans could expect persecution and suffering. He had reluctantly come to the conclusion, he said, that the missionaries had better leave Burma. Remaining would attract official attention and expose the converts to even greater danger.

He had been privately convinced that Maung Thahlah and Maung Byaay would lose heart and abjure Christianity rather than face the prospects he described. Mung Nau was the only one of whom he felt sure. Maung Nau had told him on the way down-river that he would follow the missionaries to any part of the world. His only fear was that he would be a burden in case his ignorance of another language prevented his earning a living.

But to Adoniram's delighted surprise, his words only seemed to increase the zeal of the three. The more he emphasized the dangers, the harder they tried to explain them away and persuade him that the mission was not in such desperate case as he thought.

Their constantly repeated question was, "Where are the teachers going?" To this Adoniram replied that the missionaries would never desert Burma, but that they would have to settle in the region around Chittagong, between Bengal and Arakan, where the murder of the missionary De Bruyn had left baptized Christians without teachers.

The real question, however, said Adoniram, was: What would these three do? Maung Nau, he knew, would follow the missionaries to Chittagong. But what about Maung Thahlah and Maung Byaay?

Maung Thahlah had already made up his mind. "As for me," he said stoutly, "I go where preaching is to be had."

Maung Byaay, however, was silent and thoughtful for some time. He had a wife and children. Burmese women were not allowed to leave the country. He would have to stay. "But," he said rather sadly, "if I must be left here alone, I shall remain performing the duties of Jesus Christ's religion. No other shall I think of."

But the issue was not settled so easily. For three or four days Adoniram and Colman inquired for a ship to Chittagong. Then one evening Maung Byaay came to the mission house with his brother-in-law, a man named Maung Myat-yah, who had lived in the mission yard several months and had often attended worship in the zayat.

"I have come," said Maung Byaay, "to petition that you will not leave Rangoon at present."

"I think that it is useless to remain under the present circumstances," said Adoniram regretfully. "We cannot open the zayat. We cannot have public worship. No Burman will dare to examine this religion; and if none examine, none will embrace it."

But Maung Byaay would not give up. "Teacher," he pleaded, "my mind is distressed. I can neither eat nor sleep since I find you are going away. I have been around among those who live near us, and I find some who are even now examining the new religion. Brother Myat-yah is one, and he unites with me in my petition." Myat-yah agreed that Maung Byaay spoke the truth. "Therefore do stay with us a few months," Maung Byaay begged. "Stay until there are eight or ten disciples. Then appoint one to be the teacher of the rest. I shall not be concerned about the event. Though you leave the country, the religion will spread of itself. The emperor himself cannot stop it. But if you go now, and take the two disciples that can follow, I shall be left alone. I cannot baptize those who may wish to embrace this religion. What can I do?"

Adoniram felt unable to reject Maung Byaay's request without consulting Colman and Nancy. The three were just discussing it when Maung Nau came in. He agreed emphatically with Maung Byaay. He was sure that several of the inquirers would become converts in spite of the government if the missionaries would only stay a little longer.

The attitude of the Burman converts brought involuntary tears to the missionaries' eyes. Perhaps Adoniram's feelings included a little shame when he compared his own doubts with the confidence of the humble men who looked up to him as guide and teacher. "We live only for the promotion of the cause of Christ among the Burmans," he assured them. "If there is any prospect of success in Rangoon we have no desire to go to another place. Therefore we will reconsider the matter."

While the missionaries tried to make up their minds, Maung Nau, Maung Thahlah and Maung Byaay were evidently exerting every effort to mobilize the inquirers who had taken up residence in the mission yard. After the evening prayer meeting a few days later, Maung Thahlah, along with Maung Byaay and Maung Nau, brought one of them to Adoniram as a reason for the missionaries to stay.

He was a quiet agreeable man named Maung Shwa-boo, who had come to live in the yard just before Adoniram and Colman had left for Ava.

In Maung Shwa-boo's presence Maung Thahlah said, "Teacher, your intention of going away has filled us all with trouble. Is it good to forsake us thus? Notwithstanding present difficulties and dangers, it is to be remembered that this work is not yours or ours, but the work of God. If He give light, the religion will spread. Nothing can impede it." Maung Byaay and his brother-in-law Maung Myat-yah had been listening as Maung Thahlah spoke, and in a few minutes Adoniram learned that still another resident of the yard, Maung Louk, was listening outside the door. Maung Louk was brought in to sit with Maung Shwa-boo and Maung Myat-yah.

The sight of the three inquirers moved Maung Byaay to enthusiasm. With great feeling, he raised his arm and said, "Let us all make an effort. As for me, I will pray. If we can get a little church of ten members, with one who is capable of administering the ordinances, then if you feel the necessity of going to another place to preach, go, and we will stay here and perform the duties of religion, in a still secret way, agreeably to the sacred writings. It is my opinion that there will be one raised up among us who is more learned than any of us, and who will be qualified to be our teacher. Though government difficulties are before us, hell is also before us, and those who are really afraid of hell cannot help embracing Christ."

"Yes," added Maung Thahlah with animation, "Christ has taught us not to fear those who can kill the body only, but to fear him who can destroy both soul and body in hell."

Maung Nau seconded Maung Byaay and Maung Thahlah. But when Adoniram questioned the three inquirers closely it was plain that although they were considering the new religion none of them as yet was willing to admit a belief in it. He suspected that much of their interest was the product of intense pressure by the converts rather than the beginning of inner conviction.

Nevertheless, as Adoniram talked the matter over with Nancy and Colman, it seemed that the prospect of making converts was better than ever. It would be impossible, they agreed, to go away and leave all these people without help. Yet it seemed foolhardy not to have an alternative base.

The missionaries talked late that night before coming to a decision: The Colmans would go to Chittagong, form a new station, and try to bring into it the Arakanese converts. Adoniram and Nancy would stay in Rangoon. If Rangoon became untenable, they could join the Colmans with as many converts as would go with them. If their fears about Rangoon turned out to be unfounded, the Colmans could return.

In the crisis each member of the embryo church seemed to grow out of himself. Never had the missionaries and converts felt such mutual affection and trust. The three Burmans revealed qualities no one knew they possessed, themselves least of all. It was almost as if new, hitherto unrealized personalities were emerging from the husks of the old.

To a Burman, with a fear of rulers ingrained by centuries under despotism, the mere thought of disobeying the mildest edict was inexpressibly horrifying. Yet the three converts were talking, in the most matter-of-fact manner possible, of defying the emperor by secretly building a Christian church, although no activity could have been more subversive in the eyes of the government.

Before the emergncy, Adoniram and Nancy had considered Maung Nau exceptionally mild and submissive by nature and almost excessively dependent on the missionaries. Now, on account of his boldness and zeal, they took to calling him "Peter" between themselves.

When they first knew him, Maung Byaay had been so timid and reserved that they had thought him sullen. He still sat with the missionaries in solemn silence, drinking in every word they had to say. But when it came to defending the Gospel among the Burmans living in the mission yard, he spoke out with the animation of an orator and the courage of a hero.

Maung Thahlah had always been quicker of mind and a better student than the other two, but even he had never shown any signs of the learning that distinguished the aristocratic scholar Maung Shway-gnong. Now he began to display an amazing facility at soaking up Scripture and applying apt passages in talking with inquirers. He also showed unexpected talents as student and as teacher.

It did really seem that the Lord was encouraging them in those dark days. In spite of the fact that meetings in the zayat were held behind closed doors, with never more than eight or ten present, two conversions occurred even before the Colmans sailed. The first, a relative of Maung Thahlah's, Maung Shway-bay, began to be interested in the idea of an eternal God on March 20, studied and prayed the next two days, and on March 24 presented a written statement of his faith with a request to be baptized the following Sunday. Even Maung Myat-yah said: "Set me down for a disciple. I have fully made up my mind in regard to this religion. I love Jesus Christ, but I am not quite ready for baptism."

The Colmans embarked for Arakan on March 27, 1820. The day after they left one of their rooms in the mission house was fitted out for evening worship and intimate conversations. This little chapel Adoniram and Nancy hopefully called "the new zayat." The old zayat was abandoned.

In May, two friends of Maung Shway-gnong, both wealthy men and well above the middle class, asked for baptism. The wife of one of them, and two or three other women, were nearly converts. The danger seemed to imbue them with a sense of urgency to seize salvation without delay, no matter what the risk.

But Maung Shway-gnong himself held back. Desperately he brought up one objection after another. Why was one day of the seven set aside by God as a special day? Why was it necessary to assemble on this day and worship? Why was the sacrament of baptism necessary? Why the Lord's Supper?

Adoniram refused to argue. There it was in the Bible, the Lord's command. Maung Shway-gnong could accept or reject. But if he accepted, he must accept humbly, know that it was not for the mind of man to question or even comprehend the reason. Neither God nor Jesus indulged in debates, nor stooped to split metaphysical hairs.

In spite of his cavils, however, Maung Shway-gnong kept sending inquirers. When he was with them, he would take Adoniram's side. He was particularly appreciative of one argument Adoniram had learned to use on men of Maung Shway-gnong's type. Adoniram called them Buddhist "semi-atheists." Rejecting Buddhism, which they had outgrown years earlier, they still believed in a kind of diffuse eternal wisdom which permeated the universe and was the only God. It was over this point that they always arrived triumphantly at what they considered the great objection to Adoniram's God: Why was not this sort of impersonal eternal wisdom of theirs the real God, rather than Adoniram's God, Who was a person? Invariably Adoniram would demolish them with three succinct phrases: "No mind, no wisdom. Temporary mind, temporary wisdom. Eternal mind, eternal wisdom." For some reason, noted Adoniram with relish:

> . . . This concise statement sweeps, with irresistible sway, through the very joints and marrow of their system. And though it may to others seem rather simple and inconclusive, to one acquainted with Burman reasoning, its effect is uniformly decisive. No sooner is this short sentence uttered, than one significantly nods his head, as if to say, there you have it. Another cries out to the opponent, you are undone, destroyed. Another says talk with wisdom, where else will you find it?
>
> The disputant himself, who was perhaps preparing a learned speech about the excellency and efficacy and eternity of wisdom, quite disconcerted by this unexpected onset, sits looking at the wreck of his system, and wondering at the simple means which has spread such ruin around him; presently he looks up (for the Burmans are frequently candid), and says, your words are very appropriate. And perhaps his next question is, How can I become a disciple of the God you worship?

But although Maung Shway-gnong savored these triumphs almost more than Adoniram, he still could not quite bring himself to full, open discipleship. Adoniram had finally come to recognize the real reason. It was less the opposition of Maung Shway-gnong's wife and friends than simple fear. For if Maung Shway-gnong took the final step, his prominence and position almost guaranteed his persecution, torture and death.

This was why Adoniram was no longer willing to cross dialectic swords with him. For although he continued to drop hints of the glories of martyrdom, he admitted: "My heart was wrung with pity. . . . The thought of the iron maul, and a secret suspicion that if I was in his circumstances, I should perhaps have no more courage, restrained my tongue."

Before his journey to Ava, Adoniram had begun translating the Epistle to the Ephesians. On his return he worked at it as fast as he could, and in spite of the weakness of his eyes finished it toward the end of April. The disciples and inquirers nearly tore it from his hands and all but quarreled with each other for the chance to read it. This translation, they thought, was much plainer than the Matthew, much more easily understood.

Meanwhile Nancy's health had been failing. She suffered intense pain from what seemed to be liver trouble. Two grueling courses of "salivation" did not help, and by late June Adoniram realized that she would have to seek medical help in Bengal. Since he was doubtful whether she could survive the voyage alone, this time he felt he would have to go with her. A ship was in the river, planning to sail the middle of July, and he reserved passage for them both and for little Emily. Lanciego — the Spaniard we have mentioned as currently victorious in the never-ending struggle with Rodgers for the collectorship of Rangoon — helped procure the passports and promised to protect the people on the mission premises.

Word of their imminent departure brought two more applications for baptism on Sunday, July 9. Adoniram recommended that the applicants wait until his return. But the next Sunday, with the ship due to sail Monday, the two came to him in great distress and said they could not be easy in mind until they were baptized. Suppose Adoniram should fail to return? They *must* be baptized before he left. Adoniram agreed; and that night they underwent the ceremony in a small pond near the mission house.

As it happened, the ship's departure was delayed. Maung Shwaygnong took this opportunity to visit the mission house. He had been absent for some time and Adoniram received him none too graciously until he learned that the Burman had been ill with a fever. As they talked, Adoniram began to be convinced that the teacher had at last really become a Christian. His account of his secret prayers, his struggle with sin, his penitence and faith — the evidence was overwhelming.

That afternoon some friends of Maung Shway-gnong came in

and the old teacher brought matters to a head. Indicating the visitors, he said, "My lord teacher, there are now several of us who have long considered this religion. I hope that we are all believers in Jesus Christ."

"I am afraid to say that," Adoniram replied cautiously. "However, it is easy to determine; and let me begin with you, teacher. I have heretofore thought that you fully believed in the eternal God; but I have had some doubt whether you fully believed in the Son of God, and the atonement which He has made."

"I assure you," rejoined the old man earnestly, "that I am as fully persuaded of the latter as of the former."

Adoniram looked the teacher full in the face. "Do you believe, then, that none but the disciples will be saved from sin and hell?"

The Burman met his look squarely. "None but his disciples," he said firmly.

"How, then, can you remain, without taking the oath of allegiance to Jesus Christ, and becoming his full disciple, in body and soul?"

"It is my earnest desire to do so, by receiving baptism," said Maung Shway-gnong. "For the very purpose of expressing that desire, I have come here today."

Adoniram could hardly believe his ears. "You say you are desirous of receiving baptism. May I ask *when* you desire to receive it?"

"At any time you will please to give it. Now — this moment, if you please."

"Do you wish to receive baptism in public or in private?"

"I will receive it at any time, and in any circumstances, that you please to direct."

For a moment Adoniram was silent. Then: "Teacher, I am satisfied, from your conversation this afternoon, that you are a true disciple. I reply, therefore, that I am as desirous of giving you baptism as you are of receiving it."

The effect of this conversation was immense. The disciples were overjoyed. The others were almost struck dumb with astonishment. For a long time they had thought Maung Shway-gnong was a Christian at heart. But they had never dreamed he would ever admit it publicly or allow a foreigner to put him under water.

Adoniram turned to one of these onlookers, a man named Maung Thay-ay, who he suspected might also be a believer. "Are you too willing to take the oath of allegiance to Jesus Christ?"

"If the teacher Maung Shway-gnong consents," Thay-ay said, "why should I hesitate?"

"And if he does not consent, what then?"

"Then," said Thay-ay, "I must wait a little longer."

Adoniram lifted his palm. "Stand by," he said. "You trust in Maung Shway-gnong, rather than in Jesus Christ. You are not worthy of being baptized."

One by one he asked the others. They were not quite ready. Finally he came to the woman, Mah Men-lay, whose husband had just decided he was not ready. After a moment's mental struggle, she said, "If the teacher thinks it suitable for me to be baptized, I am desirous of receiving baptism." This response did not satisfy Adoniram. He told her he could not baptize anyone who could possibly be easy in mind without it.

At dark the next evening, Adoniram called in two or three of the disciples and made the baptismal prayer in private. Then together they took Maung Shway-gnong to the usual place, went down into the water, and baptized him.

Back at the mission house, Adoniram learned that the woman Mah Men-lay had seen Maung Shway-gnong on his way to the pool. She had exclaimed to Nancy, "Ah! He has gone to obey the command of Jesus Christ, while I remain without obeying. I shall not be able to sleep this night. I must go home and consult my husband."

Later that night she returned, and asked to be baptized at once. Adoniram and the disciples had just finished partaking of the Lord's Supper, and he asked them if they were agreeable. They were. Without delay, he led her out to the pond by the house and by lantern light baptized the first Burmese woman. The dream of a church of ten native Burmese had come true.

At noon the next day, July 19, 1820, Adoniram and Nancy set out for the river. They were followed by nearly a hundred people, the women crying aloud, according to the custom of the country. When the two entered the little boat which was to take them to the ship, Adoniram asked the teacher Maung Shway-gnong, the woman Mah Men-lay, and one or two others to accompany them.

As the boat drew away from shore, those on the riverbank called out their farewells. Above the confusion of cries Adoniram and Nancy could hear voices telling them to come back soon.

When the boat returned the Burmans to shore after an hour or so, Adoniram and Nancy stood on the quarterdeck for a long time looking at the city which contained their little Burmese church, their hearts too full for words.

Two days later the ship anchored near the grove known as "The Elephant" at the river mouth. Early in the morning of August 18 they arrived at Calcutta.

## CHAPTER XII

# Return to the Golden Feet

### [ *1820–1822* ]

THEY remained in Calcutta three months: a few days with the Lawsons, who had traveled to India with Rice on the *Harmony;* two months with the Houghs at Serampore; and not quite a month with the Reverend Mr. Townley of the London Missionary Society and his wife. Mr. Townley, noted Nancy, was one of those fortunate missionaries who had sufficient property to support himself and his wife.

Nancy's health fluctuated. Dr. Chalmers, who declined any fee, thought she had a chronic ailment of the liver. He recommended that she go to the United States, where a cool climate might help. A return to Rangoon was out of the question.

Regretfully, Adoniram reserved a passage for himself alone on the *Salamanca,* which expected to sail for Rangoon early in November. But late in October, when a Dr. Macwhirter, whose reputation was equal to Chalmers's, thought he could prescribe medicines which would permit her to go back with Adoniram, he also took passage for her.

The stay in Calcutta was quiet. The only unpleasantness was occasioned by some ugly stories about the Judsons' treatment of the dying Wheelock which were undoubtedly being circulated by his widow Eliza, who had chosen to remain in India and about this time married "a Mr. Jones of Calcutta." Nancy was doubly hurt because she knew the stories were on their way back to Wheelock's parents. A few days before they sailed she wrote a long letter about the whole matter to Mrs. Carleton in the United States, asking her to convey the truth to old Mr. and Mrs. Wheelock. She could not, she wrote, have them feel she was "so destitute of the feelings of humanity as to have denied their son anything which could have rendered him comfortable." The fact was, Eliza "was the 'root of bitterness,' she endeavored to prevent our union. But notwithstanding all her exertions to ruin our characters, we are endeavouring to cultivate a forgiving spirit, and I trust we have in some measure obtained it."

They embarked with Emily Van Someren on the *Salamanca* the twenty-third of November. The voyage was unpleasant. The ship was small and overcrowded with humans, scorpions and centipedes. They met contrary winds, squalls and the most terrifying thunder and lightning storm they had ever seen. The passage should have taken about two weeks, but six weeks elapsed before, on January 3, 1821, they sighted the Elephant at the western limit of the Rangoon outlet of the Irrawaddy.

The pilot had news both good and bad. Mya-day-men, the Wungyi, the stern spear-carrier who had been viceroy of Rangoon when they first arrived and whose wife had befriended them, was again in Rangoon as viceroy. This was the good news. The bad news was that some thirty thousand troops had recently marched through Rangoon on their way to Siam, making ready for war. It was just as well that the Colmans were preparing a refuge at Chittagong.

The ship drew near the town on the fifth. As the golden tower of the great pagoda soared up above the trees, Nancy and Adoniram strained their eyes from the crowded quarterdeck for a sight of their friends on shore. Sure enough, across the yellow water they could recognize among the many on the wharf the tall figure of old Maung Shway-gnong, his hands raised to his head in greeting. And there were Maung Thahlah, the woman Mah Men-lay, and other disciples, together with various children. They all trooped together to the examination at the customs, and surrounded the two missionaries like a flock as they made their way to the mission house.

The warmth of the greetings, the love of the Burmese disciples, the solicitude for their comfort and well-being — all these filled the hearts of Adoniram and Nancy with gratitude. Their reception was as different as could be from that lonely day more than seven years ago when they had first set foot on the soil of Burma. Then they were friendless, the language a mere babel, the name of Christ a meaningless sound. Now they had a Burmese church of ten, firm friends by the score, the language was pleasantly familiar, and the Gospel news was spreading far and wide.

Maung Shway-gnong had important news for them about himself. It was the former viceroy who had said of him ominously "Inquire further," and by those few words dismayed the people and nearly ended the mission. When Mya-day-men returned from the Golden Feet to take up the duties of viceroy again, the priests and officers of Maung Shway-gnong's village had thought they saw a chance to destroy him once and for all. He knew they were conspiring, feeling more triumphant daily, and began to be afraid he might have to flee for his life any moment.

Finally the conspiracy was complete. The leading member, who belonged to the village high court, went to the viceroy and complained, "The teacher Maung Shway-gnong is trying to turn the bottom of the priests' rice pot upwards."

Mya-day-men heard this in silence. Then he replied, "What consequence? Let the priests turn it back again." These simple words had blasted the conspiracy. Until another viceroy came, toleration seemed assured.

Adoniram and Nancy went to the government house to see Mya-day-men's wife. She received them with all the familiarity of an old friend, although she had been promoted by the Emperor to the almost supreme dignity of "Woon-gyee-gau-dau." [1] This meant she was entitled to ride in a *watu,* a sort of palanquin which was carried by forty or fifty men. They saw the viceroy, too, still stalking about restlessly with his huge spear. But he was preoccupied with grief over the death of his favorite daughter, one of the emperor's foremost wives, and said only "Ah! You are come!" before striding on.

The work of the mission continued. There were more inquirers. Even the man Maung Yah, the very first inquirer of years before, returned. Maung Ing, who had been away all of this time at the town of Bike, below Rangoon, turned up too. Long a convert, he had not yet been baptized. Now he received baptism on the fourth

[1] Its translation today, "Mrs. Wungyi," does not convey its import in the 1820's. After all, "Duchess," in a sense, merely means "Mrs. Duke."

of March. A few days later he went back to Bike with a load of tracts. Mah Men-lay of her own accord opened a school in her house, to teach the native boys and girls to read, so they would not have to go to the priests.

But Adoniram spent less time in the zayat than before. He was busy with something more important. The disciples could spread the message of Jesus; it was up to Adoniram to supply that message, in the form of a more complete translation of the Gospel. He had already translated Matthew, the Epistle to the Ephesians, and the first part of Acts. Now, with Maung Shway-gnong's help, he hoped to revise everything he had done so far and produce a better, more accurate version. By mid-May he was able to send the manuscript of Ephesians and the first part of Acts to Hough at Serampore, with a request that six hundred copies of each be printed.

There were many other things to do. There were the Sunday services — one for the few Europeans in Rangoon, another for the Burmese. There were prayer meetings Tuesday and Friday evenings. A woman, Mah-Myat-lay, was baptized. Adoniram decided to employ Maung Shway-bay as a sort of assistant pastor. Maung Thahlah spoke better, Maung Shway-gnong had far more learning and authority, but Maung Shway-bay was graver and more devoted and had a "*humble* and *persevering* desire" for the post, which to Adoniram counted most of all. Adoniram also made a map showing where the events of the Bible occurred, and went over this with the converts.

All this work filled Adoniram's days from dawn to dark. By the middle of July, he had finished the Gospel and Epistles of St. John, "those exquisitely sweet and precious portions of the New Testament," and was working on the latter part of Acts.

But sickness was striking again. Earlier in the year he had an attack of cholera. In the late summer, both he and Nancy came down with a fever. For several days they lay in the same room, unable to help each other, having to depend on Emily for the most personal services. And in spite of salivation with blue mercury pills Nancy's liver trouble was growing much worse. Adoniram felt sure that she would die soon unless something drastic were done at once. August 6, he decided she must go to Bengal for help, and then probably home to America.

August 21, 1822, Nancy embarked for Calcutta with Emily Van Someren, no longer "little Emily," who was to leave her and travel on to Madras, her former home. Emily had been a member of the family for seven years. They had brought her up as their own daughter, but in the surviving letters of that past day she is seldom mentioned. She entered Nancy's and Adoniram's lives, and goes out of them, a shadowy figure.

With Nancy, Adoniram sent a letter to Hough, saying in part:

> I send you herewith Mrs. Judson, and all that remains of the blue pills and senna, and beg you will see the articles all well packed and shipped for America by the earliest safe opportunity. . . . It is said that man is prone to jest in the depths of misery; and the bon-mots of the scaffold have been collected: you may add the above specimen to the list if you like. I feel as if I was on the scaffold, and signing, as it were, my own death warrant. However, two years will pass away at last.

He went on in the same vein:

> I have been occupied in making up my mind to have my right arm amputated, and my right eye extracted, which the doctors say are necessary in order to prevent a decay and mortification of the whole body conjugal.

His right arm and right eye Nancy certainly was. But there was no help for it. For at least two years, he must resign himself to carrying on the mission without her.

When the ship bearing Nancy and Emily had slipped out of sight down the river, Adoniram left the wharf and turned with misting eyes to the mission house. For the next month he applied himself entirely to the zayat and to translation. But in September he had to close the zayat again.

Both Nancy and he suspected that the present state of toleration was too good to last. Although the viceroy and his wife had encouraged them privately, by telling them they would try to present their case favorably before the Emperor on his intended trip through Rangoon on his way to the Siamese border, they admitted that "toleration" could mean freedom only for *foreigners* to worship as they pleased. Even then they did not realize that any Burman had renounced Buddhism and become Christian. That was known only to a small circle in the mission.

But Maung Shway-gnong's conversion could not be concealed from his village. Soon its chief, together with several priests, presented a document to the viceroy accusing Maung Shway-gnong of "having embraced sentiments which aimed at the destruction of the Boodhist religion, and prejudicial to the existing authorities." The viceroy could not overlook this open accusation. He said that if it were true, Maung Shway-gnong deserved death. But he did not hurry to act.

The teacher heard the news at once — his friends had been watching the proceedings carefully. He immediately procured a boat and put his family on board, while he hurried to the mission house to warn Adoniram and pick up a supply of tracts and printed portions of Scripture. Then he went up the river about a hundred miles, to the town of Shway-doung. Here he settled down to spread the Gospel news.

As usual, the viceroy's words scattered the inquirers around the zayat like quail. Adoniram restricted his meetings to the mission house. Even so, he baptized one new convert, but he also lost one by the sudden death from cholera of Maung Thahlah, the second convert. Meanwhile, he spent almost all of his time alone, translating.

The months passed quietly. When government pressure seemed light, Adoniram spent more time teaching. When a shadow of danger appeared, he spent more time translating.

December 13, 1821, a new couple came with their infant daughter to live in the mission house: Dr. and Mrs. Jonathan Price. Price, a tall, awkward, gangling man with a bristle of light-colored hair, was almost a caricature of all the Yankees of legend, except that he lacked taciturnity. Everything he thought and felt came out in words, without any filtering; and almost every idea that occurred he tried to execute at once. He was extremely absent-minded, and, somewhat to Adoniram's disgust, almost completely indifferent to neatness and cleanliness.

Price was a medical man with a whittler's interest in surgery, particularly eye surgery. His medical studies had been financed under the Baptist Board's patronage. In a very short time he had a good-sized practice. He was good at removing cataracts, had no fear of tackling them, and his fame soon spread over all lower Burma. To the Burmese, a man who could remove those blinding white growths was a magician. And his knowledge of the language grew as fast as his practice. His grammar was weak, his vocabulary small, his construction poor; but he had a good ear and soon was chattering away to the Burmans like a magpie, his volubility diminished not at all by the fact that they did not always know what he meant.

January 20, 1822, meant another season of rejoicing as Hough and his family disembarked at the Rangoon landing. Hough knew the language pretty well now and still could print faster than Adoniram could translate. In Price, with his surgical necromancy, they had a means of spreading favorable word about themselves even faster than the word of the Gospel. However, along with rejoicing came tragedy: on the second of May, Mrs. Price died of dysentery. She was buried beside little Roger, and her little daughter was sent to the Lawsons in Calcutta, where she could receive better care than in Rangoon.

Word of the physician's cures of cataract were not long in reaching the Golden Ears at Ava. On July 20, an order came from the Golden Lips themselves commanding Price to appear at the Golden Feet.

Price could not possibly go alone. Adoniram would have to accompany him, although he did not want to. He had translated the New Testament as far as the Epistle to the Romans, having finished a new version of Matthew, Mark and Luke. The Burmese had to have the Bible, he felt, and he was the only person alive capable of giving it to them in their own language. But there was no help for it: translation would have to wait.

At least, this trip would be at government expense. Because of that, there was a delay while officialdom made the necessary arrangements, protracted by the death on August 20 of the old spear-stalker Mya-day-men. They did not actually leave until August 28, exactly a week after Adoniram had baptized the eighteenth Burmese convert. Price and Adoniram arrived at Ava a month later — September 27, 1822. They found that the work of rebuilding Ava as the new capital, in accordance with the old custom that each new king should rule from a new place, was nearly complete.

This time there was no delay in reaching the Golden Feet. The emperor was interested in Price's medical skill and had many questions to ask. He took no notice of Adoniram except as interpreter. But Maung Zah, the Atwinwun who had arranged for Adoniram's introduction to the emperor on his previous visit, remembered him. In the Golden Presence, Maung Zah asked him about his welfare. After the audience he spoke a few cautious words about religion and even gave Adoniram a little private encouragement to stay in Ava awhile.

On October first they had another audience with the emperor. This time, after some questions to Price, the Golden Eyes fell on Adoniram, who was dressed in his usual rusty black. Without the white robe he had worn on his first visit two years ago, the emperor had not recognized him.

"And you, in black, what about you?" asked the emperor. "Are you a medical man too?"

Adoniram shook his head. "Not a medical man, but a teacher of religion, Your Majesty."

The emperor asked a few desultory questions about Christianity. Then he came out with a question which froze Adoniram to the marrow of his bones: "Have any embraced your religion?"

"Not here, in Ava," Adoniram evaded.

The king persisted. "Are there any in Rangoon?"

"There are a few."

"Are there any foreigners?"

Adoniram hesitated. An honest answer could involve the whole little church in ruin. But a dishonest answer was unthinkable. Finally he replied, "There are some foreigners and some Burmans," and waited for wrath to descend.

It did not. His Majesty was silent a few moments. Then, dropping that subject, he began to ask Adoniram questions about religion of a kind he could answer fully, and finally came to geography and astronomy. On such matters as the roundness of the earth, and how the earth circles about the sun, along with the planets, Adoniram was on safe ground. Some questions, he remembered, "were answered in such a satisfactory manner as to occasion a general expression of approbation in all the court present."

Later, when the emperor had withdrawn, a Thau-dau-sen, one of the royal secretaries, conversed with him for some time and asked him a number of questions about Christianity as if he really wanted to know. Adoniram was so relieved that he would have talked happily about anything. The emperor knew at last that some native Burmese had become Christians, and had withheld his wrath!

Adoniram might not have felt so much relief if he had known that one of his listeners was that very Atwinwun who, years ago, had had his own uncle tortured nearly to death for becoming a Christian.

## CHAPTER XIII

# Royal Reception
## [ *1823* ]

THE emperor was unwilling to let Price go. Within a few days the missionaries were moved into a house he ordered erected for them. It was merely a shelter which scarcely kept out the rain and the gaze of passers-by, but it was near the palace and next to the wall surrounding the residence of the eldest half brother of the king, a "Prince M.," who had been visited by Price. The prince's arms and legs were very weak and badly contorted. Unable to get about, he had taken an interest in foreign science and wanted to hear about it from Adoniram.

Adoniram visited Prince M. a number of times in the next few weeks, but never was able to interest him in religion. He seemed to be amused with what Adoniram told him, as if it were a matter of no personal concern whatever. He did, however, once say that his brother the emperor would probably not persecute any of his subjects who wanted to become Christians. "He has a good heart," said the prince, "and he wishes every one to believe and worship as they please." But the young prince wanted more to hear what Adoniram could tell him about astronomy. He simply could not admit that the earth and planets revolved around the sun. But he also admitted that he could not answer Adoniram's arguments, and that, if they were correct, the whole basis of Buddhism collapsed.

Prince M.'s wife, "the Princess of Sarawady, own sister of the king," took a liking to Adoniram and was much pleased with the copy of Nancy's catechism which he gave her. They told Adoniram, "Do not return to Rangoon. When your wife arrives, call her to Ava. The king will give you a piece of ground on which to build a kyoung" — a house set aside for sacred characters to live in. Adoniram began to think that if he took their advice, and could continue talking to the royal family, he might win toleration for the mission and spread the Gospel even faster than before.

In November he decided to test his idea of appealing directly to the crippled young prince. He told him briefly how he had become a Christian himself and warned him he should consider the matter before it was too late. For a moment the prince seemed to take Adoniram's words seriously. Then he shrugged his shoulders. "I am young yet, only twenty-eight. I want to study all the foreign arts and sciences. Then my mind will be enlarged, and I will be able to judge whether the Christian religion will be true or not."

"But suppose," countered Adoniram, "Your Highness changes worlds in the meantime?"

The prince's face fell. "It is true," he said soberly. "I do not know when I shall die."

"Pray to God for light," urged Adoniram. "If you receive light, you will be able at once to distinguish between truth and falsehood."

The prince made no promises, but Adoniram left feeling that he had been impressed. A few days later Adoniram called on him again. This time Adoniram thought he was almost ready to give up Buddhism — until two Buddhist teachers came in. Then the prince fell in with them and contradicted everything Adoniram said.

The crippled Prince M. and his wife were by no means the only people around the throne whom Adoniram saw. Over the months, several of the officials and Atwinwuns and retainers became interested. A few, he thought, were hopeless cases; but more and more he believed there might be good reasons for trying to stay in Ava, especially since Colman at Chittagong, he now learned from a letter, had died on the fourth of July. It seemed doubly important to try to win toleration directly from the emperor while the Houghs held the foothold in Rangoon. Certainly it would be a shame to leave now, when he was finally gaining some idea of how the government was organized.

Ava was already a great city, of perhaps 700,000, he thought. Some 40,000 houses had been moved from Amarapura, the old capital, in these few years since the king had taken the throne. More would move yet. The whole court was in Ava: the four Wungyis, the highest public ministers, who ranked next to the royal family; the six or seven Atwinwuns, who made up the king's privy council; and the many Wundauks and their subordinates. Among all these, he was on good terms with a respectable number, from the emperor and members of the royal family, such as Prince M. and his wife, down to royal secretaries, the Thau-dau-sens. He could not afford to waste these connections.

With this in mind, he petitioned the emperor in late November for a certain piece of land within the city walls "to build a kyoung on." The petition was granted, provided the ground was found unoccupied.

He finally got a royal land measurer to accompany him to the place. The measurer found that the land was not occupied, but he reported to the Atwinwuns that it had once before been the location of a kyoung; therefore it was sacred and could not be given away. Even so, Adoniram pressed his case, with bribery, and at one time actually had the king's order for it passed through the levels of decision to the chief Wungyi. But the Wungyi told the king that the ground was sacred. Adoniram was present at the audience. There was nothing more he could say. The king kept silent for a moment, then remarked, "Well, give him some vacant spot."

Disappointing as this was, one incident had given Adoniram a good deal of encouragement. He had attended an audience with the emperor with Price and two Englishmen who were present in the capital. As the four sat cross-legged together, dressed in conventional European costumes (except for shoes, which they had left outside) the emperor, apparently attracted by their unusual appearance, came over to talk to them.

For some reason, this time he was interested by Adoniram. The emperor could often be pleasant — in fact, he seemed unusually good-humored now that he had consolidated his position and at thirty could look forward to many years of unchallenged rule — and this was one of the times. He asked about the Burmans who had "embraced your religion. Are they real Burmans?"

"Oh, yes, Your Majesty," Adoniram assured him.

"Do they dress like other Burmans?"

"Yes, they are just like all the other Burmese."

Adoniram mentioned, after answering a few other questions, that he preached every Sunday. The emperor was curious. "What! In Burmese?"

"Yes."

"Let us hear how you preach," commanded the emperor.

Adoniram was taken aback. The whole court had heard the imperial order. The huge audience room fell profoundly silent. After a brief hesitation, he began what he later described as "a form of worship, which first ascribed glory to God, and then declares the commands of the law of the Gospel" — probably words borrowed from his first tract: "God is a spirit, without bodily form. Although omnipresent, it is above the heavens that He clearly discovers His glory. His power and wisdom are infinite. He is pure and good, and possessed of everlasting felicity. . . Have faith in the Saviour. Love God supremely. Love others as yourself. Set not your hearts on worldly goods and riches, but look forward to those riches which are free from defilement and eternal in the heavens. Suppress haughtiness, pride and insolence, and cherish a humble, meek and lowly mind. Return not evil for evil, but have a disposition to forgive the faults of others. Love your enemies, and pray for them. Be compassionate to the poor and needy, and give alms. Covet not the property of others; therefore, take not by violence, steal not, defraud not in trade. Trespass not on the property of others. Speak no falsehood. . . ."

Adoniram stopped. "Go on," said an Atwinwun.

"Before this world was made," continued Adoniram, "God remained happy, surrounded by the pure and incorporeal sons of heaven. In order to display His perfections, and make creatures happy, God created the heavens, the sun, moon, and all the stars, the earth, the various kinds of brute creatures, and man."

Here the Emperor interrupted him. He had heard enough. But later he asked what Adoniram thought of the Buddha, the great Gautama.

"We all know that he was son of King Thog-dau-dau-nah," said Adoniram, choosing his words carefully. "We regard him as a wise man and a great teacher. But we do not call him God."

"That is right," broke in an Atwinwun, who had not been very friendly to Adoniram before, but now thought he saw how things were going. And the man went on to tell the king about what

Adoniram had related to him some days before: "The Christian idea that there is only one Being Who exists eternally, and how there are three united in One: God the Father, God the Son, and God the Holy Ghost."

Even Maung Zah was encouraged, and said, "Nearly all the world, Your Majesty, believes in an eternal God. All except Burma and Siam, those little spots!"

His Majesty remained silent. Then he asked Adoniram a few desultory questions about his health, and his wife; and suddenly rose and left.

A week or so later, Adoniram saw the king again and told him he meant to return to Rangoon. His Majesty was interested. "Will you go from there to your own country?"

"Only to Rangoon," said Adoniram. The king nodded.

Maung Zah, the friendly Atwinwun, said: "Will you both go, or will the doctor remain?"

Price would remain, Adoniram assured him. As for himself, he would return "if it was convenient."

The king nodded acquiescence, and said of Price, "Let a place be given him."

Maung Zah told Adoniram that night that he believed there was an eternal God, and that "Gaudama and Christ, and Mohamet, and others, are great teachers, who communicated as much truth respectively as they could; but that their communications are not the word of God." Adoniram did not dare press argument very far on a man whom he considered "a Deistic Buddhist, the first that I have met in the country," who had obviously thought deep and long about his beliefs and become fixed in them. But when they left, Maung Zah said, "This is a deep and difficult subject. So you, teacher, consider further, and I also will consider."

Meanwhile, Adoniram continued looking for a place to build a kyoung. He finally found a little piece of land on the riverbank about a mile from the palace and just outside the walls of the town. But the chief Wungyi had already built a fence around it, with the idea of erecting a sort of private zayat there. Adoniram began to pester him for it. He even wrote him a petition, and followed him around with money, waiting until he could slip both into the official's hand. When caught, the Wungyi read the petition, smiled, and said, "You are indefatigable in your search for a place. But you cannot have that. It is for my own use. . . . Search further."

Adoniram waylaid him again — no easy task, for he was harder to get at than the king himself. He found him one night at his house, "lying down, surrounded by forty or fifty people." Adoniram forced himself into the front rank and held up a small bottle of perfume. One of the Wungyi's officers took it and gave it to the Wungyi. For some reason, he was very much pleased with it. He sat up and demanded, "What kind of house do you intend to build?"

Just a small one, Adoniram told him, for one family. "But I have no place to build on, my lord."

The Wungyi reflected. Abruptly he decided — "If you want the little enclosure, take it!"

With profuse thanks, Adoniram prepared to leave. But he could not get away without repeating — but at even more length — the form of his preaching before the king. Every time he stopped, the Wungyi ordered him to go on; until all at once that official lost interest, lay back on the cushions, and let the preacher slip quietly away.

The next night Adoniram brought the money for the property. But the Wungyi would not take it, explaining: "Understand, teacher, that we do not give you the entire owning of this ground. We take no recompense, *lest it become American territory*. We give it to you for your present residence only; and when you go, shall take it again." This was enough for Adoniram. He managed to get assurance that another missionary to follow him could also occupy it; but if no one lived there, it would go back to the Wungyi.

The building of a crude shack took only two days. When it was finished, Adoniram arranged for one of his disciples to live there until he returned. Then, with a final farewell to Prince M., for whom he promised to translate all the Scriptures, and to the king, explaining he meant to return with his wife and household goods, he left Ava on January 25, 1823.

The future looked bright.

## CHAPTER XIV

# The New Testament; Nancy Returns

## [ *1823* ]

THE mission had suffered, he found on his return to Rangoon. Of the eighteen disciples, only three or four were at the mission house. One he knew was at Ava, guarding the hut there. But some had fled across the river to escape the exactions of the tax-hungry new viceroy. The neighbors of others had reported them to the authorities, who had demolished their houses. One, Mah Myat-ya, had died. Her sister told Adoniram she had not feared death. She had put her trust in Christ, and had looked forward to meeting Him in heaven. Nor had Hough done much. Preaching and teaching were not his strong points; and he could not print until he could get type from Bengal.

Thus, although the long-range prospects were good, the immediate outlook was discouraging. As usual when nothing else could be done, Adoniram immersed himself in translation. By July 12, 1823, he had completed his translation of the entire New Testament in Burmese and written a summary of the Old Testament in twelve sections. This latter included a brief account of Scripture history from the beginning to the coming of Christ, and an abstract of the most important prophecies about the Messiah, in which he used, so far as he could, the actual words of the Bible.

The whole made up a sort of textbook which the converts found absorbing. But Adoniram fretted because it could not be printed, particularly the complete New Testament. Meanwhile, he busied himself with revision until Nancy should return. He had not heard a word from her in ten months, and had not seen her for two years.

Before she arrived, he did one small job of translating that gave him a certain amount of amusement. Maung Shway-bay wrote a letter to the Reverend Dr. Baldwin, in Boston, which Adoniram turned into English so that Dr. Baldwin could read it.

Addressing him as "Beloved Elder Brother," Maung Shway-bay explained that, "Though in the present state the places of our residence are very far apart, and we have never met, yet by means of letters, and of the words of Yoodthan, who has told me of you, I love you and wish to send you this letter." He recounted the satisfaction his religious experiences gave him. But, he admitted, it was difficult to be a Christian in Burma: "For, elder brother, I have to bear the threatening of my own brother, and my brother-in-law, who say, 'We will beat, and bruise, and pound you; we will bring you into great difficulty; you associate with false people; and you keep a false religion; and you speak false words.' " Nevertheless, the convert knew *their* religion was the false one, the religion of death, and he persevered. He concluded:

In this country of Burmah are many strayed sheep. Teacher Yoodthan, pitying them, has gone to gather them together, and to feed them in love. Some will not listen, but run away. Some do listen, and adhere to him; and that our number may increase, we meet together, and pray to the great proprietor of the sheep.

Thus I, Maung Shway-bay, a disciple of teacher Yoodthan, in Rangoon, write and send this letter to the great teacher Baldwin, who lives in Boston, America.

Nancy came back to Rangoon on December 5, 1823. With her came another pair of missionaries, Jonathan and Deborah Wade, of Edinburgh, New York. The Wades arrived knowing a little Burmese. Nancy had been teaching them ever since they had left Boston.

Nancy was "the Ann Hasseltine of other days," Adoniram wrote, his happiness "inexpressible." They had much to tell each other about those twenty-seven months they had been apart, but there was much to do first.

For Adoniram had only been waiting for Nancy to return to Ava. With the Houghs, and now the Wades, in Rangoon, the capital was the place for the Judsons. He had a boat all ready in the river. Nancy's baggage was not even taken to the mission house. It was transferred directly from the ship to the boat — including a rocker and a little work table which Elnathan, Adoniram's brother, had given her in Baltimore. Their household goods followed, and they started upriver — with three or four of the disciples, including the faithful Maung Ing and Koo-chill, a Bengali cook Nancy had brought from Calcutta — on December 13, a week to the day from Nancy's arrival at Rangoon.

The boat was small, the headwind steady, and the downstream current strong. Their progress was slow. But to Nancy, this merely added delight to the trip. It was another honeymoon. She felt well — better than Adoniram, who had suffered much from cholera the past year — and the weather was pleasant. They had plenty of time to catch up on the story of her travels.

She arrived in Calcutta all but dying. The doctors insisted she go to a cold climate. But the American captains had full cargoes; the only passage she could get would have cost fifteen hundred rupees. Fortunately, Mrs. Thomason, wife of the East India Company's chaplain, found a "pious captain" who would take her to England for five hundred, provided she would go in a cabin with three children. She accepted, and then found that their father insisted on paying her passage.

In England, her health improved. She met Mr. Joseph Butterworth, a Methodist and Member of Parliament, who took her into his home. She had become, she found, something of a celebrity. From Mr. Butterworth's house she went to Cheltenham for several weeks for the mineral waters, and then was invited to Scotland. She could pay for nothing. Well-wishers took care of all her expenses.

She did not leave England until August 16, 1822, and arrived in New York September 25. After a week or so in Philadelphia she went home to Bradford. But the cold climate, the excitement of seeing family and friends, and the hundreds of visitors who poured in on her, weakened her. All day long they thronged the house until she could hardly bear the sight of a human face. For six weeks she had not one quiet night of sleep.

Fortunately, Elnathan was now a government surgeon in Baltimore. He invited her to spend the winter in the warmer climate with him. She accepted, and on December 3 arrived at his boarding-house.

Here she found rest and seclusion while she underwent more

courses of "salivation" with mercury. Soon she felt better and resumed work on a book about the mission which Mr. Butterworth
and others had urged her to write. The easiest way to do it, she
found, was in the form of a series of letters addressed to him. In
spite of her racking cough and the pain in her side she finished the
book in March and oversaw its printing in Washington, under the
title of *An Account of the American Baptist Mission to the Burman
Empire.*

Late in the spring she returned to Bradford for a few days,
and after a whirlwind round of visits to Plymouth, Saugus, Charlestown, Cambridge and Salem, sailed with the Wades on June 22,
1823.

In Calcutta, she and the Wades were advised not to go on to
Rangoon because war between England and Burma was imminent.
The chief secretary of the Bengal government had even privately
painted the background for her. The Burmese throne, successful
for generations in wars of conquest, had coveted the riches of
Bengal for a long time. The imperialist expansion of British power,
as represented by the East India Company, was bound to bring it
into conflict with Burma eventually. But in this particular case the
English had not been anxious for war. Teak was almost all that
Burma had to offer of a really attractive commercial nature, and the
Company already had as much as it could use easily. Therefore, its
local officers along the borders had always been warned to maintain
a conciliatory attitude.

The English mistake lay in not realizing how abysmally ignorant
the Burmese government was of British power. To the Burmese,
England was only another Siam which they meant to conquer as
soon as they had overrun Siam, Assam, and a few of the nearer
countries. This was why Chittagong and Calcutta had buzzed for
years with rumors of war.

But the old emperor, Bodawpaya, had been able to control his
ministers. The new emperor, Bagyidaw, the one Adoniram knew,
was not. Now Maha Bandula — handsome, popular and dashing —
who fancied himself a great military leader, had won ascendancy
over the king. Even now Governor-General Amherst knew the
Burmese people were about to invade Cachar. But Cachar was a
"protected state," under British suzerainty. Its passes opened into

Eastern Bengal. If the Burmese took it, they would certainly be in Bengal soon. Thus, willy-nilly, the English had to defend Cachar.

Burma threatened even more immediately in the Chittagong region. There Burmese raiding forces had been kidnapping British parties hunting elephants around Cox's Bazaar on the pretext that they were trespassing on Burmese soil. They fired on British subjects proceeding up and down the Naaf River. This past September, they had rushed and taken a British outpost on the island of Shahpuri, well on the British side of the river. A letter of protest from Lord Amherst had been interpreted as a sign of weakness. The Burmese envoys had used it as a cue for further insolence, and the kidnaping of two British naval officers whom they trapped by inviting them to negotiate the various border difficulties.

All this Nancy told Adoniram as they traveled up the broad river. It was hard to believe, on that peaceful stream, that anything so terrible as war could happen. But at Tsen-pyoo-kywon, a hundred miles below Ava, they had direct confirmation of the rumors.

Up to this point the trip had been delightful. Nancy had enjoyed the crowds that followed her through the villages when they went ashore. They had never seen a foreign woman before, and, she noted, "all were anxious that their friends and relatives should have a view. . . some, who were less civilized than others, would run some way before us, in order to have a *long* look as we approached them."

But at Tsen-pyoo-kywon they found a whole army encamped — Bandula's, reputed to number some thirty thousand. As Adoniram knew, a pass threaded the mountains to Arakan on the seacoast, adjoining British territory. Bandula was obviously preparing a sudden descent in force on Bengal. The men Adoniram met made no secret of it.

Adoniram and Nancy wasted no more time on land, but promptly returned to their boat. A few miles up, they saw across the river a huge fleet of golden war boats, dark with huddled masses of soldiers, each dressed in a campaigning jacket of black cloth, wadded and quilted with cotton, each armed with a musket or spear. The boats looked something like huge canoes, with uprearing sterns where the helmsmen stood. Each boat was scooped from the trunk of a single immense teak tree, some six or eight feet wide. Bright flags and banners by the hundreds fluttered from them, and they made a weird, terrifying spectacle as their paddlers drove them down the river to the beat of the martial music played on board. In the center of this fleet floated the golden barge of Bandula himself.

It was impossible to escape observation. Within moments, one of the golden war boats sped across the river to intercept the missionaries' vessel, but they were allowed to go when Adoniram explained that he and Nancy were *Americans*, not English, and were on their way to Ava by express command of the Golden Presence itself.

They arrived at Ava January 23, 1824, after a six weeks' journey. A few miles below the city, Price met them in a small boat to warn them that he and all foreigners were now out of favor at the court. They were almost as suspect as if the government believed them spies. All the old Atwinwuns had been turned out of office. The new ones were strangers who had no interest in Price or in foreigners. Price urged that Adoniram and Nancy stay at his new brick house, across the river from the capital.

But his house was so damp that within a few hours Nancy began to show signs of fever. The hut Adoniram had had built on his own plot of ground was uninhabitable. Their only recourse was to live on the boat for the two or three weeks it would take to put up a proper shelter.

While this work was under way, the widow of Mya-day-men called at the boat to see Nancy. With her spear-carrying husband's death her honors had ended, and she was now only a private person. There were no other callers. Adoniram took Nancy to meet a number of members of the royal family, but their reception was not what he had expected. He visited the palace two or three times, but the emperor's attitude was cold. Adoniram's friends were not in evidence. The desire to see a foreign woman had evaporated. Soon he could not even pay visits, for the great new palace at Ava was finally finished and the king, queen, royal family and most of the officials retired five miles up the river to Amarapura, the old capital, to make ready for the great ceremony of taking formal possession.

There was not much to do but stay on the boat, await the completion of their little house, and hope that on royalty's return to Ava it would feel more kindly disposed toward American missionaries.

## CHAPTER XV

# Foreigners Must Be Spies
## [ *1823–1824* ]

THE little house — three rooms and a veranda — was finished exactly two weeks after they arrived. Nancy liked its location on the bank of the river, out of the dust of the town, but it was hot as an oven. Although it was raised on stilts some four feet above the ground, so air could pass under, only brick would be able to keep out the stifling 108-degree and higher temperatures of the approaching summer season. But Adoniram had intended this house only as a temporary dwelling. He went ahead at once to secure bricks and hire masons for a brick house next door.

They settled down into a routine almost at once. Adoniram was too busy with other things to translate, but he kept the manuscript of his Burmese New Testament with him against the day of its printing. Meanwhile, he preached Sundays at Dr. Price's house across the river to an audience of eighteen or twenty who lived in the neighborhood.

Nancy began a little school with three small girls whom she taught to read, sew and do household tasks. Two of these girls were daughters of an insane mother, whose father, Maung Shway-bay, had given them to her to bring up. She named them "Mary Hasseltine" and "Abby Hasseltine" after her sisters in Bradford. "One of them," she wrote to her family, "is to be supported with the money which the 'Judson Association of Bradford Academy' have engaged to collect. They are fine children, and improve as rapidly as any children in the world."

At this time, too, they met Henry Gouger, one of the very few white men in Burma whom they did not already know. Gouger, still in his middle twenties, had found service in the East India Company too slow; had raised some money, secured a ship, and taken it to Ava more than a year before with the idea of making a fortune fast. Irrepressibly cheerful, a genius at making friends, he had soon caught the attention of king and court. When he had discovered how the Burmese almost literally fought over his goods, which he considerately let them have at a profit of some 800 or 1000 per cent, he had gone back to Bengal, secured another ship, and returned to Ava in the fall of 1823. He had already become wealthy, but he had run into the problem that had baffled every European trader in Burma before him: he could not get his riches out of the country. The law forbade his removing gold or jewels or precious metals, and teak was so bulky that his profit would have vanished in the hire of the ships necessary to remove it.

Meanwhile, he enjoyed life in a way that would have scandalized many Englishmen. He wore his own version of native clothing — including the Burmese sandal, which he found infinitely more comfortable than European shoes; he employed two rascals named "the Red Rat" and "the Red Gold" to transact his more questionable dealings; he gave not a thought to propriety. He had no trouble securing meat, a difficulty for most Europeans on account of the Burmese taboo against killing animals for food. It was amazing how many goats and cows died "by accident" in the cellar beneath Gouger's quarters. Officialdom made no complaint, because a quarter of the cow or kid which had suffered mishap always went to one or two key officials who had a taste for a nice roast themselves.

Seeing war on the way, Gouger had sent his ship down-river. Meanwhile he amused himself hunting — which, strangely, was not forbidden — riding, and even, on occasion, helping to draw the emperor's buggy. The buggy, a richly ornamented vehicle which had been the gift of some English embassy, was never drawn by horses. Instead, when the emperor went riding a number of Burmese (who were thus highly honored) stepped between the shafts and galloped off dragging the embuggied monarch behind them. Acting as an honorary horse tickled Gouger and helped his relations with the emperor.

Gouger and Adoniram took to each other at once. Each enjoyed the other's cheerfulness and keen sense of the ridiculous. Adoniram liked Gouger's worldly wisdom, which appealed to something in his innately proud, ambitious nature that he was not always successful in sinking in humility. Gouger respected Adoniram's intelligence and sincerity, and was able to sympathize with his occasional fits of deep depression — while confessing at the same time that Adoniram's almost obsessive neatness and cleanliness, combined with his complete unconsciousness of the weird cut of his clothing (product of a Bengalese tailor's conception of the garb of the well-dressed Englishman) amused him intensely.

By contrast, the other white men in Ava had little to offer. Rodgers — "Yadza" as the Burmese called him — considered himself a Burman, as did Lanciego. Besides this, the competition between Rodgers and Lanciego had ripened into personal hatred and such quarreling that other Europeans avoided them so as not to be present at a possible encounter.

As for Price, he seemed almost to have taken leave of his senses. Lured by the magnetic attraction of imperial power, he had used such crude tactics of insinuation that the emperor had actually once turned his back on him. This had occurred at a Burmese "boxing match" — a peculiar sport in which each contestant tried to seize the other with his stiffly outstretched left arm while he hammered him on top of the head with the clenched fist of the other. Adoniram had thought it unbecoming for a man of religion to attend this match, but Price had lost any such scruples. Here, seeing Gouger in a place of honor by the emperor, Price had taken the gross liberty of entering the Golden Presence without invitation. His Majesty had immediately fallen silent, frowned, and turned his back in a snub under which even the thick-skinned doctor slunk away. Now Price was even more out of royal favor than was Rodgers.

But the doctor had capped even his early folly. He had next attempted an operation on an almost blind woman of Siamese descent which resulted in her losing even the little sight she had before. Price had thereupon decided to marry her "by way," conjectured Gouger, "of compensation. . . as her plainness of person. . . was repulsive, nor was there any other conceivable motive." Horrified, Adoniram refused to perform the ceremony: whereat Price issued an ultimatum even Adoniram could not withstand: "Brother Judson, the law of America and of nature provides for cases where a minister is not to be found!"

It is understandable, then, that Gouger fell into the habit of spending his evenings at the little wood house standing on its stilts beside the river. He attended family devotions and was impressed almost more by the converts than their converters because "it was impossible not to be struck with the reverence of demeanour, the propriety of language, and above all the knowledge of the New Testament and its saving doctrines which some of them manifested in their extempore prayer. No one who heard could doubt their sincerity."

Up to this time Gouger had considered missions useless if not worse, an opinion Price's behavior had not altered. But the many evenings he spent, that spring of 1824, with Nancy and Adoniram changed his ideas completely. If these two people represented the missionary movement, then the missionary movement was the best thing that had happened in the Orient for centuries.

Although Adoniram and Nancy had avoided the boxing matches, elephant tamings, and other amusements which went along with the celebration of the emperor's dedication of his new palace at Ava, they did see his triumphal entrance into the city.

I dare not [Nancy wrote] attempt a description of that splendid day when majesty with all its attendant glory, entered the gates of the golden city, and amid the acclamations of millions, I may say, took possession of the palace. The saupwars of the provinces bordering on China, all the viceroys and high officers of the kingdom, were assembled on the occasion, dressed in their robes of state, and ornamented with the insignia of their office. The white elephant, richly ornamented with gold and jewels, was one of the most beautiful objects in the procession. The king and queen alone were unadorned, dressed in the simple garb of the country; they hand in hand entered the garden in which we had taken our seats, and where a banquet was prepared for their refreshment. All the riches and glory of the empire were on this day exhibited to view. The number and immense size of the elephants, the numerous horses, and [the] great variety of vehicles of all descriptions, far surpassed any thing I have ever seen or imagined.

But the installation of the emperor in the new palace failed to bring any relaxation in the royal attitude toward Europeans. Instead, an order was soon issued that henceforth no foreigner would be allowed to enter it except Lanciego, Akoupwoon of Rangoon.

At the same time the war talk in the Court grew louder and louder. The Prince of Sarawady, the king's brother, would expound to Adoniram half an hour at a time: "The English are the inhabitants of a small and remote island. What business have they to come in ships from a great distance to dethrone kings and take possession of countries they have no right to? They contrive to conquer and govern the black strangers with caste, who have puny frames and no courage. They have never yet fought with so strong and brave a people as the Burmans, skilled in the use of sword and spear. If they once fight with us, and we have an opportunity of manifesting our bravery, it will be an example to black natives, who are now slaves to the English, and encourage them to throw off their yoke."

The women were even more outspoken. The sister of the king told Adoniram that "the English were afraid to fight; that their conduct on the frontier was mean and cowardly; that they were always disposed to treat and not to fight; and that upon some occasions, when the Burman and British troops met, the British officers held up their hands to entreat the Burmans not to advance."

Gouger, circulating like Adoniram in quarters where he was still welcome, heard much the same. As a consequence, the foreigners were forced more and more into seclusion. Adoniram and Nancy did not mind too much. Nancy went on with her school, and Adoniram, having succeeded in assembling all the materials for a brick house, found masons and set them to work, and soon the walls had risen to a respectable height. In the evenings Gouger continued to visit them and along with the news regaled them with stories of his past adventures at court. For instance, once, he told them, when the emperor's meal was being taken away on a veritable procession of gold platters, he had brashly stepped up to one and lifted the cover. Underneath he found a number of what he thought were fried grasshoppers, looking a little like fried shrimp. He picked up one or two in his fingers and ate them. They were delicious, he solemnly assured the Judsons. But there was a variety of woodworm, a sort of white caterpillar about three inches long, served fried,

which he had never been able to bring himself to eat. The dead-
black head on the end, and the eyes looking up at him from the
plate, were just a little too much. He had tried again and again,
but every time he lifted one in his fingers to take a bite the reproach in those eyes made him lay it down again with a deep feeling of guilt and a sudden loss of appetite. . . . Henry Gouger would
tell Adoniram and Nancy such stories as these while Adoniram's
book would be neglected in his lap and Nancy, sitting in the rocker
Elnathan had given her, the little work table by her side, would
forget her sewing. Then Gouger would burst into a peal of laughter,
thinking of the fried worm or the time he was a human horse between the shafts of the king's buggy, or the time the king promised
him a three-hundred-and-fifty-pound bar of solid silver if he could
lift it — and he would have, too, had not the sharp edges cut his
fingers. And Adoniram and Nancy would laugh with him.

Thus there was a good deal of cheerfulness that spring among
the three of them, even though the prospects for English merchants
and American missionaries grew dimmer by the day. As Gouger
and Adoniram exchanged views in sober moments, however, they
agreed peace could not last much longer. Yet neither of them made
a move to get out of the country. Gouger was bound to his un-
movable treasure by a cord of greed. Adoniram and Nancy trusted
in the fact that they had come to Ava on invitation from the
Golden Voice.

One Sunday evening — May 23, 1824, to be exact — Henry
Gouger took a canoe and paddled across the Irrawaddy to Dr.
Price's house in the village of Sagaing, where they were in the
habit of meeting for Sunday worship. The house was in a singularly
beautiful location, and surrounded by trees which framed the broad
Irrawaddy rolling almost at their feet, catching glints of the dying
sun in fading pink, soft yellow and steel gray.

This time the congregation consisted only of Gouger, Price,
Nancy and Adoniram.

There was a peculiarly impressive character to the devotions
that evening. All four knew by now that a storm was about to
break over them, but of what kind, or when, or from what direction, they could not guess. None of them was received at the palace

any more. Even the contacts of the heavily pursed Gouger were failing him, and for inside information he now had only his two spies, the Red Gold and the Red Rat.

They were just concluding services in the doctor's living room and Adoniram was making a final prayer when a native messenger burst into the room. The news he chattered out made their hearts stand still.

A British fleet had arrived at Rangoon, had bombarded the city, and taken it. The native population had fled. There were no details: nothing about the safety of the Wades and Houghs, nothing about Richardson, Gouger's assistant, who had been sent downstream with his ship.

The war had begun. The Burmese were in the habit of killing or enslaving their prisoners of war. What would they do with the foreigners in Ava?

The four talked the matter over disjointedly. Gouger was in the worst position by far. He was an Englishman, in Ava for no purpose but trade; he had wealth. More than one high official must be considering thoughtfully what he could do with that fortune if it should come into his keeping. Gouger had numerous connections with the Bengal government. His correspondence with India was heavy, and he had many financial transactions with banking houses in Calcutta. He had even acted as banker and financial agent for the Judsons. He would certainly be suspect as a British agent.

The missionaries were in a different position. They had no commercial interests. More important, they were Americans. Their safety would depend on their completely separate nationality. In the future they would have to emphasize that. Price, Adoniram and Nancy all agreed that from this night on they must have no contact with Gouger. If he were taken, they might be able to help him from outside. But if they were seen together, they might all be taken together. Gouger simply must not visit any of them any more. Ruefully, Gouger concurred.

They were not worried about Rodgers. He would carefully avoid all of them. He was a completely naturalized Burmese subject. He would count on that and his long experience in court intrigue to save him. As to Lanciego, as the only foreigner allowed to enter the palace, he seemed to stand high.

No, the real problem was Gouger. He would have to go into a sort of quarantine.

Gouger paddled alone across the river to his own house. The Red Rat was waiting for him. He approved the decision made at Dr. Price's house. Henceforth, Gouger would be a political and social leper. Within a day Lanciego, whose house was nearby, sent him a message to tell him so explicitly. Lanciego, like Rodgers, was being more than careful to keep his own skirts clear. Gouger prowled his house moodily, blaming himself for his stupidity in not going earlier, treasure or no treasure, and blaming the Judsons for their idiocy in hoping to advance Christianity in an Ava obviously about to commence war with a Christian nation.

In a few days Adoniram and Nancy heard that the king's brother, the Prince of Sarawady, had sent a message to Gouger saying that "the few foreigners residing in Ava had nothing to do with the war and should not be molested." This word from such a high source made them feel easier. They would not have felt so easy if they had known that the actual tenor of the message had gone something like this: "The Prince of Sarawady presents his compliments to Mr. Gouger, and, having formed a partiality for him, would be sorry to see his throat cut, and recommends him to come quickly to his Palace, where the Prince would like to see the man who dares to touch him. *P.S.* — Mr. Gouger had better bring his wine and beer, gold and silver, for safety."

Gouger consulted with the Red Rat, who looked at him with a sort of contempt when he saw that Gouger actually took the message seriously.

"Sahib," he said, "if the Prince were to know what I am going to tell you, my life would not be worth a day's purchase. This offer is only made that he may get you and your property in his power. You would then find a grave in his garden, as many persons have done before when it suited his purpose. He knows you have a great deal of gold and silver, and thinks he may as well get it as anyone else. When you came to be demanded by the Hlut-dau, as you would be, the only answer he could give would be that you had died, and there the matter might end. You will stand a better chance by remaining quiet, and allowing yourself to be apprehended by the Wungyis, and disposed of according to their pleasure."

This advice made sense to Gouger. He dispatched a reply to the effect that, "With a thousand thanks for his benevolent intentions, I have such perfect confidence in the promise of protection given me by His Majesty, that I repose without fear, knowing he would not permit any violence to be done to a stranger, who lives under his favour."

But this Adoniram and Nancy did not know. And in a few days they saw a change of sentiment in the city which they thought might work in their favor.

After the first rage at Rangoon's loss, a curious satisfaction came over the people. They decided, from the emperor down, that the ignorant British had entered a trap, and feared only that the invaders might plunder Rangoon and leave before Bandula's army could arrive. Some feared, too, that the British might see Bandula's army and run away before slaves could be taken. Maung Ing and other disciples brought the news of the palace feeling. One young courtier told a Burmese officer, "Bring me six white strangers to row my boat." The wife of a Wungyi had a similar request, "Send me four white strangers to manage the affairs of my house, as I understand they are trusty servants."

Every day, from their little wooden house on the river shore, Adoniram and Nancy could see the war boats passing, and the warriors. Often, Adoniram would see them dancing on the decks as they went down the river. "Poor fellows!" he would think, shaking his head. "You will probably never dance again." But the soldiers proclaimed in song and gesture how they would lead those foolhardy English back to Ava with rings through their noses.

That was the first Burmese reaction. The second came within a few days. How could those English ships have appeared before Rangoon so unexpectedly, when Bandula had intended to make the first onslaught upon the English himself? Foreign strangers had arrived in Rangoon within the last year or so. Foreign strangers had arrived in Ava. They must be spies. All the Burmese plans must have been reported to the English as soon as they were made.

Now something happened to give color to this suspicion.

There was a Captain Laird, a Scot who had sought to be the Prince of Sarawady's agent in Rangoon for the sale of teak from the Prince's great forests. At the Prince's order Laird had been brought by force from Rangoon to Ava shortly before the English fleet had appeared before Rangoon. Fortunately for him, he had not carried enough money on his person to find a resting place in the bottom of the Prince's garden. He had arrived in Ava only a few days before the news of the capture of Rangoon.

Laird had carried a recent Calcutta newspaper, one paragraph of which indicated that the British government was considering an expedition against Rangoon. He had shown the newspaper to Gouger in the presence of the Prince. And with insane folly he had let it be translated to the Prince at the same time.

Within a few days, Adoniram and Nancy learned that Gouger, Laird and Rodgers had been taken in custody for questioning, under suspicion of having withheld the news in the paper from His Majesty. Gouger, furthermore, was accused of making maps of the country. Actually, they had been crude sketches of temples and scenes around Ava which he had made for a friend; but he had used measuring instruments to get the proportions right. He was also accused of being "brother-in-law to the East India Company" in disguise. As for Adoniram and Price, they were soon questioned too. They had written many letters. Were they reports to foreign countries? No, explained both men. They had written for years to friends in the United States. But that was another country, thousands of miles from England. They had never written to British officers, or the Bengal government.

For the present, they were allowed to return home.

The examiners turned to Gouger's financial records. They soon discovered that Adoniram and Price had received substantial amounts of money from him, paid on orders to Bengal commercial houses. Gouger insisted this was standard European business practice — he simply cashed the missionaries' checks, the checks were forwarded to Calcutta, and the money deposited to his credit there.

The Burmese examiners looked at each other with significant

smiles. Who ever heard of such a lame explanation? The very thought of a man paying out money to another man merely on a slip of paper — the real author being at a distance — was ridiculous. The conclusion was obvious: *The Americans must be in the pay of the Englishman. They too must be spies.*

## CHAPTER XVI

# Imprisonment

## [ *1824* ]

LATE in the afternoon of Tuesday, June 8, 1824, about two weeks after the first news of the attack on Rangoon, Adoniram and Nancy were in their little wooden house getting ready to sit down to dinner. Outside, the masons were at work on the brick house. The neighborhood sounds filtered in through the board walls as usual — the high cries and laughter of children, the penetrating voices of women, the deeper tones of the masons conversing as they worked on the walls.

All at once there was a commotion. Adoniram and Nancy stopped their preparations and looked at each other in wonderment. Before either had time to say a word, the door of the house flew open and a dozen or more native Burmese men rushed in. One was an official who carried a black book. With him was a man who bore a circle or spot tattooed on each cheek. They knew what he was — a "Spotted Face" — a branded criminal who had been turned into an executioner and keeper of the prison. The Spotted Faces, feared by everyone in Burma, were called "Children of the Prison." They lived outside the pale of society and married only their own kind. Some had the name of their crime branded into their foreheads or chests. The ears of some had been cut off. Others had no noses, or had been deprived of one eye. They took joy in inflicting similar acts of mayhem on those who fell into their hands.

"Where is the teacher?" called out the official.

Adoniram stepped out in front of him. "Here."

"You are called by the king," said the officer — the formal words used in arresting criminals. The words were no more than spoken before the Spotted Face sprang at Adoniram and threw him on the floor. Kneeling on him, he brought forth the dreaded small, hard cord carried by Spotted Faces and from behind slipped it around Adoniram's arms above the elbow.

The cord was used almost more as an instrument of torture than of control. It cut deep. Often it dislocated the arms of its victims. It could be pulled back so hard as to cut off the breath. Sometimes, drawn tight enough, it could make blood spurt from the nose and mouth of the prisoner until he dropped dead.

Nancy caught hold of the arm of the Spotted Face. "Stay!" she pleaded. "I will give you money."

"Arrest her too," ordered the official. "She is also a foreigner."

Adoniram, struggling to his knees, begged the official to leave Nancy alone until he had specific orders to take her. Nancy, meanwhile, offered money again and again to the Spotted Face if he would remove the cord. Koo-chil the cook and the Bengalese servants, who had been about to serve dinner, stood aghast. Their fear of the officials was hardly greater than their incredulity at the way Adoniram was being treated.

But the Spotted Face dragged Adoniram out of the house, followed by the officials and his retainers. Nancy had to be dragged apart from her husband.

By now the whole neighborhood was in turmoil. The workmen on the brick house took one look, threw down their tools, and ran for their lives. The people living for blocks around had collected in the street. The little Burmese children cried and screamed with fear.

The Spotted Face paid no attention. Nancy, standing in the doorway with a handful of silver, now saw Adoniram hauled away. With a quick inspiration she handed the silver to Maung Ing, who was pale as a ghost beneath his bronze. "Take it and follow," she said. "Perhaps you can make the Spotted Face loosen the cord." Maung Ing followed, at a respectful distance. Only a few hundred feet from the house the Spotted Face threw Adoniram flat on the ground again, and tightened the cord still harder.

Maung Ing tagged after the party closely. Once he managed to slip ten ticals in silver into the Spotted Face's hand. The cord was loosened a little, but even so Adoniram was dragged, sometimes walking, sometimes jerked off his feet by the cord, to the palace used as courthouse. Here the governor of the city and his staff were collected. The governor was shocked by the harshness the Spotted

Face had used, and told him to take off the cord. But already Adoniram's arms were swollen and bleeding.

One of the officers read the official order. The teacher was consigned to the dreaded *Let-may-yoon*. In Burmese the expression meant "Hand Shrink Not," but the English foreigners called it "the Death Prison."

Maung Ing followed on the long hot walk to the Death Prison. He saw Adoniram taken inside the stockade. He saw the door close. Then he turned and went slowly home to tell Nancy what had happened.

The ruler of the prison met Adoniram at the gate with a grin which was to become familiar. The word branded on his breast, Adoniram saw, was *Loo-that*: "Murderer." He addressed Adoniram as "beloved child" — all the prisoners were his beloved children, so he said, and insisted that they in turn call him "Aphe" — "Father."

In the center of the prison yard stood a block of granite. Two of the Spotted Faces lifted Adoniram's feet to the block, and Father joked while riveting three pairs of ankle fetters with an iron maul.

"Now, walk, my child," he chuckled. Adoniram took one step and fell on his face in the hot dust. With a laugh the Spotted Faces picked him up and hustled him through the bamboo wicket of the prison building. By now his face was covered with dirt, his hair in disarray, his clothing tattered from the dragging.

Inside the windowless prison he stood blinded by darkness, overwhelmed with heat, almost gagging at the indescribable stench. But he had no time to reflect. Another Spotted Face — an apprentice still serving out his own time in fetters, but allowed to carry a club — half led, half pushed him with the club into a far corner and forced him to lie down on the littered floor.

The guard warned him to keep silence. He did, but as his eyes slowly adjusted to the deep gloom he saw Henry Gouger in the corner, next to Captain Laird. Even Mr. Rodgers was there.

Now Adoniram could see that the prison consisted of one room about thirty feet wide by forty long. It lacked windows and had only one small door, but a little light filtered in through the cracks. Perhaps fifty prisoners lay fettered on the teakwood floor, all nearly naked. Not all were men. A few women lay among them. Some were obviously near death. About a dozen men lay with one or both ankles in a huge set of stocks, which consisted of one heavy log lying on another. Here and there were other smaller sets of stocks, each holding one or two men.

Hanging from the ceiling was a long, horizontal bamboo pole, suspended from pulleys. A block-and-tackle arrangement at the ends permitted it to be raised or lowered. Whispering, Adoniram asked Gouger what it was, but the Englishman could not tell him. In the center of the room stood a tripod on which had been placed a large earthen cup filled with earth-oil, crude petroleum. At dusk the fettered guard lighted it. The feeble, smoky flame supplied only a little light, but that little was nearly as much as leaked in from outside.

Before it was quite dark, the wicket opened once more and Price was brought in. He too showed signs of rough handling. He turned to the guard and began a voluble complaint. The guard flourished his club in the doctor's face, and for a moment Adoniram and Gouger thought Price, even in fetters, would spring at him. But the club made him think better of it, and after a little grumbling he allowed himself to be led over to the other foreigners, where he lay down silent and at least momentarily subdued.

In a little while night fell. Father entered with a couple of his assistants. With jests and jokes, they lowered the long horizontal bamboo pole from the ceiling, passed it between the fettered legs of the prisoners, re-secured it at the ends, and hoisted it up with the aid of the block-and-tackle. Gradually the feet of the prisoners rose into the air until only their shoulders and heads rested on the floor. When Father made sure of the height — he told them he wanted to protect their lives — he wished them a good night's rest and departed.

The young guard trimmed the lamp, lit his pipe at the flame, and lit pipes for the other prisoners. Everyone smoked to try to counteract that awful stench.

Next to Henry Gouger on the bamboo was a prisoner named Kewet-nee. In a low voice he told the foreigners about the tortures he had seen. He left no doubt that they might expect them too. Other prisoners agreed.

Gouger, Adoniram learned, had been in custody in stocks near the king's stables for nearly two weeks while the examiners questioned him and examined his records. Now it was plain that the government had decided all the white men were spies. They could only hope death would come without the usual tortures.

Gradually the sounds died, except for low nightmare groans and the rustling of the vermin in the debris on the floor.

Adoniram, his hair and neck in filth, his arms sore from the cut of the cord, his ankles already chafed raw from the three pairs of heavy iron fetters on his elevated feet, was alone with his thoughts.

They were bitter and depressed. What had he brought to those who depended on him? Nothing but death. Death for Harriet Atwood — for in a way, he had been responsible for her becoming a missionary. Death for his only son. Now death for himself, probably death for Nancy. And what was there to show for it? Eighteen converts in the twelve years since he had left Salem. Of those, probably only a few would remain faithful — if they survived. Eighteen souls for all those years and lives. And the Burmese New Testament. But most of that was in manuscript, in the little wooden house by the river. Almost certainly it would be destroyed or lost. That left only the souls. The thought of those souls beside him at the throne of God would ordinarily have seemed compensation, but this dreadful night it did not. Deep in depression he lost hope for himself and for Nancy.

Nancy was nearly frantic that evening when Maung Ing returned with the news that Adoniram had been taken to the Death Prison. She calmed her little girl pupils as well as she could, but the Burmese converts and the Bengali servants knew only too well what the Death Prison meant.

After a few minutes she retired to her room and prayed as she had never prayed before for strength to bear what was to come. But she had little time, for presently the magistrate came up on the veranda and began shouting for her to come out and be examined. After repeated commands she came, but not until she had rushed through the house and destroyed all her letters, journals and writings. It would be suicidal to let the government know that she and Adoniram had corresponded with friends in England and kept a day-by-day account of the details of their life in Burma.

When the destruction was finished, she went out and submitted to the magistrate. He asked her every entrapping question he could think of; but he got nowhere. He went away unsatisfied. Before he left he ordered the gates of the compound to be shut and directed that no one should be allowed to enter or leave. To enforce his command, he left "a guard of ten ruffians."

By now it was dark. Nancy took the little girls with her into an inside room and barred the doors. The guards immediately became suspicious. From outside they ordered her "to unbar the doors and come out, or they would break the house down." Nancy refused to obey. She threatened to complain of them to their masters in the morning. They gave up their attempt but took revenge by placing the two Bengali servants in stocks in the most painful position they could think of. This had the desired effect. Nancy "called the head man to a window, and promised to make them all a present in the morning, if they would release the servants."

After threats, arguments and much bargaining they agreed. Nancy went to bed but not to sleep. All night long she lay wakeful, inventing and discarding one fantastic plan after another.

In the morning she sent Maung Ing to see whether Adoniram was still alive, with food in case he was. Maung Ing soon came back with word that the foreigners were still living, but in the heart of the Death Prison, confined with three pairs of fetters each, and strung up on a long pole. The news struck nearly as much terror into Nancy's heart as if she had heard Adoniram were already dead. But she persisted: when the magistrate returned she pleaded with him to let her present the missionaries' case before some of the government officials. He refused. He said he did not dare let her go, for fear she might escape. As a last resort, Nancy wrote a note to the sister of the king, the wife of the crippled Prince M., whom she had come to know fairly well, asking her to beg someone in authority to let the teachers go.

In a little while the note was returned with a message. The king's sister "did not understand it." Actually, Nancy learned later, she wanted to help but dared not brave the queen's wrath — that sorceress whom everyone feared even more than the king.

There was nothing more Nancy could do. The day dragged on. As evening approached, she gave tea and cigars to the guard, in the successful hope that they would let her sleep in her room with out threatening her. In bed she lay awake for a long time. Finally, exhausted, she slept fitfully.

In the Death Prison, dawn brought a spectacle that Gouger was to remember nearly forty years later as "The sleeping convicts awoke one by one with a yawn, clanking their chains and shaking the swarm of loathsome vermin from their rags, only to scatter the plague upon their neighbors."

Some of the native convicts began to intone their morning hymn in Pali. It consisted of just a few words, repeated over and over. The song had a certain haunting, melancholy beauty that would have been pleasant in another time and place. Now it was merely irritating.

With daylight Father appeared. Grinning broadly, he asked the prisoners solicitously how they had enjoyed the night. He lowered the bamboo to within about a foot of the floor. Slowly the blood began to circulate once more in numbed feet and legs. At about eight, the inmates were taken, eight to twelve at a time, into the prison yard for about five minutes to relieve themselves. This was the only time during the day they were permitted outside the inner prison.

At nine o'clock food came. Maung Ing had brought something for Adoniram, who by now was so bedraggled that his closest friends could hardly have recognized him. One of Gouger's servants, a baker, courageously brought his employer some breakfast wrapped up in a towel. By similar means the other foreign prisoners received something to eat. Most of the natives had food delivered to them by friends and relatives. The others had to depend on the charity of good-hearted Burmese who, mostly women, considered it an act of virtue to supply food for the prisoners. Especially during festival time huge baskets of rice and *ngapi*, wrapped in large, thick, glossy plantain leaves, were sent in. But since a week might go by with nothing, the friendless recipients rolled what was left over in the plantain leaves, pinned the rolls together with bamboo slivers, and saved them. In time both food and leaves — the latter accumulating inside the prison in heaps — decayed and added to the stench. There was a rumor that the king allowed a basket of rice a month to each prisoner, but no one had ever seen any of it.

Just as he finished his breakfast, Gouger was ordered outdoors by a jailer. The others could not say good-by to him on account of the ban on talking, but the looks they gave him were eloquent. He shuffled slowly and painfully out the door, the fetters chafing his raw ankles, almost relieved that he was to know his fate. At least, he would have a breath of fresh air for a few moments before death came.

But he was not to be executed. He was to be questioned by an assistant to the city governor, a Myo-serai (today a "myosa"), who was seated in a shed in the prison yard opposite the inner prison examining another prisoner.

The young man being examined was accused of robbing the house of a high-ranking personage. He denied the charge and to Gouger, a fair judge of men, he had not the look of a robber. But the magistrate considered his denial merely obstinacy. To help the prisoner talk, he was seated on a low stool, and his legs tied together above the knees by a cord. Two executioners each took a long pole, inserted the pole between his legs, and began to lever them up and down in opposite directions.

Gouger, his eyes bulging with horror, expected to hear the thighbones snap. But although the youth screamed in agony he still denied the accusation. At length he fainted. The guards threw cold water over him and thrust him back into his cell, promising something even better for him tomorrow.

This trifling matter disposed of, the Myo-serai turned his attention to Gouger. It was unusual for a Myo-serai to appear within the prison compound, and he considered it rather below his dignity to have to make prison examinations. Moreover, he was actually a man of inherent benevolence who preferred not to order torture.

Gouger did not know that, at the time. Yet for some reason unknown to himself, he felt unusually calm. He had spent the night anticipating torture and death and felt nothing could be worse than the agonizing deaths he had already died in anticipation. He was sure, of course, that the purpose of the examination was to get him to confess he was a spy.

He was mistaken. All the Myo-serai wanted was a schedule of his property and a list of everyone who owed him money. Gouger was relieved. The officials undoubtedly already had all of his property they could discover. As to the rest, including money owed him, they were welcome if they could collect. He immediately gave the magistrate the most accurate account he could. The total was very large. When the list had been written down, Gouger was taken back to the prison. He viewed this procedure as his last settling of accounts before his departure from earth.

During Gouger's absence, the bamboo pole had been removed from between the prisoners' legs and hoisted up to its daytime position beneath the ceiling. A certain amount of subdued talking began among the inmates. The guard did not interfere, and tones grew louder through the morning. Adoniram somewhat recovered his spirits, and he and Gouger even began a certain amount of grim joking. Here and there, in spite of the discomfort, low laughs and chuckles could be heard occasionally from the other prisoners scattered on the floor.

But as three in the afternoon approached, the talking and joking strangely diminished. Voices fell to whispers, or died away altogether. Finally the whole prison population was in a deep hush.

Promptly at three, a great gong hung in the Palace yard nearby was struck. As its deep tones pulsated through the air, the faces of the prisoners grew pale. The vibration did not fully die away before the wicket opened and two Spotted Faces appeared. Each went straight to a man; those two prisoners rose without a word. Each had to follow a Spotted Face. There was never a sound except the scuffing of bare feet, and the clank of the fetters. Then the wicket closed. Those who had not been taken could breathe again — they had escaped death for another twenty-four hours.

Later that afternoon, the European contingent was increased by two. One was a Greek named Constantine, a native of Constantinople. The other was a fairly well-to-do young merchant named Arrakeel, an Armenian. The other white men had never seen either one before and had never known, until now, that they lived in Ava.

These were the events of the day. At nightfall, Father supervised the raising of the prisoners' legs on the bamboo. The young jailer with the club lighted the lamp and the prisoners' pipes, and once again the *Let-may-yoon*, the prison Hand Shrink Not, fell into silence.

The next day was much like the first. This time it was Adoniram's turn for questioning. He saw the conclusion of the examination of the young man accused of robbery. The young man's wrists were tied behind his back and the rope drawn up by a pulley until his toes barely touched the ground. After a while, just before his shoulders dislocated, he "confessed" by implicating two respectable citizens of Ava. This was intelligent. The officials now had two well-to-do men to fleece instead of one. The young man was returned to the prison nearly maimed. But as soon as the fleecing of the men he denounced was completed some days later, he was released in consideration of his services to the cause of justice.

Like Gouger, Adoniram had to give a list of his property. Unfortunately, he had also to admit that Gouger had supplied him with money. On his return he agreed with Gouger that the outlook now seemed hopeless.

Meanwhile Nancy had not been supine. That same day she had sent a message to the governor of the city, asking permission to pay him a visit in order to give him a present. This inducement had had its effect: soon orders came to the guards to allow the teacher Yoodthan's wife to go into town.

She found the governor not uncourteous. When he asked her what she wanted, she told him that the foreigners were in the Death Prison and badly treated. The teachers, at least, were Americans. They came from a different country from the English, and had nothing whatever to do with the war.

The governor considered this statement. Finally he said, "It is not in my power to release them from the prison, or from their irons. But I can make them more comfortable." He indicated an official nearby. "There is my head officer. You must consult with him, as to how this is to be done."

To Nancy, this man's appearance "presented the most perfect assemblage of all the evil passions attached to human nature." He took her aside and told her bluntly that the prisoners and she herself were completely at his disposal. What would be done for any of them would depend entirely on her liberality. Furthermore, any gift-giving must remain unknown to any other officials.

Nancy nodded. "What must I do to obtain a mitigation of the present sufferings of the two teachers?"

"Pay me two hundred ticals, two pieces of fine cloth, and two pieces of handkerchiefs." Nancy had that much money with her — it amounted to about $100 in American currency — but of course not the cloth. She could not go home for the cloth and return to the prison — a four-mile round trip — in time to see Adoniram that day. She offered the money to the official and begged him not to insist on the cloth. He hesitated. Finally, unable to let so much silver out of his sight, he took it. In a few moments she had an order from the city governor, written on a palm leaf, as was customary, permitting her to enter the prison.

At the prison the guards scrutinized her order and grudgingly let her go as far as the bamboo wicket leading into the inner prison. Here they stopped her while they called Adoniram.

As it happened, Gouger had been called at the same moment to pick up a bundle of food. He had no wish to have her see his chains, and spoke to her as briefly as he could with courtesy. But she had scarcely more than a glance for him. She may not even have noticed his fetters, for her eyes were fixed on the darkness within.

Then she saw Adoniram coming out of the murk, *crawling*. Two days in prison had turned the most fastidious man she knew into a haggard, unshaven scarecrow, his usually spotless white starched neckcloth a filthy rag, his neat black broadcloth suit disheveled, torn and smeared with fragments of rotting plantain leaves. She could scarcely recognize him. She gave him one long horrified incredulous look, and hid her face in her hands. This much Gouger saw before he turned his back. But that look and that gesture burned themselves into his memory forever.

For a moment Nancy gave way. Death she could face with some semblance of calm, perhaps even torture. But this degradation . . .! She was not prepared for it. It was too much to bear.

Soon, with a supreme effort, she conquered herself. They exchanged a few words of greeting, which she made as cheerful as she could. Adoniram had an idea about securing their release. Bribery would do it, if she went high enough up. But before he could say more, the Spotted Faces commanded her to go. She showed them the order from the city governor. She pleaded. "Get out," they insisted harshly. "Get out or we will pull you out." Weeping, the palm leaf inscribed with the useless order dangling from her hand, her tall figure drooping in the gorgeous silk Burmese costume she habitually wore, she went forlornly out the gate.

But the order was not ineffective. Before sunset, Adoniram, Price, Gouger, Laird, Rodgers and the other foreigners were moved out of the prison building into the open shed where the magistrate had sat. They were still as heavily fettered as ever, but here there were no vermin and rotting plantain leaves. Here air and sunlight streamed through the open side of the shed. True, from this unscreened place they could not help seeing the daily torture of prisoners undergoing interrogation with pole, cord and iron maul; and from so close the screams and cries rang in their ears unmuffled. But to such sights and sounds they were already becoming toughened. And meanwhile they rejoiced in the persistence, courage and love of Nancy Judson, and blessed her very name.

## CHAPTER XVII

# Death Prison Days
## [ *1824* ]

NANCY now resolved to try to get a petition to the eyes of the queen. It was impossible to go directly, but Nancy knew her brother's wife, whose liking she had won in better days.

She found this exalted lady "lolling on her carpet. . . with her attendants around her." As usual, Nancy brought a present, but instead of waiting to be asked what she wanted, according to convention, she boldly spoke out that the missionaries were being treated unfairly. They had nothing to do with England, or the war. Yet they were treated like criminals and were being tortured. Would the queen's sister-in-law help?

The princess opened Nancy's present but avoided meeting her eye. "Your case is not singular," she replied with head down. "All the foreigners are treated alike."

"But it *is* singular," insisted Nancy. "The teachers are Americans. They are ministers of religion, and have nothing to do with war or politics, and they came to Ava in obedience to the king's command. They have never done anything to deserve such treatment. Is it right they should be treated thus?"

"The king does as he pleases," said the princess. "I am not the king. What can I do?"

"You can state their case to the queen and obtain their release," Nancy proposed earnestly. "Place yourself in my situation: Were you in America, and your husband, innocent of crime, thrown into prison, in irons, and you a solitary, unprotected female — what would you do?"

In spite of herself, the princess displayed a little feeling. "I will present your petition," she said. "Come again tomorrow."

Nancy went home feeling more hopeful. There she learned that

Gouger's property, amounting to some fifty thousand dollars, had been carried to the palace. The officials who had done it soon came to her door, greeted her with bows, and told her politely, "We shall visit your house tomorrow."

As soon as they had gone she gathered together most of the silver and all the small articles she could lay her hands on. After dark she buried them in the garden. Scurrying around for one thing after another, her eye fell on the manuscript of Adoniram's translation of the Bible and his voluminous notes. This material she wrapped carefully in a bundle which she buried in the garden a safe distance from the other treasure.

Sure enough, the next morning she had visitors — no less than the Royal Treasurer himself, Prince Sarawady, the Chief Wun and Koung-tone Myoo-tsa, attended by a royal secretary and some fifty followers, as befitted his rank. Nancy welcomed them at the door, a well-bred New England hostess, smiling and gracious. The prince ordered the crowd to stay outside. Only the three officials and a royal secretary entered. Nancy ordered the servants to give them chairs and held the chair for the prince herself. She served them tea and sweetmeats, as self-possessed as if they came at her express invitation. The Burmese officials drank and ate, sitting uneasily on the edges of their chairs. But Nancy's composure suddenly broke. She began to sob quietly into her handkerchief.

The three officials apologized for the necessity of their visit. "It is painful for us to take possession of property not our own, but we are compelled to do so, by order of the king," they said.

When Nancy recovered control of herself a little, the confiscation began. Nancy prepared herself inwardly to contest every step.

The Royal Treasurer began: "Where is your silver, gold and jewels?"

"I have no gold or jewels," said Nancy, "But here is the key of a trunk which contains the silver. Do with it as you please."

The servants brought out the trunk. The silver was weighed on a portable scale. "This money," Nancy pointed out, knowing full well that the Burmese disliked taking religious offerings, "was collected in America by the disciples of Christ, and sent here for the purpose of building a kyoung, and for our support while teaching the religion of Christ. Is it suitable that you should take it?"

"We will state this circumstance to the king," said one of the officers. "Perhaps he will restore it. But is this all the silver you have?"

It was not, of course. Most of the silver was in the garden. Nancy could not lie but she could evade. "The house is in your possession," she said. "Search for yourselves."

"Have you not deposited some silver with some person of your acquaintance?"

"My acquaintances are all in prison," retorted Nancy. "With whom should I deposit silver?"

"Have you already given any silver to anyone in the government?" she was asked.

Nancy could not evade this question and perhaps even welcomed it. "Yes," she admitted; and being questioned further told of the two hundred ticals she had paid to the city governor.

The next step was a thorough examination of all of the trunks and furniture. In deference to Nancy's feelings, only the secretary went with her on this search. Everything "nice or curious" he took to the three officers. When he displayed in this manner whole armfuls of clothing, Nancy begged that at least these be left. "It would be disgraceful," she pleaded, "to take clothes partly worn into the presence of His Majesty, and to us they are of unspeakable value."

The officers agreed. They decided to take only a list of the clothing, the books, the medicines and similar articles. For a moment she thought they would take her little work table and her rocking chair, her presents from Elnathan; but in the end they merely added them to the list and went away.

They had scarcely left before Nancy hurried to the queen's brother's palace, to learn the effect of her petition to the queen. His wife, still cool and distant, said, "I stated your case to the queen, but Her Majesty replied, 'The teachers will not die. Let them remain as they are.'"

Nancy had pinned all her hopes on the petition. Now they were dashed. With heavy steps she went to the prison, to be turned back at the gate.

For the next ten days she went to the prison every day and every day was refused admittance. She bribed a jailer to carry messages;

but he was caught, beaten, and put in the stocks. She had to bribe Father with twenty ticals to get him out again.

Very little that went on in government circles in Ava could be kept a secret. Nancy soon learned that the officers who visited her house had said to the king: "Yoodthan is a true teacher. We found nothing in his house but what belongs to priests. In addition to this money there are an immense number of books, medicines, trunks of wearing apparel, and like things, of which we have only taken a list. Shall we take them, or let them remain?"

"Let them remain," ordered the king charitably. "And put this property by itself, for it shall be restored to him again if he is found innocent."

So much had Nancy gained.

The foreign prisoners, lodged in an open-sided shed during the days, quickly settled into a routine. As they went to the gate for their food, they seized the opportunity to exchange a word or two with the bearer. Soon each had a little white pillow. Nancy wrote a note to Adoniram on a flat cake, afterwards baked and hidden in a bowl of rice. He replied on a tile invisible when the tile was wet, visible when it dried. But this was too cumbersome. Presently she hit on the simple device of inserting a rolled-up note in the long nose of the teapot in which she brought his tea.

The prisoners received fresh clothing, too. The shirts they could put on, but with leg-fetters they thought it would be impossible to put on or take off trousers without cutting them. Then one of the jailers, who had guarded a trouser-wearing prisoner before, told them how to solve this problem.[1]

Of all the prisoners, Gouger probably bore himself with most equanimity. Adoniram was anxious about Nancy as well as himself; and the dirt drove him nearly to distraction. Laird was a fatalist. Twice he had been shipwrecked and each time had been one of the few to escape alive. He was convinced these escapes proved he would not die now. The others thought that if his experience proved anything at all, it was that he was not fated to die by drowning. Laird, incidentally, was the ugliest of all the prisoners.

---

[1] But the method was not told — at least in print — by Gouger, who recounted this incident.

His face had been so discolored and ravaged by smallpox that the king, when Laird was first presented as a native of Scotland, had innocently asked whether all the Scottish were as ugly as he was. But his heart was good and he made an equable prison companion.

Rodgers, the only white prisoner who thought the Burmese could defeat the English, was sure he was going to be tortured to death. To escape it, he had resolved to poison himself and had asked his wife to send the necessary poison. She never did, but every day when his rice bundle came, the others watched with horrified fascination his painstaking search for the poison and his visible disappointment when he failed to find it.

The other two foreigners spoke no English and very little Burmese. The Greek, Constantine, hated the English and they on their part thought he had leprosy. They avoided each other as much as possible. The young Armenian, Arrakeel, they liked better. He kept his spirits up and made no disturbance, but conversation with him was impossible.

They had been in the shed only a few days when all but Adoniram were suddenly ordered back inside to the same gloomy corner they had occupied before. It was a long time before they knew why. Nancy had been the unwitting cause.

When the Royal Treasurer's delegation had returned to the palace, they had confronted the city governor and demanded the two hundred ticals Nancy had given him. Giving up the money threw him into a rage. As soon as Nancy heard of it, she went to him. "You are very bad," he stormed at her. "Why did you tell the Royal Treasurer that you had given me so much money?"

"The Treasurer inquired. What could I say?"

"Say that you had given nothing, and I would have made the prisoners comfortable. Now I know not what will be their fate."

"But I cannot tell a falsehood," insisted Nancy. "My religion differs from yours. It forbids lying. If you had stood by me with your knife raised, I could not have said what you want."

Fortunately for Nancy, the governor's wife, who was sitting beside him, came to her rescue. "Very true," she affirmed. "What else could she have done? I like such straightforward conduct. You must not be angry with her."

Nancy had brought with her a very beautiful opera glass she had received from England just before the war. Now she gave it to the governor and begged him not to make things worse for the prisoners because he was angry with her. "I will try to make you presents which will make up for your loss," she promised.

This mollified him a little. "You may intercede for your husband only," he ruled. "For your sake he may remain where he is. But let the other prisoners take care of themselves."

Nancy pleaded that at least he exempt Price; but it took ten days and the promise of two handkerchiefs and a piece of broadcloth before Price rejoined Adoniram in the shed. The other foreigners remained in the dark inner prison, where their little white pillows made, Gouger remembered, a ridiculous sight on the floor, "glittering like so many stars in a firmament of unspeakable dinginess."

But in or out, there was no water for washing. The grime on their faces grew thicker and thicker. Vermin appeared in their hair. This was worse than their own smells, which were becoming insupportable. They borrowed a pair of scissors from Father — almost the only favor he ever did them — and clipped themselves bald. The Burmese, proud of their long locks, did not follow their example, and the Englishmen became the laughingstock of the prison community; but they were more comfortable.

So the time passed. After a few days, the prisoners heard the booming of a single gun by the river. They learned by the prison grapevine that this meant news from the war front. The king had commanded that after a battle the boat bringing the word should fire one gun; if the Burmese had won a victory, two guns; if the English had been driven back into the sea, three guns.

Thus the one gun meant no victory. Before the day was over the Spotted Faces were gloomy, their tempers vicious. The prisoners heard that the British had charged out of their lines and carried the Burmese stockades with the bayonet, killing hundreds.

The rumor was correct. During the whole war, "the worst managed in British history," [2] the British were to receive only one repulse, and although thousands of troops were to die of disease only hundreds would perish in battle. The individually brave but undrilled Burmese soldiers, their officers far in the rear and invariably the first to run, could not stand up against European discipline in

[2] D. G. E. Hall, *Europe and Burma*.

defending stockades. The sight of orderly lines of men steadily approaching with bayonets, closing up without faltering as some dropped under musket fire, advancing even when bleeding, dismayed the Burmese, and they almost always soon broke in panic. The legend spread that British soldiers never stopped even when arms or legs were cut off, because after the battle the old limbs were picked up and sewed back in place by the surgeons. At the beginning of the war a Burmese recruit could be secured for four or five ticals. Within months volunteers against these English were scarce at a hundred ticals apiece.

But this the prisoners did not know as yet. They only knew there had been a defeat and were afraid their heads would roll on account of it. When the fateful afternoon gong sounded that day and they remained alive, they took heart.

Outside the prison Nancy was still working for the prisoners from daylight until late at night, in the face of every kind of threat and extortion. Once she was officially summoned to the courthouse, and, standing at the foot of the steps in the presence of a crowd of hundreds, was officially accused of having given to the care of a Burmese officer a string of pearls, a pair of diamond earrings and a silver teapot. She must answer the truth, or die. Had she done this? By now, she had courage to face anybody. "It is not true," she replied boldly. "If you, or any other person, can produce these articles I refuse not to die." And she immediately began to beg for Adoniram's release.

Day after day she visited the queen's sister-in-law until the woman's looks told her she had better stay away for a while. Nearly every day she called on some official or member of the royal family. She gave as many gifts as she could. Here and there she found friends who would drop hints in the palace that the missionaries had nothing to do with the war. Some of these secretly helped Nancy with gifts of food.

There were, of course, annoyances. Some days the prisoners were not allowed to speak to each other or to anyone bringing them food. Sometimes the bearers had to pay extra bribes to bring in food. Often Nancy would be so busy with her palace rounds that

she could not go to the prison until dark. After the two-mile walk
home it might be nine at night before she could throw herself into
her rocking chair, weak with anxiousness and activity, shed a few
tears, and after a few minutes' rest try to think again of some way
she might gain the prisoners' freedom. Occasionally her thoughts
would turn to Bradford and her friends in America, but seldom for
more than a moment. All her energies were concentrated on her
job in Ava.

One day the prisoners heard another signal gun. Another defeat.
Shortly afterwards a new prisoner was brought in, an iron ring
around his waist with a length of chain dangling from it, by which
he was staked to the floor like a bear. He was an Irishman named
Cassiday, a private in the East India Company's Madras European
regiment. He had been captured while wandering away from the
camp looking for pineapples.

Late that night he was interrogated by a group of Wungyis,
Rodgers interpreting. Later Rodgers regaled the other prisoners
with the highlights of the interview.

THE WUNGYIS: What do the Kulas want by coming to
Rangoon?

CASSIDAY: I believe they are going to march up to take the
country. (*A loud laugh from the Wungyis at this preposter-
ous statement.*)

THE WUNGYIS: How many men have they brought with
them?

CASSIDAY: About three thousand British soldiers, besides a
good many black troops.

THE WUNGYIS: What do you think will become of them,
when they are attacked by one hundred thousand of our army?

CASSIDAY: I think we should make very short work of your
army, if they are no better than those we met in the stockades.
My regiment has great experience with the bayonet. (*Great
excitement, tinged with consternation, on the part of the
Wungyis.*)

There was more to the interview; but this, and the loud laugh of
the Wungyis when Cassiday innocently asked what kind of rations
the Burmese allowed to their prisoners, were what the three Englishmen relishfully rolled over and over in their minds.

Well along in the summer, Nancy's efforts began to have some effect. The foreign prisoners were moved out of the inner prison and each given a tiny cell or hut along the inside edge of the stockade enclosing the prison yard. Each hut was about six feet long and five wide, barely high enough for a man to stand erect where the peak of the roof rose in the center. But it was heaven compared to the inner prison. Nevertheless, their nights they spent in the inner prison, as before.

As usual, Gouger promptly set about organizing the best possible life for himself. One of the jailers had a very pretty sixteen-year-old daughter who took a great fancy to him. She supplied him with water for washing, an inexpressible boon. He in turn supplied her and her father with rats, a great delicacy to Spotted Faces, which he speared after luring them out of their holes with grains of boiled rice. He took immense pleasure in talking with the girl, but when she was not with him he could amuse himself further by peeking through the cracks in the stockade wall of his cell at the traffic outside.

Nancy was now permitted to spend an hour or two at a time with Adoniram in the open shed. Eventually, she was even allowed to build him a little enclosed shed of bamboo where he could be by himself. With this new privacy, and a little water to wash in, he felt he had achieved nearly the utmost goal of ambition.

Not that he had lost all others. When they could talk his thoughts turned to his New Testament manuscript. Nancy told him how she had wrapped it up and buried it. But it could not be allowed to remain thus in the garden, for it would soon rot. Finally Adoniram thought of a plan. Let Nancy take the translation and pack it into a pillow so hard and uncomfortable, and so poor in appearance, that no jailer could possibly covet it. Then let her give it to him; he would guard it himself as well as he could. This she did, and from then on he cushioned his head on the only complete copy of the Burmese New Testament in existence.

With the translation in Adoniram's hands, Nancy began to think what else she could do. The wretched food she had to bring him, usually nothing but rice with *ngapi*, disturbed her. Finally she decided to surprise him with a real reminder of home. She managed to procure some buffalo meat, and after some experimentation with plantains eventually produced a very good approximation of a New England mince pie. But the day she meant to bring it she was detained and had to send Maung Ing instead, having carefully explained to him that this was a native food of Americans, and something Mr. Judson would particularly relish. Thus Adoniram was curious when he received the mysterious package from the smiling Maung Ing. But when he opened it, and realized what it was, memory was too much. The very thought of eating closed his throat. With the pie on the ground beside him, he rested his head on his knees and wept. Then, blindly, he thrust his gift into the hands of the amazed Price, hobbled hurriedly to his little shed, and there secluded himself for hours.

Nancy's mince pie had been only too successful. Plymouth — Bradford — his father and mother and brother and sister . . . like a flood, carefully repressed memories overwhelmed him. And in the misery of his thoughts there was one which, at any other time, would have given him the greatest pleasure. Now, it was most bitter of all.

Nancy was pregnant. The baby would be born, as far as they could determine, in late January or early February.

## CHAPTER XVIII
# Prison Life; Little Maria
## [ *1824–1825* ]

T HE Burmese army had been defeated twice now, once when led by the Kyi Wungyi, once under the Thonby Wungyi. The latter had been killed in July by one of his own fear-frenzied men while bravely defending his stockade. The court began slowly to admit to itself that it might possibly have formed a wrong estimate of the enemy.

It certainly had. Moreover, it had formed a wrong estimate of the whole war. Bandula had been sent over the mountains with most of the army that he might fall upon the British on the Arakan seacoast in the direction of Chittagong and Bengal. Where the Burmese had almost no forces, at Rangoon, the British had appeared with their whole strength, with unassailable ships and even with a steamboat, the first ever seen in Burma. But Bandula, when facing negligible British forces, had driven off minor detachments and hence was credited with victories. The king, convinced by these that only Bandula understood how to fight foreigners, commanded him to return to Ava and win victories in Rangoon. His army was brought back from Arakan and sent down the river. New — and reluctant — troops were raised and sent after it.

Life in the Death Prison went on as usual. When the news was bad the foreigners were confined days at a time in the inner prison. When it was better, they were allowed to use their huts.

Various events marked the days. Once a woman was brought in covered with pustules of smallpox. The Spotted Faces, themselves concerned, had sense enough to clear a little open space on the floor. Luckily, after about twenty-four hours she was taken away.

By what miracle the fifty or so other prisoners escaped the disease no one understood, even Price. This was the only case that made an impression on his peculiar nature. Already that summer he had undertaken one piece of surgery that had made Adoniram and Gouger fear for their lives.

One of the Spotted Faces had had a large swelling on an eyelid, probably a fatty cyst. For days the doctor had itched to get a knife on it. Finally he persuaded the Spotted Face to let him remove it with the only tool in the place, the stump of an ordinary penknife. Adoniram and all the Englishmen tried to dissuade Price from trying the operation. They could imagine only too vividly the consequences to all of them of a mishap. But Price would not listen.

The prisoners watched the operation in horror. None of them had ever seen such hacking. As Gouger expressed it, "after many ejaculations and contortions on the part of the patient, the operator succeeded in whittling out something which very much resembled in appearance two or three inches of a large dew-worm; when, I suppose, not knowing what to do with it, or unable to extend his discoveries further, the disgusting string was snipped off."

But to the amazement of everyone except Price, when the wound had healed the swelling was gone and the Spotted Face still had his eyesight. There was only one slight difficulty. In removing the cyst Price had somehow also severed a muscle or nerve and the eyelid now lay inert over the eye like a curtain. But, explained the ingenious surgeon, this was really an advantage in disguise. "The eye will keep all the better. When you want it, all you have to do is lift the lid with your finger; and when you have done with it, let it drop again." Occasionally the Spotted Face suspected a flaw in this reasoning. But he was never able to lay a finger (or an eye) on it, and nothing happened to the doctor or the other prisoners.

The incident illustrated Price's uncanny ability to make the jailers think his wildest ideas were practicable. Once he actually persuaded Father to give him some bamboo and a lump of clay. Out of this he promised to make a clock which would keep the prison time. Adoniram and Gouger thought he had gone completely crazy. After a great deal of work, even Price realized the job was impossible; but as usual he snatched victory out of defeat. He used the clay to model a human head. On it he marked the "phrenological compartments" — the location of the qualities of will, love, hate, intelligence, forbearance and the like, as conceived by medicine of the time — and lectured learnedly to as many prisoners and Spotted Faces as would listen. The immensity of amazement he aroused was matched only by the minuteness of knowledge he instilled.

Adoniram and Gouger, not being surgeons or inventors, hit on another way of passing the time. They decided to play chess. The game was well known in Burma and the Spotted Faces would not think the players were hatching plots or making magic. With Price's knife-stump and bits of discarded bamboo (from Price's clock) they carved out a set of crude pieces. In one corner of the prison they found an old piece of buffalo hide. The cup of earth oil — crude petroleum — which served as a lamp was crusted with fine carbon. This they smeared into squares on the hide. Henceforth they lay on the floor or sat cross-legged for hours absorbed in chess.

Rodgers and Laird had fewer resources. But even they managed to get along by talking to their fellow prisoners at times when conversation was permitted. Rodgers, particularly, enjoyed hobbling from one group of prisoners to the other, learning all about themselves and their families and discussing the news of the day.

Even humor in the prison had a macabre flavor. At best, all prison life was grim; at worst, it seemed unendurable. Once, for instance, Father stamped with heavy wooden shoes on the face of a prisoner in the stocks until he was nearly dead, then finished him off with a club. The slave of a prince, the prisoner had committed the crime of falling in love with another slave. The prince had ordered him to be assassinated quickly. The Spotted Faces had started to starve him to death but he made too much noise. After his body had been removed it was noted in the prison register that he was an opium-eater and died for lack of opium.

Once the jailers marched into the inner prison about a hundred captive Sepoy soldiers. The hundred, added to the fifty already there, packed the place until there was barely standing room. The prisoners came to the verge of death from heat and lack of air before the wicket door was opened. Fortunately, all of the new-comers except eight officers were taken away the next day. Seven of these eight slowly died of starvation. The eighth, a Brahmin named Davy Singh, owed his life to his caste. He refused to eat rice cooked by the Burmese but asked for it uncooked and nibbled it raw, grain by grain. Rationing his rice this way, he managed to live through the long periods when he was given nothing. But although he survived the war, he became stone blind from vitamin deficiency.

It was not surprising that tempers gave way now and then, as on one notable occasion. At this period Adoniram and Price occupied adjoining sleeping places. Price could never go to sleep unless he lay on his side with his knees bent up to touch his nose. In his frequent nightmares, he would straighten out his knees with tremendous force. Weighted with the heavy fetters, they would crash into the small of Adoniram's back like a cannon-ball.

For some time Adoniram had been trying to achieve the "quietism" of Madame Guyon, a French Catholic of the seventeenth and early eighteenth century, whose doctrines had long interested him, but after two or three of these experiences in a single night quietism failed him. He blew up. "Brother Price," he exploded, "you are a public nuisance! I insist on your sleeping as other people do!"

Price replied that his thrashings were unintentional. Adoniram retorted that they were done on purpose. After some bickering Adoniram offered to fight Price. Gouger might have enjoyed the spectacle of a fight between two missionaries, but the Death Prison was not the place. He averted it by offering to sleep between them. From then on, whenever Price's knees thudded into Gouger, he would wake the doctor and smoke a pipe with him. Then he would persuade him to go to sleep on the other side, where the next blow would fall on Rodgers.

But on the whole, all the foreigners agreed, they got on together pretty well. Something interesting was always happening. Prisoners were constantly coming and going in the Death Prison — sometimes high officials of the government who had momentarily fallen under court disfavor, sometimes whole families. From them they learned the latest gossip. The servants of all of them remained faithful, and without pay continued to provide food. Gouger's baker even set up in the business of providing hard rolls for the army, and thus earned enough not only to take care of himself and Gouger but also to provide him with occasional delicacies and bits of clothing. Every week that passed and found them still alive was a triumph. Every prisoner's entire energy was directed to a single object: survival.

Meanwhile Nancy was as busy in their behalf as her advancing pregnancy would permit.

By September, Bandula was in fact Acting King of Burma. He had been loaded with honors and given the full direction of the war. Contingents of new troops went down-river every day. Soon, the court war party hoped, he would lead them to victory over the British.

Nancy resolved, with Adoniram's approval, to make one last appeal to Bandula himself. It was a dangerous step. Some friends at court advised her against it. Most likely he did not even know the prisoners were alive. If he were reminded, he might order their execution. She decided to take the chance. Adoniram wrote the petition, including every argument he could think of that might affect Bandula favorably.

With fear and trembling Nancy took it to the great man through the surrounding crowd of courtiers. A secretary read it aloud. Bandula actually listened, and rather pleasantly asked her several questions about the teachers. Her answers seemed to satisfy him. He promised to think about the subject. She should come again and he would give her a decision.

Elated, Nancy hurried to the prison. Adoniram agreed that the chances looked good that he might be released, and probably Price as well. But when Nancy told the city governor what she had done, he was amazed at her rashness, and predicted that she had probably cost all the foreigners their lives.

In a day or two she went back to Bandula's house. This time she brought the most valuable present she could. But Bandula was not home. His wife received Nancy, accepted the present, and told her that Bandula had said he was too busy preparing the Rangoon expedition to do anything just now. As soon as he had recaptured Rangoon and driven the British out of Burma he would return to Ava and set the prisoners free.

This closed the door on any hope of release. Henceforth Nancy devoted her time to doing what she could to make the prisoners' lot easier. She spent most of every other day at the governor's house. His wife, who had stood up for her when she had admitted giving the governor the two hundred ticals, became her firm friend.

The governor himself took a great liking to her. He had an almost childlike curiosity about America, and would question her for hours about the American government, the manners of the people, their customs, their clothing, their houses, their ships, their money, and every detail of their lives. Every day Nancy enthralled him with stories about Bradford and Salem and Washington and New York. She told him about the cold and snow and how they lived through the winter. And when she was sometimes kept from an appointment, he would be as disappointed as a child deprived of its favorite bedtime story.

This relation, even more than gifts, enabled her to procure little favors for the prisoners. For herself, she had a pass, usually honored by the Spotted Faces, permitting her to visit Adoniram any time of the day.

In October Bandula left for Ava. Thousands of additional troops accompanied him helter-skelter, armed with a bewildering conglomeration of spears, swords, shields and muskets. Gouger, recovered from a fever which had nearly killed him, peered through crannies in the wall and saw them pass. He was sure they were going to certain destruction. Some of the Burmese convicts thought so, too. At one time twenty stewards of townships which belonged to various princesses and other palace women of importance were imprisoned. They told Adoniram that the king had been persuaded into the war by the military leaders, especially Bandula. Adoniram asked one of them, "Suppose the English should retire and leave things as they were before the war?"

"Oh!" the man said feelingly. "How good that would be!"

One prisoner, who had been in one of the early battles, told Gouger that the British shells were charmed and knew exactly whom to look for. He knew that of his own knowledge, for he had been standing near his superior officer, whose title was "Tsekai." All at once a huge iron ball came sailing through the air, the fuse on it slowly revolving and hissing "Tsek-tsek-tsek!" Sure enough, it found the Tsekai and burst directly over him, blowing him to pieces.

By November, Bandula was entrenched outside of Rangoon with a force of sixty thousand men. He had told the Prince of Sarawady, "In eight days I shall dine in the public hall at Rangoon and afterwards return thanks in the Shwe Dagon pagoda." It seemed he should be able to do it. Facing him, the British had thirteen hundred Europeans and twenty-five hundred Sepoys — a total effective force of less than four thousand. But they knew warfare. They had mounted twenty guns on the commanding platform of the Shwe Dagon pagoda and had placed gunboats in the Rangoon River and one of the creeks, where they could enfilade Bandula's stockades.

On December 1, 1824, Bandula advanced, launching his main attack on the pagoda, the strongest point in the British position. The attack was decisively defeated, but the exhausted British were too few to follow up the retreat. Luckily for them, Bandula did not retreat out of reach; he obligingly waited until they had rested, and a few days later the British stormed the Burmese position. Bandula's whole army dissolved like a lump of wet sugar; Bandula was able to hold together only seven thousand men with whom he beat a retreat up the river to Danubyu.

The news arrived in Ava toward the end of the year. The Princesses of Pugan and Shwedong and the queen mother sent for Nancy at once. By now, Nancy was finding it difficult to get around, but they were anxious for her advice. The Princess of Pugan told Nancy: "The Bandula's troops have piled up their arms for the use of the foreigners. They have all dispersed, and the enemy has nothing to do but march to Ava, clapping their hands."

They asked, what should they do? Should they run away, or stay? If they stayed, would they be safe? Would Nancy protect them from the English and speak well of them? This was a new tune for the vain, despotic Burmese royalty, but in their dismay they credited the English with supernatural powers, like the demons called Balus that eat human flesh.

Nancy reassured them. The English were disciplined. They would not hurt Burmese women unnecessarily, particularly royalty. In any case, she would do what she could when the time came if *they* would do what *they* could for the prisoners.

This was almost the last contact Nancy had with the court. For on January 26, 1825, a daughter was born to her. She named the little girl Maria Elizabeth Butterworth Judson.

Twenty days later Nancy appeared at the prison gate with the baby in her arms. It was a pale, puny, wailing infant that Adoniram saw, but to the Spotted Faces her whiteness made her an object of wonder. Adoniram's feelings were a mixture of love, frustration and sadness. For weeks before Nancy's confinement he had been consumed with fear. Now that the baby was born, Nancy could get around again, but what did the future hold? Their first baby had been buried at sea. The second, Roger, lay beside Mrs. Price beneath the battlefield at Rangoon. The prospect for little Maria looked no brighter.

After Nancy had left with the baby, he secluded himself for a long time in the little bamboo hut in the prison yard. He was composing a poem which began:

> Sleep, darling infant, sleep,
>     Hushed on thy mother's breast;
> Let no rude sound of clanking chains
>     Disturb thy balmy rest.

# CHAPTER XIX
# Take Care of Yourself
## [ *1825* ]

FEBRUARY passed. The Pakan Wun himself was thrown into the Death Prison. He had been next in command under Bandula, from whom he had learned the art of war in the conquest of Assam. Now he was suspected of treason.

The morning the Pakan Wun arrived, just before the gate opened to admit him, a strange-looking hen with feathers growing every which way, the only domestic animal in the prison yard, had crowed lustily. The hen was a special favorite of the Spotted Faces. The fact that it crowed — or rather, croaked — won for it their belief that it had the gift of prophecy. This was why they had not eaten it long ago. Now they all but worshiped it. Its crowing was thought to mean that good luck was coming in the form of a prisoner of importance who could give enormous bribes. Gouger realistically concluded that with so many eminent prisoners arriving, now that the war was going badly, the wall-eyed warty bird could hardly be wrong no matter when it crowed.

The Pakan Wun hated the English. Even in the Death Prison he never troubled to hide his feelings. He looked at them with such murderous malevolence that, in spite of their satisfaction at seeing so exalted a personage in jail, they almost wished for his release. But there he was, glaring at them whenever they passed near. Only Laird placed any trust in him, for he had told Laird that if he ever got out he would try to do something for the prisoners.

The first day of March found the Europeans each in his little cell against the stockade wall. Towards evening on that day a Spotted Face went to each cell and brought out the man in it. Not a word was spoken, but the Spotted Faces' expressions showed that ominous business was afoot. The prisoners glanced at each other as they assembled in silence around the granite block in the prison yard.

Each man already wore three pairs of fetters. Now each received two pairs more. When the job was finished, Father pointed to the wicket of the inner prison. Freighted with so much iron, they could barely stagger inside and sink down into their places. Late that night, their legs hung high on the familiar bamboo, they discussed the meaning of it in whispers. As their new fetters had been riveted on, they had seen other Spotted Faces demolishing the little bamboo hut Nancy had built, and snatching up their pillows, mats and other small belongings. All evidence of their ever being in the yard had been removed, and the jailers had already divided their possessions.

It could mean only one thing, they agreed: they were to be assassinated secretly, where they lay. A whisper ran around the crowded room that the execution was to be at three in the morning. Outside, they could hear the Spotted Faces sharpening their knives on whetstones.

The sibilant *wheet-wheet* of the blades on stone gave Gouger a certain sense of relief. He had a peculiar dread of being strangled. He listened with grim satisfaction. The steel would be a boon compared to the cord. He had learned to pray in the prison. He made a silent prayer of thanks to God.

Adoniram's emotions were a little different. He felt bitterness and regret that he would have no chance to say good-by to Nancy and the baby. But perhaps, he decided, this way was better. He had not seen her that day. Tomorrow she would come again and he would not be there. She might even have reason to be glad he had no more to endure. For herself, he believed she would come to no harm. The Burmese had always treated her with respect. Her steadfast courage, persistence and utter honesty had won their admiration. She might even be treated better now, especially with the arrival of the British imminent. He wondered idly, almost with detachment, about the pillow concealing his precious translation of the New Testament. There were some passages he would like to improve. He had seen one of the Spotted Faces with it. No matter. Someone else would do the work again.

One thing he felt sure of. The war would advance the Kingdom of God in Burma. He had told Gouger, more than once: "Here I have been ten years preaching the gospel to timid listeners who wish to embrace the truth but dare not, and beseeching the emperor to grant liberty of conscience to his people but without success, and now when all human means seem at an end, God opens the way by leading a Christian nation to subdue the country. It is possible my life will be spared; if so, with what ardor shall I pursue my work! If not — His will be done. The door will be opened for others who will do the work better."

That was still true. He felt a certain sense of relief. Not all the prisoners did. Some broke down in a last agony of fear. Their sobs echoed through the crowded prison. Their trembling rattled their chains.

Three o'clock came and went. The prisoners remained alive. Dawn came. They were not allowed to go outside for any purpose. But they were still alive.

They spent the day inside. The bringers of their food were carefully kept from seeing them. When a stranger came into the prison yard, the foreigners were hidden from sight. When one of the prisoners went near the wicket for a breath of air, he was unceremoniously hustled back into the depths of the dark prison room. But they lived through the day.

That night they were allowed to go outside for a few moments, but only very late, when no one was on the streets. They began to hope they might live a little longer.

But why were they being hidden?

The first morning after they were thus immured in the inner prison, a message came from Adoniram to Nancy. One of the Spotted Faces, with involuntary respect for her, had allowed word to leak to Maung Ing that Adoniram and all the white prisoners were back in the inner prison, in five pairs of fetters each; that his little hut had been demolished, and that his mat and pillow had been taken by the jailers.

The blood drained from Nancy's face when she heard. She was far too experienced, by now, not to know that something dreadful impended. She hurried at once to the house of the governor, which stood in an enclosure almost directly opposite the prison gate. The governor was not at home, but his wife had a message from him to Nancy. Nancy, it said, must not "ask to have the additional fetters taken off, or the prisoners released, for *it could not be done*."

The cryptic message increased her terrors. She hurried out to the prison gate. She was not allowed to enter. She could glimpse the yard inside through the cracks in the gate. There was not a sign of the little hut, not a sign of the white prisoners. They might as well have disappeared from the earth.

Nancy had to return the two miles to her own house to nurse little Maria, but in the evening she went back to the governor's house at a time when she knew he would be home.

She found him in his audience room. When she entered he looked up at her in a peculiar way, not speaking, his expression showing anger which she sensed was not real, and shame which was.

"Your Lordship," Nancy said earnestly, "has hitherto treated us with the kindness of a father. Our obligations to you are very great. We have looked to you for protection from oppression and cruelty. You have often eased the sufferings of the unfortunate innocents in your charge. You promised me especially that you would stand by me to the last, and even though you should receive an order from the king, you would not put Mr. Judson to death. What crime has he committed to deserve such additional punishment?"

Nancy's plea melted the old governor's heart. He began to weep like a child. "I pity you, Tsa-yar-ga-dau" — the name by which he always called her. "I knew how you would make me feel. Therefore I forbade your application. You must believe me when I say that I do not want to increase the sufferings of the prisoners. When I am ordered to execute them, the least that I can do is to put them out of sight. I will now tell you what I have never told you before, that three times I have received suggestions from the queen's brother to assassinate all the white prisoners privately. But I would not do it. And now I repeat it: Though I execute all the others, I will never execute your husband. But I cannot release him from his present confinement, and you must not ask it."

Nancy had never known him to show such feelings; nor had he ever denied any favor so firmly. She realized fully now by what a rapidly fraying thread the prisoners' lives hung. Meanwhile she took what consolation she could from the fact that the old governor was at least keeping them out of sight in the hope they would not come again to the mind of the Prince Menthagee, the queen's brother. He hated foreigners and was all powerful. But so far he had never given the governor a written order. If he did, the end would be certain and quick.

But even with this knowledge, Nancy never gave up. She visited the governor nearly every day with offers of money. He refused them. She did succeed in getting permission for the prisoners to eat their food in the air outside of the dismal inner prison. Sometimes she was allowed to go to the door of the inner prison and stand looking inside for as much as five minutes. She was afraid that the confinement alone would kill the men within. Perspiring incessantly in the furious heat, they had no appetite and were beginning to look more dead than alive.

About the end of March *two* guns were heard from the message boat. Bandula had won a victory! General Cotton had made an attack on Bandula's entrenchments at Danubyu. It had been beaten off. Ava went into transports of delight. Bandula was invincible. No name was heard but his.

But a few weeks later, on the first of April, Bandula was killed by the explosion of a British shell. With one accord his entire army fled the entrenchments and scattered. When the news came to the palace, the king "heard it with silent amazement, and the queen, in Eastern style, smote upon her breast, and cried *Ama! ama!*" ("Alas! Alas!")

In Ava the people's panic was complete. Their attitude ranged from terror to fury. When Bandula's brother came to the capital with dispatches from the now deserted front, his head was cut off on the theory he might have had something to do with the defeat. In any case there was no reason why he should be allowed to live when his brother was dead.

No one could imagine who might fill Bandula's place. The common people were muttering rebellion. So far they had borne the entire burden of the war. They supplied the men and the money. Not a tical had been spent from the Royal Treasury, for there was no regular system of taxation in Burma. The king merely called for a special forced contribution each time money was needed for war, a new palace, or a coronation.

At this juncture the Pakan Wun sent the king a message from the

Death Prison that he had a plan which would surely win the war. The king sent for him immediately, and actually received him in the palace, although ancient custom forbade any who had ever worn fetters at the king's command to enter the palace gates.

The Pakan Wun offered himself as commander of a new army, which he would raise on an entirely new plan. With brazen confidence, he promised the king that with this army he would quickly drive the British back through Rangoon and into the sea. He would raise the army by paying every soldier a hundred ticals *in advance*. He would make sure of every man personally by receiving the money and paying it out himself.

His stupendous effrontery persuaded the king, who at last had come to realize that his kingdom might be in danger. The Pakan Wun was promptly given all the power in the kingdom.

He began by arresting Lanciego, the only European still at liberty. He was charged with giving the island of Negrais to the British for a large amount of money. Now he was ordered to give up the money to the king. Lanciego was tortured in the prison yard by twisting a lever in a small cord around his wrists. When he came into the prison to join the others, his fingers were coal-black, the ends nearly bursting, his wrists nearly cut through. But even under the torture he admitted nothing.

About the time of Bandula's death, Adoniram came down with a serious fever. Nancy learned about it from notes they exchanged in the spout of his teapot. (One of the notes was discovered and she nearly landed in jail herself.) She was afraid he would die unless something was done. She moved from her own house and put up a one-room bamboo shack in the governor's enclosure to be closer to the prison. From here she badgered the governor a dozen times a day to let her take Adoniram from the inner prison and make him more comfortable.

As usual, she also tried to win the favor of other officials. One day she walked several miles to the house of a Wungyi on such an errand. She had to leave early in the morning and after she arrived was kept waiting until noon, only to have her request refused when she did see him. As she turned to go, he seized her silk umbrella. It was the hot season, and Nancy told him she needed the umbrella for shelter from the sun on the long walk home. She had no money with her and could not buy another. At least, if he took it, let him give her a paper umbrella for protection. The Wungyi laughed. "Only fat people are in danger of sunstroke," he said. "The sun can't find people as thin as you." And she had to leave without the umbrella.

At length the old governor, worn out by her importunities, gave in. The Pakan Wun was now head of the state anyway, and he certainly knew Adoniram was in the Death Prison, having been there himself. The governor gave her the necessary order, and personally ordered Father to let her go in and out any time of the day with medicines and food. Again she built a bamboo hovel for Adoniram, so low that even she could not stand upright in it. But it was a "palace in comparison with the place he had just left." Adoniram even recovered his translation-stuffed pillow from the jailer, by exchanging for it a better one.

But governor or no governor, it always took her a long time to persuade the Spotted Faces to open the gate and let her in. To avoid argument, she would bring Adoniram's food herself. This got her past the gate. Once in, she would stay with him for as long as she could — usually an hour or two, sometimes only a few minutes — until the jailers drove her out.

She had done this one morning — May 2, 1825, to be exact, a month after Bandula's death — and stayed longer than usual, because Adoniram was so feverish he felt unable to eat, when all at once an urgent message came from the governor. Nancy must see him at once. Adoniram — like all the prisoners oversuspicious of anything unusual — was disturbed. Such a summons was unprecedented. But Nancy reassured him. She promised to come back as soon as she learned what the governor wanted.

Adoniram's anxiety had affected her in spite of herself. When she walked into the governor's audience room she breathed a sigh of relief when she found he merely wanted to ask her about his watch, a present from a prisoner. It was not keeping time. Could a European watch be adjusted? He was unusually pleasant and talkative, and kept her for a long time.

When she left, she was almost smiling for the first time in months. She was just going into her little hut in the enclosure across the street from the prison when one of her servants came running to her, pallid under the bronze.

"The white prisoners have all been taken away," he gasped.

Nancy could not believe it. She had just talked with the governor, who would surely have mentioned such a thing! But the man seemed so certain that she returned to the governor's house. Grave this time, the old man admitted the truth. He had learned himself what was to happen only minutes before the order went into effect. That was why he had called Nancy and kept her with him until it was over — to spare her.

Nancy waited to hear no more. Frantic with fear, not even stopping to thank the governor, she ran out of his house. She ran into one street after another around the prison, asking every person she met if they had seen the white foreigners or heard where they were going. No one would answer her. Most averted their faces. They were deathly afraid of the Pakan Wun. Finally she found an old woman who told her the prisoners had been taken toward "the Mootangai," a stream tributary to the Irrawaddy. She ran the half mile to the little river but could not find them. She decided the old woman had been lying; and, steps dragging, returned to the bamboo shack. Meanwhile, some of her friends had run to the regular place of execution, but the prisoners were not there. Finally, in despair, she went once more to the governor's house. He had received news.

"The prisoners are to be sent to Amarapura. Why, I know not. I will send off a man immediately to see what is to be done with them."

Then he looked at her with significant concern: "You can do nothing more for your husband. *Take care of yourself.*"

## CHAPTER XX

# Oung-pen-la
## [ *1825* ]

DURING Nancy and Adoniram's last meeting, the walls of the little hut which gave them privacy had also prevented their seeing certain events quietly taking place just a few feet away. In those minutes of the Judsons' seclusion, the seven other Europeans had been hastily removed from the inner prison and led to the familiar granite block in the yard. Here their fetters had been struck off and they had been tied together in pairs by ropes at the waist. The rope between each pair was long enough to allow a Spotted Face assigned to the task to handle it like reins, using his spear as a goad. Coupled in this manner they had been driven like cattle, while passing Burmans looked the other way, out of the prison gates to the building which served as courthouse. Thus they were already beyond the Death Prison and out of sight up the street when Nancy emerged from the hut in response to the governor's urgent message which had so alarmed Adoniram.

As soon as the stockade gate closed behind her a Spotted Face rushed inside the hut, dragged Adoniram by one arm into the yard, expertly stripped off all his clothing except his shirt and trousers, took his shoes, hat and bedding, struck off his fetters, and hurried him off to the courthouse after the others, where he was coupled with Laird.

Command of the four pairs of men was now handed over to the Lamin Wun (today, "Lamaing Wun": Commander of the Lamaing area). While he led the way on a horse, the Spotted Faces drove the prisoners on foot.

They had been in prison eleven months. No one who had known them when they entered could possibly have recognized them when they left. Their hair was matted, their eyes hollow, their bodies

skin-covered skeletons clothed in rags so greasy and tattered their
original purpose could not even be suspected. They could scarcely
hobble.

It was the hot season, the temperature over a hundred, the blazing sun directly overhead. Adoniram was ill. He had been unable
to eat that morning. To make matters worse, his obsessive nicety
about his personal appearance had led him to persist in wearing
shoes in prison although the others had discarded theirs long before,
and his feet were as tender as when he entered, whereas theirs were
at least a little toughened. Within a few score yards blisters formed
on his soles; in a few yards more these burst; from then on, each
step was made on a raw wound.

At the end of half a mile the little procession reached the bridge
across the Mootangai. Adoniram looked over the side. At this season most of the bed was dry and full of rocks. It was at least a
thirty-foot drop down to them. Up the long, hot road beyond the
bridge — itself a torture ending no one knew where or when —
waited the iron maul, the ax, the knife or the cord.

Adoniram turned to Gouger, who was just behind him. "Gouger," he urged, "the parapet is low. There can be no sin in our
availing ourselves of the opportunity."

But Adoniram was coupled to Laird, and Laird, a big sturdy man
who would have to go with him, was a fatalist convinced that
death would find him when it was ready; he would not seek it.
And in any case, the moment soon passed for the guards prodded
them on. But for that moment, Adoniram was ready to destroy himself, sin or no sin.

From the bridge the road led over a parched desert of sand and
pebbles, searing hot. Within minutes the soles of every prisoner's
feet — not only Adoniram's — were covered with blisters which
burst as soon as they formed. Only Gouger was relatively immune.
The youngest, and fully recovered from his illness of a few months
ago, he had eaten a good breakfast. Now that his first panic was
over, he actually began to enjoy the view of the Irrawaddy in the
distance and the forested Sagaing hills on the other side.

Before they had gone a mile, the Greek Constantine collapsed.
He was an old man with a tendency to fatness, and the sinews of
his legs had contracted and hardened. When he fell on the hot

gravel, the guards tried beating him with their spears, then pricking him with the points. This worked for a little way, but finally he merely lay where he fell, his hands clasped over his head in supplication. The guards dragged him a while with the rope, while the rest of the procession went ahead. But this was too much work, and finally they sent for a cart.

By the end of the second mile Adoniram was almost as far gone as Constantine. The soles of his feet were now nothing but raw flesh. Once, when they stopped for water, he begged the Lamin Wun to let him ride the horse for a mile or so. The Lamin Wun did not even deign to reply. In desperation Adoniram asked Laird to let him lean on his shoulder, to ease the unbearable pain of putting his feet on the ground. The goodhearted Laird agreed, but after a mile found the burden too much. It was all Laird could do to carry himself.

Adoniram was ready to follow the example of Constantine, when one of Gouger's old Bengali servants came running up. He had heard the prisoners were being driven to Amarapura and had followed at full speed to be near his master when he died. With one look he took in Adoniram's difficulty. He ripped his turban from his head, tore it into four pieces, and bound up Adoniram's feet with two of them. It was a difficult job, because the procession was not allowed to stop even for this act of mercy. The Bengali next performed the same service for Gouger. Then he returned to Adoniram and offered him his shoulder the rest of the way.

At Amarapura, the exhausted party stopped. They had marched only four miles — not a long walk for healthy men, but one that had drained the last bit of energy from the prisoners. Soon a solid-wheeled cart creaked up with Constantine. He was in a coma. In an hour or so he died.

Amarapura was as far as the Spotted Faces went. The prisoners were turned over to a new set of keepers, who told them they still had four miles to go: they were to be put in a prison at Oung-pen-la, a country village. But even the direst threats could not get the prisoners off their feet. They were ready to die where they were. The guards, not being Spotted Faces, finally decided to stay in Amarapura overnight. The prisoners crawled into an old shed. Here the Lamin Wun's wife, who had come from Ava out of curiosity, found them. The sight of them aroused her sympathy and she secured some tamarinds and sugar. They could not thank her. They merely ate, and collapsed again on the floor of the shed — all except Gouger, who found himself a shelter under a cart by the side of the road.

When morning came, the youthful Gouger was the only one who could take even a step. If life depended on walking, they would have to die here.

Eventually the new guards procured a cart and the Lamin Wun's wife mercifully saw that the prisoners had some boiled rice before they started off.

The journey was slow. It was two o'clock before their vehicle with its squeaking solid wheels covered the four miles to the prison at Oung-pen-la, about a quarter of a mile outside of the village. It was a lonely place on a grassy plain, once a rice field. The prison, the only building in the vicinity, had been deserted for years. Its bamboo-and-thatch roof had fallen in long since. It lacked a door. A row of stocks running the length of the interior stood up inside like stumps of rotting teeth. Once there had been a stockade around the building, but now only a few drunkenly leaning posts remained of it.

As in most Burmese buildings, the floor stood four or five feet above the ground. This floor was still in place, and the space beneath was solidly packed with dry faggots, which were the only new-looking objects about the building. The prisoners puzzled over this in a tired way until someone remarked what a strange place this was to store *firewood*.

Then they remembered. They had heard a rumor in Ava that they were to be taken out and burned.

Back in Ava, Nancy, frenzied with despair, had been making arrangements to follow the prisoners.

After the governor had spoken the ominous words, "Take care of yourself," he had been unwilling to let her go into the streets. He advised her to wait in his yard until night. When darkness fell, he ordered a cart for her. She took this to the house by the river, where she loaded it with two or three trunks, the medicine chest and a few other valuables. Maung Ing and the one remaining Bengal servant promised to look after the house for her. Late that night she deposited the trunks in the governor's house. Outside, she found Gouger's servant, the one who had followed the prisoners. He had returned to tell her Adoniram was alive at Amarapura, and that the prisoners were to go on the next day to a village beyond it, he did not know where.

She spent the night in the little bamboo hut in the governor's premises with little Maria, now three months old; the two Burmese children, Mary and Abby Hasseltine; and Koo-chil, the Bengalese cook. In the morning she managed to obtain a pass, rent a covered boat, and with the children and the cook set out up the river to Amarapura. Near Amarapura they landed and she found a cart in which she placed her little party.

It was two miles from the landing to the government building at Amarapura. The day was blazing hot. The cart pitched like a bucking horse. Its wheels stirred up thick clouds of choking dust. The tired children cried continually.

At the government building Nancy learned that the prisoners had gone on to Oung-pen-la. The cart driver refused to go any farther. After another hour in the blazing sun — while Nancy held the wailing Maria in her arms — Koo-chil managed to find another cart. The city governor supplied a guide, and off they creaked to Oung-pen-la.

It was dusk when Nancy arrived at the decrepit prison. The prisoners, still chained two and two, were huddled in a little patch of shade under the remains of an old projecting piece of roof. Eight or ten Burmese were busy on top of the building, trying to repair the fallen thatch with palm leaves.

Nancy left the cart and, with Maria in her arms, hurried to the prisoners. Adoniram, almost dead, looked up at her dully. "Why have you come? I hoped you would not follow. You cannot live here." And he relapsed into a stupor.

Nancy looked around her. She had no food. There seemed no place to buy any. There was no shelter for the night.

She asked one of the jailers if she could put up a little bamboo shelter near the prison. He refused. It was not customary. She pointed to the children. Could he possibly find her a place to stay until morning? Perhaps tomorrow she could look for a place to live.

The jailer took pity on her. His own house was a little distance away. It had only two rooms. His family lived in one. The other was half full of grain: she could have that place. Here Nancy took the children. Koo-chil heated water. There was no tea, and this was all their supper. They went to sleep that night on mats spread over the floor and the piles of grain.

Meanwhile the prisoners' feet had been put in the stocks. They had already concluded that they were not to be burned soon, else why would the jailers be repairing the roof? The next day they learned, to their relief, that the firewood had been stacked under the jail to prevent their escaping through the rotting floor.

It was full dark, when, to their surprise, they felt the stocks slowly rising into the air, carrying their feet with them. Somewhere out of sight, behind a wall, the guards were snickering over a great joke. In a moment they realized what it was. Their feet were being hoisted up by the stocks as they had been in the Death Prison, by the bamboo; but the mechanism was worked from the outside, where the prisoners could not see it. They were used to spending the night in this position, but not to what happened next. In the darkness mosquitoes swarmed off the stagnant rice field and settled on the raw soles of their feet, with torture that was excruciating. After a while the guards took mercy and lowered the stocks enough for the prisoners to fan away the insects with their hands.

Thus they spent the first night.

The next day things began to organize themselves. Koh-bai, the chief jailer, a surly man but no Spotted Face, let the prisoners go outside to enjoy the air on the "veranda" of the prison. The first morning Gouger was the only one able to get to his feet and take advantage of the privilege, but the omen was good.

A friend of Price's brought cold rice and vegetable curry from Amarapura for the prisoners' breakfast and Nancy and the children received some. There was no market, but Nancy felt confident she could buy at least rice in the village. Other things might be procured somehow. Adoniram was unable to stand up, but she did not think he would die. She was most worried by the fact that the girl Mary Hasseltine, Nancy's only helper, was down with a fever, and breaking out with spots which suggested smallpox. A little before noon Gouger's faithful baker appeared from Ava with a bag of biscuits and some salt fish. Henceforth he not only brought biscuits himself two or three times a week from Ava, but as before earned money to provide other necessities. The food problem was solved.

The first week passed. Nancy's fear that Mary Hasseltine had smallpox was realized. Nancy herself had been vaccinated in America, but of course the children had not. Considering what to do, she finally decided to take the risk of inoculating Abby and little Maria from Mary before she had become too infectious. She had heard of such a thing and thought she might as well try it, as both children were sure to catch the disease from Mary sooner or later. The jailer's wife saw what Nancy was doing with the needle and asked Nancy to inoculate her children too.

Mary Hasseltine developed an extremely bad case of smallpox. For a long time she was delirious and almost covered with pustules. Maria's inoculation was not effective. But Abby and the jailer's children had the disease so lightly that their play was hardly disturbed. Nancy became known all over the village as a wonder-worker. Soon nearly every village family had brought its children to Nancy for inoculation. Hoping for the best, she pricked them all with the needle and told them to be careful of their diet. Luckily, no bad effects followed. But after another week or so, little Maria caught the disease from Mary, and had it nearly as seriously.

While Nancy was caring for smallpox, arranging for food, inoculating the village children and running back and forth from village to prison, the situation of the prisoners was slowly improving. They had lighter chains, no vermin, water for washing, less abuse, and fresh air. When a new stockade had been completed around the prison yard and Koh-bai realized his charges were not dangerous, he let them hobble about outdoors during the day.

The prison also received a new prisoner, a Roman Catholic priest named Ignatius Brito, of Portuguese extraction but largely of Burmese blood. He could speak no English, the favored language of the other prisoners, but they sometimes conversed in Burmese. He hated England and the English, but otherwise was not an unpleasant companion. He liked music and composed a dance which he called "Deliverance from Prison." He used to hum the music to the other prisoners as an accompaniment to his dance, which suffered somewhat from having to be performed in fetters. Often, too, he would sing Latin chants in honor of the Virgin Mary in an excellent voice — sometimes in the middle of the night — to the pleasure of his companions. Gradually, the others realized that he was insane, though harmless.

A day or so after the arrival of Brito another prisoner arrived. This one came in the middle of the night in a huge cart. They first heard roars, over the rumblings of wheels from a mile or so away; then the cart was driven into the stockade and left there in spite of loud expostulations from Koh-bai.

In the morning they learned the new prisoner's identity: a huge lioness confined in a cage mounted on wheels. No one, not even the jailer, could understand the reason for the order that placed a full-grown lioness in the stockade. Some thought it was because the lion was the emblem of England. Gouger and Adoniram thought it more likely that the Pakan Wun meant to feed the prisoners to the lioness when he got around to it.

Whatever the purpose, there the lioness was, pacing up and down the cage and glaring at them when they passed. But no orders came to feed the animal. It began to starve. Its roars of hunger kept them awake all night. After two weeks Koh-bai threw a pariah dog into the cage with it, but by this time the lioness lacked strength to kill it. A few days later she died, and was taken away and buried.

But the cage remained — large, airy, and with a fine floor and roof. Adoniram, weakened by fever, thought it would be a fine place for privacy and rest. He applied to Koh-bai for permission to occupy it. His request was granted, and from this time on Adoniram lived by himself in the lion's cage and was locked up like a lion at night instead of being put in the stocks.

Meanwhile, just as Mary and Maria began to recover a little from the smallpox, Nancy fell ill herself, probably with dysentery. She could hardly make her way from the grain storage room where she and the children lived to the prison. In this state she took a cart to Ava for medicines and better food, leaving Koo-chil to care for the children. At Ava, she suddenly became so much worse she thought she was dying. But she managed to get the medicine chest from the governor and by taking two drops of laudanum at a time for several hours, recovered enough to get on a boat for Amarapura. Here she found a cart which took her to Oung-pen-la. At the hut, she collapsed, so changed and emaciated that when Koo-chil came out to help her he burst into tears. With his assistance she crawled into the grain storage room and fell on a mat, completely unable to help herself.

Koo-chil forgot his caste in order to take care of Nancy. In the morning he found food, prepared it and took it to Adoniram. The rest of the day, until time for Adoniram's evening meal, he devoted himself to her.

But the problem was little Maria. She had to have mother's milk to live. Her cries of hunger at night became unbearable. Although Nancy could not move, she could talk. Koh-bai's wife brought him in to see her, and she offered him presents if he would let Adoniram out of prison for a few hours — safely fettered, of course — to take the baby around the village to the nursing mothers. If one or another would supply a little superfluous milk, perhaps Maria could live.

Koh-bai agreed. Every day Adoniram was released for a time from the lion's cage, taken under guard to the jailer's house, and allowed to carry the baby around the village begging a little milk here and there from generous Burmese mothers. The expedient worked. Somehow the baby lived on from day to day and so did Nancy. On exceptional days Adoniram was allowed to spend an additional hour or two with Nancy in the grain storage room. The rest of his time he spent by himself in the cage in the prison stockade.

His spirits had never been so low. Ever since he had first been put in prison he had tried to console himself by imitating Madam Guyon's meek acquiescence. He used to repeat, to Gouger, Cowper's translation of her verses:

> No bliss I seek, but to fulfill
>     In life, in death, Thy lovely will;
> No succour in my woes I want,
>     Except what Thou art pleased to grant.
> Our days are number'd — let us spare
>     Our anxious hearts a needless care;

'Tis Thine to number out our days,
And ours to give them to Thy praise.

But now this philosophy failed him. His daughter was starving before his eyes; Nancy was nearly dead; his translation was lost; he himself was marked for death. The thought of death was tolerable. But the indignity, the protracted petty misery of day to day, were not. Merely to drag out a few hours more of life he had to meet the daily extortions of the jailers. One day he was allowed to visit Nancy. Another day, for no apparent reason, he was refused.

He knew there must be a just Plan and a loving Planner in all that was happening. Everything was doubtless for God's good purpose. But his finally rebelling mind refused to accept it. . . . So his despairing thoughts went as he mused by himself in the lion's cage. But he did not quite give up. Every day he somehow took up the battle to stave off death. And somehow he lived, and Nancy lived, and Maria lived.

Meanwhile the war seemed to be standing still. In his wretchedness, Adoniram hardly knew or cared what was happening, but Gouger was still interested. The English had settled down at Prome. The Pakan Wun took the opportunity to reorganize his own forces, which he repleted by large bounties from the Royal Treasury. The new recruits were of poor quality, the scouring of the cities, but at least he had them in large numbers. Other large units were brought in from the tributary Shan States under the command of their own princes.

And now Gouger, who had become well acquainted with Kohbai, learned some things which had no good effect on his peace of mind. The Pakan Wun had been born in Oung-pen-la. The very name of the village could be translated as something like "Field of Victory." A pattern emerged. The name, the association of the location, the lioness, all indicated that the Pakan Wun had something impressively and dreadfully symbolic in mind for the white prisoners.

Rumor soon supplied the explanation. When the Pakan Wun was ready to proceed against the British, he planned to assemble his headquarters staff at Oung-pen-la, where the white prisoners were to be offered up to propitiate the spirits of war by being buried alive at the head of the army. Planting their bodies in the Field of Victory could result only in a harvest of victory.

The prisoners never found out whether the rumor was really true, for on May 28, three days before the sacrifice was to take place, Gouger's trusty baker came hurrying up to the prison from Ava. He was almost exhausted, but good tidings glowed from his face like a beacon. As soon as he could catch his breath he burst forth with them: The Pakan Wun was dead!

"Where did you get the news?" questioned Gouger, standing amidst all the prisoners, who had clustered around when they saw the approach of the excited baker. "Are you sure?"

"I saw it myself," beamed the baker. "He was dragged and beaten through the town to the place of execution, and there trodden to death by elephants!"

The haggard faces of the prisoners brightened. For the first time in all these weary months there was hope. Their joy was almost hysterical. A couple attempted a feeble cheer. One or two danced impromptu jigs in their hobbles.

Later they heard a reason for the sudden execution of the hated leader. The Pakan Wun had asked for command over the troops of the Shan princes. This was refused on the ground that a subject could not command royalty. Then he asked that the king's personal bodyguard be put at his disposal to accompany him to the wars. The king was already becoming suspicious of him. This request heightened his suspicions. The Pakan Wun next asked the king to go to the Mengoon Pagoda, some miles outside of Ava, site of one of the largest bells in the world, and pray for success.

Command of king's forces . . . Command of the Royal bodyguard . . . The king to leave Ava . . . to the king, all this looked like a plot. In rage he broke out: "Ha! He would take away my guard and then have me leave my throne!" Before the Pakan Wun could say another word he was dragged by the hair from the Golden Feet and beaten and kicked all the way to the execution place, where the elephants did their work in a very few minutes. Immense treasures, it was said, were found in his house afterwards — money withheld from the Royal Treasury for paying recruits.

After this news, the prisoners felt fairly sure that they were in no further danger of execution, except through some high official's sudden outburst of rage at the English. And even this seemed unlikely. Sooner or later the British Army would move. The more it moved, the more valuable would the prisoners become as hostages.

The summer passed. Little Maria held on to life by the sympathetic nursing mothers of the village. Slowly Nancy began to recover. She was almost as emaciated as the prisoners and almost too feeble to move. But it seemed that her life had been spared. The prisoners, existing drearily but peacefully, felt as if they had been forgotten by the Government.

But about August they learned they were remembered. One day a band of Burmese officials arrived at the prison, with orders to transport them in carts to Amarapura. There at the house of the governor of the city each was placed in a separate room. It turned out that they were to translate a document discussing terms of peace from Sir Archibald Campbell, the British commander. In order to rule out any collusion, each prisoner was to translate the document separately and the results were to be compared.

Sir Archibald had offered to make a treaty. The prisoners — particularly Gouger — had no optimistic ideas about the probable success of the peace negotiations, but they did feel that from now on their services would be required often and they could expect better treatment.

Their estimate was correct. The ministers of the court viewed the British proposal as a face-saving device. The fact that the enemy commander had offered to discuss terms meant to them that he must be weak. The inactivity of his forces seemed to confirm their view. Rumors flew about that cholera was destroying the British forces, that war had broken out elsewhere, that the army would be withdrawn. Then in late October the Kyi-Wungyi blandly informed Sir Archibald Campbell that the Burmese had never heard of a custom of giving up territories or paying indemnities. The chagrined British general realized that the Burmese had merely been playing for time while they amassed their forces, and the fighting began again.

But powerful individuals at Ava had begun to realize interpreters would be needed. Peace would have to come sometime, and not a single person in the Burmese camp could speak and write English. Nor could a single one of the British speak and write Burmese.

On November fourth, a messenger came to Nancy from a friend, the former Koung-tone Myoo-tsa, now the governor of the North Gate of the palace, that an order had been given in the palace for Adoniram's release. That evening it came. In the morning, Adoniram's fetters were struck off. Nancy joyously set about preparations to leave. But the jailers decided to keep her in Oung-pen-la on the ground that the orders did not include her name. She pointed out that she was not a prisoner and never had been, but they refused permission to let anyone in the village rent her a cart. Finally Adoniram was brought out of the prison to the house of the jailers. For once he was in a position to bargain. He threatened them the wrath of the Golden Presence and sweetened the threat with promises of rich gifts. A large load of food had just come to Nancy from Ava; the jailers finally agreed to let Nancy go if they could have it. At noon, after a whole morning of haggling and cajoling, Nancy, with little Maria in her arms, Mary and Abby Hasseltine, the cook Koo-chil and Adoniram took their places in a creaking cart and began rolling slowly to Amarapura in the custody of a jailer.

They were sick and very tired. The children were fretful. The cart was slow and uncomfortable. But as the prison of Oung-pen-la finally receded from sight, their hearts were full of joy.

## CHAPTER XXI

# Release and Triumph

## [ *1825–1826* ]

A<small>T</small> Amarapura they once more were separated. Adoniram was taken to the house of the Amarapura governor and thence to the hall of justice in Ava. Nancy, with the children and the faithful Koo-chil, procured a boat and went down-river. She reached her own house on the riverbank before dark. In the morning she saw her old friend the City Governor, who had just been elevated to the rank of Wungyi. He told her that Adoniram was considered still in prison, but only while certain necessary orders were being prepared. He was to go to the Burmese camp at Maloun, to translate and help deal with the British.

Early the next morning, November 7, 1825, she saw the Wungyi again. Just that moment, he said, Adoniram had been given twenty ticals for expenses — about ten dollars — and was to go immediately aboard a boat for Maloun. But the Wungyi had arranged for him to stop a few minutes at Nancy's house, which was directly on his way. Nancy hurried home, hastily got together some food and clothing, and went with Adoniram to the boat. For sleeping, all she could provide was a mattress, a pillow and a blanket. Everything else had been looted.

But any annoyance was minor compared to Adoniram's pleasure at learning that his Burmese translation of the New Testament was now safe in the house. The day he had been taken to Oung-pen-la, one of the jailers had stripped the cover off the hard pillow which contained it. Then the pillow itself, which looked like a useless roll of hard cotton, he threw away. Some hours later the faithful Maung Ing, searching for some relic of Adoniram to cherish, had found the uncovered pillow and had taken it home.

Consoled by this news Adoniram took his place in the tiny boat

— too small to lie at full length — and made the three-day trip downriver to Maloun. He had one servant. For supplies, he had the twenty ticals and a bag of mildewed refuse rice supplied by the government. The nights were cold and damp. He arrived at the Burmese camp almost disabled with fever.

Here he was placed under guard in a bamboo hut on the glaring white sand of the broad river beach. His fever grew worse. He was ordered to go to the Burmese commander, the Kyi-Wungyi. When he pleaded that he could not move, his guards, thinking he was shamming, threatened him. But the reality of his illness was only too evident, and, leaving him in the hut on the sand, they brought him papers every hour or so for translation. He tried to make sense of them, but gradually he lost consciousness. For a day or two he lay in delirium. At times he had a vague idea that a shaven-crowned, yellow-robed Burmese priest was with him. Other times he thought he was being taken from the prison at Oung-pen-la to be burned alive. When the fever broke and he returned to consciousness, he found himself in an enclosure made by hanging a mat from the outside eaves of a cookhouse.

He was still too weak to move; but he found his mind more clear and active than at any time since before the war. As he read and explained the papers brought to him in increasing numbers, he began to study the Burmese leaders carefully.

He could see plainly that they must get used to the idea of giving up territory and paying indemnity. But in doing so they must come to think of him as a friend, or he would be lost. They were in mortal terror of the British. But they had not the slightest conception of official negotiations or statements. A paragraph of gossip in a Calcutta newspaper carried exactly the same weight as a formal proposal from Sir Archibald Campbell. Insofar as negotiations were concerned, they simply believed that obviously the conqueror would keep what he got.

Adoniram finally began to give a regular course of instruction in the nature of agreements and contracts between civilized nations. His lectures generated personal admiration for him but little confidence in the British. The Burmese officers would exclaim "Ah, that is noble! That is as it should be!" Then they would shake their heads and add, "But the teacher dreams. He has a celestial spirit and he thinks himself in the land of the celestial beings." But as evidence of their great esteem for him and their recognition that he was a true friend of Burma, they gave him another blanket (or rather, a cotton rug) large enough to cover a six-year-old child. This he attached to his own blanket with slivers of bamboo, to double its thickness in the center. Henceforth, with the aid of a good deal of contortion to stay under the double part, he managed to keep fairly warm at night.

All this time the Burmese emissaries were meeting the British in a boat moored in the middle of the river. Eventually a treaty was actually signed by both parties. The terms included giving up Arakan, Tenasserim, Assam, Manipur, and one *crore* of rupees — about a million British pounds sterling. The British granted a fifteen days' armistice for the treaty to be carried to Ava and ratified by the king.

At the end of the fifteen days nothing had been heard from the Burmese. The British realized that their antagonists once again had been playing for time. They began to advance on Maloun.

Adoniram had served his purpose. On December 17, on five minutes' notice, he was loaded in a boat and taken upriver to Ava. When the British stormed the stockade and took the camp they found the original treaty. It had never been transmitted to Ava at all. But as the king would undoubtedly have sliced off the head of anyone rash enough to present it, perhaps no one could be blamed too much.

But of all this Adoniram knew nothing. He knew only that he would soon see Nancy. He disembarked on the riverbank late at night on December 29, and was led directly past his own house. He could see a feeble light inside, but in spite of his entreaties his guards refused to let him enter it even for a moment. They were not unsympathetic, but their orders were positive. Instead, they took him to the courthouse, where he was kept in an outbuilding until morning. From there, pending his early return to Oung-pen-la, he was moved, after a brief examination, to a shed.

Here, after a day without food, he was found in the evening by Maung Ing, who had heard of Adoniram's return from the servant who had accompanied him downriver. Nancy, said Maung Ing, had already told him to go to the friendly governor of the North Gate to see whether Adoniram could not be spared a return to Oung-pen-la. Little Maria was well, too, Nancy had said. Adoniram must not worry.

Adoniram was so relieved to see Maung Ing that he did not realize until after he had gone that there had been something oddly evasive in Maung Ing's words. Two or three times Adoniram had directly asked Maung Ing whether Nancy was well. Maung Ing had replied either that Nancy had given him instructions about applying to the governor of the North Gate, or that Maria was well. Maung Ing's tone had been so reassuring that he had felt no anxiety at the time, but now, the recollection of this unusual indirectness made him uneasy.

The governor of the North Gate acted promptly. That same night he presented a petition to the highest court for Adoniram's release, offering himself as security. In the morning the old official summoned the prisoner to his house to be given the news. After thanking him profusely, Adoniram hurried to his own house. It was December 31, 1825.

When Adoniram entered the open door the first thing he saw was a fat Burmese woman squatting beside a pan of coals. She was holding a baby on her knees, a baby so very thin and dirty that it never occurred to him it might be Maria. He hurried into the bedroom. "Across the foot of the bed, as though she had fallen there, lay a human object that, at the first glance, was scarcely more recognizable than his child. The face was of ghastly paleness, the features sharp, and the whole form shrunken almost to the last degree of emaciation. The glossy black curls had all been shorn from the finely shaped head, which was now covered by a close-fitting cotton cap, of the coarsest and . . . not the cleanest kind."

As he leaned over the motionless figure he could hardly credit his eyes. But yes, it was Nancy. Was she dead? His breath on her cheek must have fanned some remaining vitality, for she opened her eyes. She was still alive, just barely alive.

Deathly ill though she still was, Nancy had passed the real crisis fully a month before. Her health had declined steadily after Adoniram had gone downriver. After about two weeks she had been attacked by the dreaded spotted fever, cerebral spinal meningitis. She recognized the disease and was certain it would be fatal. Luckily, the same day a Burmese wet nurse offered to come in and nurse Maria. Soon Nancy lost consciousness. She had been in a raging fever for at least two weeks when Price arrived. Just out of the Oung-pen-la prison for another translating task, he had managed to secure permission to see her. Price was sure she had only a few hours to live, but as a last resort he ordered her hair shaved and blisters applied to her head and feet. The Burmese neighbors who came to her said, "She is dead. If the king of angels should come in, he could not recover her." But somehow she lived. After nearly a week, she began to return to consciousness. The loyal Koo-chil persuaded her to drink a little wine and water. Slowly she improved. Before Adoniram's return, she had been able to ask that a watch be kept for him; but she could not yet sit up. Thus it was that he found her.

When she could be moved, Adoniram took her from the river house to the house of the governor of the North Gate, where he had been invited to live. They would have had to move out of the river house in any case, for early in the new year 1826 the British began pressing up the Irrawaddy. All Ava fell into panic. Until now the court had always believed that one way or another the British would be driven out of Burma — by new armies and leaders summoned from somewhere, by uprising in their other territories, by disease, by treachery, by trickery, or perhaps by sheer boredom. But the British advanced remorselessly.

Adoniram and Price were called to the courthouse for consultation every day. Two recently captured British officers, a Dr. Sandford and a Lieutenant Bennett, were also consulted. But although all four were treated as oracles, they could convince the Court but of one thing: the treaty signed at Maloun (the king knew about it now) had provided for an indemnity of a *crore* of rupees, a million British pounds sterling. On payment of this the English agreed to withdraw their forces and leave Burma to the Burmans, except for the coastal provinces. But the Burmese court could not believe the British would keep their promise. As Gouger wrote, "Such an unheard-of thing as conquering a country and then restoring it was incredible! Measuring British faith and honor by their own standard, they concluded the intention was first to impoverish them, and then to march on the Capital."

Eventually the government concluded that the two captured Englishmen might be used to induce Sir Archibald Campbell to yield easier terms. Adoniram was selected to go with one of them to the English headquarters. Of all missions, this was the one Adoniram feared most. The slightest suspicion of his good faith, and he and his family could lose their heads. Price, however, wanted to go. Adoniram managed to convince officialdom that Price could do the job as well as he.

A complicated security system was set up. Price was to go with Dr. Sandford. Adoniram would be hostage for Price. Lieutenant Bennett would be hostage for Dr. Sandford. The king generously gave each of them a hundred ticals for expenses. Dr. Sandford promptly sent Gouger twenty-five of his through Gouger's baker, who was now, as Gouger expressed it, flying "backward and forward between Ava and Oung-pen-la with the rapidity of a weaver's shuttle." [1]

Late in January Price and Sandford set off down the river with a Burmese official. Meanwhile, true to its principle of trusting nobody, the government went on with furious efforts to fortify the city. Nancy noted:

> Men and beasts were at work night and day, making new stockades, and strengthening old ones, and whatever buildings were in their way were immediately torn down. Our house, with all that surrounded it, was levelled to the ground, and our beautiful little compound turned into a road and a place for the erection of cannon. All articles of value were conveyed out of town, and safely deposited in some other place.

When news came that Price's and Sandford's boat was on its way upriver, thousands of Ava's inhabitants anxiously lined the bank. The court were thunderstruck to see Dr. Sandford return when there had been nothing to stop his breaking his parole and staying

---

[1] Knowing his master, the baker spent some of the money for what he knew Gouger had most coveted for two years — a cup of arrack. Gouger was still smacking his lips over it thirty-five years later: "Oh! who can tell the comfort a daily glass of strong waters administers to a frame ready to sink with exhaustion? It is indescribable."

with his own forces. Sandford merely said it was nothing very surprising. Sir Archibald would have made him return even if he had not wanted to, since that was his agreement. Such behavior was the established custom of Europe. The court still could not understand it, but for the first time they began to believe these crazy British might actually be so foolish as to keep their word, even with all Burma defenseless for the taking.

Price gave the British answer to the seated members of the government at the Hlut-dau. The palace gates were crowded with watchers.

"The general and commissioners," he said, "will make no alteration in their terms, except that the indemnity may be paid at four different times. The first quarter must be paid within twelve days, or the army will continue their march. In addition, the prisoners in the hands of the Burmese must be given up immediately."

Also, the British commander had specifically commissioned Price to demand Adoniram, Nancy and little Maria; but of these three the king fumed: "They are not English, they are my people. They shall not go." He had learned the value of Adoniram's services. As to the territory, the Burmese government agreed to give that up. It could be taken back later when the English had gone away. But the money, the *crore* of rupees! Surely there must be some way to get rid of the English without paying all of it! Perhaps they could be given just a taste of the first installment, enough to make them think they would get the rest soon. Then they might go away. Or perhaps another army could still be raised.

Price and Adoniram told the king, the queen and the court plainly that the English would never make peace on any other terms. It would be useless to go down to them again without the money. Some of the officials said to the two missionaries: "Probably you are on the side of the English. You did not try to make them take less. If you do not agree, your families will suffer for it."

At this time there was one general, Layar-thoo-yah, who still thought he could defeat the English. They had not yet quite reached the ancient capital of Pagan, down the river. He could fortify it, make it impregnable, and from here sally out and drive them away. Rather than give up so much money from the Royal Treasury, the king and queen agreed to let him try. He was dubbed "Lord of the

Setting Sun." Some fifteen thousand new troops were raised by an advance payment of a hundred and fifty ticals to each man. The men of this new army, named "The Retainers of the King's Glory," went down to Pagan and strengthened the city, spending their sudden wealth on the way for fine clothing. The British attacked them with nine hundred men. They broke and ran. Layar-thoo-yah appeared before the king and asked for new troops.

The king was infuriated. His commander had delayed the negotiations and irritated the British commander. The Lord of the Setting Sun was "hurled from the palace, and beat all the way to the courthouse — where he was stripped of his rich apparel, bound with cords, and made to kneel and bow towards the palace. He was then delivered into the hands of the executioners, who, by their cruel treatment, put an end to his existence, before they reached the place of execution." Immediately afterwards the king had it announced that Layar-thoo-yah was executed because he had violated the royal command *not to fight the English*.

That same night Price was sent down again with some captured British, with instructions to persuade the enemy to accept about a quarter of the first installment. In a few days he returned. The British general was very angry, he reported, and refused even to talk with Dr. Price. He was now within a few days' march of Ava and ready to move on the city.

Even with this news the king might have temporized, but the queen asserted her old dominance and decreed that the money must be raised at once. The palace was in an uproar. Gold and silver vases, pitchers, dishes — all were melted down. The king and queen themselves took charge of the weighing. Silver bars were carried from the Royal Treasury to boats. By the following evening the entire first installment was loaded and ready to go down the river.

But the sight of so much silver changed the royal mind again. How did they know the British would stop after receiving it? They would send down a quarter of it, as before. Then, if the British stopped, they would promise the rest.

At this moment some of the officials thought of Adoniram, who was walking on the streets observing what was going on. They sent out men who took him by the arm and told him he must go aboard at once with the Wungyi and Wundauk, who were empowered to make peace. A few more British officers, and, to Adoniram's delight, Henry Gouger and the Armenian Arakeel had just been released from Oung-pen-la and were going down at the same time.

Sir Archibald Campbell reacted exactly as Adoniram had expected. He refused even to accept the quarter of the first installment. He refused to stop his march but was willing to advance slowly until the money arrived. He promised Adoniram he would halt and make peace if the complete installment reached him before he reached Ava. Furthermore, he authorized Adoniram to round up all the foreigners in the vicinity of Ava, and ask them, in the presence of government, whether they wished to remain or go. If they wished to go, they must be delivered to the British at once or there would be no peace.

Adoniram delivered this news to the king on his return to Ava about midnight. The Wungyi and Wundauk gloomily confirmed his words. Adoniram had all the foreigners — including those left at Oung-pen-la — rounded up and the question asked. Those who wanted to stay — poor old Rodgers, so long committed to Burmese service, was among them — were set free.

Once more some of the officials wanted Adoniram to stay. "You will not leave us; you will become a great man if you will remain." Adoniram, thinking of the future of the mission, did not want to refuse point-blank. Diplomatically, he said his wife had said she wanted to go, and of course he must follow her.

The prisoners and silver — the complete first installment, this time — soon set off down the river in six or eight golden boats. Adoniram, Nancy and little Maria, Maung Ing, the wet nurse and Koo-chil were in one. Their friend, the governor of the North Gate, came down to the waterside to see them off.

It was a cool, moonlit evening. Maria slept in Adoniram's arms. All their worldly possessions were with them in the boat. About midnight, at the Burmese camp below, they were detained for about two hours. The Wungyi and some of the officers had insisted the Judsons should wait while Price went ahead with the treasure, to make sure the British would accept it and stop where they were. But Adoniram insisted on going on. Reluctantly the Wungyi consented; he could ill afford to antagonize the American teacher now.

Once more the boat floated down the quiet Irrawaddy under the light of the brilliant moon. Adoniram and Nancy looked at each other with quiet satisfaction. He was thin and haggard, in appearance an old man. Nancy was emaciated and pale, almost wraithlike, as she leaned back on the cushions. Her hands were so thin they were almost translucent. Little Maria too looked weazened and old, her baby face pinched, her arms and legs like little sticks. But she slept quietly. All three were ragged as scarecrows.

At the same time these two, who had come so far from peaceful Bradford and gone through so much, tonight were utterly peaceful and happy. They were free at last. Heaven, they thought, must feel something like this.

In the morning they saw the masts of the steamboat *Diana*, that mysterious, magical craft which had done much to make the Burmese think the British were invincible. Here Nancy and Maria were taken on board, while Adoniram continued a few miles down to Yandabo to see Sir Archibald Campbell. From now on, Nancy was treated like royalty. The night before, she and Adoniram had believed they were experiencing a foretaste of heaven. Now, to the British, she seemed an authentic angel.

The next day both Adoniram and Nancy went to General Campbell's headquarters. He had a tent with a veranda, by far the largest in the camp, pitched for them next to his own, and they dined with him at his own table. In Nancy's words he treated them "with the kindness of a father." She wrote to Elnathan, "I presume to say, that no persons on earth were ever happier, than we were during the fortnight we passed at the English camp."

Meanwhile the first few days were occupied with the peace treaty known to history as the Treaty of Yandabo. Henry Gouger, resplendent in clothing given him by Sir Archibald's son John, helped Adoniram frame the final details. At its conclusion, General Campbell decided to give a state dinner for the Burmese commissioners.

He wanted to impress them with British pomp, and the job was done well. Every flag and banner that could be found was flown in a blaze of color. Gold and crimson cloth and hangings were displayed everywhere to awe the somewhat reluctant guests.

The dinner hour was announced by a regimental band in full

regalia. Solemnly the whole company assembled in couples, the Burmese commissioners following suit as well as they could, and marched to the long dinner table. General Campbell, in his dressiest full-dress uniform, saved for just such an occasion, walked alone in front of the rest.

As he came opposite the Judsons' tent, next to his own, the music stopped and the procession halted. Wonderingly the Burmese craned their necks to see what would happen next. The British (and Adoniram), having some idea, kept their faces impassive. The general went into the tent. In a moment he reappeared with Nancy on his arm, her thin face demure but her eyes dancing with some of the mischief of the Nancy Hasseltine of old. Ceremoniously he led her to the head of the table and seated her on his right hand.

These Burmese officials knew Nancy very well. For a year and a half she had abased herself before them for the smallest favors. She had endured rebuffs and insults without a murmur of anger. Now this victorious British lord and general, most likely own brother to the East India Company, and probably even a brother of the British king, gave her the position of highest honor. As they cringingly took their own seats, they looked with fearful eyes at the pair at the head of the table, the wife of the American missionary and the commanding general of the British army. If she cared to tell what she knew — and if she were anything like a Burmese, she would — almost every one of them had something to fear: probably death, certainly torture.

Nancy knew what was in their minds. She was too human not to let a little of what she felt show in her eyes. General Campbell, suspecting it, had difficulty repressing a smile.

"I fancy these gentlemen must be old acquaintances of yours," the general said as food was placed among them. "Judging from their appearance you must have treated them very badly." The Burmese did not know English, but they could tell he was talking about them. One of them in particular showed fear. As he tried to eat, the food slipped off the fork he held in his trembling hand. The man's behavior attracted General Campbell's attention. "What is the matter with the owner of the pointed beard over there?" the general went on. "He seems to be seized with a fit of ague."

Nancy looked at him carefully, warm recognition in her expression. "I do not know," she said, "unless his memory may be too busy. He is an old acquaintance of mine. Probably he considers himself in danger now that he sees me under your protection."

And she told the story of how Adoniram had been placed in five pairs of fetters and thrust into the Inner Prison, half dead from fever, and how it was to this man's house she had walked early one morning to see if he would help a little. It was this man who had kept her waiting in the hot sun until noon, who had heard her request indifferently and refused it with contempt. It was he who had seen her silk umbrella as she turned to leave and snatched it out of her hand. It was he who had laughed and said, "Only fat people need to fear sunstroke. The sun can't find a woman as thin as you."

The English officers ranked along one side of the table found it difficult to keep a courteous silence as she told the story. But their looks at the shrinking official spoke even louder than their few indignant words. By a sort of intuition he seemed to know what Nancy said. His face writhed with fear. His hand shaking uncontrollably, he tried to wipe the perspiration that oozed from his death-pale face.

Nancy took pity on him. In Burmese she reassured him softly, "You have nothing to fear." She explained to General Campbell what she had just told him. Conversation turned to other subjects, Nancy and Adoniram translating polite remarks back and forth. But the dinner was not a success for the Burmese commissioners. They ate little and shook much. The white men were painfully correct, but no more.

After the dinner, alone in their tent, Adoniram and Nancy rocked with perhaps un-Christian laughter. "I never thought I was over and above vindictive," confessed Adoniram between gasps, "but really, it was one of the richest scenes I ever beheld."

## CHAPTER XXII

# The Black-sealed Letter

## [ *1826* ]

MARCH 6, 1826, Adoniram and Nancy left Yandabo for Rangoon aboard the gunboat *Irrawaddy*. They arrived at the mission house, a ruin, but still standing, March 21. They had been away from it for two years and three months.

The Houghs and the Wades had gone back to Calcutta. They had been peacefully at work printing Adoniram's Burmese dictionary that day in 1824 when the British had attacked Rangoon. They had been imprisoned, and their deaths decreed, when the invaders' bombardment began. Fortunately for them, their captors had fled in panic when the British entered the city.

The war had dispersed almost all of the little congregation. Maung Shway-bay had remained in the mission house. The learned Maung Shwa-gnong, they heard, was alive somewhere in the interior. Mah Men-lay and her sister had been at Prome and returned with them to Rangoon. But most had died or disappeared. The work had all to be begun again, and without Price. He had decided to remain at Ava in the employment of the king.

The treaty of Yandabo had left Rangoon in Burmese hands. Adoniram and Nancy saw no reason to suppose there would be any more religious toleration in Burmese-ruled territory than before. There might even be less, as an expression of vindictiveness.

The distinguished orientalist John Crawfurd had been named civil commissioner under the British governor general, Lord Amherst. One of his first tasks was to select a new capital for the provinces which had passed to English control, and he asked Adoniram to go along. Adoniram, knowing the value of a secure base for missionary activity, agreed, and ten days after arriving in Rangoon left with Crawfurd aboard the steamboat for Martaban, in the direc-

tion of the Salween River. At the mouth of the Salween was a
harbor with good anchorage. The peninsula at the river's mouth
was selected as the best site for a capital. Here, April 6, 1826, the
British flag was hoisted, a salute of guns fired, and the place given
the name of Amherst. Adoniram concluded the ceremony by reading the sixtieth chapter of Isaiah, an apt dedication of a new city,
and offering prayer.

By April 10, Adoniram was back at Rangoon with Nancy. He
was enthusiastic about the place, and certain it would become a
great center from which they could propagate the Gospel. He immediately had the old zayat torn down and arranged for shipping
the boards to Amherst for use in making a shelter against the coming rainy season.

Nancy too was elated. There would be plenty of Burmese to
convert, and, most important, they would "have no longer to solicit
the patronage of a haughty monarch for the establishment of our
mission, or to court the favour of the Woongyees, to prevent the
persecution of the converts." By April 26 they had sent ahead four
of the native Christian families, among them Maung Ing and Maung
Shway-bay to prepare dwelling places.

Adoniram and Nancy did not get away until the end of June
because of a proposal made by Crawfurd. The Treaty of Yandabo
had provided for negotiation of a commercial treaty between the
East India Company and the Burmese government, to "open the
gold and silver road," as the Burmese version expressed it. With
merchants able to take out gold and silver, as in other countries,
and relief from some of the other peculiarly vexatious Burmese
impediments to trade, commerce was expected to develop rapidly.
Crawfurd was to negotiate the commercial treaty and wanted Adoniram above any one in Burma as translator and adviser.

Adoniram declined. He had no desire to serve the East India
Company, and such a role might link him, in Burmese eyes, with
the hated British. But Crawfurd finally brought out an irresistible
inducement: he promised to try to get an article inserted in the
treaty guaranteeing religious freedom to all the people of Burma.
When Nancy heard this, she would not hear of Adoniram's refusing.

Because for a missionary the salary would be very large, Adoniram
decided to settle once and for all the question of whether a mission-

ary should enter any service but that of the mission — and especially whether, if it were necessary for a time, he should keep the money he received. He decided any such money should be considered the property of the organization supporting him, not his own. Therefore, on June 10, he recommended to the corresponding secretary in Boston a set of rules covering the matter. Following his own recommendation, he later turned over to the Board some 2000 rupees realized from presents made him at Ava and 2500 rupees paid him by the East India Company.

But before leaving for Ava with Crawfurd, he wanted to see Nancy and little Maria properly settled. On June 29 they left Rangoon aboard the *Phoenix*, and on July 2 landed at the mouth of the Salween River. Captain Fenwick, civil superintendent of Amherst, turned over to Nancy a temporary house he had just erected for his own use.

Nancy was delighted with Amherst. She liked the air of the country and the pioneer feel of the new town. It had only about fifty houses, mostly native, a mile or so from the military post on the west side of the peninsula. Maung Ing's and Maung Shway-bay's houses, which were among the first to be built, actually edged into the jungle "and disturbed the deer and wild fowl which had been the undisputed occupants of the peninsula."

She set to work at once to start a school and to supervise the building of a mission house, but Adoniram stayed only long enough to see her safely settled. Three days after their arrival, he left for Rangoon on the *Phoenix*. Preparations for the embassy to Ava kept him busy through the rest of July and August. September first the steam-driven *Diana* started upriver with a full party of officers assisting Crawfurd, a medical officer, Adoniram, and a botanist who was to evaluate the teak resources of the country. Accompanying the steamer were five Burmese boats carrying writers, drafts-men, baggage, presents to the court and a guard of honor consisting of twenty-eight picked grenadiers and light infantry of His Majesty's 87th Regiment and 15 picked Sepoy grenadiers. Adoniram was traveling in style.

At Ava it became clear that the war had not changed the character of the Burmese government. Delay followed delay. The second installment of the indemnity was three months overdue and the British army was waiting for it in Rangoon. The principal object of the Burmese negotiators was to avoid paying it. The business dragged out in meeting after meeting. As to the commercial treaty, that got hardly anywhere. The Burmese simply could not understand the idea of letting gold and silver move freely in and out of Burma as money; and it became more evident every day that there was no hope of a clause providing for religious toleration.

Perhaps the best example of the court attitude was the account of the recent war which the royal historian had written and recorded in the official Burmese chronicles and which Adoniram translated for Crawfurd:

In the years 1186 and 87, the Kalu pya, or white strangers of the East, fastened a quarrel upon the Lord of the Golden Palace. They landed at Rangoon, took that place and Prome, were permitted to advance as far as Yandabo; for the King, from motives of piety and regard to life, made no effort whatsoever to oppose them. The strangers had spent vast sums of money in their enterprise; and by the time they reached Yandabo, their resources were exhausted, and they were in great distress. They petitioned the King, who, in his clemency and generosity, sent them large sums of money to pay their expenses back and ordered them out of the country.

As October drifted into November, Adoniram fretted. He was wasting his time. But he had committed himself to the embassy and had to stay with it.

Occasionally he received a letter from Nancy. They had parted cheerfully and the same cheerfulness prevailed in her letters. One dated November 14 went in part:

I have this day moved into the new house, and for the first time since we were broken up at Ava, feel myself at home. The house is large and convenient, and if you were here, I should feel quite happy. The native population is increasing fast, and things wear a rather favourable aspect. Maung Ing's school has commenced with ten scholars, and more are expected. Poor little Maria is still feeble. Sometimes I hope she is getting better; then again she declines to her former weakness. When I ask her where Papa is, she always starts up and points toward the sea. The servants behave very well, and I have no trouble about any thing, excepting you and Maria. Pray take care of yourself, particularly as it regards the intermittent fever at Ava. May God preserve and bless you, and restore you in safety to your new and old home, is the prayer of your affectionate Ann.

The news about Maria disturbed him, but he viewed it as hopefully as he could. Perhaps the better climate at Amherst would help her through her first year, now that her mother could give her the loving care a baby needed.

Early in November Adoniram had a letter from Captain Fenwick mentioning that "Mrs. Judson is extremely well." But he had not received a letter from Nancy herself since that one written in the middle of September, and he wondered why she had not written again.

He found out in another letter from Captain Fenwick dated October 18, which he received about the middle of November:

I can hardly think it right to tell you, that Mrs. Judson has had an attack of fever as before this reaches you, she will, I sincerely trust, be quite well, as it has not been so severe as to reduce her. This was occasioned by too close attendance on the child. However, her cares have been rewarded in a most extraordinary manner, as the poor baby, at one time, was so reduced, that no rational hope could be entertained of its recovery; but at present a most favourable change has taken place, and she has improved wonderfully. Mrs. Judson had no fever last night, so that the intermission is now complete.

Adoniram's mind was relieved. No wonder Nancy had not written! Busy night and day with Maria until she came down with fever herself, she certainly had no time to pen letters, even to her husband. As for little Maria, he feared she would have a hard fight. Word of her illness was no surprise. For a long time he had felt it necessary to be prepared for worse.

Then on the twenty-fourth of November, Adoniram received another letter. The man who had brought it up the river handed it to him with the words, "I am sorry to inform you of the death of your child." Adoniram took it and went up to his room in Price's house at Sagaing, where the embassy had been staying for almost a month. It bore a black seal, and even as he turned it over in his hands he felt grateful that at least Nancy was spared.

He sat down, broke the seal, and began to read. It was dated more than a month ago, October 26, 1826, and from Captain Fenwick's assistant. He braced himself for the task of absorbing the details of little Maria's final illness. He read several lines before his mind grasped the real import of the words:

> My DEAR SIR: To one has suffered so much and with such exemplary fortitude, there needs but little preface to tell a tale of distress. It were cruel indeed to torture you with doubt and suspense. To sum up the unhappy tidings in a few words — *Mrs. Judson is no more.*

He stopped, the words swimming before his eyes. He seemed to feel no emotion but a kind of iciness and a sensation that time had stopped. For a moment the room seemed to turn over. For the next five or ten minutes, Adoniram forced himself little by little to read the rest of the letter. . .

> Early in the month she was attacked with a most violent fever. From the first she felt a strong presentiment that she would not recover, and on the 24th about eight in the evening, she expired. Dr. R. was quite assiduous in his attentions, both as friend and physician. Capt. F. procured her the services of a European woman from the 45th regiment, and be assured all was done, that could be done, to comfort her in her sufferings, and to smooth the passage to the grave. We all feel deeply the loss of this excellent lady, whose shortness of residence among us was yet sufficiently long, to impress us with a deep sense of her worth and virtues. It was not until about the 20th that Dr. R. began seriously to suspect danger. Before that period, the fever had abated at intervals; but its last approach baffled all medical skill. On the morning of the 23rd, Mrs. Judson spoke for the last time. The disease had then completed its conquest, and from that time up to the moment of dissolution, she lay nearly motionless, and apparently quite insensible. Yesterday morning, I assisted in the last melancholy office of putting her mortal remains in the coffin; and in the evening her funeral was attended by all the European officers now resident here. We have buried her near the spot where she first landed; and I have put up a small rude fence around the

grave to protect it from incautious intrusions. — Your little girl Maria is much better. Mrs. —— has taken charge of her; and I hope she will continue to thrive under her care.

This was the substance of the letter. Adoniram's eyes mechanically went back over three or four lines to make sure again of the sense of the handwriting.

All at once desolation overwhelmed him. The letter fell to the floor. He began to weep, softly at first, later with hoarse, racking sobs. Finally, as the full, crushing weight of the letter's meaning descended upon him, he leaned forward over the writing table in front of him and pillowed his head on his arms.

PART THREE
# To the Golden Shore
[ *1826–1850* ]

# CHAPTER I
# The Shadows Fall

## [ *1826–1827* ]

IT is doubtful whether Adoniram himself ever knew quite how
he got through the next few weeks. After the first "bitter, heart-
rending anguish," he was able to comfort himself to a certain extent
with the Gospel's assurance that Nancy's spirit was rejoicing with
the angels. But even so, the pain was almost too much to bear.

There was no reason to leave Ava, so he remained with the embassy. He could do nothing for Nancy. She had been buried a
month before he had known she was dead. He could do nothing
for little Maria. She was receiving better care than he could give
her himself.

Three days after the news of Nancy's death, Price's wife died
of cholera morbus. She had been far advanced in pregnancy, and
the disease had induced premature labor. She lived only a few
hours after its onset, the baby remaining unborn. Such a combination of circumstances placed the court in a peculiar dilemma. Price
was a servant of the king's, and as such a spectacular public funeral
for his wife's remains was obligatory. On the other hand, Burmese
law forbade any ceremony at all to a victim of cholera; and to
complicate the problem, custom required that the body of a woman
dying in labor without giving birth be treated in a certain especially
gruesome manner and then buried privately, even furtively.

The dilemma was resolved in typical court style. Official announcement was made that Mrs. Price had died in childbirth *after*
delivering the child. The appropriate public rites were then carried
out with great and impressive solemnity. Price himself, weakened by
imprisonment, was to die of tuberculosis in little more than a year.
Nor was Rodgers to live much longer. The Death Prison and Oung-
pen-La were exacting their first toll.

Meanwhile the Crawfurd embassy dragged on to the conclusion of a nearly meaningless commercial treaty, Adoniram keeping himself mechanically busy with translating. On December 13, 1826, about three weeks after the arrival of the black-sealed letter, the embassy started down the Irrawaddy. Low water and frequent strandings of the *Diana* on sand bars made a slow passage, while Adoniram fretted.

By this time his profound grief had dulled to a persistent ache — he even, perhaps, entertained a bewildered feeling that the letter, with its awful meaning, was in some way unreal. His sense of reality told him that he would never see Nancy again. But another part of him insisted just as stubbornly that she would be waiting to greet him at Amherst — for printed on his memory for all time was his last sight of her in front of Captain Fenwick's house, little Maria in her arms, smiling cheerfully. He knew this feeling was a delusion, but he could not shake it off.

Rangoon turned out to be beleaguered on all sides by Peguan rebels. For those on the armed steamboat, entry into the city by a ladder to the wharf was easy, but it was impossible to go outside the encircling defensive stockade. Here in the intervals between his official duties Adoniram asked about little Maria, but no one could give him any word. His old teacher, Maung Shway-gnong, had died of cholera on the way down from Ava.

The mission house was too close to Peguan muskets for Adoniram to visit, but by climbing on a high roof inside the stockade he could catch a glimpse of it. This building was a ruin. Only the posts and part of the roof were left. All the houses outside the stockade and along the river had been destroyed. Brushes between Peguans and Burmans occurred frequently; and one fair-sized sortie or small battle for possession of the Shwe Dagon pagoda took place the day of the embassy's arrival. After the few obligatory ceremonial courtesies with Rangoon officialdom there was no reason for the embassy to stay. The *Diana* paddled on down the river, and on January 24, 1827, dropped Adoniram at Amherst.

Jonathan Wade was waiting to meet him at the landing place; it was Wade and his wife Deborah who had sailed with Nancy from Philadelphia more than three years before. They had barely escaped with their lives from Rangoon at the outbreak of the war and,

Wade told Adoniram, had returned to Amherst about a month after Nancy's death. They had moved at once into the house Nancy had built and immediately taken charge of little Maria. She was still alive, but very feeble, said Wade.

As Adoniram and Wade walked together to the house, the converts — the two men Maung Shway-bay and the faithful Maung Ing, and the two women Mah Men-lay and Mah Doke — ran out to meet him, the men weeping and the women wailing and loudly lamenting. Their distress brought Adoniram sharply back to reality. All at once his sorrow grew fresh as on the day he received the black-sealed letter.

His grief swelled when, on the veranda, instead of Nancy, he saw Deborah Wade holding little Maria in her arms, "a poor little puny child, who could not recognize her weeping father, and from whose infant mind had long been erased all recollection of the mother who loved her so much." He tried to take the baby in his arms, but she shrank away.

Rebuffed, he asked Wade to show him Nancy's grave. It was almost next door, in front of a house Henry Gouger had built during Adoniram's absence, close by the garden. A hopia tree or "hope-tree," grew at the head of the grave and a crude fence had been constructed around it.

He looked at it awhile, lost in a confusion of thoughts and memories. "But who ever obtained comfort there?" he wrote bitterly a few days later to Nancy's mother. He knew Nancy's body must be under the hope-tree. They had told him so. But he could not see her. He could not hear her voice.

He turned from the grave and walked to Captain Fenwick's house, where she had been living when he went away with Crawfurd. He looked at the place where they had knelt in prayer before he had left, and where he had kissed her in farewell. He could see the place. He remembered the farewell. But there was no Nancy now.

He returned to the house she had built during his absence, where he would live by himself. He climbed the stairs to the room where she had died. From the window he could see the hope-tree and the top of the fence. Every moment he half expected to see her, or at least hear her voice or footstep. But every sound was made by others: his own slow footsteps, little Maria's wailing, the quiet movements of the Wades. There was no Nancy.

He asked for Dr. Richardson, who had attended her. But Richardson had moved to Moulmein. He plied the Burman disciples with questions, as if cross-examination could somehow force answers that might magically bring her back.

They told him that Nancy had said little during her illness. Her mind had seemed to be affected and sometimes her thoughts wandered. But they did remember her saying, "The teacher is long in coming and the new missionaries are long in coming. I must die alone and leave my little one, but as it is the will of God, I acquiesce in His will. I am not afraid of death, but I am afraid I shall not be able to bear these pains. Tell the teacher that the disease was most violent and I could not write. Tell him how I suffered and died. Tell him all that you see; and take care of the house and things until he returns."

When she was scarcely aware of anything else, she would still call for little Maria, who was being cared for by Mrs. Whitlock, wife of an officer and the only European woman in Amherst. When Mrs. Whitlock would bring the baby, Nancy would tell her again and again to be kind to it and be sure it had everything it wanted until its father should return. But the last few days she did not even do this. She lay on one side without moving, apparently almost unconscious, her head on her arm, her eyes closed. About eight o'clock one evening she gave an exclamation of distress or pain in Burmese and at that moment stopped breathing.

This was all the disciples could tell Adoniram.

He was dissatisfied. He wished Henry Gouger were still in Amherst. But Sir Archibald Campbell had decided that a place opposite Martaban called "Maulamyaing" or "Moulmein," some twenty-five miles upstream where the Salween was met by two smaller rivers in a lakelike islanded confluence, offered a better military location than Amherst even though it lacked a harbor for large vessels. When Campbell made Moulmein his headquarters, Amherst began to lose population. Gouger, in spite of his house and several months' service as a magistrate there, had decided to leave Amherst to its fate. He had departed from Burma forever. His wealth still remained in Ava, uncollectable. His health had been damaged. But he was young, with most of his life still ahead of him. He was content to leave the past behind and start again somewhere else.

Gouger being unavailable, Adoniram decided to visit Moulmein at the first opportunity and see Dr. Richardson. Meanwhile he mechanically resumed his missionary duties on Sunday, January 28, 1827 — four days after his return — by recommencing worship in Burmese. Only about 20 people were present, but it was the first Burmese service he had held in two and a half years. A few days later the little Burmese girl "Abby Hasseltine" died — the younger of Maung Shway-bay's two daughters who had lived with Nancy through the war years in Ava and Oung-pen-la. After the funeral, Adoniram began to pick up the threads of his partial translation of the Old Testament.

Early the next week Adoniram carried out his intention of visiting Dr. Richardson. He was well impressed, both as to the doctor's competence and his kindness and attentiveness to patients. Richardson told him that he had seen Nancy twice a day and had sometimes spent most of the night by her bed. From the beginning, he said, Nancy had been certain she would not recover; but even in the face of death "her mind was uniformly tranquil and happy." She seemed to regret most leaving Maria, the converts and the school before Adoniram or some other missionary could arrive. But she seldom complained even about this. Her last two days, said Richardson, she had no pain and her attention seemed to be turned inward so that it was necessary to question her again and again about how she felt before she would arouse enough to answer. But she did say, "I feel quite well, only very weak." These were the last words Richardson heard her speak.

The doctor was certain that Amherst's climate had nothing to do with her death. In his opinion, the real cause was exhaustion from the privations of Ava and Oung-pen-la.

Not only did Dr. Richardson confirm the disciples' account; more important, he allayed a certain feeling of guilt that had troubled Adoniram since the day of the black-sealed letter — a feeling that if he had been present he might somehow have been able to prolong Nancy's life. Now he was convinced — at least consciously — that his absence had contributed nothing toward her death.

With his guilty feelings about Nancy's death abated at least temporarily, Adoniram plunged once again into the work of the mission, hoping that time and activity would heal the remainder of his sorrow. There was certainly plenty to do. Some of the Amherst natives were showing interest in the Gospel. Another building was begun for a school. A great deal of work was put into clearing trees and brush from the mission premises. Maung Ing, appointed a teacher and preacher by his own request, went off down the southward coast to Tavoy to spread the Word.

Meanwhile, under Mrs. Wade's tender care little Maria began to improve until Adoniram thought with a mixture of gratitude and regret that the baby believed Mrs. Wade was her own mother. But the improvement was only temporary. Maria suffered a bowel complaint; recovered again; then, in April, relapsed. Adoniram and Mrs. Wade took her to Dr. Richardson in "Maulmain" (Moulmein). The doctor could do little, and on the twentieth, after some days in Moulmein, they returned to Amherst.

During their absence two new missionaries had arrived at Amherst and installed themselves — George Dana Boardman and his beautiful blue-eyed wife Sarah, with their own baby girl, barely six months old. But though the meeting with the Boardmans was pleasurable, Adoniram had little time for them, for Maria continued to sink rapidly. Four days after the return to Amherst, at three in the afternoon of April 24, 1827, Maria Elizabeth Butterworth Judson died. She had lived two years and three months.

Adoniram and the Wades and Mrs. Boardman "closed her faded eyes and folded her little hands on her cold breast." Boardman built her coffin himself.

The next morning [wrote Adoniram to Nancy's mother] we made her last bed in the small enclosure that surrounds her mother's lonely grave. Together they rest in hope, under the hope tree, which stands at the head of the graves; and together, I trust, their spirits are rejoicing after a short separation of precisely six months. And I am left alone in the wide world. My own dear family I have buried; one in Rangoon, and two in Amherst. What remains for me but to hold myself in readiness to follow the dear departed to that blessed world,

"Where my best friends, my kindred, dwell,
Where God, my Saviour, reigns"?

The Death Prison and Oung-pen-la had claimed another victim.

Once again Adoniram threw himself into missionary work. He exhorted and debated with inquirers as of old. He made an astronomical and geographical catechism to inform the Burmese about the world they lived in. He began the translation of Psalms. He considered how the enlarged missionary forces should be disposed. With Amherst still shrinking and Moulmein growing, it was decided the Boardmans should settle in Moulmein on ground Sir Archibald had offered for a mission station. They left in May. Adoniram joined them in August. The Wades and the native converts moved in November. At Moulmein Adoniram helped set up better facilities: a room in front of the new house for a zayat; a school for girls and one for boys; a "reading zayat" conducted by Maung Shway-bay; and a "preaching zayat" conducted jointly by Wade and Maung Ing, who had returned from Tavoy; each zayat in its separate shed.

But these labors were largely mechanical. The fact was, the more work of this kind Adoniram did, the less it seemed to involve the real wellsprings of his thought and feeling. For deep inside, his energies were wrestling with a question which might be stated, so far as such questions ever *can* be stated: Why did he feel such overwhelming, persistent grief for an earthly loss?

At times the belief that Nancy and the babies Roger and Maria were happier than they ever had been on earth would make him feel glad that they were in heaven, and he would yearn for the bright prospect of seeing them in the company of the angels. But then the shadows of appalling sadness and regret and loneliness would descend again. These shadows, like shadows in a darkling woodland, were interlaced in a confused pattern with strange haunting questions and guilty feelings of self-blame. What meaning, what purpose, lay behind the deaths of those he loved most? Did he carry death with him, like a contagion? In the beginning there had been Harriet Newell and her baby, and Newell, who had died a few years later in Bombay, a broken man. Then his own son Roger. Then Nancy. Now his daughter Maria. He hoped — he believed — he carried the gift of happy life eternal in the next world. But why did he carry the gift of death in this? And, most important: Since these dead were happy, why did he grieve?

Two additional deaths helped deepen these melancholy thoughts. In July Adoniram received word that his father had died the previous November at Scituate, Massachusetts. Objectively, there was no reason why his father's death should have distressed Adoniram unduly. Mr. Judson had reached the ripe old age of seventy-four, more than the Biblical three score and ten. He had adopted Adoniram's denominational views and been a Baptist for the past ten years. He had become surprisingly prosperous for a poor minister of small income, for as money came to him (partly, apparently, through subdivision and sale of lands in Plymouth) he had invested in stocks of banks in and around Boston. At his death his estate was appraised at more than seven thousand dollars, of which fifty-five hundred dollars was bank stock. All of this, except for twenty dollars to each son, he left to his widow and daughter, who were thus well provided for by the standards of the time.

But it was not these facts, which could well have called forth more admiration than grief for that stern, noble old man, which impressed Adoniram. What overwhelmed the son was a flood of poignant memories. All at once Adoniram recollected those glowing ambitions his father had held in front of his eyes from his earliest days. He remembered his father's predictions that the child Adoniram would surely grow up to become a great man; his bitter despair when Adoniram became an "infidel"; his pride when Adoniram accepted the Gospel again at Andover; and his disappointment when Adoniram refused the assistant pastorate of the Park Street Church in favor of a mission to Burma. Reliving these memories, Adoniram began to realize that no matter how he had rebelled, his father had succeeded in instilling in him, consciously or unconsciously, a goal of *earthly* ambition, an intense determination to surpass his fellows.

He began to suspect that his real motive in becoming a missionary had been not genuine humility and self-abnegation but ambition — ambition to be the *first* American foreign missionary; the *first* missionary to Burma; the *first* translator of the Bible into Burmese: *first* in his own eyes and the eyes of men.

He had a lust to excel. That was why he enjoyed the company of important men — ambassadors, generals — such as Crawfurd and Sir Archibald Campbell. He knew they liked and admired him, and their liking and admiration were like heady wine. In their company he glowed, and his wit flashed sparks like fire.

He had always known that his forwardness, self-pride and desire to stand out were serious flaws in his nature. Now he began to suspect that they were more than flaws. They made his entire missionary career up to now a kind of monstrous hypocrisy, a method of securing prominence and praise without admitting it to himself. He had deluded himself. But he had not deluded God. Perhaps here was the intention in all these deaths: to teach him true humility.

There was another death in September, that of the native sister Mah Men-lay. Almost half of her little wealth — one hundred and fifty rupees — she had left to the missionaries. A letter from Amherst on one of her last days told Adoniram, "She is not inclined to converse much; but how delighted *you* would be to hear her, now and then, talk of entering heaven and *of meeting Mrs. Judson,* and of other pious friends! The other day, after having dwelt for some time on the delightful subject, and mentioned the names of all the friends she should rejoice to meet, not omitting *dear little Maria,* she stopped short, and exclaimed, 'But first of all, I shall hasten to where my Saviour sits, and fall down, and worship him, for his great love in sending the teachers to show me the way to heaven.' "

To Adoniram, the letter must have been gall and wormwood. He and Nancy had converted Mah Men-lay in those long-ago days in Rangoon. Now she had looked forward to meeting Nancy, and Maria, and to thanking the Master in person for sending His Word through Adoniram. Adoniram had brought that Word — but through what motives!

No wonder it took death itself, by wholesale, to teach him better. For Adoniram's mission, God had approval; for Adoniram and his self-love, a harsh lesson.

So it seemed.

## CHAPTER II

# The Hermitage; Give Us a Writing

## [ *1828–1831* ]

EARLY in 1828 the missionaries decided to spread out from Moulmein, and in late March the Boardmans moved to Tavoy, one hundred and fifty miles or so south of Amherst down the Tenasserim coast. At this time Boardman was 27. A native of Maine, he had been graduated in 1822 from what is now Colby College, then "The Maine Literary and Theological Institute." Inspired by Colman's death that year he had chosen a missionary career, and studied at Andover, many of whose 150 students were now preparing to become missionaries. More than six feet tall, thin, light-complexioned, he was unlike Adoniram in appearance. But in drive, intellectual brilliance, flair for languages, and charm the two men had much in common.

As Colman's death had influenced Boardman's choice of career, so it had been responsible for his meeting his wife Sarah, who in her own way was as remarkable and well suited to him as Nancy had been to Adoniram.

Sarah, now 24, had been born to Ralph and Abiah Hall on November 3, 1803, in Alstead, New Hampshire, but the family had moved to Salem when she was a little girl. She was the eldest of thirteen children, and much of the care of her younger brothers and sisters had fallen on her shoulders. Nevertheless, by putting every spare minute into study, she taught herself almost single-handed rhetoric, logic, geometry and Latin, and even acquired a good grounding in theology. Even in her childhood she kept a journal and by her teens she was writing articles and verse for religious papers.

Colman's death had affected her much as it had Boardman and a poem by her about him had appeared in one of these papers. Boardman, deeply impressed by it, had tracked down its author. When he discovered she was a stunningly beautiful eighteen-year-old blue-eyed girl with light brown hair, shy but gracious, who taught school, took the lead in church activities and had considered missions for herself, the outcome was inevitable. They were engaged within a few months, and were married in the First Baptist Church of Salem on Sunday, July 3, 1825, a few weeks before their departure for India.

Sarah's poem about Colman had also resulted in her meeting Nancy, when on her American visit Nancy had addressed a Salem missionary gathering. It was already known that Sarah would some day join the Judsons, and when at the end of the meeting some well-meaning person proposed that Sarah should read her poem to Nancy, who had actually known Colman, the audience welcomed the suggestion with enthusiasm. Blushing and trembling, the protesting Sarah was all but dragged before what were to her the awe-inspiring dignitaries, and a copy of the poem forced into her unwilling hands. She got through it somehow, but it was not an experience she ever recalled with much pleasure.

The Boardmans had waited out the Anglo-Burmese War at Chittapore, near Calcutta, with the Wades and Colman's widow. With their help and that of a native Burman teacher they soon acquired a remarkably good knowledge of the Burmese language. They had proved themselves as pioneers at Moulmein, which was a most dangerous post in its early days, infested with robbers from Martaban, across the Salween, and with cobras, tigers and leopards from the jungles and hills above the cleared patches along the river.

One morning at Moulmein, for instance, they were awakened by a before-dawn sound to discover that robbers had cut into their bamboo hut, ransacked their trunks and boxes, and gone off with Boardman's watch, a mirror, the silver spoons, and even their keys. Even more unnerving, a long slash directly above their heads had been made in the mosquito net around their beds. Evidently the visitors had looked in and considered whether to slit their throats before thinking better of it. Another day, a guard assigned to their house by Sir Archibald Campbell had been mauled — fortunately not seriously — by a wild beast on their very veranda.

With them to Tavoy the Boardmans took a Siamese Christian, four of their schoolboys and a 50-year-old convert, as yet unbaptized, who was to prove one of the most famous apostles to his own people, and become an almost legendary figure.

This man, Ko[1] Tha Byu by name, belonged to a wild jungle nation who lived in the mountains of lower Burma. Adoniram and Nancy had seen small parties of them straggling past the mission house even in their earliest days in Rangoon and had been told "that they were called Karens; that they were more numerous than any similar tribe in the vicinity; and as untamable as the wild cow of the mountains; [and] . . . that they shrunk from association with other men, seldom entering a town, except on compulsion."

Ko Tha Byu had been a "wicked and ungovernable boy" who had left home at the age of fifteen, become a robber and murderer, and by his own estimate been involved in at least thirty murders. After the war he had entered Hough's service at Rangoon. Leaving Hough, he fell into trouble and was up for sale as a slave for debt when Shway-bay came across him, bought him, and took him as a servant. But he had an uncontrollable temper and Shway-bay had been glad to turn him over to Adoniram for the debt. Slowly Adoniram had made an impression on Ko Tha Byu. He learned to read the Burmese Testament. His entire personality changed. Eventually he became a Christian, and, his immense energies focused in this new direction, became the virtual father of Karen Christianity.

It was no wonder that the Boardmans, sensing his ability, took him along with them to a region abounding in Karens. It was no wonder that the Boardmans were the natural choice for the Tavoy mission. And it was no wonder that Adoniram should miss them.

Although the Boardmans' departure — particularly that of Sarah and her daughter, who must have reminded him of Nancy and his own little Maria — may have intensified Adoniram's melancholy, it was not responsible for the development of his underlying feelings of guilt or self-blame, or his apparently only partly conscious conclusion that he had been punished, and deserved further punishment, for his self-love and self-serving motives of ambition in performing the otherwise good work of bringing the Gospel to the Burmese. At any rate, these inner feelings continued to deepen

[1] "Ko" is a title applied to mature men, just as "Maung" is applied to younger men.

throughout all of the year 1828, and with them came all kinds of attempts to make atonement through what looks from this distance of years remarkably like self-punishment.

Securing the testimony of the Burman converts and Dr. Richardson about the details of Nancy's death had been Adoniram's first action in trying to assuage these feelings. Now, as he restudied the "quietism" of Madame Guyon, long a favorite of his since even before the Death Prison days, he came further under her influence and the mysticism of Thomas a Kempis, Fénelon and other writers, mostly of a distinctly un-Baptist sort, who expounded almost abject humility, solitary asceticism, and variously disguised forms of self-mortification.

Even before the Boardmans left for Tavoy he began by dropping his Old Testament translation — a labor of love — after doing thirty of the Psalms, and spending his days in one of the most hateful environments he could think of, a zayat "in a little shed, projecting into one of the dirtiest, noisiest public streets, in Moulmein." Wade occupied a somewhat similar zayat in another part of the city.

Little by little he continued cutting himself off from the world and divesting himself of anything that might conceivably support his pride or promote his pleasure.

Sir Archibald Campbell and other British officials had been in the habit of inviting him for dinners, which he keenly enjoyed; now he told them he would no longer dine out of the mission. He had received letters of commendation and praise from them which he valued highly; these he destroyed. In 1823, Brown, his alma mater, had conferred on him the degree of Doctor of Divinity; this he renounced in a letter to the *American Baptist Magazine*.

But these privations were of no more permanent help than a tiny dose of a drug is to one who is becoming an addict. He tried bigger doses.

When he left the United States he had brought with him a fair-sized amount of money, some of it earnings, some of it gifts from relatives and friends. Over the years this had grown at interest to some twelve thousand rupees, about six thousand dollars. He gave it — all his private wealth — to the Baptist Board. A little later, along with Wade, he offered to give up one twentieth of his missionary salary to support missions, plus another twentieth if a hundred

Baptist ministers in America would do the same. Later, he asked that his salary be reduced by an additional one quarter.

But he still was not satisfied. Toward the end of October he built a little hut, which he dubbed "the Hermitage," in the jungle some distance from the Moulmein mission house — itself no very safe location, as the Boardmans had discovered. He moved into the hut on October 24, 1828, the second anniversary of Nancy's death, and from it that night wrote to Mary and Abigail Hasseltine in Bradford:

> It proves a stormy evening, and the desolation around me accords with the desolate state of my own mind, where grief for the dear departed combines with sorrow for present sin, and my tears flow at the same time over the forsaken grave of my dear love and over the loathsome sepulchre of my own heart.

Nancy's grave. . . his own heart a "loathsome sepulchre." There was some mysterious equation in thought between Nancy in the grave with her body moldering, and his own inner corruption — his soul moldering, with his own eventual destination, his body too undergoing dissolution — *his*, Adoniram Judson's, in physical person neatest and cleanest of men. He was obsessed with such thoughts. Try as he would, he could not free himself from them, and from his feelings of guilt and self-disgust. Presently he concluded that it was a mistake to try. Perhaps he should immerse himself in them until he could accept them with resignation.

So he had a grave dug near the Hermitage and for days sat beside it, deliberately considering the stages of the body's decay in all its gruesome detail, in hopes that he might thus rise above fleshly considerations and through solitary reflection bring himself close to some intimation of Divinity. He apparently had in mind the Abbé de Paris, who "after having tried various modes of self-denial, in order to subdue his spirit, and gain the victory over the world, at length selected a crazy man to be the inmate of his miserable hut."

But this grave-watching period did not last long, for in addition to his doubts about such self-inflicted austerities some remaining sense of the ridiculous must have come to his rescue. After all, the grave was not a real grave. There was no more sense in sitting beside it, staring into it, than in sitting beside and staring into any other excavation.

Nevertheless, solitude and self-denial — less obvious forms of self-punishment — still held their attractions, as became clear when early in 1829 he began writing in a mood far more mystical than his original orthodoxy, in some ways even faintly resembling the New England Transcendentalism Emerson was to enunciate in another decade or so. For example, when Sir Archibald Campbell left Moulmein Adoniram wrote him a letter of warning about his soul:

> True religion is seldom to be found among mitred prelates and high dignitaries. It consists not in attachment to any particular church, nor in the observance of any particular forms of worship. . . . True religion consists in a reunion of the soul to that great, omnipresent, infinite Being, from whom we have all become alienated, in consequence of the Fall.

He developed some aspects of his thoughts further in a tract, called *The Threefold Cord*, which he wrote primarily for the guidance of repentant Burmans. The three cords if grasped with "the hand of faith" would draw the convert infallibly to heaven. The first cord was secret prayer.

The second cord — to which he gave the most space — was self-denial:

> Self-love, or the desire of self-gratification in the enjoyment of the riches, the honors, and the pleasures of this world, is the ruling principle of fallen man. . . . And the way to dispossess self-love is to cease indulging it; to regard and treat self as an enemy, a vicious animal, for instance, whose propensities are to be thwarted, whose indulgences are to be curtailed, as far as can be done consistently with his utmost service-ableness. . . . Adopt a course of daily, habitual self-denial . . . fast often; keep thy body under. . . . Cease adorning thy person. . . . Occupy a poor habitation; suffer inconveniences, yea, prefer them ever to slothful ease and carnal indulgence. Allow no amusements. . . . Get rid of the encumbrance of worldly property. . . . "Not only be content, but desirous, to be unknown, or being known, to be condemned and despised of all men, yet without any faults or deservings, as much as thou canst." Finally, renounce all terms with this world, which lieth in the arms of the wicked one.

This way of life would lead to God's graciousness and was a way of following in the steps of Jesus as He bore the Cross.

The third cord was that of doing good, which strengthened the "principle of holy benevolence."

How literally Adoniram took this principle of self-denial and cutting off all ties with the world he loved, we have already seen. And he went farther with it. Soon he wrote Abigail at Plymouth to destroy all his old letters, even those to her and their mother, except three or four recent ones "which you may wish to keep as mementoes." And he enforced his demand by making it a condition of signing a quitclaim against his father's estate: ". . . I am so very desirous of effecting a complete destruction of all my old writings, that you must allow me to say positively (as the only means of bringing you to terms) that I cannot send you the instrument you desire until I have an assurance, under your hand, that there is nothing remaining, except as mentioned above."

Self-denial. Seclusion. No matter how far he carried it, self-denial failed to bring him the spiritual peace he sought; perhaps deeper seclusion might help. After all, although he lived alone in the Hermitage, his days had always been at least partly occupied with exhortations in Moulmein, writing and translating. At some time during this period of melancholy he decided to drop all these activities for a while and try solitary meditation. So, his Bible under his arm, he went over the hills behind Moulmein, deep into the tiger-infested jungle, until he found a place that suited him near a long-abandoned, moss-overgrown pagoda. Here he began spending his days reading, reflecting, praying. Each evening he returned to the Hermitage.

He thought he was completely alone in his wilderness; but he was not, for at first he was secretly followed and watched by Ko Dwah, devoted deacon of the little native church. Ko Dwah even braved the jungle's dangers one evening after Adoniram had returned to the Hermitage to make a "rude bamboo seat" and weave some branches into a canopy. Next morning Adoniram found the shelter, but he never knew who placed it there.

The forty days Adoniram spent in this solitary meditation by the old pagoda, his entire diet nothing but a little rice, probably marked the extreme in his search for some sign that God had forgiven him. It failed. As he wrote on October 24, 1829, the third anniversary of Nancy's death, to Abigail and Mary Hasseltine: "Have either of you learned the art of real communion with God, and can you teach me the first principles? God is to me the Great Unknown. I believe in him, but I find him not."

But at least by this time he was becoming resigned. The paralyzing melancholy was slowly lifting. He was beginning to resume some of his activities. The Hermitage had been moved a little nearer to the mission house, so that he was within sound of a bell that called him to meals when he felt like eating with the missionaries. At other times, Mrs. Wade sent him food.

Thus he was able to bear up better, and even find some consolation, when he learned in mid-December of 1829 that Elnathan had died in Washington May 8, at the age of thirty-five. Long ago, when Adoniram and Elnathan had left Plymouth for Adoniram's wedding and ordination, they had dismounted from their horses and knelt in the snow beside the road while Adoniram had prayed for Elnathan's soul. So far as Adoniram knew, however, his brother had never experienced religion.

But now Dr. Sewall wrote:

A few hours before his death, and when he was so low as to be unable to converse or to move, he suddenly raised himself up, and clasping his hands, with an expression of joy in his countenance, cried "Peace, peace!" and then he sunk down without the power of utterance. About ten minutes before he expired, it was said to him, "If you feel the peace of God in your soul, open your eyes." He opened his eyes, and soon after expired, and, as we believe, in the triumph of the faith.

Of this, Adoniram wrote Abigail, "When I read this account, I went into my little room, and could only shed tears of joy . . ." [2]

The turning point had been passed. All through the year 1830, Adoniram continued climbing out of the depths. Sadness still shadowed his spirit, but he was slowly concluding that neither solitary

[2] Elnathan's family did not long survive him. His daughter, Ann H. Judson, died May 30, 1832, at the age of seven. His wife, Ellen Young Judson, died November 25, 1832, aged thirty.

reflection nor self-denial in and of themselves would bring him relieving happiness or a sense of communion with God. Instead, he was turning more and more to the third principle of *The Threefold Cord*, that of good works, of useful activity. Of course, he had never entirely ceased practicing good works, except during the forty days of meditation beside the old mossy pagoda, but neither since Nancy's death had he thrown himself into them so completely as he began to now.

It was an encouraging time for missionary activities. Reinforcements were arriving, activity was increasing, conversions were being made steadily — although success itself stirred up opposition, as when the mother of one of the girls in the mission school, on hearing that her daughter was ready to embrace Christianity, waylaid her, hit her on the head with an umbrella, and threatened to sell her as a slave. The mother of another, who had been baptized, ran one day into the schoolroom, dragged her daughter into the yard by the hair, and was arming herself with a stick of wood from the woodpile when Mrs. Wade intervened to save the girl's life. A sixty-year-old man was driven out of his house by his wife and family after his baptism, and forced to take refuge with the missionaries. Some women were threatened by their husbands — a man tore a child from his wife's breast and chased her with a knife. Curiously, he soon became interested in Christianity himself, and Adoniram eventually reported that he "has become a lamb."

Adoniram himself was now a venerated figure among missionaries and Burmans alike. In fact, his forty days in the jungle were proof to the Burman Christians that a miracle had occurred. Everybody knew that tigers were bigger, stronger, fiercer and less reluctant to attack men than lions — and if Daniel's survival in the lions' den, as recounted in the Bible, was a miracle, then the survival of the teacher Yoodthan in the tigerish jungle, which they had witnessed themselves, was far more miraculous.

In January of 1830 Mr. and Mrs. Cephas Bennett arrived at Moulmein with their two children. Bennett was a printer. Now tracts could be produced in quantity. Also, the Bennetts' arrival freed the Wades, for an attempt to revive the mission in Rangoon.

Not long after the Wades' departure, Sarah Boardman returned to Moulmein. Her health had been poor since the birth of her third child and second son, Judson Wade Boardman, and she had not recovered from the previous summer — when, together with her family, several hundred women and children and a few Europeans and Sepoy troops, she had undergone a siege by rebellious Tavoyans in a six-room wooden building on the Tavoy wharf until rescued by the ubiquitous steamer *Diana*. Her eldest child, Sarah Ann, had died just before the rebellion; her son George had been ill to the brink of death; and she and her husband had adopted the two sons of Dr. Price, who by now had died in Ava. It was not surprising that she needed rest and Moulmein's medical care. Boardman remained behind, but he had been suffering from an ominous cough for months and was shortly to join Sarah in Moulmein.

Meanwhile, the Wades had written Adoniram that Rangoon offered encouraging prospects — would he join them? As soon as Adoniram learned that Boardman would presently be in Moulmein, so that with both the Boardmans and Bennetts on hand the Moulmein station would be amply served, he set out for Rangoon.

He arrived May 2, 1830, to find the Wades living in the center of the city, where they had a great many visitors and inquirers — some of them, thought Adoniram, most promising. The viceroy of Rangoon turned out to be an old acquaintance of Adoniram's — an Atwinwun he had met on his first visit to Ava with Price; this dignitary now invited Adoniram to stay under his protection. One of the Wades' inquirers was another acquaintance, a man of rank and close friend of the old governor of the North Gate at Ava who had stood security for Adoniram at the war's end to prevent his return to Oung-pen-la.

But Adoniram did not stay long in Rangoon . . .

for every day deepens in me the conviction that I am not in the place where God would have me be. It was to the interior and not to Rangoon, that my mind was turned long before I left Maulmain; and while I feel that brother and sister Wade are in the right place, I feel that I am called elsewhere. Under these impressions, I am about proceeding up the river, accompanied by Maung Ing, Maung En, Maung Dway, Maung Dan . . . and Maung Like . . . The boat on which we embark will take us to Prome, the great half-way place between this and Ava, and there I hope and pray that the Lord will show us what to do.

This party left Rangoon on May 29, 1830. The trip up river had almost the quality of a triumphal procession, so many Burmese wanted tracts. For instance, wrote Adoniram, only a dozen or so miles above Rangoon, "I went on shore, entered into conversation with several, and gave away a dozen of the old tracts; and it was amusing and gratifying to see the groups of boatmen, about sunset, employed in reading and listening to the truth; and some would be constantly coming to our boat for a tract. I could have given away a hundred to advantage . . ." At a village farther up, he gave away thirty and was sure he could have distributed two hundred.

By now Adoniram had learned a certain guile.

It is my way to produce a few tracts or catechisms, and after reading and talking a little, and getting the company to feel kindly, I offer one to the most attentive auditor present; and on showing some reluctance to give to every person, and on making them promise to read attentively, and consider, and pray, they get furious to obtain a tract, many hands are eagerly stretched out, and "Give me one, give me one," resounds from all sides.

On the Irrawaddy, the missionaries were so badgered for tracts that late one evening the captain decided to push a little way out into the river so the party could get some rest, out of reach of inquirers.

However, it would not answer: for they came to the shore, and called out, "Teacher, are you asleep? We want a writing to get by heart." And, on being promised one if they would come and get it, they contrived to push off a long canoe . . . and got so near that they could reach a paper stuck in the end of a long pole. . . . Once, during the evening, our captain went on shore and said that in almost every house there was some one at a lamp, reading aloud one of our papers.

Everyone in Burma seemed to want to learn about the new Gospel. Sometimes after the missionaries' boat had started up the river from a village, people would even put out in boats after it to secure tracts. Adoniram had to write for more tracts, and suggest the printing of another edition.

But towards Prome, the atmosphere began to change. Listeners were more inclined to raise objections. Fewer wanted tracts. In one village some of the townsmen even treated Adoniram "rather uncivilly."

At Prome a European was living. He invited Adoniram to stay in his house and took him to the governor and deputy governor of the town. They heard Adoniram preach and read, "but seemed to be more taken with the sound than the sense." When Adoniram tried to rent a house in Prome he found that the common people were afraid to deal with a foreigner. Major Burney was in Ava on a mission to the Golden Feet, and ever since his passage up the river the country had resounded with alarming rumors. Prome was already terrorized and debt-ridden from one war. Now the Burmese foresaw another, and even the face of a white man scared them. Adoniram could understand why people would be afraid to talk to him. But without conversations, how could there be conversions?

Being unable to rent a house, Adoniram decided to build one. He found an old zayat with some vacant land around it in the center of the city and petitioned for permission to buy it. After a few days of negotiation the deputy governor and magistrates agreed to let him have it. The zayat was a good-sized building, forty-five by twenty-five feet, the teak posts, roof and floor still in fair condition, but the whole was overgrown with wild creeping vines and made "a pretty venerable ruin."

He moved in Saturday, June 26, 1830, with good hopes. If the population feared him, at least the officials were friendly. After worship the next morning with Maung Ing and other disciples, he spent the rest of the day at the great San-dan (San Daw) pagoda, Prome's equivalent of Rangoon's golden-spired Shwe Dagon. It happened to be the Burmese day of worship and the pagoda was thronged. Adoniram and the disciples settled down in a zayat beside it, "and some heard with attention."

But in less than a week he found himself under Government suspicion of being a spy. Maung Ing returned from a nearby town to report the same suspicion spreading everywhere. People were afraid to listen to missionaries, whether Burmese or white. By the next

Sunday "All smiles and looks of welcome are turned away; people view me with an evil eye, and suffer their dogs to bark at me unchecked." Still, he "found a vacant place under a shed built over a large brick idol" near the great pagoda. Here he sat on the ground and talked with a few small groups. "But it is really affecting to see a poor native when he first feels the pinch of truth. On one side he sees hell; on the other side, ridicule, reproach, confiscation of goods, imprisonment, and death." At least, he discovered, the suspicions attracted attention. On the following Sunday, he seated himself as before "on a brick under the shed over the big idol." Crowd after crowd came to hear. "Some became outrageously angry, and some listened with delight. 'Some said, He is a good man; but others said, Nay, he deceiveth the people.'"

He was closely questioned by the magistrates — not on religion, but on all his actions in Burma. The record was sent to Ava. The magistrates were ostentatiously neutral, but Adoniram foresaw the outcome. "At Ava I have been regarded as a suspicious character ever since I deserted them at the close of the war, and went over to the British."

Meanwhile, he learned there was no doubt that Boardman had tuberculosis. Barring a miracle, he could not last long. Wade was planning to leave Rangoon for Moulmein. Adoniram began to wonder whether he should not return to Rangoon to take Wade's place; but he finally decided to stay in Prome a little longer because he had noticed that although most of the spectators thronging around him in the zayat were hostile, there were always some "in distant corners" who listened attentively.

By September first, the disturbance Adoniram was stirring up in Prome had been brought to the attention of Major Burney in Ava by the king's ministers. Burney noted in his journal that they charged Adoniram with "abusing the Burmese religion, much to the annoyance of the king. I told them that Dr. Judson is now exclusively devoted to missionary pursuits; that I possess no power or authority over him, but that I know him to be a very pious and good man, and one not likely to injure the Burmese king or government in any manner." Burney warned them tactfully that "the Burmese king and government have always enjoyed a high reputation among civilized nations for the toleration which they have shown to all religious faiths; that there are thousands in Europe and America, who would be much hurt and disappointed to hear of any change in the liberal policy hitherto observed by the King of Ava, and that I hoped the ministers would not think of molesting or injuring Dr. Judson, as such a proceeding would offend and displease good men of all nations."

The minister replied that of course they would not hurt Adoniram — that was why they had come to Major Burney. Could he not write Adoniram about the king's feeling toward him? This Burney finally agreed to do, after explaining that he could not and would not give any orders whatever, and that Adoniram must act according to his conscience.

Actually, the king's order had been peremptory. The ministers, as usual, had hoped to use Burney to do their work for them. But of this Adoniram knew nothing at the time. For before anything was done he had left Prome for Rangoon, partly because Rangoon was a better center for combining translation with exhortation. But he viewed his stay in Prome with a good deal of satisfaction. He felt that he had gone into the heart of the enemy's country and, in a manner of speaking, thumbed his nose at them. Something of that lighthearted feeling came out in a letter he wrote in the middle of September:

> Afloat on my own little boat, manned by none other than my three disciples, I take leave of Prome and her towering god Shway San-dau, at whose base I have been laboring, with not the kindest intentions, for the past three months and a half. Too firmly founded art thou, old pile, to be overthrown just at present; but the children of those who now plaster thee with gold will yet pull thee down, nor leave one brick upon another.

Adoniram had distributed some five hundred tracts in Prome and made at least one convert, though the man was still unbaptized. Adoniram gave out another five hundred tracts on the way down the river.

In Rangoon, he found that the Wades had left and the mission had dropped once more to "a very low ebb." Men had actually at one time been "stationed at a little distance, on each side of the house, to threaten those who visited the place, and take away the tracts they had received. Reports were circulated that Government was about to make a public example of heretics; the crowds that used to come for tracts all disappeared, and Pastor Thah-a, who continued to occupy the house, became intimidated, and retreated to his own obscure dwelling."

There were still a few stouthearted inquirers and disciples around, of course, and these he saw often. But most of the time he spent translating. By now, he was well into the Old Testament.

He was visited here by a traveling Englishwoman, a Miss Emma Roberts, who was most anxious to see this missionary now celebrated throughout the civilized world. She found him in his "Burmese habitation, to which we had to ascend by a ladder; and we entered a large, low room through a space like a trap door. The beams of the roof were uncovered, and the window frames were open, after the fashion of Burman houses. The furniture consisted of a table in the centre of the room, a few stools, and a desk, with writings and books neatly arranged on one side."

The two talked through a good part of the afternoon, but . . .

As we were thus conversing, the bats, which frequent the houses at Rangoon, began to take their evening round, and whirled closer and closer, till they came in almost disagreeable contact with our heads; and the flap of the heavy wings so near us interrupting the conversation, we at length took our leave and departed. And this thought I, as I descended the dark ladder, is the solitary abode of Judson, whom after ages shall designate, most justly, the great and the good.

In this garret he pressed on with his translation, while the disciples taught and gave out tracts in the room below. A little after the beginning of the new year of 1831 he had finished Psalms, the Song of Solomon, and Daniel. There had been several conversions. But most impressive to Adoniram was the development of a "spirit of inquiry that is spreading every where, through the whole length and breadth of the land."

I sometimes feel alarmed [he reported] like a person who sees a mighty engine beginning to move, over which he knows he has no control. Our house is frequently crowded with com-

pany; but I am obliged to leave them to Moung En, one of
the best of assistants, in order to get time for the translation.
Is this right? Happy is the missionary who goes to a country
where the Bible is translated to his hand.

Although the missionaries never gave away a tract without being
asked for it, they found themselves giving away hundreds every
day. The great annual festival at the Shwe Dagon pagoda fell this
year on February 25. To be ready, Adoniram wrote Bennett for
fifteen or twenty thousand copies. On March 4 he wrote that during the festival he had distributed . . .

nearly ten thousand tracts, giving to none but those who ask.
I presume there have been six thousand applications at the
house. Some come two or three months' journey, from the
borders of Siam and China — "Sir, we hear that there is an
eternal hell. We are afraid of it. Do give us a writing that will
tell us how to escape it." Others come from the frontiers of
Kathay, a hundred miles north of Ava — "Sir, we have seen a
writing that tells about an eternal God. Are you the man that
gives away such writings? If so, pray give us one, for we want
to know the truth before we die." Others come from the
interior of the country, where the name of Jesus Christ is a
little known — "Are you Jesus Christ's man? Give us a writing
that tells about Jesus Christ."

## CHAPTER III
# The Burmese Bible; Sarah
### [ 1831–1834 ]

**B**UT, as always, along with the triumph there was tragedy. During the Shwe Dagon celebration, Adoniram received word that Boardman had died a few days before while returning to Tavoy from the mountain Karens.

Though he knew his days were numbered, Boardman had insisted on making the arduous expedition. He had become a great leader to the shy Karens, and had promised to visit them and help baptize them. So, carried on a cot by the Karens, and accompanied by Sarah, his two-year-old son George, and Francis Mason, a newcomer to the Tavoy mission, he had journeyed for three days into the hills to a bamboo chapel the Karens had built beside a stream at the foot of a mountain range. Here he saw thirty-four of the Karens baptized by Mason. On the way home, thundershowers had soaked the whole party. Boardman, wet and cold, was permitted to lie on the porch of a house by the river belonging to a native of Tavoy. In the morning a boat was brought up to take him the rest of the way. But it was too late. He had hardly been placed aboard when he died.

Adoniram wrote to Sarah a few days after he learned the news. His opening words may have been cheerless, but he knew he could tell her the truth:

> You are now drinking the bitter cup whose dregs I am somewhat acquainted with. And though, for some time, you have been aware of its approach, I venture to say that is far bitterer than you expected. It is common for persons in your situation to refuse all consolation, to cling to the dead, and to fear that they shall too soon forget the dear object of their affections. But don't be concerned. I can assure you that months and

months of heart-rending anguish are before you, whether you will or not. Yet take the bitter cup with both hands, and sit down to your repast. You will soon learn a secret, that there is sweetness at the bottom. . . .

He added that he hoped she would stay on as a missionary to the Karens. As for her son George,[1] she was promised that, when the boy was old enough to leave Burma, Adoniram would try to secure for him the best education she could wish. Or, should Sarah herself die unexpectedly, if she would commit George to Adoniram: "I hereby pledge my fidelity to receive and treat him as my own son, to send him home in the best time and way, to provide for his education, and to watch over him as long as I live."

For a while after Boardman's death Sarah thought she should return to America, particularly on account of her little son. Perhaps Adoniram's letter helped change her mind. At any rate, she finally decided she belonged in Burma. She knew Burmese pretty well; she knew the Karens. They liked and trusted her. She had a flourishing school which probably would not continue if she left.

The Karens, in fact, were much easier to convert to Christianity than the Burmese. They were a primitive people, jungle dwellers, not even accustomed to live in villages, and their simple animistic beliefs offered no such resistance to a highly developed religion as did Buddhism. Christianity could flow into a religious vacuum, so to speak, instead of having to displace an already well organized doctrine.

Besides, the Karens had some peculiar legends which suggested the Bible, even including one about the consequence of the eating of forbidden fruit from a "tree of death." One of these involved a Creator called "Y'wa," who had seven sons, of whom the Karen was the first-born, the white man the youngest. Y'wa was to go on a journey and invited the Karen to go with him. The Karen refused because he had to clear his field. The Burman refused, too, but he and the Karen each gave their father a gift. Finally the white brother went with Y'wa. When they reached the "celestial shore," Y'wa made a silver and gold book for the Karen, a palm-leaf book for the Burman and a parchment book for the white man. But the white

[1] The baby boy, Judson Wade Boardman, had died in September.

man kept the silver and gold book for himself, and sent the Burman with the parchment book to the Karen. The Karen, who was still busy clearing his field, scarcely looked at the book. Instead, he left it on a stump. When he burned his clearing the book was ruined and the pigs and chickens ate what was left. But, said the legend, some day the white brother would bring the Karens the lost book from across the water. Naturally, some of them took the missionaries for that "white brother" of the legend.

The Boardmans, in fact, when they first arrived in Tavoy, heard of a Karen teacher or sorcerer who had such a sacred book which the Karens of his village had been worshiping for twelve years. They brought the book to Boardman to see whether it contained the Christian Gospel. Tenderly the old sorcerer lifted a bundle from a basket, unfolded numerous wrappings, and revealed a badly worn copy of the *Oxford Book of Common Prayer with the Psalms*. Suppressing a smile, Boardman told the people that the book was good, but not to be worshiped. Worship was reserved for the God revealed in the book.

Thus, the Karens were well prepared for the missionary message. The worst problem was reaching them — they moved about so nomadically. Finally Boardman tried persuading them to settle down in villages in the hills, the first of which he named Wadesville for Jonathan Wade, who had baptized the first Karens in the vicinity.

After her husband's death, Sarah made periodic mission journeys herself into the hill country in whatever spare time she felt free to take from her school. A white woman, dressed European fashion, always accompanied by little George, she became legendary herself. One of the Karen men always carried the boy, and they referred to him among themselves as "the little chieftain." There were no roads, and once she wrote to Mrs. Mason from the jungle, "Perhaps you had better send the chair, as it is convenient to be carried over the streams, when they are deep. You will laugh, when I tell you, that I have forded all the smaller ones."

Sometimes she startled exploring white men. For instance, a young British officer stationed at Tavoy remembered meeting her deep in the jungle while he was on a hunting trip. He had taken refuge from the rain in a wayside zayat, and while his breakfast was being prepared was philosophizing to himself on the primitiveness of these desolate mountain fastnesses. All of a sudden a beautiful, smiling white woman appeared in front of him, dripping with rain, surrounded by a party of Karen followers.

"The lady seemed as much surprised as himself," it was recounted years later; "but she curtsied with ready grace, as she made some pleasant remark in English; and then turned to retire." When she returned in dry clothing, she put her stores with his to provide a better breakfast than either could have supplied alone. They talked for a long time and became good friends. But the man never forgot his amazement when intrepid Sarah Boardman unexpectedly materialized before him, a blue-eyed apparition of the mountains, in the rainy jungle deep in the wild Karens' hills.

By late July, 1831, Adoniram had finished the translation of Genesis, twenty chapters of Exodus, Psalms, the Song of Solomon, and Daniel. But he was needed at Moulmein. Mrs. Wade's health had become so bad that all the missionaries agreed her husband must take her to the United States. Adoniram waited until two new missionaries, Mr. and Mrs. John Taylor Jones, arrived at Rangoon before leaving for Moulmein himself. On his arrival he found that the church for Europeans built up by Kincaid had grown. Reports from the Karens in the north were encouraging, but not much success had been achieved among the natives of Moulmein.

Nevertheless, the overall results, measured by the standards of those early years when he and Nancy were desperately trying to make even a single convert, were amazing. It had taken Adoniram and Nancy nine years to baptize eighteen native converts. But in the first five years since the war, Adoniram was to report in a few months, 242 natives had been baptized, plus 113 foreigners. From the beginning in 1831, therefore, the total number of baptisms stood at the end of 1831 at 373, of which 217 had been made during this one year. If the missionary forces continued to grow at this rate and if they worked as hard in the past as they had recently, they might look forward to years when they would make thousands of converts — and perhaps even in some distant future to the Christianization of Burma.

By now Adoniram was the senior — he avoided thinking of himself as the chief executive — of a fair-sized group of missionaries. Some died, some left, usually some were away from Burma attempting to recover health, but the total on hand was seldom much less than a dozen.

He noted, however, that most of them had a tendency to cling in a group to the most comfortable station, Moulmein, safely under British protection. Some, like the Wades and Bennetts and Masons and Sarah Boardman, voluntarily struck into front-line areas such as Rangoon, Tavoy and the interior; but not even any of these cared to make another trial of Ava in the Burmese heartland. And from Ava he himself was barred until that unlikely time when king and court might change their feeling about him.

No one on earth was better qualified than he to pioneer in these or in other places. He knew more about the Burmese language and people than any other white man alive. And almost everything the Burmese knew about Christianity they had learned from him — either directly through hearing him, or through reading something he had written or translated, or through meeting someone he had taught.

He no longer had any ties to hold him back. Wife, children — all were dead, martyrs to the mission. He had the command of native idiom and the experience to deal with people who had never heard of the Gospel. He felt, moreover, that neither teaching in native schools nor preaching to British soldiers was not the primary task of a missionary, useful though those occupations might be. He felt, to tell the truth, that some of the missionaries were slower in learning the language than necessary merely because of their tendency to immure themselves in Moulmein where everyone knew at least a word or two of English.

His health was good. He had just turned forty-three, but he looked much younger than his age. His face was still almost unlined, his spare, slight, compact body as vigorous as ever, his step still springy and rapid as he took the long morning walks to which he credited his health. Therefore he usually volunteered to undertake pioneering trips, and in fact preferred them to staying in Moulmein.

Only one thing deterred him. This was the knowledge that the complete Bible was not yet translated into Burmese, and there was no one else to do it. So he oscillated. At times his wishes and his freedom drove him into the remote hill regions; but at other times his conscience and his fondness for scholarship chained him to a desk.

That September, for instance, he went up the "Dah-gyne" (Dagyaing today) River four or five days' journey above Moulmein to Wadesville, where Wade had baptized the first Karens. But within a week he came down with jungle fever and had to return to Moulmein. While he was recovering, the Wades returned. Their ship to America had been so buffeted about by storms that it began to sink and had to make for the Arakan coast. Here, during their two months' detention, Mrs. Wade's health improved so much that they decided to return to the mission.

But by the beginning of 1832 he was well again and at Wadesville with a small group of native converts, some of them deacons of the Moulmein congregation. From here the members of the party would go out in different directions for several days at a time, then re-unite to move farther up the river before scattering again into the jungle hill villages. The rivers were their highways. As they went farther and farther up the narrowing tributaries, they had to chop passages for the boats through trees which had fallen across the streams.

Here and there they found small clusters of disciples still strong in the faith. Others had backslid. One church member had made an offering to a demon called a "nat" when his child was deathly sick; but he repented so vociferously that the transgression was forgiven. A few presented themselves for baptism.

One woman, remarked Adoniram with amusement, the wife of a man named Loo-boo, "presented herself for baptism, with twelve strings of all manner of beads around her neck, and a due proportion of ear, arm, and leg ornaments! and strange to say, she was examined and approved, without one remark on the subject of her dress. The truth is, we quite forgot it, being occupied and delighted with her uncommonly prompt and intelligent replies."

The next day before breakfast, Adoniram mentioned the subject of female dress.

    . . . it was truly amusing and gratifying to see the said lady, and another applicant for baptism, and a Christian woman who accompanied them, divest themselves, on the spot, of every article that could be deemed merely ornamental; and this they did with evident pleasure, and good resolution; to preservere in adherence to the plain dress system. We then held a church meeting, and having baptized the four applicants, crossed the Leing-bwai on a bridge of logs, and set out for Tee-pah's village, accompanied by a long train of men, women, children, and dogs.

All through January the missionaries roamed through the jungles, sometimes crossing high mountains, sometimes fording mountain streams barefoot, cutting their feet on the sharp stones. Sometimes individuals underwent surprising changes of heart in mere hours. Once an old man of some importance in a village, a Buddhist Karen, was openly contemptuous. He would not invite Adoniram to his village, but he would not forbid his coming. Adoniram sent word to him:

I would not come, but, as he loved falsehood and darkness, I would leave him to live therein all his days, and finally go the dark way; and all my people drew off to the boat.

While we were deliberating what to do, something touched the man's heart; we heard the sound of footsteps advancing in the dark, and presently a voice. "My lord, please to come to the village."

"Don't call me lord. I am no lord, nor ruler of this world."

"What must I call you? Teacher, I suppose."

"Yes, but not your teacher, for you love to be taught falsehood, not truth."

"Teacher, I have heard a great deal against this religion, and how can I know at once what is right and what is wrong? Please to come and let me listen attentively to your words."

I replied not, but rose and followed the old man. He took me to his house, spread a cloth for me to sit on, manifested great respect, and listened with uncommon attention. When I prepared to go, he said, "But you will not go before we have performed an act of worship and prayer?" We accordingly knelt down, and, during prayer, the old man could not help now and then repeating the close of a sentence with emphasis, seeming to imply that, in his mind, I had not quite done it justice. After I was gone, he said that it was a great thing to change one's religion; that he stood quite alone in these parts; but that, if some of his acquaintances would join him, he would not be behind.

Another time, Adoniram had to leave a hostile village after trying unsuccessfully "to conciliate the children and dogs, who cried and barked in concert." But in another village, the chief himself applied for baptism and admission into the church.

Altogether, thought Adoniram when he returned to Moulmein after a six weeks' absence, it had not been an unsuccessful expedition. He had baptized twenty-five converts and as many more were "hopeful inquirers."

He remained only a few weeks in Moulmein. At the end of February he set out for the Karen villages on the Salween River. It was a dangerous expedition. In some areas the countryside was "swarming with tigers" and they had to curl themselves up in their boat to sleep. The hills back from the streams were heaped up of "craggy rocks" and the mountains were "stupendous" — the whole country a "desert," inhabited only by "scattered immortal beings." On this trip, which lasted about a month, there were nineteen conversions and one dismaying apostasy. "May Byah-ban, of whom we all had such high opinion, joined her husband, not many days after their baptism, in making an offering to the demon of diseases, on account of the sudden, alarming illness of their youngest child; and they have remained ever since in an impenitent, prayerless, state! They now refuse to listen to our exhortation, and appear to be given over to hardness of heart and blindness of mind. I was, therefore, obliged this morning, to pronounce the sentence of suspension, and leave them to the mercy and judgment of God." But Adoniram could not help sympathizing with them. "They are quite alone in this quarter, have seen no disciples since we left them, and are surrounded with enemies, some from Maulmein, who have told them all manner of lies. . . "

Back at Moulmein he found that Bennett had arrived from Calcutta with a new and complete font of Burmese type and was already beginning to print his newest version of the New Testament. The Wades had left for Rangoon, but when Wade had to return

to Moulmein a few months later on account of a serious illness
requiring medical aid, Adoniram begged him to stay on. He had
begun to see that correcting the proofs of the New Testament would
keep him in Moulmein for months and he would have no time for
expanding the activities of the mission.

As a matter of fact, he was in the grip of a bigger idea. Looking
over what he had done on the Old Testament, he saw that about a
third was done and calculated "that I could finish the whole in two
years, if I confined myself exclusively to the work. . . . " Otherwise, it might drag on for years, and possibly never be done, in view
of the "uncertainty of life."

But this meant that the Wades would have to take charge of the
Moulmein church and the nearby Karens. The Wades, recognizing
the importance of having a complete printed Burmese Bible, agreed.
Adoniram promptly prepared a room "at the end of the native
chapel." Here he shut himself up for the next two years, "and I
beg prayers of my friends that, in my seclusion, I may enjoy the
presence of the Saviour, and that special aid in translating the inspired word which I fully believe will be vouchsafed in answer to
humble, fervent prayer."

All through 1832 and 1833 Adoniram worked on translation. On
December 15, 1832, he sent to the press the last sheet of the New
Testament, about two weeks after the Wades had sailed to America
to recoup Wade's shattered health. The Wades had taken with them
Prices' children and two converts, a Burman and a Karen. Inevitable
changes had occurred. The Bennetts' two daughters, Elsina and
Mary, had sailed to the United States, leaving their brokenhearted
mother behind. But the missionaries had learned that their children
must go to a temperate zone as soon as they could travel if they
were to live to adulthood. Jones had gone to Siam, Kincaid took up
the work in Rangoon.

The printing, performed by Bennett and a new missionary named
Cutter, had become a big business. The printing house was of brick,
and more than fifty feet long. There were two printing presses and
all the materials for a stereotype foundry. Here Bennett printed, in
1832, between his arrival in March with the types and the end of
the year, 3000 copies of the New Testament, and 33,000 copies of

tracts and catechisms, including some in Karen and Taling and a Karen spelling book. Altogether, around two and a half million printed pages came out of the printing house that year.

There had been more conversions in 1832 — 126 natives, most of them at Moulmein and Tavoy. Rangoon, paralyzed under the dark shadow of Ava, received only three.

The opening of 1833 brought additional missionaries from the United States — one of them Miss Sarah Cummings, an unmarried woman. Later there were to be accessions to the mission forces. But as usual, they could not be of much real use until they became fluent in the language; and that would be a matter of years. At least one of these had come out with the understanding that his service was to be for a limited period of years. Adoniram was disturbed, like all his experienced colleagues.

> I much fear [he complained to the Corresponding Secretary at home,] that this will occasion a breach in our mission. How can we, who are devoted for life, cordially take to our hearts one who is a mere hireling? . . . I have seen the beginning, middle, and end of several limited term missionaries. They are all good for nothing. Though brilliant in an English pulpit, they are incompetent to any real missionary work. They come out for a few years, with the view of acquiring a stock of credit on which they may vegetate the rest of their days, in the congenial climate of their native land. . . The motto of every missionary, whether preacher, printer, or schoolmaster, ought to be *"Devoted for life."*

Meanwhile, Adoniram was trying to spin out into Burmese twenty-five to thirty verses of the Old Testament every day. Most of the time he secluded himself in his study. But even when he went up country for a few days or weeks he took his books with him and continued his studies.

The job he had set himself was a difficult one, for he had never been content to translate from English into Burmese. Since the English Bible was itself a translation from Greek and Hebrew, this would have required the people of Burma to read a translation of a translation. He felt this double straining would sieve out too much of the meaning. Instead, he translated the Greek and Hebrew directly into Burmese, using whatever critical and scholarly commentaries he had available — and he had a good many. For years, even before leaving Salem in 1812, he had been accumulating the necessary library, and whenever he heard of a new book that might be useful he wrote for it. Working this way he hoped to produce a Burmese Bible which, while it would certainly need plenty of revision, would not have to be done all over again within a few years.

At the end of June, 1833, only the minor prophets and the historical books remained to be done. He had hopes of finishing the entire translation by the end of the year. Nearly seven years had passed since Nancy's death. The first of those years he had descended into an emotional and spiritual valley of shadows, where he had dwelt in the chilly gloom of his memories. Now he was climbing out from the half-death of its depressing shades into the sunshine of life.

Translating, he was in isolation, yet occupied with what he was sure was the most useful work he could possibly do. He took pride in the tangible results. Some of the missionaries could preach in Burmese or Karen. All of them could preach in English. Most of them could teach. Some could print. But only he had the incomparable combination of abilities and knowledge to make a Burmese Bible that would stand for generations. This he knew full well. He leaned over backwards to avoid boasting, but deep in the recesses of his mind he must have heard again echoes of the words his father so often spoke to him when he was a boy: "Adoniram, I expect you to become a great man." The words themselves may have long been lost to conscious memory; but such words are never really forgotten.

In the work and the accomplishment, his frozen emotions began to melt. He began to participate in the feelings of others. He wrote to Mrs. Bennett about her two daughters, " . . . Those poor culprits, Elsina and Mary, do so frequently squeeze out the tear, that it is painful to think of them. I don't wonder that you say your heart is ready to break. I almost wonder that you can breathe." And to the Bennetts, when they had left for Rangoon, " . . . I never have had a *tighter fit* of low spirits than for about a week after you had gone. I sometimes went, after dinner, to take a solitary walk in the veranda, and sing, with my *harmonious* voice, 'Heartless and hopeless, life and love all gone.' However, I am rallying again, as the doctors say."

He was becoming conscious of his loneliness in a new way. It was as if deadened nerves of sensation were returning to life and once again beginning to feel. There was pain in it, but a dawning prescience that there might be pleasure, too. By cutting close personal ties, he might have cut the possibility of another pain like that of Nancy's death. But the suspicion was stirring that the sweetness of the association could be worth the pain.

In this transitional mood he wrote at the end of the year to his mother and sister:

> I still live alone, and board with some one of the families that compose the mission. After the Wades left, I boarded with the Bennetts. After the Bennetts left for Rangoon, I boarded with the Cutters. After the Cutters left for Ava, I boarded with the Hancocks, where I now am. I have no family or living creature about me that I can call my own, except one dog, Fidelia, which belonged to Little Maria, and which I value more on that account. Since the death of her little mistress, she has ever been with me; but she is now growing old, and will die before long; and I am sure I shall shed more than one tear when poor Fidee goes.

So new thoughts and feelings began to put out their delicate, seeking tendrils as the translation of the Old Testament slowly approached its conclusion. He did not finish, as he expected, by the end of 1833. But two months later, January 31, 1834, he was able to write:

> Thanks be to God, I can *now* say I have attained. I have knelt down before him, with the last leaf in my hand, and imploring his forgiveness for all the sins which have polluted my efforts in this department, and his aid in future efforts to remove the errors and imperfections which necessarily cleave to the work, I have commended it to his mercy and grace; I have dedicated it to his glory. May he make his own inspired word, now complete in the Burman tongue, the grand instrument of filling all Burmah with songs of praise to our Great God and Saviour Jesus Christ. *Amen.*

With the translation finished he suddenly felt released. He began to look around him. He began to think of the life remaining to him. He was forty-six years old.

A few weeks later he received a letter from Tavoy. It was dated February 17, 1834. It went:

My Dear Brother:
   The translation of the Bible into Burmese is an event, to which thousands have looked forward with joyful anticipation, and for which, thousands now perishing in their sins, should fall on their knees in thanksgiving to God, and through which, thousands yet unborn will praise him for ever and ever.

   My dear brother, I dare not pass encomiums upon a fellow-mortal in speaking of the Word of God; and if you think me guilty of this impiety in what I may say, bear with me yourself, and pray God to forgive me. I have, for the last four years, been in the daily practice of reading attentively the New-Testament in Burmese; and the more I study it, the better I am pleased and satisfied with the translation. I am delighted with the graphic style of the narrative part; and think many of the doctrinal passages are expressed with a force and perspicuity entirely wanting in our version. How much of this is due to your vivid manner of expression, and how much to the nature of the language, I do not know. I sometimes tell the Masons, that I should be willing to learn Burmese for the sake of being able to read Scriptures in that language.

   Last Lord's-day, while reading a portion of Scripture, I was affected to tears, and could scarcely proceed, as is often the case, in reading striking passages; and the effect was also observable on the old Tavoyan, for he managed to bring a great part of it into his prayer, which immediately followed. My scholars are now reading the Gospel of Luke; and I am reading St. John's Gospel and Revelation alternately, at evening worship.

Yours affectionately,
SARAH H. BOARDMAN

The simple warmth of the letter pleased Adoniram as much as the words of praise. She had occupied a special place in his heart for a long time. When her husband had died, she had not left Burma like the widows of other missionaries. Undaunted, she had stayed and carried on his work as well as she could. Cheerful, tactful — yes, and beautiful — she had even dared to carry the Word by herself through the tiger-haunted jungle. The vision of her fording streams and crossing the hills as she went from Karen village to village, her little son carried by one of the native converts who accompanied her, smiling and unafraid in the face of danger and hardship, rose irresistibly to his mind.

She had not tried to cut herself off from the world. She had not sat for days by an open grave. She had equably accepted what came as the will of God and kept on with His work.

She was altogether different from Nancy — calmer, less dominant, with less fire but perhaps more glow. But she reminded him of Nancy. She must, he suspected, have reminded him of Nancy a long time ago, for before her husband had died Adoniram had given her a watch of Nancy's, a watch he had given Nancy when he was still at Andover and she at Bradford. He had thought he gave Sarah Boardman the watch because he had no use for it. But he could as easily have given it to someone else, the wife of another missionary — Mrs. Wade or Mrs. Bennett, for instance.

At any rate, she was alone and he was alone. Why should they not live out their years together, and find together what companionship and comfort they could for the rest of their lives? She was thirty years old. He was forty-six. They should have a good many years.

Adoniram was not usually a man to waste time. He wrote to Tavoy.

On the first of April he left Moulmein. On the sixth he arrived in Tavoy. On the tenth, he and Sarah Hall Boardman were married by Mason. The very same day they left for Moulmein with little George.

He had no feeling — nor did Sarah — that they were betraying their late spouses. Adoniram made that amply clear in his journal before embarking:

Once more, farewell to thee, Boardman, and thy long-cherished grave. May thy memory be ever fresh and fragrant, as the memory of the other beloved, whose beautiful, death-marred form reposes at the foot of the hopia tree. May we, the survivors, so live as to deserve and receive the smiles of those sainted ones who have gone before us. And at last may we all four be reunited before the throne of glory, and form a peculiarly happy family, our mutual loves all purified and consummated in the bright world of love.

## CHAPTER IV

# Quiet Years; the Family
## [ *1834–1839* ]

THE home which Adoniram provided for Sarah and little George in Moulmein, like the houses of the other missionaries, was a glorified version of a native hut, containing "three good-sized rooms and two small ones." The cookhouse, a small separate building, stood on stilts some four feet off the ground, in the Burmese fashion. The roof was thatched, the walls made of bamboo mats. A wide, shaded porch ran the length of the front. The whole cost Adoniram three hundred dollars.

The location of the new house in the heart of the mission community signified that Adoniram's hermit life was over. The printing house — constantly being enlarged — was scarcely a hundred steps from his front porch, and the school and the other missionaries' houses nearby.

Their life together began inauspiciously. Although Sarah considered herself "pretty well," she was pale and thin. Her appetite was poor. A half-mile walk taxed her endurance to the limit. Soon she fell seriously ill. She spent weeks in bed. Occasionally Adoniram carried her in his arms from her bed to a couch to give her a little change; once even this made her worse. The doctor gave up hope for her life. He continued to prescribe medicines, but more to placate Adoniram than from any expectation they would help.

Little George, six years old, sobered and matured beyond his years by the harsh demands of life, spent a good deal of time by her bedside, reading the Bible to her or reciting hymns he had learned.

Gradually, however, Sarah began to recover. As soon as she was on her feet, Adoniram persuaded her to try his favorite specific — riding on horseback, the remedy he had learned in the early days in Rangoon. Every morning before sunrise the two went for a long ride. At first Sarah resisted. The rides simply tired her. But Adoniram insisted. After a while, somewhat to her surprise, she found her strength and spirits returning. After four or five months, her "nice little pony" died. But by now she was so enthusiastic about Adoniram's regimen of exercise that she decided to take up walking; and from then on each rising sun found them afoot, "far over the hills beyond the town."

By the end of the year the time came for her to carry out a decision she had made about George even before her marriage. If he were to live to adulthood he must go to America, like the Bennetts' children. The opportunity to send him came in December, when the ship *Cashmere* arrived from Boston with the Wades, the Osgoods, and some missionaries. The *Cashmere* was to return directly to Boston after a stop of a few weeks in Singapore. So good an opportunity to send George in careful hands might not occur again for years.

It was a heartrending parting. George was unusually dear to his mother: "and his nature had about it a clinging tenderness and sensitiveness which peculiarly unfitted him for contact with strangers."

But there was no help for it. "Oh! I shall never forget his looks," wrote Sarah to her sister, "as he stood by the door and gazed at me for the last time. His eyes were filling with tears, and his little face red with suppressed emotion. But he subdued his feelings, and it was not till he had turned away and was going down the steps that he burst into a flood of tears."

While Sarah, her heart breaking, hurried to her room and fell to her knees in tearful prayer, Adoniram carried the little boy in his arms to the small boat that would take them to the *Cashmere*, anchored in the harbor at Amherst down the river. All the way down, Adoniram comforted the boy as best he could, and reported to Sarah afterwards that "his conversation was very affectionate and intelligent." On board the *Cashmere*, Adoniram saw George's little bed properly made up in the cabin, made sure that he would be well cared for, "and then, as George expressed it, returned to 'comfort Mama.'"

It was just as well that Sarah was not to know for a long time what happened to George at Singapore. J. T. Jones and William Dean — the latter a new missionary — had taken care of him while the *Cashmere* lay fifteen miles below the city. When it was time to sail, the two missionaries took a native-rowed boat out to the ship. They carried with them a box of letters destined for America. Ten miles from shore and five from the *Cashmere*, the boat was attacked by a crew of Malay harbor pirates who thought the box contained treasure. While little George cowered under a bench, Jones was thrown overboard, and Dean, after a struggle, stabbed in the side and finally transfixed through the wrist by a three-pronged fishing spear. Luckily, when the pirates had the box they drew off and Jones, not quite drowned, was pulled aboard. Little George, terrified but uninjured, was finally taken aboard the *Cashmere;* but he never forgot the experience.

The beginning of the year 1835 marked the real beginning of Adoniram's and Sarah's married life together. Sarah had completely recovered her health. Her blue-eyed beauty, her quietly glowing disposition, her ability and experience made her an ideal wife and colleague. At last Adoniram seemed to have sailed out into calm seas. He was well fitted to enjoy his new life. His health was excellent. Although he was approaching fifty, his still luxuriant hair was without a fleck of gray, incredible when one pauses to think of the hardships he had endured. His face was unlined, his eyes bright, his energy apparently as overflowing as when he sailed from Salem in 1812.

Both Adoniram and Sarah made languages their main labor. In Moulmein was a numerous population of Talings, or Peguans.[1] They differed from the Burmese in everything but their Buddhism. Some of these people came across the Gospel message in a Burmese tract which had somehow been translated into Taling. But none of the missionaries knew enough about the dialect to give them any real help. At Adoniram's suggestion Sarah, who already knew Karen and Burmese, began to study Taling and with the help of Ko Man-boke, a Peguan Christian, to translate into it the Burmese tracts and catechisms.

Adoniram's preoccupation was the Burmese Bible. He had come

[1] Also known as the Mons people.

to feel that the making of a good translation was a life work in itself and more than important enough to justify giving a life to it. All missionary work — in fact, all knowledge of Christianity — rested on the Bible, particularly the New Testament. More, every Bible that found its way into a Burmese village was a missionary in itself, one that needed no pay, no support, and never grew tired or fell sick. No sooner, therefore, had he finished the translation of the Old Testament than he threw himself into its revision and correction for the press, utilizing every scholarly publication upon which he could lay hands to make it more nearly accurate.

But although translation took most of their time, neither Sarah nor Adoniram neglected other duties. While Sarah organized prayer meetings, classes and mothers' societies for the women, Adoniram preached seven sermons a week — one on Sunday to "a crowded assembly" and one every evening to a smaller gathering. Every morning before breakfast he met with the native assistants who spent their days going about Moulmein preaching, so that he could keep track of their work and make suggestions for improving their effectiveness. He kept charge of the native church, too, which numbered ninety-nine and was shortly to pass the one hundred mark, and performed baptisms.

Among these baptisms was one which gave him special pleasure: that of Koo-chil, the Bengali cook whom Nancy had brought with her from Calcutta to Ava on her return from the United States. It was Koo-chil's faithfulness which had kept Nancy and little Maria alive through the worst days at Oung-pen-la. Ever since he had served one or another of the missionary families.

"Though a faithful, good servant," wrote Adoniram, "he persisted for years in rejecting all religious instruction, and maintained his allegiance to the false prophet." But in 1834 his Burmese wife was baptized, and by late 1835 Koo-chil himself was won over. "But the process was slow, the struggle strong; he felt deeply the responsibility of changing his religion, and when he made his formal request for baptism, he trembled all over. Poor old man! He is above sixty; his cheeks are quite fallen in; his long beard is quite gray; he has probably but a short time to live . . . He affectionately remembers his old mistress, and frequently sheds tears when speaking of the scenes of Ava and Amherst, where he saw her suffer and die."

There were white men whom Adoniram and Sarah influenced, too. One of them was James Delaney, an artilleryman with the East India Company, one of the many soldiers who thronged the streets of Moulmein and sometimes attended services in English. Delany had been converted by Kincaid in 1831 and baptized in the Salween. In time Adoniram recognized his ability and planted in him a desire to become a minister. When he received his discharge in 1834, Adoniram and Sarah helped to arrange for his passage to America and enrollment in the theological seminary at Hamilton, New York. Sarah even gave him twenty-five dollars from her meager stock of money. He eventually settled in Appleton, Wisconsin, as a minister and remained there the rest of his life except for a period as chaplain with the Union Armies during the Civil War. But more than fifty years after leaving Moulmein, he still remembered Adoniram and Sarah with warm affection.

September 26, 1835, Adoniram completed his revision of the Old Testament. A little more than a month later, on October 31, Sarah gave birth to Abigail Ann Judson — the "Abigail" for his mother and sister, the "Ann" for the memory of Nancy. Commending little Abby to her two living namesakes, he revealed in a letter to Plymouth the next day how his feelings were beginning to soften.

DEAR MOTHER AND SISTER:

Since I have attained, in some measure, the great objects for which I came out to the East, and do not find it necessary to be so exclusively and severely engrossed in missionary labors as I have been for a long course of years, my thoughts and affections revert more frequently, of late, to the dear home where I was born and brought up; and now especially, after having been childless many years, the birth of a daughter and the revival of parental feelings, remind me afresh of the love with which my dear mother watched over my infancy, and of all the kindness with which she led me up from youth to man. And then I think of my earliest playmate, my dear sister, and delight to retrace the thousand incidents which marked our youthful intercourse, and which still stand, in the vista of memory, tokens of reciprocated brotherly and sisterly affection.

In another two months, exactly a month after he baptized the one hundredth member of the Burmese church — December 29, 1835 — he sent to press the last sheet of the Old Testament. "I used to think," he had written earlier to his mother and sister, "when first contemplating a missionary life, that, if I should live to see the Bible translated and printed in some new language, and a church of one hundred members raised up on heathen ground, I should anticipate death with the peaceful feelings of Old Simeon."

But of course, he did not. He had been away from home and in the Orient longer than any other missionary alive except three — Marshman, Robinson, and Moore of Serampore. But he certainly did not feel his life was over. In a sense, it was only beginning. Little Abby, already showing signs of becoming a "sweet, fat baby," perhaps might be only the first of a real family whom he devoutly hoped he could see grow up around him.

Toward the end of February, the ship *Louvre* arrived at Amherst from Boston with another load of missionaries. Among them was a visitor, a member of the missionary board, the first agent sent out for the specific purpose of surveying the work of the missionaries on the spot, to make suggestions and take home suggestions, and in general to gather information and settle points on which correspondence had proved inadequate. He was the Reverend Howard Malcom, pastor of Boston's Federal Street Church.

Malcom stayed with Adoniram and Sarah while he was in Moulmein and took one trip up the Dagyaing River with Sarah and another up the Salween with Adoniram in the intervals between excursions to all the missionary posts.

Of all the missionaries, it was Adoniram — by now a legendary figure to Americans — who interested Malcom most. Adoniram himself did not realize how Burmese he had become. But he had lived in Burma more than half his life now, and the Burmese language and customs were more familiar to him than those of his native land.

On his very first Sunday in Moulmein Malcom was struck with differences that Adoniram never even noticed. At morning worship with the Burmese congregation in the zayat, for instance, everyone sat — Adoniram on a chair, the audience on mats on the floor. Long horizontal bamboos about a foot and a half above the floor served as back rests. In prayer, the Americans knelt; but the Burmese merely leaned forward from their sitting position and, resting their elbows on the floor, placed their palms together. Sermon, prayer and all, were in Burmese except for one word which surprised Malcom when he heard it. As Adoniram concluded his prayer, every person in the congregation spoke the "Amen!" aloud.

About the middle of May Malcom left for Rangoon, from which place he made a voyage up the Irrawaddy to Ava, where Kincaid had been stationed several years. Missionaries were tolerated again in Ava — all but Adoniram. He had never been forgiven for his services to General Campbell in writing the Treaty of Yandabo, although many individuals remembered him with friendly feelings.

With Malcom's departure, Adoniram began a revision of the New Testament at which he worked steadily for months with only one interruption, a visit to the Tavoy station with Sarah and the Vintons. Toward the end of March, he sent the last sheet of the revised Gospel to the press. Just as Sarah had given birth to a girl shortly after the completion of the revision of the Old Testament, so now on April 7, 1837, after the revision of the New, she presented Adoniram with a son: Adoniram Brown Judson.

Both Abby Ann and the new baby flourished. A year later Adoniram wrote his mother and sister:

We have just carried Adoniram through the small-pox by inoculation. He had it very lightly, and is now quite recovered. He is one of the prettiest, brightest children you ever saw. His mother says that he resembles his uncle Elnathan. Abby is growing fast. She runs about, and talks Burman quite fluently, but no English. I am not troubled about her not getting English at present, for we shall have to send her home in a few years, and then she will get it of course. She attends family and public worship with us, and has learned to sit still and behave herself. But Fen, or Pwen, as the natives call him [the words meant *flower*], when he is brought into the chapel, and sees me in my place, has the impudence to roar out Bah (as the natives call father), with such a stentorian voice, that his nurse is obliged to carry him out again.

"Pwen" and Abby soon had another brother, Elnathan Judson, born July 15, 1838. With three children to care for, Sarah had to turn over her Peguan translation to another missionary, James Haswell. But she had produced one book, a life of Christ, and some tracts. Until Elnathan came, she had been able to keep on by letting "The little ones play in the verandah, adjoining the room where I sit all day with my Peguan translator."

Since I commenced this letter, I happened to look up, and saw a man leaning over the balustrade, looking at me very attentively. . . So I asked him what he wanted. He replied, he was looking to see me write. I immediately laid down my pen, invited him in, and he sat a long time listening to the truth.

For four years Adoniram's health had been excellent except for the low fever that came on him for a few months every fall. But late in 1838, after little Elnathan's birth, he began to be aware of a soreness in his lungs and throat. He acquired a painful cough. He began to lose his voice. Preaching became impossible and even ordinary conversation was difficult. Everyone in the mission suspected tuberculosis, the scourge which had carried off so many of the missionaries. The Moulmein doctors prescribed a long sea voyage; and on February 19, 1839, he embarked for Calcutta on the ship *Snipe*, Captain Spain.

It was the first time he had been away from Sarah and the children for more than a few days, and, as he wrote from shipboard, he felt "very low in spirits. It is sad, dull work to go to a place which you have no wish to see, and where you have no object scarcely to obtain. . . . The bosom of my family is almost the only bright spot that remains to me on earth."

Although the soreness persisted, his cough improved rapidly once the *Snipe* was at sea. Another passenger, "probably in an incurable consumption," scoffed at Adoniram "for pretending to be consumptive when I have only a slight cough, without raising anything. He says he has no doubt the trip will cure me."

Adoniram landed at Calcutta on the ninth of March. During a stay of three weeks he managed to visit all the Baptist missionaries in the city and a great many of other denominations. He spent one week end at Serampore at "old Mrs. Marshman's." The original trio of Serampore, Carey, Marshman and Ward — Ward had baptized Adoniram and Nancy so long ago — were all dead. Marshman's son John was still there, along with other missionaries. "But," observed Adoniram, "the glory has departed from Serampore."

Still, he enjoyed himself. For once he had no responsibilities except to take his watch to the watchmaker and get shoes and clothing made for the children, and this latter duty was taken over by his Calcutta hostess, Mrs. Ellis. His life was a pleasant round of breakfasts, teas, and evenings of conversation with various groups, which included opportunities to discuss the principles of translation and the standard text of the Bible with such men as Dr. William Yates, who was continuing Carey's work in translation. But he was lonely for his family — mostly for Sarah. He wrote her that the Calcutta missionaries. . .

. . . all thought that you must be a wonderful woman to make books as you do; and they all say, particularly Mrs. Ellis, how sorry they are that you did not come with me. I almost think that if I had known all things, and what good accommodations we could have had in this house, we should have come together.

And he continued with the intimate frankness of which he was capable:

I should have been *so* happy to have had you with me. If such exquisite delights as we have enjoyed with those now in paradise, and with one another, are allowed to sinful creatures on earth, what must the joys of heaven be? Surely there is not a single lawful pleasure, the loss of which we shall have to regret there. What high and transporting intercommunion of souls we may, therefore, anticipate, and that to all eternity! — intercommunion between one another, and between the "Bridegroom" and the "Bride," of which wedded love on earth is but a type and shadow.

It is not surprising that he wrote Sarah as soon as he learned the *Snipe* would sail again for Moulmein at the end of March:

How joyfully do I hope to embark! How joyfully retrace my way, and at length see the hills of Amherst and Maulmain rising in the distant perspective! And how joyfully do I hope to see your dear face, and take you to my loving arms, and find again "that home is home."

When he left Calcutta, Adoniram's throat and lungs seemed to have healed almost completely. But on the return trip he tried his voice by conducting worship in Burmese with Koon-gyah, a convert whom he had taken along on the trip. Although "the effort was very small, I was dismayed to find, in the course of the afternoon, the old soreness of lungs and tendency to cough come on." He made a partial recovery before reaching Moulmein, but no sooner had the rainy season begun in May than his throat was almost as bad as ever.

Some of the missionaries advised him to go to America for a year or two, but Adoniram felt "I should be of no use to the cause at home, not being able to use my voice." Perhaps, he thought in one of his characteristic fits of depression, "I have lived long enough. I have lived to see accomplished the particular objects on which I set my heart when I commenced a missionary life. And why should I wish to live longer? I am unable to preach; and since the last relapse, the irritation of my throat is so very troublesome that I cannot converse but with difficulty, or even sit at the table, as I have done to-day, and prepare copy for the press."

No one seemed able to diagnose his ailment. "My complaint, it is said, is very much like that of which the late Mrs. Osgood died — not common pulmonary consumption, but something in the throat which puzzled even her attending physicians, one of whom maintained, till near her death, that she was not in a consumption, and would recover."

He would prefer to die and to go to the reward he hoped was waiting for him — "But I shrink back again, when I think of my dear wife and darling children, who have wound round my once widowed, bereaved heart, and would fain draw me down from heaven and glory."

The growth of the children made him think of his own childhood and his mother and sister Abby still in Plymouth. He wrote them more often than he ever had before, telling them of his fears he would die before he could see the children grown up and happily settled. But he had passed the age of fifty. Abby Ann, the eldest, was only four, Adoniram Junior two, and Elnathan just a year old. It seemed unlikely he would live to see their adulthood.

> Abby Ann [he proudly wrote], has begun to go to school, with Julia Osgood, to Mrs. Simons. . . . Abby attends every

forenoon, and just begins to read words of one syllable. Adoniram says, "I want go school"; but he stays at home and deports himself like a little man. Elnathan has been very ill. We thought we should lose him; but he is now better, and begins to be bright and playful."

The end of the year there was a fourth child, Henry, born December 31, 1839, "but," remarked Adoniram, "there was no earthquake, nor anything."

From time to time Adoniram tried to resume preaching, but one sermon a week was all he could manage. Even this he had to deliver in a low tone of voice, barely audible to the listeners at the back of the chapel. For the rest, in the intervals of revising the Old Testament for the printer, he spent what time he could in personal conversation with converts and inquirers.

Early in February he made a brief visit to Rangoon, reading two books on Napoleon on the way. They struck him as "A history of infernals." But Rangoon was still unreceptive to missionaries. He and Ko En,[1] his native assistant, gave out about a thousand tracts when Ko En was ordered to the government house by the Ray-wun, the city governor. It was night before Captain Boothby, who had made the trip from Moulmein with Adoniram, and Mr. Staig, an Englishman who lived in the city, could see the Ray-wun and arrange for Ko En's release. All Adoniram could do was wait.

He was still unpopular with the Burmese government. They dared not touch him directly but they took every opportunity to strike through his native associates. Unable to distribute tracts, he could do little the rest of his stay but discuss religion with the Englishmen who lived in the city and the few remaining Burmese converts. In his spare time he walked out to the great golden Shwe Dagon pagoda, near the abandoned mission grounds and the grave of little Roger, who would have been a man of twenty-five by now if he had lived.

Rangoon had grown. Adoniram thought it was twice the size of Moulmein. But the war and the changes since had erased most of what had once been so dear. Memories of the early days of the mission and his life there with Nancy still stirred, but they no longer had the power to rack his heart. It was almost as if that one

[1] Formerly "Maung En."

Adoniram Judson had died with his wife and children. The new Adoniram Judson's affections centered in Moulmein, with Sarah and Abby Ann and the three little boys.

Meanwhile the church in Moulmein was declining again, with "many of the younger members falling into open sin, and the older ones cold and negligent of religious duties," as the wife of one of the missionaries wrote. On Adoniram's return he decided to do something about it. He wrote "a covenant of eight items, taken from the New Testament," which each church member was required to sign. As soon as the complete Burmese Bible had been printed and bound, he planned to make a formal presentation of a copy to the head of each family. He decided to increase the number of Sunday services for the Burmese to three.

These measures may have had some result, but probably his private meetings with church members were most effective. By now he knew the Burmese so well that they believed it was impossible to conceal a sin from him. Even at the moment "a culprit was exulting in fancied security, he would suddenly find an eye fixed upon him that was absolutely irresistible, and would be obliged, in spite of himself, to go to the teacher and confess."

One reason may have been that Adoniram never made accusations unless he was absolutely certain of the facts. Hearsay he ignored. When one member of the church would tell him of the faults of another, Adoniram would ask, "Have you told him his fault between you and him alone?"

Usually, naturally, the complainer had elaborate reasons for not doing so, but merely "thought the teacher ought to know."

"He knew us," recalled one of these Burmese Christians, "through and through, much better than we know ourselves. If we had done anything amiss, he called us pleasantly, talked so," — and he picked up a toy from the floor and ran his finger gently around the rim — "talked, and talked, and talked, till suddenly, before we knew it, he pounced upon us there" — and he struck his finger on the center of the toy — "and held us breathless till we had told him everything."

One Burmese woman remembered vividly how Adoniram had once sent for her when she planned to do something he thought might harm her spiritually. She refused to give up her project.

Finally Adoniram took a ruler from the table and marked a zigzag line on the floor. "Look here," he said. "*Here* is where you have been walking. You have made a crooked track, to be sure — out of the path half of the time; but then, you have kept near it, and not taken to new roads, and you have — not so much as you might have done, mind, but still to a certain extent — grown in grace; and now, with all this growth upon your heart and head, in the maturity of your years, with ripened understanding and an every day deepening sense of the goodness of God, *here you stand*." And he placed the tip of the ruler firmly on a point along the line. "You know where this path leads. You know what is before you — some struggles, some sorrows, and finally eternal life and a crown of glory. But to the left branches off another very pleasant road, and along the air floats, rather temptingly, a pretty bubble. You do not mean to leave the path you have walked in fifteen years — fifteen long years — altogether. You only want to step aside and catch the bubble, and think you will come back again; but *you never will.* Woman, think! Dare you deliberately leave this strait and narrow path, drawn by the Saviour's finger, and go away for one moment into that of your enemy? Will you? *Will you? Will you?*"

"I was sobbing so," the woman recalled, "that I could not speak a word. But he knew, as he always did, what I meant; for he knelt down and prayed that God would preserve me in my determination. I have made a great many crooked tracks since; but whenever I am unusually tempted, I see the teacher as he looked that day, bending over in his chair, the ruler placed on the floor to represent me, his finger pointing along the path of eternal life, his eye looking so strangely over his shoulder, and that terrible 'Will you?' coming from his lips as though it was the voice of God. And I pray, just as Peter did, for I am frightened."

## CHAPTER V
# Let the Will of God Be Done
### [ 1840–1845 ]

ON October 24, 1840, Adoniram sent to the printing house the revised last sheet of the complete Burmese Bible. Burma now had its first one-volume Bible. It was a big book, about twelve hundred pages in quarto size, and on the whole, Adoniram liked it. He felt the translation of the Old Testament still left a good deal to be desired, but the New Testament had been under sporadic revision for almost twenty years and he felt better satisfied with it "than I ever expected to be."

But as usual there was a certain frustration along with the sense of accomplishment. The Bible was ready, but, Burma proper being closed to missionary operations, there was no present way to get it into the hands of the people. There was talk about another war between Burma and England. Adoniram took little stock in it and thought the only preparation lay "in the wishes and imagination of certain individuals, here called 'the war party', who, having ruined their interest in Burma, see no hope of retrieving their affairs, but by a war." Nevertheless, the fact remained that the borders of Burma were shut; and when enough Bibles had been printed for immediate use, operations in the printing building ceased.

At any rate, one part of his life's work was done. He meant to spend the rest of it building and strengthening the native church. Once again he took personal charge of the native assistants, sending them out each day after a morning meeting to all the quarters of Moulmein and the neighboring villages to propagate the Gospel as best they could.

Presently he undertook another task. For some time the Board at home had been pressing him to prepare a dictionary when the Bible was out of the way. Long before, in 1819, he had made a crude one for his own use which had been printed in Serampore in 1826. But it was so incomplete as to be of little help to anyone who did not already know some Burmese. Adoniram's colleagues felt he could do more good with a new dictionary than in any other way. For a while he resisted, his heart not being in it. But when he found his voice constantly breaking down, he began to "dabble" at it, although the work gave him little pleasure because "it is such a chaotic affair, and seems to me so unmissionary."

Even the dictionary soon had to be set aside, however, for on March 8, 1841, Sarah gave birth to a stillborn boy who was named Luther. She "fell into a decline, and became quite confined to her bed." All the children had had whooping cough. Before they were fully recovered Abby Ann, Adoniram Junior and Henry came down with a "bowel complaint" which turned into dysentery.

An English officer, Captain Impey, offered Sarah and the children the use of his seashore house at Amherst, so that they could at least escape the worst of the hot season. Here they seemed to improve for a while. Then Sarah came down with a cold which turned into a fever. Abby Ann and Adoniram Junior grew worse until they were at the point of death. When the family returned to Moulmein they were sicker than when they had left.

Toward June the doctors, their colleagues and all their friends told Adoniram flatly that a sea voyage offered the only hope of recovery of Sarah and the two older children, although, as he wrote, "no one hardly hoped we could all get on board ship alive."

On June twenty-sixth they embarked for Calcutta. "How I managed to break up housekeeping, and pack up, and get my sick family and all the things aboard, I can hardly tell, now it is passed. But it was done somehow, and the children were stowed away in a range of berths I had made on one side of the cabin, and wife on the other, while I occupied a movable cot between the parties."

It was the season of the southwest monsoon. On the fourth night at sea the ship struck a shoal. Everyone aboard expected to drown. "I shall never forget my feelings," wrote Sarah later, "as I looked over the side of the vessel that night, on the dark ocean, and fancied ourselves with our poor sick, and almost dying children, launched on its stormy waves." Nevertheless, weak and distraught as she was, Sarah managed to fill a small trunk with things they might need in the lifeboat. Luckily, the tide was rising, the captain tacked, and after about twenty minutes the ship floated free.

In spite of the excitement, the whole family improved rapidly on the voyage. Adoniram took them to Serampore, where he rented "a nice dry house, on the very bank of the river, at forty rupees a month."

But, complained Sarah, the weather was very unfavorable. "At one time it was so oppressively hot, that we could scarcely breathe, and the next hour the cold, bleak winds would come whistling in, at the high windows, completely chilling the poor little invalids." In these circumstances, the children relapsed. Soon the doctors told Adoniram that another sea voyage was absolutely necessary. Just as he was looking for a ship bound for the Isle of France, the healthiest place in the East, Captain Hamlin of the *Ramsay*, a Moulmein acquaintance, offered a round trip there and then home to Moulmein. Thinking of the dangerous monsoon in the Bay of Bengal, Adoniram and Sarah hesitated. But the children were not improving, and there seemed no alternative.

The *Ramsay* was to sail in ten days. In the interval Sarah went to Calcutta with Abby and young Adoniram, "Pwen," to make purchases for the long voyage. Adoniram stayed in Serampore with Henry and Elnathan.

In Calcutta the two older children with Sarah promptly fell sicker. Besides his dysentery, Pwen was now attacked by fever. A physician managed to reduce the fever, but he warned Sarah that it would be all he could do to keep the children alive until they went to sea.

In Serampore, meanwhile, Elnathan grew feverish, and on July 27 little Henry suddenly became acutely ill. Until now Adoniram and Sarah had concentrated their attention on the older children, but next day, Henry was so much worse that Adoniram wrote Sarah she had better return. By evening Adoniram began to be afraid the baby might not live.

Sarah received his note the following morning. She decided to return at once, but the boat she hired could not start up the river until six o'clock, when the tide turned. At sunset, she put Abby and Pwen to bed aboard the boat and the boatmen began the long row.

It was at the neap tide; and for the last four or five miles the men were unable to row, but pushed the boat up the stream with long bamboos. The moon was setting, and I shall never forget the melancholy feelings which crept over me, while I watched the long shadows of the trees on the darkening waters.

At Serampore, meanwhile, the doctor told Adoniram he had given up hope for Henry, "and we ceased from giving him any more medicine, for he could keep none on his stomach for a single minute; and my only prayer was, that he might not die before his mother arrived."

Slowly the heavy hours passed. It was two in the morning before the boat finally nosed in at the bank by the house. Adoniram met Sarah at the door, embraced her, and told her Henry was dying. Sarah "flew to him, but oh, how changed! I had left him a bright little boy, running about the floor, with cheeks far from having lost their plumpness. Now, his eyes were dim, his cheek colourless, and his little form so emaciated, that, in the sincerity of my heart, I involuntarily exclaimed, 'Can this be Henry!' "

Sarah refused to believe he was dying, but in a few hours she had to admit there was no hope. Somehow Henry existed through the day, racked by occasional convulsions but still usually able to recognize his parents, raise his arms for help, and call out "Nahnee!" — for "naughty" — in protest. But late that night of July 30 he died. The next morning he was buried in the mission cemetery. He had lived one year and seven months.

A few weeks later they went on board the *Ramsay* and after one of the stormiest voyages Adoniram had ever experienced — during one series of squalls two topmasts, a topgallant mast and the jib boom with all their sails were carried away — they arrived at Port Louis on the Isle of France October 1, 1841.

It had been a remarkable trip in another respect. Captain Hamlin was an extremely pious man. He and Adoniram had alternated in conducting worship every evening; and Adoniram preached every Sunday. The home port of the *Ramsay* was Greenock, Scotland, and Captain Hamlin and most of the crew hailed from there. By the time the ship sailed into Port Louis nineteen members of the ship's complement, in addition to Captain Hamlin and Adoniram, had signed a covenant in the ship's Bible to try "to live as sincere

Christians ought to live, avoiding all known sins so far as possible, and striving to keep all the commands of God. . . ." Of the nineteen only two "yielded to temptation at Port Louis," and public worship was held on board the ship every Sunday while she lay at anchor.

By the time they had arrived at Port Louis, Abby Ann and Elnathan had made a complete recovery. Sarah was much better. Only young Adoniram did not improve. "The poor boy has been ill so long, that he seems to have stopped growing. . . . Elnathan, on the contrary, who has had but little illness, is nearly as thick as long, has a broad back and face, is actually stouter and stronger than his elder brother."

Food and clothing in Port Louis were "most exorbitantly dear," thought Adoniram. "A fowl is one dollar, and a common pair of shoes three dollars, and every other article almost in the same proportion." He felt certain that he would be deeply in debt by the end of the year.

They sailed from Port Louis November 1 and arrived in Moulmein December 10. Sarah was still thin but feeling well, and Adoniram Junior was at least convalescent, although his father doubted whether he could ever recover completely in the climate of Moulmein.

The religious atmosphere aboard the *Ramsay* had persisted. Captain Hamlin had been baptized as an infant, but at Moulmein, together with his first officer and two of the crew, he was baptized again by Adoniram. He had refused absolutely to accept any money from the Judsons for the cruise, although Adoniram estimated that a fair charge would have been more than two thousand rupees. Adoniram sent him four hundred rupees as " a small expression of gratitude," but the captain promptly returned it, "saying that he considered it a privilege to have been able to show some kindness to the servants of Christ." Not knowing what else to do, Adoniram finally wrote to the Corresponding Secretary of the Board and suggested that the Board send Hamlin a formal letter of thanks together with "what he would prize more than money — some valuable religious books, say a set of the Comprehensive Commentary, or such other as you shall think suitable."

February 21, 1842, a little more than two months after their return, the Judsons moved into a more comfortable house which had formerly been occupied by the Stevenses. At one corner Adoniram had a little guest house erected, "partly with a view to accommodate company, and partly in the hope that dear sister, if left alone, will think of coming out to see us. So, if the people of Plymouth get tired of you, you may be sure of a home with your most affectionate brother."

Although Adoniram did not yet know it, Abigail had already been left alone. Their mother had died January 31, 1842, in her eighty-third year, and been buried in the graveyard on Fort Hill, overlooking the harbor from the upper end of Leyden Street. But this he would not learn until late August. His thoughts had turned often to Abigail and his mother these years, and several times he had invited Abigail to Burma to live with the family. Sometimes he speculated whether after thirty years away from home he would recognize his mother and sister if he should see them. He felt sure he would know his mother, but he suspected that Abigail, who was in her twenty-second year when he left, might be too changed.

As for himself, he was certain his appearance had altered beyond recognition. He was mistaken. His features had aged surprisingly little through the years. His face was a little fuller. There were a few lines under the eyes and beside the mouth, but that was all.

But much of the Adoniram within the body's shell had changed more than once. The self-confident, almost arrogant, Adoniram had shattered under imprisonment and the impact of Nancy's death until nothing was left but a soul consumed by guilt and self-blame trying vainly to take refuge from painful reality in a mystical communion with God. This Adoniram had given away its property and income and renounced the world. Its attempt had not succeeded. The deeper Adoniram — the one which never changed — had eventually recognized the futility of the effort, come to terms with life, married Sarah Hall Boardman and created a new life out of healthy adult love. This altered Adoniram had a true humility more genuine than the spurious humility of the hermit days; the kind of humility, for instance, that gladly accepted frequent gifts of money from Abigail and his mother for the good of the family.

This new, warm, outlooking Adoniram, more realistically aware of himself and humanity and the world around him, honestly faced the fact that life must be lived to the end, that events can be molded by sheer will only a little, that what cannot be cured must be endured. This Adoniram kept on at the dictionary, disagreeable though the work was as measured by his real preference. This Adoniram, recognizing that Sarah was failing in physical health little by little, did his best within his limitations to foster the sense of security based on affection in his children.

For on July 8, 1842, Sarah gave birth to another son, this one named Henry Hall Judson in memory of the little Henry who had died at Serampore. Afterwards her health slowly worsened, although for a while she continued translating — she was working at *Pilgrim's Progress* — and trying to take care of the children.

They were quite a handful by now. Abby Ann was almost seven, the boy Adoniram five, Elnathan four. Abby could read anything easy and Adoniram could "read a little, but on account of his illness his education has been very much neglected." With the children of the other missionaries — James Haswell, Sarah and Edward Stevens, Julia Haswell and Brainerd Vinton — they made the mission compound a lively place.

There were stories, both secular and Biblical, to act out. They even had their own baptismal services, sometimes with young Adoniram acting as the minister, in imitation of his father. When Adoniram interrupted one of these he must have been reminded of his own childhood in Malden, when he gathered the neighborhood children around him and preached as he had seen his own austere father do.

December 18, 1843, Sarah gave birth to Charles Judson and on December 27, 1844, to Edward Judson. She had had eleven children in all — three by George Boardman, eight by Adoniram. Six of her children by Adoniram lived, and one by Boardman. That one, George Dana Boardman, Junior, had left Moulmein for the United States in 1834, when he was six. He was sixteen now, perhaps still dearest to her heart of all her children. But she had not seen him, nor he her, in all these ten years.

By now she was exhausted with childbearing. Her old dysentery had returned. The doctors shook their heads gravely and, as usual, prescribed a change of scene. With Abby Ann she made a trip to Mergui and Tavoy in February of 1845 at the invitation of the Civil Commissioner and his wife, while Adoniram tried to cope with the rest of the family.

From Mergui, Abby Ann sent a box of sea shells. "The boys are delighted with the shells," her father reported to her gravely, "and Henry has picked out some for his own; and they have agreed to give me for my share the large coral shell." Edward, he told her:

. . . has become a fat little fellow; I am sure you would not know him again. He begins to look pleased when he is played with. But he has not yet made any inquiries about his absent mother and sister. Indeed, I doubt much whether he is aware that he has any such relatives. Or if he ever exercises his mind on such abstruse topics, perhaps he fancies that black Ah-mah is his mother since she nurses him, and does not know what a fair, beautiful, fond mother he has at Mergui, who thinks of him every day. However, when he gets larger, we will tell him all about these matters.

When she returned, Abby Ann would have a new cot, too, a longer one. Her old one had been handed down to her brother Adoniram, his to Elnathan. And there was tragedy to report. "Both the kittens are dead, and the old yellow cat has been missing for several days." Most of all, though, her father concluded seriously, he wished that the Saviour would give her "his converting, sanctifying grace, and make you his own child." And He would if she helped, for *"If you trust in the Saviour and try to be good, he will make you good."*

Sarah returned in early April unimproved. Adoniram was appalled by her condition. It was far worse than he had dreamed. In desperation he wrote to the Corresponding Secretary of the Board in the United States:

The hand of God is heavy upon me. The complaint to which Mrs. Judson is subject has become so violent, that it is the unanimous opinion of all the medical men, and indeed of all our friends, that nothing but a voyage beyond the tropics can possibly protract her life beyond a period of a few weeks, but that such a voyage will, in all probability, insure her recovery.

. . . She is willing to die, and I hope I am willing to see her die, if it be the divine will; but though my wife, it is no more than the truth to say that there is scarcely an individual foreigner now alive who speaks and writes the Burmese tongue so acceptably as she does; and I feel that an effort ought to be made to save her life. I have long fought against the necessity of accompanying her; but she is now so desperately weak, and almost helpless, that all say it would be nothing but savage inhumanity to send her off alone. The three younger children, the youngest but three months and a half old, we must leave behind us, casting them, as it were, on the waters, in the hope of finding them after many days. The three elder, Abby Ann, Adoniram, and Elnathan, we take with us, to leave in their parents' native land.

So, all at once, his previous resolution never to return home was broken. All at once his children whom he loved were to be separated. He knew he would never again see them together, as one family. But, Sarah, mother of his children and first in his heart, must be saved. Any action, almost, seemed the wrong one. But there was no choice. The real question was: Could her life be saved? Or was it already too late?

The ship *Paragon* was preparing to sail for London late in April. In a rush Adoniram arranged for passage. Henry Hall, not quite three, he took to Mrs. Haswell in Amherst, along with his lancet and pox material, so they could be inoculated against smallpox. In Moulmein, the Osgoods took sixteen-month-old Charles and the Stevenses took four-month-old Edward, Mrs. Stevens nursing him herself along with her own baby.

The dictionary was a vexing problem. He had given it a couple of years now, and his notes and manuscripts were in such a state "that if I should die before this work is completed, or at least carried forward to a much more advanced state, all my previous labor would be nearly or quite lost." Among his native assistants, two were willing to make the trip with him. "They are both Christians, the one a settled character, a convert of long standing, formerly a government writer in Rangoon; the other a nephew of the late premier of the court of Ava, a person of noble extraction, and though not a tried Christian, I hope a sincere one."

With their help Adoniram thought he could continue work on the dictionary during the long months at sea and probably in the United States. His throat and lungs would prevent his preaching aloud, and in any case he felt he had so nearly forgotten spoken English that "I can scarcely put three sentences together in the English language. I must therefore beg the board to allow me a quiet corner, where I can pursue my work with my assistants, undisturbed and unknown."

On April 26, 1845, Adoniram, Sarah, Abby Ann, young Adoniram, Elnathan and the two assistants embarked on the *Paragon*. She set sail for Amherst on the third of May. The first month at sea was very rough, everyone was seasick, and Adoniram was busy most of the time taking care of Sarah. He seized what spare moments he had for the dictionary, but they were not many. The second month, Sarah began to improve and Adoniram "had most sanguine hopes for her recovery."

Soon after crossing the line, the *Paragon* sprung a leak. The captain decided to put in at Port Louis on the Isle of France. Meanwhile, the weather was beautiful. Many years later the boy Adoniram recalled how

. . . crossing the Indian Ocean, one night, when the wind had died away and the stars were out, the ship stood still in a calm, the family gathered on deck and Mother sang to the group, which included some of the sailors and officers of the ship. The hymn was "the Star of Bethlehem," beginning:

> When marshaled on the nightly plain
> 　The glittering hosts bestud the sky,
> One star alone of all the train
> 　Can fix the sinner's wandering eye.
> Hark! Hark! to God the chorus breaks
> 　From every host, from every gem,
> But one alone the Saviour speaks,
> 　It is the star of Bethlehem.

As the *Paragon* approached Port Louis, everything was optimism. Sarah was much better; the latter part of the voyage had been delightful. Adoniram and Sarah, discussing the matter together, began to believe she would not need Adoniram's care the rest of the way to London. Adoniram belonged in Burma. There would certainly be a ship bound for Moulmein at Isle of France. It would be hard to separate, but they could hope to meet each other, if not the children, in a few years.

This was the decision, as much Sarah's as Adoniram's. The thought brought to life Sarah's long-neglected habit of verse. Within sight of the Island she penciled, on a scrap of paper:

> We part on this green islet, Love,
>     Thou for the Eastern main,
> I, for the setting sun, Love —
>     Oh, when to meet again?
>
> My heart is sad for thee, Love,
>     For lone thy way will be;
> And oft thy tears will fall, Love,
>     For thy children and for me.
>
> The music of thy daughter's voice
>     Thou'lt miss for many a year;
> And the merry shout of thine elder boys,
>     Thou'lt list in vain to hear.

She went on through the next stanzas to mention Henry's death, when they had been together and could console each other; but at least, though parted, their souls could "hold communion sweet, O'er the dark and distant sea." And eventually, they would be reunited in Burma, and after that in heaven, never to be separated again. Meanwhile,

> Then gird thy armor on, Love,
>     Nor faint thou by the way,
> Till Boodh shall fall, and Burmah's sons
>     Shall own Messiah's way.

The *Paragon* dropped anchor on the fifth of July. Adoniram found a ship bound for Moulmein almost immediately. He sent the two assistants home by this vessel, while he tentatively engaged passage for himself on another which was to sail for Calcutta in two or three weeks. Meanwhile, they found an American vessel in port, the bark *Sophia Walker*. Captain Codman, her master, told Adoniram that Sarah and the children were more than welcome to transfer to her on better terms than they received aboard the *Paragon*. Codman was sailing directly home to Boston. Sarah could expect to land at "the very doors of her friends" a month sooner than if she went to England and transhipped there.

Adoniram accepted Codman's offer gratefully. Then, while they were waiting, Sarah suffered a relapse. In a few days she was deathly ill again, even worse than when they had left Moulmein. Adoniram could not possibly leave her now. Once more all their plans had to be changed. When the *Sophia Walker* sailed out of Port Louis on July 25, Adoniram was aboard.

After a while, in the cold weather off the Cape of Good Hope, Sarah grew much better and Adoniram had high hopes that she would recover. But soon she began to sink again. She would improve for a day or two at a time, but even Adoniram began to lose hope for her. As the vessel approached the island of St. Helena in late August, it was obvious she had not long to live.

The *Sophia Walker* arrived at St. Helena on the twenty-sixth of August and anchored in St. James's Bay. Sarah was sinking fast. She knew she was dying, and Adoniram had even expected she might have to be buried at sea. Adoniram spent most of his time in the cabin with her. Sometimes the children came in for a few minutes, sobered and apprehensive, but not quite able to grasp what was happening to their mother.

On one of these occasions he said: "My love, I wish to ask pardon for every unkind word or deed of which I have ever been guilty. I feel that I have, in many instances, failed of treating you with that kindness and affection which you have ever deserved."

"Oh," she said, "you will kill me if you talk so. . . . I . . . should ask pardon of you. . . . I only want to get well that I may have an opportunity of making some return for all your kindness, and of showing you how much I love you."

In spite of her tranquillity, she had some regrets. She told Adoniram she wished she could see Salem again after twenty years, and her son George, and the three children left in Moulmein. Between these wishes and her longing to leave life, she said, "I am in a strait between the two — let the will of God be done."

The last few days, wrote Adoniram later . . .

> Her mind became liable to wander; but a single word was
> sufficient to recall and steady her recollection. On the evening
> of the 31st of August, she appeared to be drawing near to the
> end of her pilgrimage. The children took leave of her, and re-
> tired to rest. I sat alone by the side of her bed during the hours
> of the night, endeavoring to administer relief to the distressed
> body, and consolation to the departing soul. At two o'clock in
> the morning, wishing to obtain one more token of recognition,
> I roused her attention, and said, "Do you still love the Saviour?"
> "O, yes," she replied, "I ever love the Lord Jesus Christ." I
> said again, "Do you still love me?" She replied in the affirma-
> tive by a peculiar expression of her own. "Then give me one
> more kiss;" and we exchanged that token of love for the last
> time. Another hour passed, life continued to recede, and she
> ceased to breathe. For a moment I traced her upward flight,
> and thought of the wonders which were opening to her view.
> I then closed her sightless eyes, dressed her, for the last time,
> in the drapery of death; and being quite exhausted with many
> sleepless nights, I threw myself down and slept.

In the morning he was awakened by the three children. They
were standing around their mother's body, weeping bitterly, and
crying out for her to answer them. Adoniram and everyone aboard
the ship had been prepared for Sarah's death. The captain and
friends on shore had even had mourning suits made for the children
and sent on board. But Abby Ann, young Adoniram and Elnathan
could not realize until this terrible September first exactly what
impended and what death meant. Now they knew.

But there was no time to waste. A coffin was sent from shore. A
minister of the town, the Reverend Mr. Bertram, offered a prayer
in the cabin, and the funeral party — a strange little flotilla towed
by a rowboat — followed Sarah's body, itself in a single boat behind
the one occupied by the oarsmen, to the land.

The shops of Jamestown were closed in respect as the funeral
procession passed silently through the town, the coffin now borne
forward by stalwart seamen, with four "chief women" of the island
serving as pallbearers.

A grave had been dug "in a beautiful shady spot" beneath a banyan tree in the cemetery next to that of Chater's wife, who had died like Sarah on the way home from Ceylon. Here Sarah was buried at about six in the evening. Bertram and the members of his congregation took Adoniram and the children into the home of one of them for a few hours.

A little later Adoniram and the children, exhausted with their grief, went aboard the ship. She set sail immediately. When the children, weeping afresh, woke him in the morning, they were in the open ocean, out of sight of the lonely rocky island.

> For a few days, in the solitude of my cabin, with my poor children crying around me, I could not help abandoning myself to heart-breaking sorrow. But the promise of the Gospel came to my aid, and faith stretched her view to the bright world of eternal life, and anticipated a happy meeting with those beloved beings whose bodies are mouldering at Amherst and St. Helena.

> It was a long, sad voyage home.

But the human spirit has nearly endless reserves of buoyancy. By the end of six weeks, when the *Sophia Walker* dropped anchor in Boston Harbor, the children were eagerly anticipating their future in the country they had never seen. Even Adoniram was looking forward, half with hope, half with dread, to the experiences that awaited him in his almost forgotten native land.

## CHAPTER VI

# America

## [ 1845 ]

THE United States Adoniram had left in 1812 had been not much more than a loose aggregation of seaboard states. It faced east, to Europe. Its only sources of wealth were in agriculture and foreign trade. The few rich men were great landowners or merchants. Although with the Louisiana Purchase the boundaries of the young nation had come to lie somewhere along the Rocky Mountains, the real frontier extended no farther than the Ohio and Mississippi Rivers. Its visible prosperity could be seen mostly in the proud, busy ports of Salem, Boston, New York and Philadelphia. Roads were few and poor. On land men traveled afoot, by stagecoach or on horseback; or along the shore by coastal sailing vessels.

When Adoniram returned in 1845, after an absence of thirty-three years, the nation had turned to face west. The frontiers were in Texas and along the course of the Missouri River, and in rapid movement. It was clear to everyone that all the continent from the Atlantic to the Pacific must belong to the United States, the claims and objections of Mexico notwithstanding. A major issue of the preceding year's presidential election campaign — which the dark horse James K. Polk had won — had been the annexation of Texas; a major slogan, "Fifty-four Forty or Fight," with reference to the nation's northwest boundaries. The news of Polk's nomination had been flashed to Washington by the new electric telegraph. Manufacture had become a great source of wealth. Whole new industrial cities, like Lowell, in Massachusetts, had sprung up around water power sites along the rivers. The clanking machinery in other factory towns was turned by hissing steam. A new class of wealthy men had emerged — the industrialists. There was swelling an intoxicating consciousness here and there of the unbelievable mineral wealth —

copper, coal and iron, perhaps even precious metals — that lay beneath the earth. There were many roads now; the northeastern
states were crisscrossed with canals; fleets of steamboats were plying
the Great Lakes and the Mississippi; and railroads radiated out from
all the large cities, extending tentacles that would in time, everyone
knew, link together the whole sprawling country.

There were new problems. In 1812 it had been the freedom of
American ships to sail the high seas as a neutral while the great
powers of England and France were at war. Now, as the great
period of territorial expansion approached its climax, the problem
of slavery was beginning to loom darker and huger. The nation
was already starting to divide. Even the foreign missionary movement had begun to feel it. There had been an acrimonious debate
over whether Christianity sanctioned the owning of slaves. Some
Northern churches and individuals had refused to contribute to
foreign missions if their money went into a common treasury with
that of slaveholders. At a state convention, Alabama supporters of
Baptist missions sent to the national headquarters resolutions de-
manding "explicit avowal that slaveholders are eligible and entitled
equally with nonslaveholders" to appointment as missionaries by
the Mission Board. The Board replied in as conciliatory way as
possible, but did feel constrained to say that "if anyone should offer
himself as a missionary having slaves, and should insist on retaining
them as his property, they could not appoint him."

The Southern churches promptly severed their ties with the
Board and formed "The Southern Baptist Convention" — whereupon a special session of the General Convention was called in New
York in September of 1845, while Adoniram was at sea, and organized the "American Baptist Missionary Union."

When the *Caravan* had set sail for India in 1812, Salem's vessels
were among the fastest and largest under the American flag and
Salem itself one of the most prosperous ports in the country. Now
in 1845 Salem, its harbors too shallow for the new fast clippers, was
becoming a backwater, already beginning to live in the memory
of past glories.

As for those four eager young missionaries who had sung hymns
joyfully together in their cabin the night before the *Caravan* sailed,
three had long been dead. Harriet Newell had slept in the cemetery

at Port Louis on the Isle of France for more than thirty years; Samuel Newell in Bombay for twenty-four; Adoniram's Nancy under the hopia tree at Amherst for nineteen.

Of the four signers of the petition to the General Association which Adoniram had presented at Bradford the day he met Nancy, Adoniram believed himself to be the only survivor. Mills had died at sea in 1818, returning from Africa. Of the two whose names had been removed in order not to frighten the Association with too many applicants at one time, Richards had died in Ceylon in 1822 and Rice in 1836, never having resumed service as a foreign missionary. Rice had worn himself out in the United States promoting foreign missions and Columbia College in Washington. Financial difficulties of the college had brought him under reproach, and his life had ended in sadness. Gordon Hall, who had been ordained at the Tabernacle in Salem with Adoniram, Nott, Newell, and Rice, had died in India in 1826.

To Adoniram, as the *Sophia Walker* dropped anchor in Boston Harbor, it seemed as if they had all gone: all his early associates. Only he was left, with his three motherless children who had never seen their homeland. And of his own boyhood family only his sister Abigail lived on in Plymouth.

He felt like another Rip Van Winkle. Nothing was familiar, everything was strange. He expected to make arrangements for the children and settle down in quiet obscurity, perhaps with Abigail, until it should be time to return. He expected no attention. Who knew him any more except those with whom he had corresponded? He expected to be ignored, and he welcomed the thought.

He could not possibly have been more mistaken.

Before going on shore, he had been worried about where to look for a place to spend the night. This new, bustling, unfamiliar Boston intimidated him.

But as he stepped off the ship he found crowds of people waiting to receive him. The *Boston Traveller* reported his arrival. "A hundred houses" were "at once thrown open to him," a hundred families competed for the honor of receiving him.

As he shyly received homage, murmuring his thanks in the low, husky whisper that was all his throat permitted, he began to feel as intimidated by these crowds of welcomers and their all but worshipful welcome as he had been by Boston itself. He began to realize with a certain feeling of discomfort that he had become even while living a legendary figure of awesome proportions.

The *Caravan* leaving Salem had left in its wake the seed of that legend. The almost foolhardy daring of that first foreign missionary attempt, the youth and sincerity of the young missionaries, something almost pathetic in their determination to risk everything to bring the Gospel to the heathens, had been discussed far and wide. For every one who thought the missionaries merely zealots, a score were stirred with sympathy. The death of Harriet Newell at nineteen had quickened the growth of the legend. Within a short time Leonard Woods, Abbot Professor of Christian Theology at Andover Theological Seminary, had brought out a memoir of Harriet telling, largely through her letters and extracts from her journals, the whole story of her life and death. The memoir went into edition after edition.

The religious magazines — the *Panoplist,* the *American Baptist* and other publications — had been steadily printing every scrap of missionary news that came into their hands. Nancy's *Particular Relation of the American Baptist Mission to the Burman Empire* had been followed after her death by Knowles' *Memoir of Mrs. Ann Judson,* which, like Harriet's memoir, had gone into many printings and been read by hundreds of thousands. At every religious fireside its descriptions of the horrors of Ava had been read aloud with a breathless excitement few novels could hope to arouse. The lives of the missionaries — particularly those of Adoniram, Nancy and Sarah — had come to be viewed as a never-ending story, packed with hair-raising episodes, pathetic scenes of grief which brought tears to the eye, and periods of suspense lasting as long as two years — such as the one when Adoniram and Nancy were out of communication with the world during the Anglo-Burmese war. And, most exciting of all, *it was all true.* And no one knew how it would "come out in the end."

Adoniram had been the subject of thousands of sermons, the theme of hundreds of thousands of prayers. Thousands had named their children for him. The country was full of men and women who had been hearing all their lives about the great missionary

Adoniram Judson, the saint of Burma. But although the Judson legend had been growing for thirty-three years, few now living had ever seen the man himself. This was their chance. Scarcely any celebrity, any public figure, any hero, could hope to rival the interest aroused by the visit of Adoniram Judson to the United States.

He had no sooner arrived that October Wednesday in 1845 than a public meeting of welcome was arranged at the Bowdoin Square Church in Boston. The meeting was to be held Friday. There was no time for public announcements. The news spread by word of mouth. Nevertheless the church was packed and even the aisles filled long before time for beginning.

As Adoniram sat on the platform with the dignitaries the sheer size of the crowd almost appalled him. He was tired and sick, the cold weather had aggravated his sore throat, he was still exhausted with grief for Sarah and worry for the children. Perhaps worst of all, as he heard himself the sole theme of everything that was said, saw himself the attraction, he began to suspect that he was simply being shown off as a curiosity, like an exotic wild animal. But that thought he dismissed as unworthy. Certainly nothing in this particular meeting could lend credence to such an idea.

The meeting produced one surprise. After a psalm and a prayer, Dr. Daniel Sharp, pastor of the Charles Street Church and president of the Mission Board, gave an address of welcome. Adoniram rose to reply. But the penetrating voice of his youth was gone. His husky whisper could not be heard, and William Hague, pastor of the Federal Street Church, stepped to his side and repeated his expressions of thanks sentence by sentence. When Adoniram sat down, Hague continued with a review of Adoniram's career. But as Hague spoke, heads began to turn. An elderly gentleman was slowly working his way from the back of the church through the crowded aisle to the platform. He mounted it and crossed over to Adoniram, whose attention had been attracted by the slight disturbance. Suddenly he recognized the man, rose to his feet, clasped him by the hand and embraced him.

It was Samuel Nott. Adoniram had thought him long dead, but here he was, still alive. He and Adoniram were the only two survivors of that first missionary group of 1812. Together, he and

Adoniram had laid down the ultimatum to the American Board in 1811. When others questioned Adoniram's motives in becoming a Baptist, in Calcutta long ago, Nott had defended him. Ill health had forced Nott to leave India in 1816. Now he was pastor of the Congregational Church in Wareham.

As man after man on the platform joined the group around the two men, Hague stopped in midspeech. Dr. Sharp introduced Nott to the audience. The poignancy of the reunion and the memories it aroused brought tears to many of the watchers. Nott himself was shaken by emotion as he recalled aloud that he gave Adoniram "the right hand of fellowship" as part of that ordination ceremony long ago in the Tabernacle Church in Salem. When Adoniram became a Baptist, he did not withdraw it.

Nott was well aware — more than Adoniram, because he had been in the United States since 1816 — of the bitterness of some of the controversies that had raged at home over Adoniram. Adoniram's impetuousness had offended some. His conversion to Baptism had outraged others. Still others had insisted that Samuel Mills was the father of American foreign missions, not Adoniram. For that matter, neither Mills nor Adoniram had ever claimed the honor, but each had been praised by some overzealous supporters and blamed by his detractors as if he had.

The fires of those arguments had faded long since, but the ashes were still warm. Therefore, said Nott to the audience, what impressed him most this night was that, out of the five who went to India, three were dead. Soon the remaining two would be gone, but the thing they went out for, the Word of God, would stand fast and eventually prevail. And that was what mattered rather than the details of creed. As to whether Adoniram Judson or Samuel Mills was the originator of foreign missions, "he deemed it a very trifling question. . . . Samuel Nott, Jr., certainly was not. They were all mere boys, but with God's blessing on their puerile efforts, they had begun an influence which is spreading over the world."

These conciliatory reflections of Nott, a Congregationalist speaking from a Baptist platform, probably summed up the conclusions of all but a few diehards. They *had* been boys when they went out. Their mistakes had been the mistakes of youth's inexperience. But with all their inexperience — perhaps partly through the sheer foolhardiness it gave them — they had begun something much bigger than themselves. And as for their mistakes — the mistakes had all been paid for many times over.

The remarkable meeting brought forth one more surprise. The audience had no sooner settled down than still another missionary pioneer was discovered in its midst. He was Hiram Bingham, a graduate of Andover Theological Seminary in the class of 1819, who with his classmate Asa Thurston went out that same year on the first mission to the Sandwich Islands — Hawaii, "Owhyee." The crowd must have returned home that night more than satisfied, for had they not seen, besides Adoniram Judson, the only living associate of his earliest days and one of the two first missionaries to the scented islands of the Pacific?

As for Adoniram, he spent a sleepless night. The crowds and the excitement were cause enough, but they were not all. There was rising in him a feeling of distaste for all this adulation and praise. He could not believe it wholly sincere. He knew himself too well to believe he deserved it. He could not preach or speak because of the condition of his throat. He could only allow himself to be looked at. With disgust, he felt he was becoming merely an exhibit — and he began to feel hostility for those who wanted to stare.

The meeting at the Bowdoin Square Church was only the beginning. There seemed to be a new welcome ceremony every night. Even his days were not free. His own Board held a special meeting of welcome for him October 20, 1845, the Monday after his arrival. He was suffocated by visitors.

About a week later he fled north to see the Hasseltines and consider what to do with his children, and perhaps to visit Ralph and Abiah Hall, Sarah's mother and father. A few years later they were living in Skaneateles, New York, but at this time might still have been in Salem.

He traveled to Salem on the railroad which had been built north from Boston in 1838. Salem, like everything else, had changed. The old life around the wharves was gone. The railroad was becoming the commercial center of gravity in the town with the result that the Tabernacle Church, where he had been ordained, was now on the fringe of the business section. The railroad station, a small

wooden structure, stood where the central dock of the South River
had been. Most of the land had been filled in since. A bell, originally
a convent bell captured at the siege of Port Royal, announced the
departure of each train. Across the way stood an old red warehouse
which served as waiting room and ticket office.

Almost all the people he knew in Salem were gone. Lucius Bolles,
who had been secretary of the Mission Board, had died only the
preceding year. Samuel Worcester, Adoniram's indefatigable friend
and supporter, had been in his grave for more than twenty years.
But the Tabernacle Church still stood. Revisiting it, he found that
the settee on which the candidates for ordination had been seated
was still there, and he sat on it once more.

From Salem he took the stage to Bradford. John Hasseltine,
Nancy's father, was dead but his wife still survived in the comfortable old homestead between the church and Academy, an old
woman of eighty-four with a single year of life ahead of her. Nancy's
sisters Mary and Abigail Hasseltine were still living with their
mother, and Abigail had been head of Bradford Academy, now
grown much larger, for many years.

Bradford, too, had changed. It seemed to have mellowed and
slowed down, like an aging person. It was now merely a quiet
suburb of Haverhill, across the river. Haverhill had burst out of its
village swaddling clothes to become a booming industrial city, its
factories stretching up and down the river humming and clacking
with machinery.

Adoniram arrived in Bradford with a severe cold, but there was
to be no rest. A huge meeting had been scheduled in his honor in
Haverhill for the night after his arrival. He dreaded it, but felt that
"as it has been appointed, I suppose I must attend." But he begged
the secretary of the Board "that I may be excused from attending
any more such meetings, until I get a little better." After the meeting and the continuous stream of callers, which spoiled most of
the pleasure he had expected from Bradford, he meant to go to
Boston for a few days and then to Worcester. He thought wist-
fully that "if I could spend the next Sabbath alone in some chamber,
I should feel it a great privilege, both as a refreshment to the soul
and a relief to the body."

All this while he had been trying to decide what to do with his three children, young Adoniram, Elnathan and Abby Ann. Shaken and insecure among strangers in a strange country, they could not help feeling neglected as their father was called away for meeting after meeting, his time taken by visitor after visitor. People were kind to them, but they needed their father. He had decided against taking them back to Burma. He could not even take them on the many trips he foresaw himself soon making around the country. He finally decided to place the two boys with Dr. and Mrs. Newton, friends in Worcester with whom George Boardman, Jr., Sarah's son, was staying, and to leave Abby Ann with his sister Abigail in Plymouth.

On the thirteenth of November he took the boys to Worcester on the railroad, while he sent Abby Ann down to Plymouth in the care of his sister Abigail. It may have been on this day, when he took his seat in the cars at Worcester after leaving the weeping boys, that a newsboy came along with the daily papers. Adoniram accepted one and began to read. The boy stood waiting for the money until a lady sitting with Adoniram told him the boy expected to be paid for his paper. "Why!" exclaimed Adoniram in surprise, "I have been distributing papers for nothing in Burma so long that I had no idea the boy was expecting any pay."

A few days later he visited Abby Ann at Plymouth and from there went down to Providence for a great meeting. The next day he spent at Brown University where the whole student body assembled to see him. The Philermenian Society, to which he had belonged, held a special meeting for him and so did the Society for Missionary Inquiry.

From Providence he went to New York, where the Triennial Convention of the Baptist Church was holding a special session. Here he saw at first hand how the issue of slavery was not only dividing the country but even disruptively affecting the foreign missionary movement.

There was already a debt for missions of some forty thousand dollars which weighed heavily. The disaffiliation of the Southern churches meant that this had to be assumed by the Northern group, to which it was obvious most of the missionaries abroad would adhere.[1] As a result, there was talk of contracting missionary activities,

---

[1] Eventually they all did, except a Reverend Mr. Shuck, who was stationed in China.

and even abandoning the Arakan mission. This was too much for Adoniram, and he protested. As his voice failed, Dr. Spencer H. Cone, who, while they were both shut up in Baltimore by the British Army in 1815, had heard Luther Rice tell about Adoniram's conversion, repeated his offer to go himself to Arakan if the Baptists were willing for him to give up the dictionary. Kincaid and Abbot, who had served with Adoniram in Burma, were present, and they added their words to Adoniram's. It was enough. The final decision was to enlarge the missionary movement, not to abandon stations.

At the end of November, a few days after returning to Boston from New York, Adoniram received a letter from Moulmein. Little Charlie had died early in August at the age of a year and a half. While they were at sea and Sarah's life had still a month to run before ebbing away, little Charlie was already gone. Perhaps, thought Adoniram, when Sarah arrived in heaven she was pleasantly surprised to find Charlie, a baby angel, waiting there for her.

This left only two of the children in Burma — Henry and Edward, the youngest, still not quite a year old. With Abby Ann at Plymouth and the two older boys at Worcester, he had done what he could for his children in America. His thoughts began to turn once more to his duty in the East — not only to his children, but to the unfinished dictionary.

## CHAPTER VII

# Fanny Forester
## [ *1845–1846* ]

IN December, Adoniram was invited to attend a series of missionary meetings in Philadelphia. To make sure of his accepting, the Reverend Dr. A. D. Gillette of the Eleventh Street Baptist Church of that city visited him in Boston with an offer to accompany him on the trip.

Between New York and Philadelphia the train was held up for two or three hours by a railroad accident. Gillette, a solicitous companion, borrowed for Adoniram's entertainment a copy of a newly published book which he saw in the hands of a friend. He had read it, he said, and it was attracting a great deal of deserved attention. Adoniram looked at the cover doubtfully. It read *Trippings in Author Land,* and it bore the name of a woman, Fanny Forester. He did not think he would be interested. An elderly missionary, a scholar — he had no interest in tripping through morasses of gush about author land. But there was nothing else to do.

He took the book and idly riffled the pages. It consisted of sketches — half brief stories, half impressions — with titles such as "The Bank Note," "Nickie Ben," "The Chief's Daughter." Here and there a phrase caught his eye. In a few minutes he was absorbed. The subjects may have been trivial, but the writing had a lightness and vividness that held the reader. Fanny Forester, whoever she was, had the ability to create reality.

Gillette had left Adoniram when he saw the book had his attention. On his return he found Adoniram enthusiastic. "Who is Fanny Forester?" he asked. "This writing has great beauty, great power." He repeated emphatically, "Great beauty and power."

Her real name was Emily Chubbo[u]ck, Gillette told him. She had been a teacher at a seminary in Utica, in central New York. A few years ago she had attracted the attention of N. P. Willis, editor of the *New York Mirror*. Willis — worldly wise, superficially frivolous, with a keen eye for what women liked to read, nevertheless possessed taste, and integrity — the latter derived perhaps from his youth in Boston, where his father had been a deacon on "Brimstone Corner," or perhaps from the sober influence of his undergraduate days at Yale. It was Willis who had told Emily Chubbock, when she bewailed the fact that she was getting nowhere in literature, "How can you expect anything better? Who will read a poem signed 'Chubbock'? Sign yourself 'Fanny Forester' and you will see the change." Whether or not the change of name was responsible, the name of Fanny Forester had skyrocketed to literary fame within the past two years.

To Adoniram, Fanny Forester's bright personality was a refreshing contrast to the unrelieved sadness and soberness of recent months. He would willingly exchange a few hours of conversation with a woman like that for any number of panegyrics at missionary meetings. Ever since Sarah's death he had felt himself almost dead. People spoke of him in his presence as if he *were* dead and they giving funeral orations. Even the farewells to his children were like deathbed leavetakings. Now Fanny Forester's lively pages flaunted a colorful banner of persistent life and happiness. She knew death and misery existed. That was plain in several of the sketches. But the pert life in her character defied them.

It would be too much to expect a woman like this to have religious feelings. Adoniram asked Gillette, "Is she a Christian?"

When Gillette assured him that she was, Adoniram put his wishes into words. "I should be glad to know her. A lady who writes so well ought to write better. It is a pity that such fine talents should be employed upon such subjects."

Gillette smiled. "You can meet her soon and tell her yourself. She is a guest at my house."

Arrangements had been made for Adoniram to stay at the home of Mr. and Mrs. W. S. Roberts, but he wasted no time in calling on the Gillettes the next morning, Christmas Day. Sure enough, the authoress was at home. In fact, that very moment she was being vaccinated against smallpox. When Adoniram was led into her presence and introduced, he found her informally but smartly garbed in morning dress, one arm bared, while the doctor made ready to introduce the vaccine.

Adoniram studied her silently during the vaccination. He saw a slender, self-possessed, dark-eyed woman of middle height. She seemed to be in her late twenties—thirty at most. Her nose and mouth were too large for beauty, her lips too thin. But she had something better than beauty — life, and a humor that bordered on playfulness. As Emily Chubbock she displayed the same spirited personality that appeared in her writing as Fanny Forester. Adoniram forgot the homeliness of her features as he saw their response to the emotions that lighted them. She seemed to find fun even in a vaccination.

No sooner had the doctor put away his instruments and left the room than Adoniram led her to the sofa, sat down beside her, and said he wanted to talk to her. With a smile, she replied she would be delighted and honored.

Bluntly Adoniram asked, "How can you reconcile it with your conscience to employ such noble talents in writing so little useful and spiritual as those sketches I read?"

Emily was anything but meek. Ordinarily, such an abrupt attack would have brought a sharp retort. But like most people she found it impossible to take offense when the attack came from Adoniram. Respect alone would have put a leash on her tongue, but it was not respect which made her heart soften to him so suddenly. It was that peculiar candor of Adoniram's, the warmth and sweetness he was capable of radiating as a lamp radiates heat and light.

She understood at once that he was not blaming her — he really wanted to know. She told him honestly how she came to be Fanny Forester. Her childhood in central New York State, near Hamilton, had been one of poverty and bitter struggle. Her father, a hard worker, had never been able to make ends meet. His large brood of children never knew from one day to another whether they would have anything to eat. Emily had to go to work at the age of eleven in a woolen factory splicing rolls. With unbelievable effort she somehow managed to acquire an education of sorts, taught here and there, and finally settled down in the Utica Female Seminary, which was kept by two sisters with the interesting names of Urania and Cynthia Sheldon. Here she quickly manifested an extraordinary literary talent.

After a good many of her products had appeared in local newspapers, it occurred to her that she might be able to earn money by writing. Her first book — a little volume of moral stories for children called *Charles Linn* — sold fairly well and earned her something more than fifty dollars. Popular magazines began publishing her work. Book followed book and eventually she was able to buy a small mortgaged home for her parents, who were now almost entirely dependent on her support. But her earnings only became substantial when she took on the name and literary character of the frivolous Fanny Forester. As Fanny, her writings were not quite the kind she preferred but they were not immoral. And could Adoniram blame her, she asked him seriously, turning toward him on the sofa, if she felt it necessary to use her only talent this way for her parents' sake?

No, Adoniram admitted, he could not blame her. She might not be employing her talents to the highest purpose, but certainly she had the best of reasons for using them as she did. He changed the subject. He had been looking, he told her, for someone who could prepare a memoir of Sarah. It was this, partly, that had made him want to meet her as soon as he read her book. Would she be interested in helping him?

Emily would, of course. A devout Baptist since girlhood, she had thought of becoming a missionary herself when she was twelve or thirteen and read about the tragic deaths of Nancy and little Maria. Once in her teens she had even written to her pastor inquiring how to go about becoming a missionary. She had followed the careers of the Burma missionaries ever since.

The two promptly set to work discussing the matter — discussions that in a day or so were taking up nearly all their waking time. In spite of their different experiences, they seemed to have everything in common. Her religious faith was not equal to his own — but neither had been Sarah's in her early years with him. And Emily certainly had an innate goodness and determination to do right that formed a solid foundation for the building of faith in the future. Within a few weeks, probably January 5, 1846, the day he noted in a personal chronology as having "commenced an acquaintanceship with Emily Chubbock," Adoniram made up his mind that she should not only write Sarah's biography — she should take Sarah's place.

The decision made, he acted in the same quick way as always. In the most vivid language at his command he painted for her the East where he had worked so long: rich, beautiful, ornamented, but peopled with hungry souls. He described his life there: full of labor, dangers and frustrations, but completely satisfying because he was filling those souls with the truth and guiding them to heaven.

Emily listened with fascination. No man whom she fully respected had ever made love to her. Now here was the great Dr. Judson, revered around the world, offering her the most useful of all work, offering to take care of her, offering to lift her burdens, offering love. And offering with a fire and impetuosity and charm that seemed to belong more to a man of thirty than of fifty-seven. For that matter, he looked like a man of thirty. His hair was still untouched by gray. His movements were active as a youth's. Only the huskiness of his voice betrayed the ravages of his life. But that husky voice did not lack passion, and volume was unnecessary. After all, she was not a congregation.

She felt she could not withstand him, yet his proposal frightened her. She was a public figure. What would Mr. Willis and the literary coterie in New York say when they learned that Fanny Forester — gay, witty, frothy Fanny Forester — meant to give up a career just at the rise, and bury herself among the heathen of Burma? Worse, she felt no real call to be a missionary. Entering such a life seemed like entering a kind of death.

Adoniram brushed aside her objections. She could not deny they were a completely congenial pair. Their tastes, their natural gifts, even their exuberant humor, matched. His children needed a mother. He needed a companion. She revered him; but most of all he called forth her love.

Less than a month after their meeting he sent her the watch which had been worn by Nancy and Sarah, and with it a formal proposal:

*January 20, 1846*
I hand you, dearest one, a charmed watch. It always comes back to me, and brings its bearer with it. I gave it to Ann when a hemisphere divided us, and it brought her safely and surely

to my arms. I gave it to Sarah during her husband's lifetime (not then aware of the secret), and the charm, though slow in its operation, was true at last.

Were it not for the sweet sympathies you have kindly extended to me, and the blessed understanding that "love has taught me to guess at," I should not venture to pray you to accept my present with such a note. Should you cease to "guess" and toss back the article, saying, "Your watch has lost its charm; it comes back to you, *but brings not its wearer with it*" — O first dash it to pieces, that it may be an emblem of what will remain of the heart of

Your devoted,
A. JUDSON.

It was the kind of letter a Fanny Forester might have written; certainly not what one would expect of the dean of American foreign missionaries.

Emily accepted the watch.

Four days later she wrote to Miss Sheldon at the Female Seminary in Utica, "My good doctor has now gone away, and I have just said to him the irrevocable *yes,* though I must acknowledge that I have acted it slightly before."

That same day, Adoniram left for Washington and Richmond, Virginia, while Emily waited for the temperature in Utica to rise above zero so that she could go home and make the necessary arrangements for embarking on her new life.

The engagement raised a storm of talk over the country, much of it — perhaps most of it — critical. Everywhere Adoniram had gone, people had insisted on regarding him as something more than human. On platform after platform he was so extolled, much to his own distaste. In reaction, he had been cold, almost insulting, to the men and women who persisted in viewing him as a plaster saint. Time after time he had disappointed audiences by refusing to discuss his adventures and instead repeating to them the simple message of the Gospel they heard every Sunday from their own ministers. They could see for themselves, so he thought, that he was a man like other men, with a family and family cares, with the frailties and foibles of other men. Nevertheless, many preferred the legend to the man.

Now they learned that the saintly Dr. Judson planned to marry a woman scarcely more than half his age! Worse, a woman who wrote light fiction for popular magazines! Still worse, a woman who wrote under an *assumed name!*

The legend was shattered. Those who had held to it most blindly now savagely took most pleasure in attacking the fragments, forgetting that Adoniram had children still in Moulmein who needed a mother, overlooking the fact that Emily Chubbock had begun her literary career with a series of religious books and that she turned to polite literature only when she had to do something to support her parents.

The criticism from the religious world was matched by that from the literary. Editors and readers alike blamed Adoniram for bewitching Emily by some dark sorcery. They thought of him almost as a seducer. How else could she be induced to give up her brilliant career at its most promising moment in order to bury herself in the Orient with a man old enough to be her father?

By the time the full storm broke, Emily had settled down in Utica while Adoniram continued his travels. They wrote every day. She was less prepared than he to withstand the gossip. Early in April she wrote disconsolately:

> I wish they would just let me alone. Give me some place to be quiet in, if it be only a hovel, and I will be grateful. I am heart-sick now, and if the feeling be not wicked, would rather die than live. It is not enough that I have resolved on a step which is almost death — forgive me, dearest — I am troubled, and do not consider what I write. I shall be very happy with you, I know; but now I am most miserable. It seems that all New York is alive about the affair. It is the common subject of conversation on steamboat and in hotel, in parlor and in grog-shop. H. Anable, who has just returned from New York, says there is no place or circle where my name is not heard. There is even talk of preventing such an insane proceeding as F. F.'s "throwing herself away." They say such a senseless sacrifice is unparalleled. . . .

Adoniram, at his best under opposition, took a certain amount of wry amusement out of the furor. He was staying with the children at Plymouth and a letter of his crossed hers:

The children are mightily amused at their papa's marrying Emily Chubbock. Abby Ann had found out from some neighbors that it was Fanny Forester: but she is quite sure that Fanny Forester must be very good, since she wrote *Effie Maurice*, one of her favorite books. Our affair, I find, has been, not the town-talk but the country-talk, for a fortnight or month past. The Philadelphia announcement, that "marriage was intended between the Rev., etc., and the dear, delightful Fanny Forester," opened people's eyes a bit. Even that slow, deliberating —— committed it to memory, and was able to repeat it verbatim, which I made him do. He did not know, not he, but I had found a jewel, but timidly inquired whether you would be arrayed in other jewels and finery! — evidently fearing that you would come dancing through the country, like other Fannies, in the style laid down in Isaiah, chap. iii. . . . The truth is, it is not strange that there should be a great wonderment; we calculated on it. But we need not care for it. We can both of us, perhaps, afford to be pretty independent of it. And we know it will soon pass away, and still more, that a reaction will probably take place. . . .

Perhaps Emily sometimes thought uncomfortably that it was the experience of his two previous marriages that enabled Adoniram to keep so cool about the whole matter. She continued to protest that she felt as if she were "set up in a pillory. . . . It does not agree with my mental or moral constitution to occupy such a conspicuous position. I grow unamiable every day, and shall be a perfect Xantippe before we get to heathendom." She felt all kinds of fears. She was "so nervous that the slightest thing startles and alarms me." She dreaded "the coming of something that may separate us, or make us less happy in each other."

Adoniram reassured her from Boston:

As to what the newspapers and the public say, can you not receive it with that cool, quiet composure which best becomes you, nor let any one but me know that it disturbs you? In fact, be not disturbed. There is nothing that ought to disturb one of your pure and high purpose. Before God we are indeed full of sin; but we may still feel that the path we are treading is one which the common people have neither capacity to investigate, nor right to judge.

He added that the opinion of one man such as President Wayland of Brown University was "worth that of ten thousand and here it is under March 26th: 'I know not where you are, but hear you are tripping in author-land under the guidance of a fair Forester. I am pleased to hear of your engagement, as far as I know of it. Miss C. is everywhere spoken of as a pious, sensible, cultivated and engaging person. I pray God it may prove a great and mutual blessing.' " He admitted however, that it was easier for him than for Emily. "I have been so cried down at different periods of my life . . . that I suppose I am a little hardened. But I feel for you, for it is your first field."

Meanwhile, he had other cares.

I have just been having a good cry here alone, in Mr. Colby's chamber, about my poor dear children. I left the two boys crying yesterday as they set off in the cars for Worcester. Abby Ann I took on to Bradford, and this morning I left her crying at the Hasseltine's. And thoughts of the children bear my mind to their departed mother, and I review the scenes on board the *Sophia Walker* and at St. Helena. And then I stretch my way to my two little forsaken orphans in Burmah; and then I turn to you whom I love not less, though but a recent acquaintance. What a strange thing is the human heart!

But at least, he comforted himself, his children were settled for the present. George Boardman was to enter Brown in the fall. And Adoniram had money enough to care for his children and for Emily's parents, "so that you can write as much or as little as you choose, and if you take any remuneration, you can have the pleasure of presenting it, through the missionary treasury, as an expression of gratitude to Him who gave His life for you, and is now preparing your seat and your crown."

Clearly, this was not the Adoniram who, long ago, after Nancy's death, had given all his property to the mission board as part of his self-punishment. But his recovery, his marriage to Sarah, the family which resulted had brought him to a more realistic attitude. Since then he had kept the sums his sister and mother had sent him. Possibly, too, well-to-do admirers had arranged for his own and the children's care.

At any rate, Emily replied contritely, "You do take all the trouble away so sweetly! I don't know why you should be so good and kind to me when I get out of patience. Yes, I do know that you will never repent the step you have taken, though the whole world should disapprove of it, and with full faith that I will not be disturbed by trifles. I know these are all trifles — things I shall laugh at when I get away from them; but sometimes they seem terrible now. They shall not any more, though; I will rest in your love and in a holier . . ." And as for his children, "Do not call them 'orphans' any more. I will love them and watch over them, and when I fail in any thing, you will point out the faults and teach me better."

A few days later Adoniram went to Maine for a week. Other engagements kept him busy the rest of April, but early in May he was able to visit Emily in Utica. Together they went to Hamilton for a few days with her parents. Adoniram had lent Emily enough money to pay off the mortgage on the house she had bought for them so that at least it was theirs free and clear. She was to repay him from future royalties on her books.

At Hamilton that Sunday he was overjoyed to meet his old Andover professor Leonard Woods, who had preached his ordination sermon in the Tabernacle Church in Salem in 1812, and who preached again this day. Adoniram sat with him on the platform. After the sermon he told the audience how he had first gone to Andover, "a poor blind skeptic," looking for enlightenment, and how he had received it from Dr. Woods. His hearers were thrilled — more so than those of the Morrisville church, where Emily had been baptized years before. That building had been so small he felt he could speak to the congregation without injuring his throat. Although the day was rainy, the church had been crowded with people who had learned he would have something to say. After the sermon he had spoken for some fifteen minutes "with singular simplicity, and . . . touching pathos," as Emily thought, of the love of the Saviour, "what he has done for us, and what we owe to him."

> As he sat down [Emily recollected] . . . it was evident, even to the most unobservant eye, that most of the listeners were disappointed. After the exercises were over, several persons inquired of me, frankly, why Dr. Judson had not talked of some-

thing else; why he had not told a story . . . On the way home, I mentioned the subject to him.

"Why, what did they want?" he inquired; "I presented the most interesting subject in the world, to the best of my ability."

"But they wanted something different — a story."

"Well, I am sure I gave them a story — the most thrilling one that can be conceived of."

"But they had heard it before. They wanted something new of a man who had just come from the antipodes."

"Then I am glad they have it to say, that a man coming from the antipodes had nothing better to tell than the wondrous story of Jesus' dying love."

From Hamilton they made the short journey to Eaton, where Emily had been born. They had tea in Underhill Cottage, which she had described in *Trippings*, and explored the alderfringed stream which was to give her next book its name, *Alderbrook*.

But the interlude in Hamilton had to end — Adoniram had engagements in New York and Philadelphia. Emily had arrangements to make before the wedding. Together they returned to Utica, and there they parted.

Their letters reflected their many concerns. From discussions of terms with publishers for her next book — "Will you try to make a bargain for me with Lippincott?" — she turned abruptly to clothing. "I think of you now and then between exclamations concerning pretty frocks. Oh, that is a charming blue! and that purple, how exquisite! You don't know what absorbing things new frocks are, for you, poor man, never had any. . . ." She dreaded the voyage. ". . . The mention of the ship sends my heart down into my shoes. How nice could we but sleep a half year, and then awake in our own dear home." She suggested that they take Abby Ann back to Moulmein with them — "She is your only daughter, you love her so much, and it will be so hard for the little creature to stay behind."

Between religious meetings, Adoniram saw publishers for her. She wanted her new book to be a complete edition of her stories and sketches; her publishers did not want to include any material already in book form. So, wrote Adoniram:

I have got the stereotype plates out of the hands of Paine &

Burgess, and had them packed up, ordered to be sent, and deposited at Lewis Colby's. They cost $190. P. & B. have also paid me $70 for you, being the percentage on the whole edition, beside what they have already paid you. So that your business with them is closed. The $70 I will send you, and take a receipt, dear, to avoid mistakes. . . . [New York publishers were not interested in the new miscellany.] People's minds are full of the Mexican war, and probable rupture with England and all the world. Too much stern reality to allow time for fiction; too close engagement with Mars, to allow time for flirting with Venus and the Muses. You can arrange for the purchase of the additional lot, if you please, for $300, before I come, and for the fence at $50. I shall be able to let you have as much of the sum appropriated for your outfit, that is $200, as you may wish. . . . Is not this a beautiful letter, full of gold and pearls, and costly array? Do not wear it in your hair. It will be contrary to Scripture . . .

And later:

Notwithstanding the nonsense I write you, I am full and overflowing with most serious, joyful thoughts. The past, the present, and the future are before me. If I should attempt to write, I should not know where to begin or end. May we meet in "love and happiness." May God crown our union with his blessing, that we may be blessings to one another through life and to all eternity!

June 1, 1846, Adoniram was in Hamilton again. The next day they were married in Emily's home by Dr. Nathaniel Kendrick, the elderly minister, now in the beginning of his last illness, of whom Emily had once inquired about the prospects of her becoming a foreign missionary. It was a quiet wedding. Only her immediate family and a few close friends were present. After the ceremony they spent a few days in Hamilton together, and a few more in Utica. Then they began a series of whirlwind visits to New York, Boston, Plymouth and Bradford, making last farewells. For their ship, the *Faneuil Hall*, Captain Hallet, was to sail from Boston on July 1, bound for Moulmein.

The sailing was delayed, but a huge farewell meeting was held on schedule, the afternoon of June 30, in the Baldwin Place Church. Other missionaries were to accompany the Judsons — the Norman

Harrises, the John S. Beechers, and Miss Lydia Lillybridge, who had been a school friend of Emily's in Utica.

But Adoniram and Emily were the center of attention. The storm aroused by their engagement had died down. Churchgoers had begun to learn that the new Mrs. Judson was a sincere Christian and not a light lady after all — though many of them felt (as did Emily herself, for that matter) that her consecration to religion and to missions was not quite as deep as could be wished in the spouse of so venerated a man.

The literary world, too, had come to the conclusion that the marriage might be a good thing. As N. P. Willis wrote to Emily, "The more I think of your marriage, the more I think you are doing the best for your happiness." He had met Adoniram in New York in May, and thought he had "a prodigal largeness of nature, and the kindest and most affectionate of hearts." And, he felt, "Dr. Judson's errand abroad will soon draw on your volcanic enthusiasm, and the vent will be healthful to soul and body."

Emily had sent Willis money for some books, but he had returned it. He would give her a box of books from his own library. Moreover, he had spoken to Secretary of the Navy Bancroft at a party in Washington, and Mr. Bancroft "was, of course, proud of the opportunity to present you with his books, and so will be Prescott and Longfellow . . ."

In this letter Willis announced his intention of being present at the sailing, "and see you, with a tearful Godspeed, off the shore." But a week or so later he wrote that he had changed his mind. "A little closer approach to the scene which that embarkation would probably be — with the number of Mr. Judson's friends and the enthusiasm felt for him — made me shrink from compelling you to reserve for me any of the attention which those friends will expect from you at the parting hour, and still more to shrink from adding to the emotion of that troubled hour the pain of parting with one who must be dear to you as the foster-father of your genius. I see that it is better that we exchange our farewells, as we have exchanged all other feelings, on paper."

Adoniram seized the delay in the sailing to go to Worcester on July 4 and visit the two boys for the last time. After another missionary service on the fifth, he went to Bradford on the ninth to say farewell to Abby Ann. These leave-takings, painful as they were, at least helped him to escape the flood of callers in Boston. Emily bore the brunt of that, and complained to her sister, "I have been crowded almost to death with company. Sometimes my hand has been so swollen with constant shaking that I have not been able to get on a glove, and I have been obliged to use my left hand."

On July 10 Adoniram wrote short, sad notes to his sons and to Abby Ann and his sister. His sister did not go to Boston to see him off. But her feelings had already revealed themselves when Adoniram had left Plymouth. She had closed the door of his room, leaving everything in it as he had left it. Thenceforth, so long as she lived — nearly forty years — nothing in it was ever to be moved or disturbed.

On July 11, 1846, "amidst the tearful adieus of hundreds," they boarded the ship and sailed. Among those they saw on this last day were the family of Gardner Colby, who had entertained them in lordly fashion; the Gillettes; the Lincoln family; and, closer to Adoniram's heart, George D. Boardman, Jr., Sarah's only surviving child by her first husband.

As the ship sailed out of the harbor and the land dwindled to "a speck in the distance," as Emily wrote to her mother in a letter she sent back by the pilot-boat, Adoniram must have thought of the last time he had left the United States that freezing February morning in 1812. Then, instead of hundreds on the wharf, there had been only a few to see the missionaries leave on their doubtful mission. Of the four who had sailed then, only he still lived. Nancy slept beside little Maria under the hopia tree at Amherst. All his living children, those he left in America and those he was returning to in Moulmein, were Sarah's, now resting in the shade of the banyan at St. Helena. He had sent a stone for her grave in April. Emily, his companion now, had not even been born when he sailed the first time.

He would never see his native land again, of that he was sure. But although he felt sadness, he had no regrets. He still felt like the Adoniram Judson of 1812. He was still capable of work and love. And he still looked forward to the future with confidence and even joy.

# CHAPTER VIII
# When We Shall All Shine Together

[ *Moulmein; Rangoon: 1846–1847* ]

TO Adoniram, the voyage was the pleasantest he had yet experienced. His cabin was comfortable, the food was good, Emily proved to be an excellent sailor, and Captain Hallet was more than considerate. Worship was held on board every evening; Sundays there was a service for the crew, and a Bible class.

To Emily it was enjoyable but far from uneventful. The sea so fascinated her that she found herself incapable of fear. In a gale off the Cape of Good Hope she described it:

. . . lashed into perfect fury, rising and sinking in strange contortions, wresting our little floating nutshell from the hands of the crew, to leap, and plunge, and wrestle, as though born of the mad billows which bellow as they rise, and, bursting, cover it with their foam. The water is of inky blackness in the hollows; but each billow, as it bounds upward, becomes green and half transparent, and bursts at the summit, the long wreaths of foam circling over and over each other, tumbling to the bottom, and disappearing like immense piles of down. . . . And still we go on rearing and plunging, reeling and tumbling, as though the centre of gravity was surely lost, and our frail teasaucer capsizing itself, and then pausing on the top of a billow, quivering in every spar before venturing another plunge, which it seems must be fatal. [One of these nights she dreamed she could see the center of gravity "in the shape of a *bull's eye*" sinking too low for safety.] I watched every plunge with trembling breathlessness — a kind of night-mare feeling — a little more, just a little more, and we were lost for ever! At length it came. I bounded from my berth, staggered, and tumbled headlong, grazing my shins most beautifully."

[Later there was an even stronger gale] . . . a perfect hurricane, but it was astern, and so swept us on our way at a furious rate. A Dutch bark came within a few rods of us, and I assure you my heart went pit-a-pat when I saw it reeling and tumbling, though I was told that it went on quite as sedately as we did. At one minute it seemed leaping to the clouds, and at the next not even the top of the mast was visible, so low had it sunk behind the mountain billows. But the beauty of the scene was the showers of rainbows, for the sun was gloriously bright. . .

Her descriptions were vivid. In a sudden squall, "the tarpaulins scramble, racing after each other up the rigging like so many rats, and shouting a chorus something in the tone of a bellowing bull. . . " Or "a supper of dolphins, which, but for their being fried in rancid lard, would have been delicious." She had an eye for color. The dolphin was "rich brown on the back, and blue, and green, and gold, shaded into each other along the side to the belly, which becomes of a deep salmon hue, then pale rose, and then white." A Portuguese man-of-war, that strange living jelly, had a sail "of ribbed silver, fringed with pink and purple; the body seems silver, and then the long strings of purple beads."

While Emily occupied herself with observing and describing, Adoniram did what he could on the dictionary. Without the native assistants he had sent home during Sarah's last illness there was nothing he could add, but at least he could occupy himself with revising and transcribing the first part. He had scarcely finished when, in late November of 1846, after a voyage of more than four months, the first cry of "Land ho!" rang out from overhead.

Emily had proved an exquisite companion. Her lack of physical fear; the boldness of her thought; the sharpness of her eye, and her ability to put into words what she saw and felt; her sensitivity; and, most of all, the delicious completeness of her love — all these together had given him a kind of happiness he had never known before. Each of his wives had brought with her love a distinctly different personality. Nancy with her dark youthful beauty had brought the fire of incomparable resolution and a pure singleness of purpose that matched his own. Most of the three, she was another aspect of himself. Sarah had brought sweetness and serenity, an ability to accept what came to her without frantic struggle. Emily, lacking their physical beauty, brought a subtly compounded blend of character. She was piquant, spicy, bold but meltable, independent yet deeply feminine, deeply responsive. She was his equal, with her own accomplishments, which she prized; yet she revered him. She could throw off her adulthood in a way that encouraged him to throw off his; they could play and tease together like children. Whatever happened, they could never be bored with each other.

Now he stood at the rail with her, keenly savoring the pleasure of seeing the familiar coast with her fresh eyes. The first land looked to her like "a succession of dark rich purple festoons . . . turning their convex side to the sky. . . . " Another purple island sat "like a pyramid upon the water." The shores of Burma appeared as "a long chain, made up of irregular links, which it seems that a breath might dissever." The purple changed to emerald. The trees looked like shrubs. They borrowed a telescope from the captain, and the tiny sails of the inshore fishing boats stood out, and the point of Amherst. Then "tree by tree becomes visible as it appears in relief against the sky — the palm, the cocoa, and the tamarind."

And one other tree. Adoniram took the telescope and found it on a "green bank sloping to the water." He pointed it out to Emily. It was the hopia tree over Nancy's grave.

They took on a pilot, "a Portuguese, fat, square, and heavy," on the twenty-seventh. The next morning the ship dropped anchor in the harbor. Emily thought the country "queer, ridiculous, half-beautiful, half-frightful, extremely picturesque." And that day she saw in one incident the whole reason for Adoniram's life. She described it in a letter to her sister before the sun went down.

We were scarcely anchored this morning when a boat of six or seven men came bounding toward us, who, by the fluttering of gay silks, and the display of snowy jackets and turbans, were judged to be something above mere boatmen. [Adoniram], who had been for some time silently watching them from the side of the vessel, leaned far over for a moment gazing at them intently, and then sent forth a glad wild hail. In a moment the glancing of oars ceased, a half dozen men sprang to their feet to the imminent peril of the odd nut-shell in which they floated, and a wilder, longer, and if possible more joyous cry showed that the voice of the salutation was recognized. Christian [1] beckoned me to his side. "They are our Amherst friends," he said; "the dear, faithful fellows!" . . .

In a few moments the men had brought the boat along side, and were scrambling up the sides of the vessel. . . . How the black eyes danced beneath their grave brows, and the rough lips curled with smiles behind the bristling beards! Then came a quick grasping of hands, and half-choked words of salutation, in a strange, deep guttural, which he only to whom they were addressed could understand; while I, like the full-grown baby that I am, retreated to the nearest shadow, actually sobbing; for what, I am sure I do not know, unless I might have fancied myself a sort of floodgate for the relief of other people's eyes and voices.

However, though it had been pretty strongly intimated that "mamma" must not be out of sight, just at present, I do not think her madamship was missed until she had made herself tolerably presentable, and then she was again beckoned forward.

The Burmans gave my hand a cordial American grip, but their dusky palms were so velvety that I do not think even your fingers would have complained under the pressure. Then a venerable old man, who, as I afterward learned, is a deacon in the church, came forward, and bending his turbaned head respectfully, commenced an animated address, waving his hand occasionally to the troop behind him, who bowed as in assent. I have no doubt it was a rare specimen of eloquence, but, of course, I could not understand a word of it, and could only curtsy and simper very foolishly in acknowledgment. You will laugh when I tell you I have seldom been so embarrassed in my life.

I soon learned that the men had reserved nicely matted seats for us in the boat, and that several of their wives and daughters were waiting at the jetty, with cart and oxen, to take me up to the village. Off ran I for my bonnet, but somebody very peremptorily interfered, declaring that a certain pair of thin cheeks were quite thin enough already for their owner's good; and, moreover, that it was very foolish to waste life by keeping the heart all of a flutter, asserting that mine made a dozen trills

[1] One of Emily's pet names for Adoniram. She was referring to the "Christian" of *Pilgrim's Progress*.

and quavers, while that of a sensible person took but one moderate step.

Our visitors had brought us bottles of milk, eggs, fish, shrimps, yams, sweet potatoes, plantains, and oranges for our comfort, and while they were unloading their treasures, I borrowed the captain's glass and took a long look at the jetty. I could see now that I knew they were actually there, the women grouped along the beach, and another object, which I was told was the cart and a pair of cream colored oxen, standing farther back upon the greensward. My feet fairly ached to press that soft carpet of earth and vegetation, but even the strong man who came for me acknowledged that "mama" was too small for the undertaking, and so went away alone.

Now, darling, you know I am not a Niobe; you know I always did try to steer clear of certain sentimental indulgences, because they were sure to bring on headache without leaving any mortal good in return. You know I say that I am not one of "earth's sorrowful weepers," but somehow I did get *overtaken* this time. Down into my cabin I went, every nerve in me quivering, and treated my pillow to a regular tear-bath. "Twice of a single morning?" you ask. Twice of a single morning, dear — or what is nearer the truth, the quarter deck operation continued. I was deep in the melting luxury, when the door was softly opened, and I knew that some person stood beside me. I did not move; but kept my face covered with the tolerably well wetted bit of linen, that had divided my favors with the pillow; fortifying meanwhile my voice in anticipation of a question.

Presently I heard words, but though spoken close to my ear, they were not addressed to me. How that low, mellow voice crept down into my heart, calming its foolish agitation, imparting the strength of faith, illuminating its tremulous, shadowing depths with hope, and elevating it to a still, serene reliance on Him who can be touched with the feeling of our infirmities, simply because His nature though sinless, has vibrated to every earthly emotion.

Then how strange to be so thoroughly comprehended! Any body else now would have thought I was in a pet from the disappointment of not going on shore, or something else of the kind.

He knew, I can not tell how, but he told it all in that prayer as I never could have done — he knew just how a faint heart feels, suddenly pressed upon with a view of moral sublimity to which it is for the moment inadequate; he knows what it is to have the doors of time, all shut and barred, and the long vista of eternity stretching in solemn perspective before the shrinking soul, and he knows just what it needed at such a crisis.

I remember a soothing, balm-distilling influence, a feeling of perfect security and serenity, and then I went to sleep. When I awoke, the jolly boat with the officers and gentlemen passengers, Christian among them, had gone on shore and with the exception of a half-hour devoted to the hopia tree, I have been writing to you ever since.

Three days later, on Monday, they were rowed up the river to Moulmein by a crew of the Amherst converts in what looked to Emily "very much like a long watering-trough, whittled to a point at each end, and we were all nestled like a parcel of caged fowls under a low bamboo cover . . . " Nothing looked or sounded like home. The birds — "the white rice-bird, or a gayer stranger, with chameleon neck and crimson wing"; the flowers — "rich blossoms of new shapes and hues. . . some in clusters, and some in long, amber wreaths, stained here and there with amber and vermilion"; the oarsmen in their "gaudy *patsoes*," with "bare, brawny shoulders, and turbaned heads"; the luxuriant, wild tropical trees and the vines trailing down into the water — it was all strange, strange as the manners and language of the people. But she was delighted with the "picturesque beauty — a mingling of awkward simplicity with magnificence quite as clumsy and awkward — a rich gorgeousness, a fantastic extravagance, a rudeness sometimes annoying, but oftener ludicrous. . . "

To all this the houses of the missionaries in Moulmein offered a sharp contrast. They were "the plainest possible, built of teak boards, and furnished with the same kind of wood, without varnish. The partitions between the rooms are mere screens, reaching a little above the head, so that a word spoken in one room is heard all over the house." Nevertheless, she liked them. "I think I was made for an uncivilized land."

She took the children, Henry and Edward, now four and two years old, to her heart. One night in December when Emily had just put them to bed Adoniram wrote to the two sons in Worcester, "Henry is singing and talking aloud to himself; and what do you think he is saying? Your new mamma has just called me to listen. 'My own mamma went away, away in a boat. And then she got wings and went up. And Charlie, too, went up, and they are flying above the moon and the stars.'"

By late December they had settled down, but Adoniram had not yet returned to the dictionary. Moulmein, he felt, was not the place for it. Rangoon, where he could have the help of learned Burmese scholars, would be better. Ava would be better still. He had been considering a move to Rangoon even before leaving Boston and had discussed it with Emily. But although the ease of working on the dictionary was an important factor, it was not the real reason. He had never felt that Moulmein was really Burma — and Burma was where he belonged. He thought it possible he might at least be tolerated in Rangoon. If so, perhaps he could regather a small congregation and continue at least part of the time with missionary work.

But he was sure he was not needed in Moulmein. Nearly thirty missionaries were there already — far too many, he thought. The work had been departmentalized. Stevens was in charge of the native church; Howard and Birney each had a school; Ranney functioned as business manager and had charge of the printing office; Haswell superintended the printing of the New Testament in Peguan; Stilson oversaw the printing of Burmese elementary books for schools.

All of these jobs were being done at least as well as he could do them. But he had longer experience than anyone else in the regions not under British control; in Rangoon and Burma proper there was not a single missionary; and no one was as qualified as he to make the dictionary. He decided to go to Rangoon alone for a few weeks and find out for himself whether it was possible to settle there with a family.

Meanwhile Emily was becoming accustomed to life and the duties of a wife in a strange land. She opened her journal on New Year's Day of 1847 with the bewildered observation:

Actually in Burmah! And is it really myself? Is the past year a reality, or am I still dreaming up there in Dominie Gillette's chamber, where I lay down (seemingly) a year ago? If it *be* a dream, I pray God that I may never wake, for I believe it would break my heart to be other than I am. Thank God, it is a reality — a blessed reality; and I am in the very spot I so longed to plant my foot upon, years and years gone by.

*January 2.* I have got a teacher, and made a beginning in the language, but the children absorb so much of my time that I can not study much. They are dear little fellows, but *so* full of mischief! . . .

*January 5.* It seems to me as though I do nothing but get up, turn around, and then go to bed again! I believe there never was such a novice in housekeeping; and then the children, and the language, and the thousand and one other botherations! I expected to make a rush at the language, take it by storm, then get a parcel of natives about me, and go to work in "true apostle style." . . .

*January 10.* This taking care of teething babies, and teaching darkies to darn stockings, and talking English back end foremost to teetotum John, in order to get an eatable dinner, is really very odd sort of business for Fanny Forester. . . . But I begin to get reconciled to my minute cares. I believe some women were made for such things; though when I get settled, I hope to put in a mixture of higher and better things, too. But the person who would do great things well, must practice daily on little ones; and she who would have the assistance of the Almighty in important acts, must be daily and hourly accustomed to consult His will in the minor affairs of life.

Adoniram had procured passage for Rangoon on the schooner *Cecilia*, Captain Crisp, and was to embark on the eighteenth of January. It was their first separation since their marriage. Even before he left Emily found herself frequently weeping and unable to sleep — and to her surprise, and consolation, she found that Adoniram could weep too. "If men who have been through prison and all perils weep at such separations," she wrote, "surely such a weakling as I should not be put in a strait-jacket. The truth is, we poor humans are utterly baffled in attempting to estimate each other's sufferings. I will venture to assert that it required a far greater effort in Ann H. Judson to leave her husband (*such* a husband!) in Rangoon, and go to America alone, than to play the heroic part in his presence, and for his sake, that she did at Ava.

But Dr. J's going to Rangoon for two or three weeks is not my going to America, and I must not try to be quite a fool."

By the nineteenth, the *Cecilia* had dropped out of sight of Moulmein and was near Amherst. On the way down the river Adoniram occupied part of the time writing to Emily, wondering how she and the children were spending their time that day. "It seems as if I had been associated with you for many years; and hardly knew how to deport myself in your absence."

But he felt "in excellently good spirits in regard to making the attempt at Rangoon," though he doubted the success of the effort. However, he meant to do his best "and am quite willing to leave the event in the hands of God. 'Trust in God and keep your powder dry,' was Cromwell's word to his soldiers. Trust in God and love one another is, I think, a better watchword." The thought sent him into one of his characteristic lover-like homilies:

> Let us do the duties of religion and of love, and all will be well. Conjugal love stands first. Happy those who find that duty and pleasure coincide. Then comes parental love and filial love; then love to associates, and then love to all that come within our reach. I have been talking to Crisp this two hours, and you see I have become quite ethical. Sweet love, I wish I could reason out the subject, and come to a satisfactory solution on your lips.

The next morning as the *Cecilia* passed out of Amherst harbor, the sight of the hopia tree over Nancy's grave, still just visible, reminded him of "conjugal love" in a way it had when Sarah was still living:

> I seem to have lived in several worlds; but you are the earthly sun that illuminates my present. My thoughts and affections revolve around you, and cling to your form, and face, and lips. Other luminaries have been extinguished in death. I think of them with mournful delight, and anticipate the time when we shall all shine together as the brightness of the firmament and as the stars for ever and for ever.

He disembarked at Rangoon January 23, 1847, and stayed for about ten days. He met the city governor — an old acquaintance to whom he had been introduced some twenty years before — and after an interview decided it would be safe to move the family. The governor had invited him to settle and promised him a location for an English church, so that the English might have some place to worship. But he made it clear, without saying so explicitly, that Adoniram was expected to confine his ministrations to the foreigners. The dictionary aroused genuine interest in the governor. He promised to mention it favorably to His Majesty and even held out some hope that Adoniram might someday go to the capital and look for royal patronage at the Golden Feet.

But none of this implied religious tolerance. The new reign [2] was perforce a little more friendly to foreigners than the previous one; but as to the natives, they had less freedom of faith than when Adoniram first came. But Adoniram had already met quietly with some of the converts for worship. He was sure something could be done in secrecy.

Once he had made up his mind, Adoniram proceeded to rent a place to stay. In Moulmein he had heard of a large brick house in a "street of Mussulmans." He found it — a huge, gloomy, prison-like building. The upper floor was for rent, for a hundred rupees a month. Adoniram beat the owner down to fifty, and took it. He wrote Emily that he hesitated to take her into it, but at least it had six or eight rooms, some large, and it was the best he could find. Living would be expensive. "Two or three bottles of milk for a rupee, and eight loaves of very poor bread; but fowls and fish are cheaper."

He returned on board the *Gyne*, which anchored on February 5 in front of Amherst. Emily already knew of the impending move and was packing. Once more the sight of that port which he had helped locate and dedicate moved him to reflections. Waiting for the tide to change, he wrote to Emily:

Here we lie, with Amherst in sight from our cabin window. Amherst, whither I brought Ann, and returned to find her grave; Amherst, whither I brought Sarah, on returning from

2 King Bagyidaw had become insane. In 1837, the "Tharrawaddy prince" ("Sarawady") had deposed him. Tharrawaddy in turn became sadistically insane and died in confinement in 1846. He was succeeded by his eldest son Pagan Min, a debauched tyrant atop a crumbling central administration riddled with gangster dacoits. See D. G. E. Hall's account in *Europe and Burma*, or Mrs. Ernest Hart's *Picturesque Burma*.

my matrimonial tour to Tavoy, and whence I took her away in the *Paragon*, to return no more; Amherst, the terminus of my long voyage in the *Faneuil Hall* with Emily. The place seems like the centre of many radii of my past existence, though not a place where any of us have lived for any length of time. Ann never saw Moulmein; Sarah never saw Rangoon. If we should remove to the latter place, it would seem to me like beginning my life anew. May it be under more propitious auspices, and may the latter part of life make some atonement for the errors of the former. May you, my dearest, be happy, and useful, and blessed there! May we be luminaries to Burmah, and may our setting sun descend in a flood of light! . . .

Your devoted husband

A. JUDSON

## CHAPTER IX

# Bat Castle
### [ *Rangoon: 1847* ]

THE *Gyne* entered the Moulmein River mouth just in time to meet the *City of London*, on which Adoniram had engaged passage to Rangoon for his family some weeks earlier. She was to sail in about a week, and Adoniram and Emily had to move fast to get their belongings and the children on board.

They embarked on February 15, 1847, and at the end of five days were in Rangoon. Ill with a bowel complaint, Adoniram suffered through the lengthy custom inspection, which took only two days because, asserted Emily, he "dispensed presents right and left." Until their goods could be moved, they stayed with Captain Crisp of the *Cecilia*, whose house was built "in English style," and "the best but one in town." Adoniram had known Crisp's father, who also lived in Rangoon, before the war; and the son, thought Emily, was "very kind."

A few days more saw them in their own house. Emily promptly dubbed it "Bat Castle." She described it in a letter to her sister Kitty, comparing it with the "Loggery," the house of their childhood:

I write you from walls as massive as any you read of in old stories and a great deal uglier — the very eyeball and heart-core of an old white-bearded Mussulman. Think of me in an immense brick house with rooms as large as the entire "loggery" (our centre room is twice as large, and has *no* window), and only one small window apiece. When I speak of windows, do not think I make any allusion to glass — of course not. The windows (holes) are closed by means of heavy board or plank shutters, tinned over on the outside as a preventive of fire. . . . Imagine us, then, on the second floor of this immense den, with nine rooms at our command, the smallest of which (bathing-room and a kind of pantry) are, I think, quite as large as your dining room, and the rest very much larger. Part of the floors are of brick, and part of boards; but old "Green Turban" white-washed them all, with the walls, before we came, because the Doctor told him, when he was over here, that he must "make the house shine for madam." He did make it shine with a vengeance, between white-washing and greasing. They oil furniture in this country, as Americans do mahogany; but all his doors and other wood-work were fairly dripping, and we have not got rid of the smell yet; nor, with all our rubbing, is it quite safe to hold too long on the door. The partitions are all of brick, and very thick, and the door sills are *built up*, so that I go over them at three or four steps, Henry mounts and falls off, and Edward gets on all-fours, and accomplishes the pass with more safety.

But the worst trial was the bats. The many beams overhead sheltered

. . . thousands and thousands of bats, that disturb us in the day-time only by a little cricket-like music, but in the night — Oh, if you could only hear them carouse! The mosquito curtains are our only safeguard. . . We have had men at work nearly a week trying to thin them out, and have killed a great many hundreds, but I suppose their little demoniac souls come back, each with an attendant, for I am sure there are twice as many as at first. Every thing, walls, tables, chairs, etc., are stained by them.

As if bats were not enough . . .

We are blessed with our full share of cockroaches, beetles, lizards, rats, ants, mosquitoes, and bed-bugs. With the last the woodwork is all alive, and the ants troop over the house in great droves. . . . Perhaps twenty have crossed my paper since I have been writing. Only one cockroach has paid me a visit, but the neglect of these gentlemen has been fully made up by a company of black bugs about the size of the end of your little finger — nameless adventurers.

This was the house in which they settled down to work: Adoniram at the dictionary; Emily at the biography of Sarah, housekeeping, and the care of the two little boys.

Rangoon cast a peculiar spell of unreality over both of them.
Wrote Emily later:

> I have seen all this before! was a feeling that flashed upon me
> more frequently at Rangoon than here, producing a momentary
> confusion of intellect, that almost made me doubt if "I was I";
> and then came the reflections, when? — how? — where? and
> finally it would creep into my mind; why, I learned about it
> in Sabbath school when I was a little child. . . . There I was in
> the identical town of which I had read with such eager curiosity
> when I was a little child away in the central part of New York;
> and which then seemed to me about as real as a city belonging
> to the moon. And stranger still, I was actually associated with
> one of the movers in scenes, the bare recital of which had, in
> years gone by, thrilled on my nerves with greater power than
> the wildest fiction.

This feeling came when Adoniram took her to the "half enclosed neglected British grave-yard":

> The first child of European parents born in Burmah had
> been buried there; and there was a strong tie between that
> mouldering little one and ourselves. Over the grave of little
> *Roger* stood, but slightly broken, the rude brick monument
> which was built thirty-three years ago; and a tall azalia, very
> much like those which perfume the forests of New York, had
> grown out from the base almost overshadowing it. It was
> strange to stand and muse beside that little grave, with one
> parent by my side, and the other so irrevocably a being of the
> past. Oh, how she had wept there! and how *human* she grew
> — she whom I had formerly only wondered at — while my
> own tears started in sympathy.

The same impression stole over her at the pool where Adoniram
had baptized the first Burman:

> . . . with a similar, dreaming, wondering feeling, as though
> walking among shadows and skeletons, I wandered about the
> grounds occupied by the old mission house. The building was
> torn down after the war, and the place is now covered by a
> garden of betel, so thickly planted that it was with great dif-
> ficulty we could make our way among the long creepers which
> had climbed far above our heads. . .

"The house must have been somewhere here," remarked one of those beings of the past (not a shadow), close to my elbow; "that mound was the site of an old pagoda, and I leveled it as you see. But there is a nice well somewhere — that will be a sure mark."

A plainly dressed, sober faced, middle aged Burman had been regarding our movements for some time with curiosity, and he now ventured on a remark.

"I am looking for a good well from which I drank water many years ago," was the reply. "It was close by my house, and was bricked up."

"Your house!" repeated the man with astonishment.

"Yes, I lived here formerly."

The Burman turned his eye on the tall betel vines with a kind of wondering incredulity; and then back upon our faces.

"It was in the reign of *Bo-dan-parah*" (the fourth king from the present reigning monarch).

If . . . some modern looking personage should walk into your parlor and announce himself as the "Wandering Jew," I doubt whether your smile and shrug would be quite so significant as were those of our new friend. There was the well, however, a proof against imposture; and the next moment it was evidently so regarded by the Burman, for he led the way to it without speaking. It was a large square well — the bricks all green with moss, or silvered by lichens — almost as good as new, and quite superior to anything in the neighborhood. It could not be looked upon without some emotion; and the man stood by us listening to all our remarks as if he hoped to hear something he might understand; and when we went away he followed a little, and then stood and gazed after us in wondering silence.

Adoniram had similar feelings. Of course, he *had* seen all this before — but on his part he felt as if he must have known Emily in some previous existence. It came out one night when he was feeling discouraged and downcast. Emily had tried to cheer him up without success. Finally she had given up and retired to her chair while he continued gloomily stalking up and down the room.

At last [as Emily told it] I turned suddenly to him and inquired, "Would you like to know the first couplet that I ever learned to repeat?" I suppose he thought I was trifling, for he only turned his head and said nothing. "I learned it," continued

I, "before I could read, and I afterwards used to write it every where — sometimes, even, at the top of the page, when I was preparing the story on whose success more depended than its readers ever dreamed." I had gained his attention. "What was it?" he inquired.

"Beware of desperate steps; the darkest day
(Live till tomorrow) will have passed away."

"I declare," said he with energy, and his whole face brightening, "if I could only believe in transmigration, I should have no doubt that we had spent ages together in some other sphere, we are so alike in every thing. Why, those two lines have been my motto; I used to repeat them over and over in prison, and I have them now, written on a slip of paper, for a book-mark." He stood for a few moments, thinking and smiling, and then said, "Well, one thing you didn't do: you never wrote 'Pray without ceasing' on the cover of your wafer box." "No; but I wrote it on my looking-glass."

Thus they worked and lived together. During the day, wrote Adoniram, "Wife and I occupy remote ends of the house, and we have to visit one another, and that takes up time." After the day's work, of course, they were together. "And I have to hold a meeting with the rising generation every evening. . . . Henry can say, 'Twinkle, twinkle,' all himself, and Edward can repeat it after his father! Giants of genius! paragons of erudition!"

For a while life in Bat Castle was enjoyable. On June 2, 1847, her first wedding anniversary, Emily could write, "Just one year to-day since I stood before good old Doctor Kendrick, and said the irrevocable 'love, honor, and obey.' It was on many accounts a day of darkness, but it has dragged three hundred and sixty-five *very* light ones at its heels. It has been far the happiest year of my life; and, what is in my eyes still more important, my husband says it has been among the happiest of his. We have been in circumstances to be almost constantly together; and I never met with any man who could talk so well, day after day, on every subject, religious, literary, scientific, political, and — nice baby-talk. He has a mind which seems exhaustless, and so, even here in Rangoon, where all the English I hear, from week's end to week's end, is from him, I never think of wanting more society. . . "

Nevertheless, at the end of this happiest of their years together, troubles were accumulating. They had left about half their household goods and possessions with the Stevenses in Moulmein. They had scarcely settled in Rangoon when word came that an incendiary had set the house on fire. The Stevenses had barely escaped with their lives, and the house and everything in it had been burned to ashes.

The loss of their Moulmein valuables could be borne philosophically. But there were other difficulties. Adoniram had begun bringing together the scattered remnants of the Rangoon church with the idea of establishing a new one. Working quietly — almost surreptitiously — he was soon meeting with a dozen or so converts and several inquirers, one of whom he baptized toward the end of March.

He knew the danger. The assistant governor of the city — the real power, since the governor was an old, weak man — was, thought Adoniram, "the most ferocious, bloodthirsty monster" he had ever known in Burma. It was common knowledge that "his house and courtyard resound, day and night, with the screams of people under torture. Even foreigners are not beyond his grasp. He lately wreaked his rage on some Armenians and Mussulmans, and one of the latter class died in the hands of a subordinate officer. His crime was quite a venial one; but in order to extort money, he was tortured so barbarously that the blood streamed from his mouth, and he was dead in an hour."

Knowing this, Adoniram had taken such precautions that he believed he was conducting his little meetings in Bat Castle without detection. He was mistaken. Saturday, May 29, he learned that orders had been issued privately to have the house watched, "in order to apprehend any who might be liable to the charge of favoring 'Jesus Christ's religion.'" Fortunately, he had time to warn his disciples to stay away from worship Sunday. And from this time on he never dared to meet with more than two or three at a time.

Even so, a week later he secretly baptized another convert, a young man of unusual qualities. Within two or three days the convert's father was arrested on charges of heresy and "frequenting the house of Jesus Christ's teacher." Luckily, the order came to the attention of the old governor, and the charges were dismissed. But Adoniram could longer deny that the prospects for real missionary work were far darker than they had been thirty years before.

There was one hope. If he could go to Ava — rather "New Ava," formerly Amarapura, which had once again become the capital — he might possibly win toleration at the Golden Feet. The old governor gave him permission to make the trip. The best season for going up the river was approaching. But this hope too was dashed by word that the annual budget for missionary expenses had been cut deeply. Adoniram's extra expenses in Rangoon for assistants and house added up to eighty-six rupees. The mission secretary wrote him that the most he could be allowed henceforth would be seventeen and a half.

When the letter came, Adoniram could not believe it. It had never occurred to him that money might be lacking. "I thought they loved me," he told Emily sadly, "and they would scarcely have known it if I had died."

It is my growing conviction that the Baptist churches in America are behind the age in missionary spirit. They now and then make a spasmodic effort to throw off a nightmare debt of some years' accumulation, and then sink back into unconscious repose. . . . This state of things cannot last always. The Baptist missions will probably pass into the hands of other denominations, or be temporarily suspended; and those who have occupied the van will fall back into the rear.

But, as it had before, his "unnatural state of excitement" (as Emily termed it) soon passed and he accepted the setback as the will of God.

On top of this disappointment came sickness. Emily became, according to Adoniram, "as thin as the shad that went up Niagara." She blamed her condition on the food.

As for living, I must own that I am within an inch of starvation, and poor little Henry says, when he sits down to the table, " I don't want any dinner — I wish we could go back to Maulmain." His papa does better, for he never has a poor appetite. For a long time after we came here, we could get no bread at all; now we get a heavy, black, sour kind, for which we pay just three times as much as we did in Maulmain. . . .

Our milk is a mixture of buffaloes' milk, water, and something else which we cannot make out. We have changed our milk-woman several times, but it does no good. The butter we make from it is like lard with flakes of tallow. But it is useless to write about these things — you can get no idea. I must tell you, however, of the grand dinner we had one day. "You must contrive and get something that mamma can eat," the doctor said to our Burmese purveyor; "she will starve to death."

"What shall I get?"

"Anything."

"Anything?"

"Anything."

Well, we did have a capital dinner, though we tried in vain to find out by the bones what it was. Henry said it was *touk-tahs*, a species of lizard, and I should have thought so too, if the little animal had been of a fleshly consistence. Cook said he *didn't know*, but he grinned a horrible grin which made my stomach heave a little, notwithstanding the deliciousness of the meal. In the evening we called Mr. Bazaar-man. "What did we have for dinner today?"

"Were they good?"

"Excellent." A tremendous explosion of laughter, in which the cook from his dish room joined as loud as he dared. "What were they?"

"Rats!" A common servant would not have played such a trick, but it was one of the doctor's assistants who goes to bazaar for us.

There is no record of their having rats again, but there was little else to eat. The Burmese Lent had begun and for four months there was to be no meat and no fowl — nothing but fish, and that half-putrid and procurable only "by stealth, and at great price."

For a while they lived on boiled rice and fruits until Emily's whole being revolted. Then some boxes of biscuits came from Moulmein. Adoniram bribed a rascally Mussulman to get them some fowls secretly. He stole most of them back later, but they managed to live on those he left.

Meanwhile the rainy season had arrived. The house had been comfortable during the hot weather; but now, wrote Emily:

We are obliged to get directly before the window in order to see, and we suffer unaccountably from the damp air. We frequently shut all up, and light candles at noon. The doctor has severe rheumatism in his writing shoulder and constant headache, but his lungs do not trouble him so much as during the first storms. For myself, I am utterly prostrated; and, although I have taken care of everything and written a little, I have not sat up an hour at a time for six weeks. I have my table by my couch and write a few lines, and then lie down. The wooden ceiling overhead is covered with a kind of green mould, and the doors get the same way in two days if they are not carefully rubbed. Now, do you think I am in any way discontented, and would go back to America to live in a palace? Not I. I am ten times happier than I could be there. . . And then we are so, *so* happy in each other. . . We are frequently startled by echoing each other's unspoken thought, and we believe alike in everything. . .

Adoniram was afraid Emily would waste away and die before his eyes. She was more optimistic. "People like me 'die' too many times to be much alarmed by anything that comes upon themselves." But she admitted that it was a bad time. Funeral processions passed the house every day. "There has been of late a funeral feast in nearly every house in our neighborhood, and the constant tap-tap of nailing up coffins in the night is dreadful."

Now came catastrophe. One Saturday night . . .

Dr. J. was seized with terrible pains in the bowels, etc., which he thought was diarrhoea. On Sunday he took laudanum injections, and was easier; but in the night the disease showed itself a dysentery of the worst form which we could find in our books. He had never had it before, either himself or in his family, and was utterly at a loss to know how to treat it. No two books agreed, and you know there is no medical advisor in the place. I begged him to take calomel, and he would have administered it to any other person, but in his own case he procrastinated. He has taken various medicines, and thus checked the disease; but last night . . . he became alarmed, and for the first time took a dose of rhubarb and calomel. I am afraid, however, it is too late, for he is in a terrible condition this morning. The last resort is a sea voyage, which at this season of the year is a

desperate thing. Nothing goes from this port but little native
vessels, with no accommodations for a well man, much less a sick
one; and they are frequently wrecked.

All these calamities Emily poured out in a letter to Miss Cynthia
Sheldon in Utica. Writing was the only way she could express her
fears without inflicting them on Adoniram and the children. And
this Friday morning in mid-June her forebodings soon drove her
again to her pen. Only an hour or so after finishing the letter to
Miss Sheldon, she began another to Miss Anable:

> The Doctor is awake, but we cannot tell yet whether he is
> better or worse. He is evidently *passing a crisis* of some sort.
> The music and mourners have set up their screeching and howl-
> ing at a house nearly opposite, and men are busy decorating
> the funeral car in the streets. We seem to be hemmed in by
> death. Suppose it should come here; there would be only serv-
> ants to bury the dead! Something is the matter with Edward.
> He was wakeful all night, and this morning he screams out
> suddenly when at his play as in pain, and runs to me as fast as
> he can. Poor little fellow! He can not tell his trouble. I have
> just quieted him, and take the moment to write while his head
> lies in my lap.

The next day Adoniram thought the "backbone of his disease"
was broken. "If it is," commented Emily, "I am afraid there are
two back-bones, for I think I never knew a person suffer so
severely." Meanwhile Henry had been seized "suddenly and vio-
lently" with a fever and was groaning on a pallet Emily had made
for him on the floor. Edward had a disturbing night "and acts as
strangely as yesterday. He scarcely ever cries, yet screams seem
forced from him as by a sudden blow. He runs to me, but recovers
in a moment, and goes back to play. There is something very
alarming in this, knowing the brave little fellow's disposition as I
do."

By next morning Edward's disease had manifested itself. His
face was shining, spotted purplish, and so swollen that his eyes
were nearly closed. "At a venture" Emily gave him a dose of
calomel. Later that day she decided he had erysipelas. By afternoon
his fever dropped and the spots on his face turned from purple to

red. It was late that night before Emily went to bed "with one of my very worst nervous headaches."

I was awakened from a troubled sleep by Edward's screams; but as soon as I raised my head I seemed to be caught by a whirl-wind, and fell back helpless. As soon as possible, I made another attempt, and this time reached the middle of the room, where I fell headlong. I did not venture on my feet again, but crept to the bed on my hands and feet, and finally succeeded in sooth-ing him. All this time the Doctor was groaning terribly, and he managed between his groans to tell me that he was in even greater agony than when he was first seized. I was unable to do anything for him, however, and so crawled over to Henry's cot. . . I expected that both Edward and the Doctor would die, and you may imagine that I had one long cry before I began to contrive what I should do in case the worst should come.

This night was the worst. Slowly Adoniram and Edward and Henry began to recover — although two weeks later Adoniram had to lance the immense abscesses which formed on Edward's head and neck. Emily saw something "angelic" in Edward's patience and calmness.

He could not help crying when his papa lanced his head; but the moment the sharpest pain was over, he nestled down in my bosom, and though quivering all over, he kept lifting his eyes to my face, and trying to smile, oh, so sweetly! He watched his papa while he sharpened the lancet to open another, and when it was ready, turned and laid his little head on his knee of his own accord. . . You will say that I write of nothing but my husband and children. Of course not; I *think* of nothing else.

Government intolerance, lack of food and money, sickness. . . If God intended them to leave Rangoon, He was making known His wishes in no uncertain terms. And Emily was pregnant. To stay longer was impossible. They decided to leave as soon as they could procure passage.

Yet later Adoniram and Emily cherished the memory of their seven months in Rangoon. Through all the horrors, except perhaps at the very worst, bright flashes of humor and affection had passed between them like sparks of electricity. Neither had ever experienced anything quite like the relation they enjoyed. Each seemed to know what the other was thinking. Each had the same ability to see something ridiculous in what should have been most depressing.

They always remembered, for instance, how once when Emily had been too ill to get out of bed — and Adoniram not much better — she had painfully raised herself on one elbow and scribbled three stanzas which she handed to him. He had read with amazement and a broadening smile:

> Vive la bagatelle!
> High let laughter swell!
>   Peal forth the song!
> Mirth's careless children, we,
> And in the path of glee,
>   Dance we along.
>
> Vive la bagatelle!
> Deep in the bosom's cell,
>   Bid Sorrow sleep;
> And 'neath the radiant flowers,
> Wreathed in Hope's blooming bowers,
>   Bury her deep.
>
> Vive la Bagatelle!
> Only bright Pleasure's spell,
>   Young hearts should hold;
> Care will gloom hours enow,
> On the shrunk, faded brow,
>   When we are old.

With difficulty suppressing the smile, Adoniram had told Emily that she deserved a rebuke for her mischievousness. Look at that last stanza! After all, he *was* old — should he feel gloomy and careworn?

Her own eyes dancing, she retorted that since he criticized the poem she would turn it into a sermon in Ecclesiastes. She took back the paper, thought a moment, then wrote a conclusion:

> Vive la bagatelle!
> Yet in Truth's crystal cell,
>   One lesson see, —

*God counts the scattered hours,*
*God gave the wasted powers, —*
*Our judge is he!*

With this Adoniram was satisfied — more so than Emily suspected, for a few days later he told the story and repeated the poem in a letter to Mrs. Stevens.

But episodes like this still did not make Rangoon tolerable. August 31, 1847, they sailed away, never to return. A week later, they were again in Moulmein.

## CHAPTER X

# Sunset; the Dictionary

## [ *Moulmein: 1847–1849* ]

IN Moulmein, life quickly settled down to a pleasant, busy routine. Emily's baby — a girl, christened Emily Frances — was born December 24, 1847. They had taken a house on the outskirts of the mission, but when the baby was two months old they moved into their old home. Emily made a quick recovery and for the next year enjoyed the best health she had ever known. Adoniram, too, felt unusually well. They rose every day before sunrise and went for a brisk walk, often as much as three miles. Sometimes several of the missionaries would go along and even, once in a while, some of the mission children. Their objective was usually the hilltop beyond the city, from which they could see the sunrise.

One of the regular features of the return was the race down the hill between Adoniram and Emily. Emily would go ahead until she was halfway down. Then Adoniram would start after, trying to catch her before she reached the bottom. Members of the watching party at the top would hold their breaths as Adoniram bounded down the path, zigzagging from rock to rock like a mountain goat, checking his speed now and then by caroming off a ledge. He became sixty years old the summer of 1848, but he seemed active as a school boy.

As usual, he had time for more than the dictionary. He exercised general oversight over the work of the mission, and preached regularly in the native chapel Sundays. For a long time his listeners remembered those vigorous sermons, sometimes tinged with humor, in the native tongue — Adoniram wearing a long black gown, standing on the low platform beside a table that served for pulpit, the congregation divided so that women were on one side of the room, men on the other — and their close with a hymn, perhaps

one of his own, such as: "I long to reach the golden shore." [1] *Golden!*
The concept was characteristically Burman, with its Golden Pagoda, the Shwe Dagon; its ruler, the Golden Presence. If these, why not a Golden Shore?

He was mellowing noticeably. Although during his sermons he would ask the mother of a crying child to take it out, when he led meetings for the twenty or so children of the mission, he liked to offer puzzles and conundrums for them to solve, as he had done in his boyhood. More and more, in fact, his life seemed to have swung around full circle. Though his creed was as conservative as ever — essentially the creed of his boyhood — the love and grace of God took a larger and larger place in his thought and teaching.

What elements of mysticism he still preserved in his thinking had transmuted themselves into reflections on the peace and sweetness a Christian could feel after giving his heart to the Saviour. During their first days in Rangoon, Emily had been "a little annoyed by what seemed to me a taint of Guionism, Oberlinism, or something of that sort." But together with Adoniram she had gone carefully into all the literature "and weighed it with the Bible and common sense." She had concluded that Adoniram was "strictly and thoroughly orthodox" — the only person she had ever known, beside herself, who was. They agreed on everything, even, she believed, on her opinion of Madame Guion, whom she considered "disgusting" and a "monomaniac," though she admitted that "notwithstanding her very apparent unamiability, she had grace."

Young Edward and Henry, however, knew little of creeds. They remembered their father's affection and how he entered into their games. Nearly forty years later, Edward could recall "how his father used to come into his room in the morning and greet him upon his first awakening with a delicious piece of Burmese cake, or with the joyful tidings that a rat had been caught in a trap the night before!"

It was Emily who supervised the boys' education. When they had first gone to Rangoon she had insisted on Henry's learning to

---

[1] This description mostly from Warburton, p. 218. The line "I long to reach the golden shore" has been literally translated by Miss Lucy F. Wiatt, as follows:

Golden land heaven enjoy I long to.
*Shwe pye kaungin san longyin le.*

tie his shoelaces himself. She had been disturbed at how dependent the abundance of native servants, waiting on them hand and foot, made white children.

Of course, she used servants herself, both in Rangoon and in Moulmein. After Emily was born she described "Granny Grunter (alias wet-nurse, alias May Bya), who does nothing but sleep and eat alternately. . . during the twenty-four hours, and who would invent a machine to lift the child and carry it to her breast if she were a Yankee"; and "his impship, teetotum John, an old Bengalee dwarf, with a smoke-colored face, no teeth, a vermillion tongue, that looks precisely like a snake's, and muscles all on the outside of his dried-up body." But he was "that wonder of wonders in this climate, an active man." And at the door, "erect as a sentinel, stands Sir Oily Longlegs — a Bengalee of the first water — Jessingh by his heathen appellation, and lady's factotum, at least at present."

He is a fine-looking six-footer, with a turban which makes him appear at least six inches taller. And what do you think he does — this magnificent specimen of humanity, with his quick eye, graceful figure, and smooth tongue? Why, any thing and everything "mamma" pleases, and as deliberately and super-ficially as Jessingh pleases. He bathes the boys, dresses and un-dresses them, sweeps the floor, waxes the tables, puts "mamma's" things to rights, even in her dressing-room, runs of errands, and lastly, though far from least, sews on all needed strings and buttons.

But at least she did everything she could to instruct the boys and make them independent and fearless. In Rangoon, she wrote, they had become "great cowards."

One night Edward, who slept in a little room by himself, called out that he was "afraid," and would not be comforted. . . . So I prayed with little E., kissed him goodnight, and left him apparently satisfied. Pretty soon, however, I heard him call out, as though in great distress, "Oh, Dod!" The poor little fellow had not sufficient acquaintance with language to know what to say next, but this up-lifting of the heart evidently re-lieved him, for in a few minutes after, he again called out "Oh, Dod!" but in a tone much softened. I stepped to the door, but hesitated about entering. In a few minutes he again repeated

'Oh, Dod!' but in a tone so confiding that I thought I had better
go back to my room and leave him with his Great Protector.
I heard no more of him for some time, when I at last went in
and found him on his knees fast asleep. He never fails now to
remind me of asking "Dod to tate tare of him," if I neglect it,
and I have never heard him say a word since of being afraid.

Emily was busy, too, not only with the two little boys and
Emily Frances, but learning Burmese. She had finished the biography of Sarah long ago in Rangoon. In fact, it had taken her only
six weeks. Acquiring Burmese took longer, but she had a remarkable facility and made extraordinary progress. She soon was able
to finish Sarah's *Scripture Questions*, keep a Bible class, and conduct
prayer meetings for the Burmese women.

All in all, it was a good year, that year 1848, a happy year, a busy
year for both Adoniram and Emily — perhaps their happiest together. And it closed with a momentous accomplishment.

For early in the new year, on January 24, 1849, Adoniram was
able to note that he had finished the English-Burmese part of the
dictionary. A quarto volume of six hundred pages, it was a prodigious accomplishment. He expected the Burmese-English part to
be about the same length. He knew, of course, that it would undergo
changes and improvements, but he judged correctly that it would
be one of the foundations for all future work on the language.
"No one can tell what toil it has cost me. But I trust it will be a
valuable and standard work for a long time."

This was all to the good. Other events were not so good. For
instance, the opening of 1849 also found Emily ill again with a
cough which kept growing worse and worse. Her appetite failed
and she lost weight. Nursing Emily Frances through a short but
severe illness pulled her down still more. For a few days she
rallied. Her usual walks with Adoniram were out of the question,
but they bought a pony so that she could ride with him — "a
beautiful, black little creature, smooth and glossy; full of spirit,
but gentle and obedient, and gallops, O, so charmingly."

But Emily used the pony only a week. The cough returned, worse
than before, and with it fever and night sweats. In a little while
she was hardly more than a skeleton. In desperation, they decided on

the usual voyage, and she took a steamer to Tavoy to visit the Bennetts. Here she grew worse, if anything, and the Bennetts began to be afraid she would die away from home. After a week in Tavoy she returned to Moulmein. Adoniram was in despair. There was no better climate in the Orient, and it was the warm, dry season, best of the year. The Houghs, now in British employ, in charge of a government school, sent their carriage for her every morning, and these short drives seemed to relieve her enough so that Adoniram and Emily decided to have a horse and carriage of their own. But they both expected her to die soon; and although wishful of a longer life, she composed herself as well as she could.

Only their physician, a Dr. Morton, held out hope. He was convinced her ailment was caused by "congestion of the liver rather than disease of the lungs." He gave her quinine for the fever and various dosages which he thought would help. To Adoniram's surprise, they did. She slowly improved through that summer, but Adoniram suspected she would always be delicate.

As for Adoniram, age seemed to improve him. He worked, wrote Emily in July, "like a galley slave; and really it quite distresses me sometimes, but he seems to get fat on it, so I try not to worry. He walks — or rather *runs* — like a boy over the hills, a mile or two every morning; then down to his books, scratch-scratch, puzzle-puzzle, and when he gets deep in the mire, out on the veranda with your humble servant by his side, walking and talking (*kan-ing* we call it in Burman) till the point is elucidated, and then down again — and so on till ten o'clock in the evening. It is this *walking* which is keeping him out of the grave."

That summer of 1849 he finally received word from America that he could go to Ava. The Board had appropriated the necessary money at last. But it was too late, for there was no longer any prospect of winning toleration. The trip would add nothing to the dictionary — only delay it — since by now Adoniram had managed to employ an accomplished Burmese scholar, once a priest in Ava, who had wandered on to Moulmein, But Adoniram hoped that the appropriation would remain available. When the dictionary should be finished — a matter of another year or so — perhaps he could use it.

## CHAPTER XI

# To the Golden Shore
## [ 1850 ]

THAT time was not to come. For late in September of 1849, just as Emily was returning to something resembling health, Adoniram contracted a severe cold, the consequence of getting up on a chilly, damp night to help Emily with one of the children, whose sudden illness had wakened them. The cold "settled" in his lungs and produced a terrible racking cough. Three or four days later he was attacked by dysentery, followed by a fever which put him to bed in late November and completely stopped work on the dictionary. From November of 1849 to early 1850, he suffered so much that he told his friends he felt as if he had never been sick before. Yet at first neither he nor Emily nor his friends had any fears for his life. Only Dr. Morton had noticed the look of age which had begun creeping over him since his return from America. When he began to recover a little, Emily took him riding in the carriage once or twice, holding the reins herself. But he did not improve fast enough, and Dr. Morton recommended a sea voyage, as much for Emily as for Adoniram. In January of 1850 they took the steamboat to Mergui for a few days. He felt a little better, and they spent a month at Amherst, so that he could have the sea air.

Something else was happening, too. As early as December, Emily noted, Adoniram had been giving more and more time to prayer, trying to complete the self-conquest for which he had struggled ever since Andover. For forty years he had been trying to love everyone else as much as the Saviour had enjoined. He had tried again and again, and failed again and again. For forty years he had considered it a sin to love himself; to have feelings of pride; to place himself higher than others in his own estimation; to love his wife and children and parents more than others. Yet he had sinned, all too often. Now, hour after hour in his bed he prayed for improvement and examined his own feelings, reporting his progress to Emily daily.

Then one day in January he lifted his head from the pillow and told her: "I have gained the victory at last. I love every one of Christ's redeemed, as I believe he would have me love them." There was a calm triumph in his voice as he discussed how it felt to have passion spent; hate, envy and ambition spent. He said at last: "And now I lie at peace with all the world, and what is better still, at peace with my own conscience. I know that I am a miserable sinner in the sight of God, with no hope but in the blessed Saviour's merits; but I cannot think of any particular fault, any peculiarly besetting sin, which it is now my duty to correct. Can you tell me of any?" Emily could not.

From now on Adoniram enjoyed a satisfying sensation of peace. But during their month at Amherst, Emily began to be frightened by his growing weakness. When he thought he was unobserved, he would cling to the furniture and walls in walking. Away from support, he would totter. His face had become ghastly pale. Several hours each day he was in intense pain. In spite of the iron self-control he tried to exercise, at times "his groans would fill the house. At other times a kind of lethargy seemed to steal over him, and he would sleep almost incessantly for twenty-four hours, seeming annoyed if he were aroused or disturbed."

When he was more comfortable, he lived much in memory, and told Emily story after story of his boyhood in Wenham and Plymouth, of his college days, of the imprisonment in France, and of the early days of the mission in Rangoon.

He spoke of the dictionary, too. The part done was already capable of becoming a bridge of communication between the Burmese and English-speaking peoples. As for the part unfinished, he hoped a mark could be placed where his own work left off.

As he weakened, Emily became more and more apprehensive. They were alone in Amherst. There was no doctor. After a month they returned to Moulmein. Dr. Morton advised another sea voyage — a longer one. Since there was not at that moment any vessel in the harbor going far enough, the doctor suggested they move out of their house, which he thought damp and unhealthy, to another one.

For a few days after the move, Adoniram seemed to rally. Then he relapsed again.

Emily was far advanced in her second pregnancy. With a baby due in a few months, there was no possibility of her accompanying him on a voyage now. They had resisted the thought of his voyaging alone; but soon it was plain he would have to go, if he were to live. His suffering had become unbearable; but neither could he bear the thought of leaving Emily. In broken phrases he would wish God would let him die in Moulmein, at once. But his strength was failing more rapidly. So far he had been able to make his way slowly from one room to another. Now one evening, as he rose from his chair, he collapsed; and if Emily had not caught him, he would have fallen to the floor. After this he spent all his time on a couch. His symptoms became more ominous. His feet began to swell. With his long experience he knew only too well what the swelling foretold.

Yet he could not quite believe he was dying. Instead, he looked forward more and more eagerly to the voyage. He told Emily he wanted to be free of the suffocating air of the hot season and feel the fresh sea breezes.

In March came news of a ship. The French barque *Aristide Marie* had come to Moulmein and was due to sail the third of April for Isle of France. Passage for Adoniram was arranged at once. By now, Emily felt certain that he would not return. She knew, of course, that he was always, in a sense, prepared to die; but she "could not bear to have him go away, without knowing how doubtful it was whether our next meeting would not be in eternity." Perhaps, too, she admitted honestly, she might still be looking "for words of encouragement and sympathy to a source which had never before failed."

Late one night she saw her opportunity. She had been busy with various small duties in his room when Adoniram suddenly aroused, and in a voice almost as strong and firm as when he had been in health, exclaimed, "This will never do! You are killing yourself for me, and I will not permit it. You must have someone to relieve you. If I had not been made selfish by suffering, I should have insisted upon it long ago."

For a moment his tone filled Emily with delirious hope. But as she replied that she was not overworked, so long as the work was for Adoniram, his expression lapsed again into slackness. And she added, "It is only a little while, you know."

He mistook her meaning. "Only a little while," he murmured sadly. "This separation is a bitter thing, but it does not distress me now as it did — I am too weak."

"You have no reason to be distressed," Emily persisted gently, "with such glorious prospects before you. You have often told me it is the one left alone who suffers, not the one who goes with Christ."

Adoniram gave her "a rapid, questioning glance," then fell silent with his eyes closed for several minutes. She knew he understood her and was considering her words. When he opened them he looked steadily at her as he said, calmly and positively: "I do not believe I am going to die. I think I know why this illness has been sent upon me; I needed it; I feel that it has done me good; and it is my impression that I shall now recover, and be a better and more useful man."

"Then it is your wish to recover?" Emily asked him.

"If it should be the will of God, yes," he insisted. "I should like to complete the dictionary, on which I have bestowed so much labor, now that it is nearly done; for though it has not been a work that pleased my taste, or quite satisfied my feelings, I have never underrated its importance. Then after that come all the plans we have formed. Oh —" he raised his voice a little for emphasis — "I feel as if I were only just beginning to be prepared for usefulness."

Emily reminded him: "It is the opinion of most of the mission that you will not recover."

"I know it is; and I suppose they think me an old man, and imagine it is nothing for one like me to resign a life so full of trials. But I am not old — at least in that sense; you know I am not. Oh, no man ever left this world with more inviting prospects, with brighter hopes or warmer feelings — warmer feelings — " He broke off. His expression did not change but the tears rolled down his face from under the closed eyelids and fell to the pillow.

Emily thought he might have some unnecessary doubts whether he was really worthy of salvation; or perhaps he simply had a lingering fear of death, or regretted leaving his family. She voiced some of these thoughts as tactfully as she could, but he rejected them.

"It is not that," he said. "I know all that, and feel it in my inmost heart. Lying here on my bed, when I could not talk, I have had such views of the loving condescension of Christ and the glories of heaven as I believe are seldom granted to mortal man. It is not because I shrink from death that I wish to live; neither is it because the ties that bind me here, though some of them are very sweet, bear any comparison with the drawings I feel at times towards heaven. But a few years would not be missed from my eternity of bliss, and I can well afford to spare them, both for your sake and the sake of the poor Burmans. I am not tired of my work, neither am I tired of the world. Yet when Christ calls me home, I shall go with the gladness of a boy bounding away from his school. Perhaps I feel something like the young bride, when she contemplates resigning the pleasant associations of her childhood for a yet dearer home — though only a very little like her, for *there is no doubt resting on my future*."

"Then death would not take you by surprise," inquired Emily, "even if it should come before you could get on board ship?"

"Oh, no," said Adoniram. "Death will never take me by surprise — do not be afraid of that — I feel *so strong in Christ*. He has not led me so tenderly thus far, to forsake me at the very gate of heaven. No, no. I am willing to live a few years longer, if it should be so ordered. If otherwise, I am willing and glad to die now. I leave myself entirely in the hands of God, to be disposed of according to His holy will."

The next day a visitor mentioned to him that the native Christians did not want him to make the voyage, and that many others agreed with them. Emily thought the words seemed to trouble him. When the visitor had gone, she asked him whether he still felt as he had the night before. "Oh, yes," he replied. "That was no evanescent feeling. It has been with me, to a greater or less extent, for years, and will be with me, I trust, to the end. I am ready to go *today* — if it should be the will of God, this very hour. But I am not *anxious* to die — at least, when I am not beside myself with pain."

"Then why are you so desirous to go to sea?" asked Emily. "I should think it would be a matter of indifference to you."

"No," he said quietly, "my judgment tells me it would be wrong not to go; the doctor says *criminal*. I shall certainly die here; if I go away I may possibly recover. There is no question with regard to duty in such a case; and I do not like to see any hesitation, even though it springs from affection." And he added, then and later, that there was something pleasing to him in the prospect of being buried at sea. He had always loved the sea — its spaciousness, its many moods, even the motion of the ship in storm. He liked the freedom, the wideness of the sea. He would rather have his body floating in watery space, with wind and current, than confined in smothering darkness, narrowness, under the weight of earth. Thoughts of earth burial brought back to him something of his horror after Nancy's death. He told Emily, a little apologetically, that it was of no real importance where he was buried, but it was only human to have a choice.

So, not quite willing to admit that he was crossing the threshold, still clinging to life but willing to have it taken, he waited for the day of embarkation.

At the last moment, when everything else was stripped away, this inner driving force still remained, the will to live, the belief in life that was central to his nature.

This, and his faith. One of the last few days in Moulmein, Emily by chance gave him what he considered confirmation of his faith.

She had found a paragraph in a paper from home, the *Watchman and Reflector*, which told how a tract published in Germany giving an account of Adoniram's mission to Ava had brought about the conversion of some Jews in Trebizond, one of whom had translated it for the others. Long, long ago Adoniram had toyed with the idea of a mission to the Jewish people but had had to drop it, as Emily knew.

She read him the paragraph and at first was a little disappointed by the light way he spoke of it, though his eyes filled with tears — as they so often did these days. But then he clung to her hand "as though to assure himself of being really in the world," and said: "Love, this frightens me. I do not know what to make of it."

"What?"

"Why, what you have just been reading. I never was deeply interested in any subject, I never prayed sincerely and earnestly for anything, but it came. At some time — no matter at how distant a day — somehow, in some shape — probably the last I should have devised — it came. And yet I have always had so little faith! May God forgive me, and, while He condescends to use me as His instrument, wipe the sin of unbelief from my heart."

On Wednesday, April 3, 1850, Adoniram was carried in a palanquin supplied by Captain Lawford, the commandant of artillery, aboard the *Aristide Marie*. At a meeting of the mission, Thomas Ranney, superintendent of the printing press, had been appointed to accompany him on the voyage. Panapah, a Coringa servant, was to be his body servant.

Doctor Morton had emphasized the extreme importance of getting Adoniram out to sea at once, and the missionaries had applied to the commissioner of the provinces to have the steamer *Proserpine*, which was going out with a cargo of troops, tow the French barque down the river to Amherst. Permission was granted. But after Adoniram had been put aboard, the troop commander refused to allow the steamer to take the barque in tow. The *Proserpine* was a military transport and not under the commissioner's orders. He refused to endanger the lives of his soldiers, he said, by towing another vessel.

Emily had spent all Wednesday on board with Adoniram. At dark she had to go home to care for the children, but Thursday morning she found that the *Aristide Marie* had dropped only a little way down the river. With the Stevenses and Mr. Stilson, she took a boat and spent the greater part of Thursday with him. He was already feeling a little better and able to take a little food, although he was not able to leave the cot which had been built for him.

Emily was a little encouraged. If she could not go with him herself, at least her Adoniram was in the best of hands. Mr. Ranney and Panapah, she knew well, would take good care of him; and the officers on the vessel, although they could not speak English, were more than considerate. The barque's captain even carried a French-English dictionary around the ship with him so that he might be able to communicate with Ranney with as little loss of time as possible.

Friday, Emily saw him again. He did not seem as well as before, and when she left the barque she thought she had taken final leave of him. Emily had sent Ko En and Ko Shway Doke, his disciples of many years, on board to fan him until the vessel reached the ocean. They had planned to stay with Adoniram until the pilot left. But now, seeing him Friday, they pleaded that he be taken back to Moulmein and be permitted to die there. They could not endure the thought of his burial at sea. They wanted his grave to be where they and the other disciples could see it. But there was no choice. To stay would be fatal; to go gave him at least a slim chance. So Mr. Stilson reminded them, and encouraged them to remember the example of Moses, whose place of burial was unknown to his own people.

Saturday, Emily learned that the *Aristide Marie* had still not reached Amherst. Desperate for one more sight of him, she took a boat in the morning and reached the barque early in the afternoon. Her heart fell when she saw him. He could scarcely whisper how glad he was to see her. The two disciples begged her again to have him taken on shore. Privately she agreed with them, but reluctantly decided that she could not overrule the doctor. When she left at dark, Adoniram's lips moved but he made no sound. He had told Ranney earlier that he was in such pain he would be more than glad to die if he could. And Ranney knew that he had hardly been aware of Emily's visit and departure, he was so absorbed in pain.

This was the last Emily saw of him. She stayed home, with nothing to do but care for the children and wait in dread for the news she was sure would come. Once the vessel was at sea, she might learn nothing for months. Meanwhile, she steeled herself. The two little boys, fortunately, did not quite grasp what was happening, although they cried from time to time because their father had gone away.

Sunday the *Aristide Marie* reached Amherst. To Ranney's surprise, Adoniram felt better. He told Ranney that the natives were too much frightened by the swelling of his feet, which they thought a sure sign of death. "But I do not," he insisted. "I have talked with the doctor about this, and have myself remarked, at different times, the swelling and subsiding. I still feel that there is so much of life in me that I shall recover."

On Monday, April 6, the *Aristide Marie* put out to sea. Adoniram was feeling still better. Maung Shway Moung, of the Amherst church, had joined the ship in the harbor, and together with Ko En and Ko Shway Doke went back to land with the pilot. They carried a letter from Ranney to Emily, telling that Adoniram was better, spoke aloud, took a little tea and toast, and was refreshed by the sea breeze. Adoniram had told Ranney to let Emily know that he had "a strong belief it was the will of God to restore him to health."

The pain came and went. His left side began to swell markedly. Tuesday afternoon he began to vomit frequently. From now on he was unable to retain food. That night and Wednesday the air was still and hot. Ranney gave him laudanum and even ether, so that he was able to sleep a little, but he was nearly ready to give up. The captain had some favorite doses which he induced Adoniram to take — making himself understood by frequent recourse to his French and English dictionary. Adoniram told him he knew the medicines would do no good, but "I do not want anyone to think I died because all was not done that could be done for me."

Fearful pains preceded each bout of vomiting. During one attack he groaned a heartfelt wish that he could die at once, "and go immediately into paradise where there is no pain."

Wednesday evening, as Ranney sat by his cot, Adoniram said, "I am glad you are here. I do not feel so abandoned. You are my only kindred now — the only one on board who loves Christ, I mean." That was a comfort, he whispered. In response to a question he said he had no fear that Christ was not near — he believed the pain and suffering were being inflicted to make him fit to die — to make him submissive to God's will.

Thursday morning he seemed already nearly dead. His eyes were dull and glassy. They remained half closed while he slept. From this lethargy he was aroused from time to time by terrible suffering ending in vomiting. "How few there are who suffer such torment — who die so hard!" he said during one of those periods. Occasionally, Ranney gave him ether, which he said helped. During the night his agony became so appalling that Ranney could hardly stand to watch it. Sometimes he called for water, but it gave relief only while he was drinking it, and was followed immediately by the pain.

Late that night Ranney felt his body. His feet were cold, his head hot with fever. He had become so weak he seldom spoke. He indicated his wants by signs.

By Friday morning it was obvious that the end was not far off. For a few minutes before noon his mind began to wander, but he quickly regained control of it. In the middle of the afternoon he spoke in Burmese to the weeping Panapah: "It is done; I am going." A little later he made a downward sign with his hand. When Ranney failed to understand, he took hold of Ranney's head, drew his ear close to his mouth, and gasped, "Brother Ranney, will you bury me? Bury me? Quick!" A little later Ranney was called out of the cabin for a moment. Adoniram spoke to Panapah both in English and Burmese, telling him to "take care of poor mistress."

These were his last words.

His pains had left him. He lay quietly, Ranney holding his hand. From time to time he pressed Ranney's hand, each time less strongly. Panapah stood at a little distance, overcome with grief. The ship's officers, passing the open cabin door on their way to dinner, forgot their meal and gathered in the doorway to watch the end.

His death [remembered Ranney] was like falling asleep. Not the movement of a muscle was perceptible, and the moment of the going out of life was indicated only by his ceasing to breathe. A gentle pressure of the hand, growing more and more feeble as life waned, showed the peacefulness of the spirit about to take its homeward flight.

At fifteen minutes after four on Friday afternoon, April 12, 1850, Adoniram Judson reached his golden shore.

Ranney, who closed the eyes of the corruptible clay, wanted to hold the body for burial until the next day, but the captain overruled him. The ship's carpenter went to work at once on a strong plank coffin. Several buckets of sand were poured into it to make it sink. The body was placed inside, and the top nailed shut.

That evening at eight the *Aristide Marie* hove to. The crew assembled silently. The larboard port was opened. There were no prayers, except those silent ones in the hearts of the living. The captain gave an order. The coffin slid through the port into the night.

The location was latitude 13 degrees north, longitude 93 degrees east, almost in the eastward shadow of the Andaman Islands, and only a few hundred miles west of the mountains of Burma.

Afterwards, in the darkness, the *Aristide Marie* sailed on toward the Isle of France.

## CHAPTER XII

# Afterwards

APRIL 22, 1850, ten days later, Emily gave birth to her second child, named Charles, for her father. The child died at birth. She did not learn of Adoniram's death until the end of August, some four months later.

There was no reason for her to stay in Moulmein. On January 22, 1851, she sailed for England with Henry, Edward, and Emily Frances. They arrived in Boston aboard the steamer *Canada* in October, 1851.

She worked with Dr. Francis Wayland, President of Brown University, assembling the material for his great biography of her husband, but her health was broken. On June 1, 1854, she died of tuberculosis.

Abby Ann became a teacher and eventually headmistress of Bradford Academy, which Nancy Hasseltine and Harriet Atwood had once attended. Adoniram, Jr., became a physician; Elnathan and Edward, ministers. Henry fought for the Union and was permanently disabled by wounds. Emily Frances married. George D. Boardman, Sarah's son by George Boardman, became a minister.

Adoniram's sister, Abigail, lived on in the old house in Plymouth until 1884, still keeping her brother's room untouched, just as he left it in 1846. She lived more and more in her memories until in the last years of her life the children of Plymouth, when they saw her antiquely garbed in rusty black, fled from her in fear as if from a witch.

As for Adoniram Judson, the man was dead but his memory lived. A college in Rangoon was given his name. A church in New York came to be known for him. A denominational press is called "the Judson Press." Then, as the decades passed and the legend faded, new events, one superimposed over another, nearly obliterated the memory, though the influence survived.

This has been an attempt to remove some of the grimy crust of time, and reveal, at least a little, the bright features underneath.

# *Acknowledgments*

Many institutions and individuals have helped bring this book into being. Not all can be named here, but specific acknowledgment must be made to:

THE AMERICAN BIBLE SOCIETY and the AMERICAN BAPTIST CONVENTION, for financial assistance in the early stages which made it possible to undertake serious work; the ESSEX INSTITUTE and its library, the PEABODY INSTITUTE, and the MARITIME NATIONAL HISTORIC SITE, all of Salem, Massachusetts; the HUNTINGTON LIBRARY at San Marino, California; the library of ANDOVER-NEWTON THEOLOGICAL SEMINARY; the library of PHILLIPS ACADEMY at Andover; the library of the AMERICAN BIBLE SOCIETY; the BROWN UNIVERSITY library, particularly the Department of Special Collections; the DARTMOUTH COLLEGE library; the HOUGHTON LIBRARY; HARVARD UNIVERSITY, library; YALE UNIVERSITY, library; the Missionary Research Library at UNION THEOLOGICAL SEMINARY; the Public Library, at Beverly Hills and at Los Angeles, California, and at Beverly, Haverhill, Malden and Quincy, Massachusetts, and at New York City, New York; the FIRST CONGREGATIONAL CHURCH and the FIRST BAPTIST CHURCH in Malden, Massachusetts; the CHURCH OF THE PILGRIMAGE in Plymouth; the FIRST CONGREGATIONAL CHURCH in Bradford and in Wenham, Massachusetts; the HISTORICAL SOCIETY of Beverly and of Wenham, Massachusetts; the OFFICE OF ALUMNI RECORDS of BROWN UNIVERSITY, and of DARTMOUTH COLLEGE, and of YALE UNIVERSITY; the AMERICAN BAPTIST FOREIGN MISSION SOCIETY; the OFFICE OF THE TOWN CLERK in Wenham, Massachusetts, and in Belfast, Maine; the REGISTRY OF DEEDS AND THE REGISTRY OF PROBATE in Plymouth, Massachusetts.

Among individuals, special thanks must not be omitted to: MR. ROME A. BETTS, for suggesting Judson as a subject, undertaking to find the initial financing, and unfailing counsel and encouragement; DR. STACY R. WARBURTON, for counsel, for warm encouragement, and for certain information which came to him too late for inclusion in his own life of Judson; MRS. MARTHA KINGSBURY COLBY, daughter of one of Bradford's great ministers and its historian, for years of search for books about Judson and his associates; the late AMOS E. JEWETT, historian, antiquarian and rare book collector and dealer of Rowley, Massachusetts, for the same and for the gift of a rare Judson engraving and for permission to borrow and quote from the "Diary" of Deacon Joshua Jewett of Rowley; the late ROBERT LULL of Newburyport for the gift of certain documents; MISS HAZEL F. SHANK, Secretary for Burma and Thailand of the American Baptist Foreign Mission Society and her assistants, scholars and acquaintances, for reading much of the manuscript and help in resolving many confusing points of meaning, identification and spelling; MISS BESSIE BARKER of Malden, for photographs; MRS. BENJAMIN L. BULLOCK of Manchester, Massachusetts, for a gracious shelter in the center of New England's "Judson country"; MISS MARGARET T. HILLS, Librarian of the American Bible Society; HENRY H. HENSTELL, M.D., MR. ANTON M. LEADER and MR. JOSEPH GAER, for many kinds of encouragement and help; MISS LUCY WIATT of Santa Barbara, California, for information about and translations of hymns by Judson; and, above all, to my wife CATHERINE and my son JAMES A. ANDERSON, for many days of reading typescript and proof, for encouragement, and, perhaps most important, for sympathetic forbearance at difficult times.

# Concerning the Sources

There have been many biographies of Adoniram Judson, most of them published in the nineteenth century within a few decades of his death. Three stand out: FRANCIS WAYLAND'S, the "official" biography; EDWARD JUDSON'S, perhaps the most interesting; and STACY R. WARBURTON'S, briefer than the others, but perhaps the first twentieth-century biography embodying new material and modern methods of research.

All the biographies draw upon the same basic material, of which Wayland remarks in his preface:

> From peculiar views of duty, Dr. Judson had caused to be destroyed all his early letters written to his family, together with all his papers of a personal character. Mrs. Ann H. Judson, from prudential reasons, during their captivity in Ava, destroyed all his letters in her possession. Manuscripts were also consumed by the burning of Mr. Stevens's house in Maulmain. Dr. Judson's correspondence with Dr. Staughton perished by the shipwreck of a vessel on the passage from Philadelphia to Washington. Last of all, his letters to his missionary brethren in Burmah were lost by the foundering of the ship which was conveying them to this country. My materials, therefore, consisted chiefly of his official correspondence, much of which had been published in missionary periodicals. To these I have been able to add such letters as had escaped destruction, together with very valuable reminiscences from the pen of Mrs. [Emily] Judson. Enough has been preserved to present his missionary character with remarkable distinctness. His opinions on many subjects can never be recovered, but the record of his deeds is beyond the reach of both fire and flood.

Wayland's words could not be improved today, although a few additional personal letters from Judson, from Nancy and from Emily have turned up within the past several years and are now in the library of the Andover-Newton Theological Seminary. Surely others exist and will yet come to light.

But a man's own writings are by no means the only sources of in-

formation about him. And with a civil war, two world wars, industriali-
zation, imperialism — the list is endless — between the early 1800's and
today, the challenge has seemed to this biographer less one of recovering
a few letters than of recovering an individual and his associates — even
an epoch and a culture.

The complete bibliography involved in such an effort would be impossibly lengthy. What follows is therefore a selection. For example, town
and village histories and probate, real estate and vital records, both
published and unpublished, have been arbitrarily omitted. So have newspaper files. But it is hoped that enough has been retained for the interested reader to follow up aspects of the subject that might seem attractive; and some titles have been included in the hope they will help
scholars who will write better biographies of Judson than this one.

## Selected Bibliography

ALLEN, JONATHAN: *A Sermon Delivered at Haverhill February 5, 1812
on the Occasion of Two Young Ladies Being about to Embark as
the Wives of Rev. Messieurs Judson and Newell Going Missionaries
to India.* (Haverhill, 1812.)

AMERICAN BOARD: *First Ten Annual Reports of the American Board of
Commissioners for Foreign Missions, and Other Documents of the
Board.* (Boston, 1834.)

————: *Memorial Volume of the First Fifty Years of the American
Board of Commissioners for Foreign Missions.* (Boston, 1861.)

————. *See also* STRONG, WILLIAM E.

*Baptist Missionary Magazine, Boston, 1803–1851.* (Entitled *Massachusetts
Baptist Missionary Magazine,* 1803–1817; *American Baptist Magazine,*
1817–1836.)

BENTLEY, REV. WM.: *The Diary of William Bentley, 1759–1819, D.D.,
Pastor of the East Church, Salem.* Four volumes. (Salem, 1905–1914.)

BEVERLY, MASS.: *Historical Sketches of the Dane Street Congregational
Church, Beverly, Mass. Prepared for the Centennial Celebration,
November 9, 1902.* (Beverly, 1902.)

BRADFORD ACADEMY: *Public Exercises at the Presentation of the Portraits
of Rufus Anderson, D.D., Mrs. Harriet Newell, and Mrs. Ann H.
Judson to Bradford Academy, March 26, 1884.* Also includes "Cir-
cular of Bradford Academy." (Haverhill, Mass., 1884.)

BROOKS, VAN WYCK: *The World of Washington Irving.* (Philadelphia,
1944.)

BUCHANAN, CLAUDIUS: *"The Star in the East": A Sermon, Preached in
the Parish Church of St. James, Bristol, on Sunday, February 26,
1809, for the Benefit of the "Society for Missions to Africa and the*

*East," Etc.* 8th American edition. 52 pages. (Boston, 1809.) The 6th American edition of Buchanan's "Works" is dated Boston, 1812 — a fact which suggests both the influence of his sermon and New England interest in foreign missions.

CAREY, S. PEARCE: *William Carey.* Two volumes. (London, 1923.)

CHRISTIAN, JOHN L.: "Americans in the First Anglo-Burmese War," *Pacific Historical Review,* Volume 5, pp. 312–314. (Berkeley and Los Angeles, 1936.)

CLEMENT, J.: *The Life of the Rev. Adoniram Judson, The Heroic Pioneer Missionary to the Tropics of the Orient, etc.* (Philadelphia, no date.) My own copy. Warburton lists this as published in New York and Auburn, 1857.

CONANT, MRS. H. C.: *The Earnest Man: The Character and Labors of Adoniram Judson.* (Boston and New York, 1856.)

CRAWFURD, JOHN: *Journal of an Embassy from the Governor General of India to the Court of Ava.* (London, 1829.) There are various editions. The date given is that on the copy in the Los Angeles Public Library. My own, the two-volume second edition, is dated 1834.

DEXTER, FRANKLIN BOWDITCH: *Biographical Sketches of the Graduates of Yale College, etc.* Volume 3, May, 1763–July, 1788. (New York, 1903.) See p. 569 for Adoniram Judson, Senior, "7th child and 6th son of Capt. Elnathan Judson of Woodbury, Connecticut . . . ")

DOWLING, REV. JOHN: *The Judson Offering.* (New York, 1846.)

DWIGHT, TIMOTHY: *Travels in New-England.* Four volumes. (London, 1823.)

EDDY, DANIEL C.: *The Three Mrs. Judsons and Other Daughters of the Cross.* (Boston, 1860.)

ELSBREE, OLIVER WENDELL: *The Rise of the Missionary Spirit in America, 1790–1815.* (Williamsport, 1928.)

EMERSON, REV. RALPH: *Life of Rev. Joseph Emerson, Pastor of the Third Congregational Church in Beverly, Mass.* (Boston, 1834.)

FUESS, CLAUDE M.: *An Old New England School: A History of Phillips Academy.* (Cambridge, 1917.)

GAMMELL, WILLIAM: *A History of American Baptist Missions, etc.* (Boston, 1849.)

GOUGER, HENRY: *A Personal Narrative of Two Years' Imprisonment in Burmah.* (London, 1862.)

HAGUE, WILLIAM: *The Life and Character of Adoniram Judson, Late Missionary to Burma, etc.* 38 pages. (Boston, 1851.)

HALL, D. G. E.: *Europe and Burma: A Study of European Relations with Burma to the Annexation of Thibaw's Kingdom in 1886.* (London, 1945.) Has bibliography.

HAROUTUNIAN, JOSEPH: *Piety Versus Moralism: the Passing of the New England Theology.* (New York, 1932.)

HART, MRS. ERNEST: *Picturesque Burma: Past and Present.* (London and Philadelphia, 1897.) Has list of "Works Consulted."

HARVEY, G. E.: *A History of Burma*. (London, 1925.)

HILL, JAMES L.: *The Immortal Seven*. (Philadelphia, 1913.)

HUBBARD, ETHEL DANIELS: *Ann of Ava*. (New York, 1913.)

HULL, J. MERVIN: *Judson the Pioneer*. (Philadelphia, 1913.)

JEWETT, DEACON JOSHUA, of Rowley, Massachusetts. (1768–1862): *Diary*. (Unpublished.)

JUDSON, ANN H.: *An Account of the American Baptist Mission to the Burman Empire, in a Series of Letters Addressed to a Gentleman in London.* (London, 1823. Also, as *A Particular Relation of the American Baptist Mission to the Burman Empire*, Washington, 1823.)

JUDSON, EDWARD: *The Life of Adoniram Judson.* (New York, 1883.)

JUDSON, EMILY CHUBBOCK ("Fanny Forester"): *Memoir of Sarah B. Judson, Member of the Mission to Burmah.* (New York and Cincinnati, 1848.) My copy, of the "15th thousand," apparently printed in Cincinnati, gives the author's name only as "Fanny Forester."

KENDRICK, A. C.: *The Life and Letters of Mrs. Emily S. Judson.* (New York and Boston, 1860.)

KNOWLES, JAMES D.: *Memoir of Mrs. Ann H. Judson, Late Missionary to Burmah, etc.* (Boston, 1829.)

LEWIS, J. NELSON: *Judson Centennial Services. A Compilation of the Addresses, Papers, and Remarks, Given at These Services, etc.* (Malden, 1888.) Contains the letter from a "prominent citizen of Haverhill" to one in Lisbon, February 12, 1812.

MIDDLEDITCH, ROBERT T.: *Burmah's Great Missionary: Records of the Life, Character and Achievements of Adoniram Judson.* (New York, 1854. Third edition.) The first edition was published anonymously and authorship was credited, by Warburton, to E. H. Fletcher. Fletcher, a Baptist, published this book in time to "beat out" Francis Wayland's "official" biography, against the strenuous objections of Emily, who accused him of taking the food out of the mouths of Judson's own children.

MILLER, BASIL: *Ann Judson, Heroine of Burma.* (Grand Rapids, Michigan, 1947.)

MISSION RECORDS (various authors): *History of American Missions to the Heathen from the Commencement to the Present Time.* (Worcester, Mass., 1840.) Includes "History of the American Board of Commissioners for Foreign Missions," compiled by Rev. Joseph Tracy; "History of the Baptist General Convention," prepared "under the superintendance of Rev. Solomon Peck, Foreign Secretary of the Board," etc.

————: *Memoirs of the American Missionaries Formerly Connected with the Society of Inquiry Respecting Missions in the Andover Theological Seminary: Embracing a History of the Society.* With an introductory essay by Leonard Woods. (Boston, 1833.)

MORISON, SAMUEL ELIOT: *Maritime History of Massachusetts, 1783–1860.* (Boston, 1921.)

NORTH, ERIC M., editor: *The Book of a Thousand Tongues: Being Some Account of the Translation and Publication of All or Part of the Holy Scriptures into more than a Thousand Languages and Dialects.* (New York and London, 1938.)

ODELL, GEORGE C.: *Annals of the New York Stage.* (Volume 2, 1798–1821. (New York, 1927.)

*Panoplist and Missionary Magazine,* 1809–1815. (Boston.)

PIERCE, RICHARD DONALD: *A History of the Society of Inquiry in the Andover Theological Seminary, 1811–1920 . . . and a Brief History of the Brethren, 1808–1873.* (Unpublished thesis in Library of Andover-Newton Theological Seminary.)

PIERSON, H. W., editor: *American Missionary Memorial, Including Biographical and Historical Sketches.* (New York, 1853.)

POLLARD, E. B., and STEVENS, D. G.: *Luther Rice, Pioneer in Missions and Education.* (Philadelphia, 1928.)

POND, JEAN SARAH: *Bradford: A New England Academy.* (Bradford, Mass., 1930.)

RAWSON, MARION NICHOLS: *From Here to Yender.* (New York, 1932.)

RICHARDS, THOMAS C.: *Samuel J. Mills, Missionary Pathfinder, Pioneer and Promoter.* (Boston, 1906.)

ROBBINS, J. C.: *Boardman of Burma.* (Philadelphia, 1940.)

ROWE, HENRY K.: *History of Andover Theological Seminary.* (Newton, Mass., 1933.)

SALEM, MASSACHUSETTS: *Visitor's Guide to Salem.* (Salem, Essex Institute, 1937.) There are later editions of this excellent guide. The 1937 edition is the one I used.

SCHNEIDER, HERBERT WALLACE: *The Puritan Mind.* (New York, 1930.)

SPRING, GARDINER: *Memoirs of the Rev. Samuel J. Mills, etc.* (New York, 1820.)

STEARNS, HALLIE, AND OTHERS: *1735–1935, Tabernacle Church in Salem, Mass., 200th Anniversary Observance.* (Unpublished. In Essex Institute.)

STRONG, WILLIAM E.: *The Story of the American Board.* (Boston, 1910.)

STUART, ARABELLA (Mrs. Arabella M. Willson): *The Lives of Mrs. Ann H. Judson and Mrs. Sarah B. Judson, with a Biographical Sketch of Mrs. Emily C. Judson, Missionaries to Burma.* (Auburn and Buffalo, 1854.) My copy is listed as "14th thousand." The book was copyrighted in 1851. Warburton lists it as by Arabella H. Willson, New York, 1858.

SWAIN, ANNA CANADA: *Ann Hasseltine Judson, Heroine of Ava.* (New York, no date. But in back, August, 1944.) A 16-page pamphlet reprinted by the Baptist Board of Education from *My Book of Missionary Heroines.*

SYMES, MICHAEL, ESQ.: *An Account of an Embassy to the Kingdom of*

*Ava, Sent by the Governor-General of India, in the Year 1795.* (London, 1820.) My copy is in three volumes, but I have seen a one-volume copy.

TAYLOR, JAMES B.: *Memoir of Reverend Luther Rice, One of the First American Missionaries to the East.* (Baltimore, 1840.)

WARBURTON, STACY R.: *Eastward! The Story of Adoniram Judson.* (New York, 1937.)

WATERS, THOMAS FRANKLIN: "Augustus Heard and his Friends," *Publications of the Ipswich Historical Society,* Vol. XXI, 1916. (Ipswich, Mass. In Essex Institute.)

WAYLAND, FRANCIS: *A Memoir of the Life and Labors of the Rev. Adoniram Judson, D.D.* Two volumes. (Boston, 1853.) The "official" biography, copyrighted by Emily C. Judson. The proceeds went to the children.

WHITE, SIR HERBERT THIRKELL: *Burma.* (Cambridge, 1923.)

WILLIAMS, DANIEL DAY: *The Andover Liberals: A Study in American Theology.* (New York, 1941.)

WINSLOW, MIRON: *A Sketch of Missions: Or History of the Principal Attempts to Propagate Christianity among the Heathen.* (Andover, Mass., 1819.)

WOODS, LEONARD: *A Sermon, Preached at Haverhill, Mass., in Remembrance of Mrs. Harriet Newell, Wife of the Rev. Samuel Newell. . . . to which are added* MEMOIRS OF HER LIFE. (Boston, 1814.) Many editions. My copy of the 8th, for instance, is datelined Boston and Utica, 1818.

————: *A Sermon Delivered at the Tabernacle Church in Salem, Feb. 6, 1812, on Occasion of the Ordination of the Rev. Messrs. Samuel Newell, A.M., Adoniram Judson, A.M., Samuel Nott, A.M., Gordon Hall, A.M. and Luther Rice, A.B., Missionaries to the Heathen in Asia, etc.* (Stockbridge, 1812.) Huntington Library copy. Warburton lists as Boston, 1812.

WOODS, LEONARD: *History of the Andover Theological Seminary.* (Boston, 1885.) Obviously not the Leonard Woods above.

WORCESTER, S. M., JR.: *A Correction of Erroneous Statements Concerning the Embarkation of the Rev. Messrs. Judson and Newell, at Salem, February 18, 1812. Reprinted from the Christian Review, No. LIV.* (Boston, March 1849.) A pamphlet, 24 pp. My copy is inscribed: "Miss A. Hasseltine. With the Author's Respects."

————: *The Life and Labors of Rev. Samuel Worcester, D.D. By his Son.* (Boston, 1852.) Two volumes.

WYETH, WALTER N.: *Ann H. Judson: A Memorial.* (Cincinnati, 1888.)

————: *Sarah B. Judson: A Memorial.* (Philadelphia, 1889.)

————: *Emily C. Judson: A Memorial.* (Philadelphia, 1890.)

————: *The Wades: A Memorial* (Philadelphia, 1891.)

YOE, SHWAY, "Subject of the Great Queen": *The Burman: His Life and Notions.* (London, 1896.)

# Index